Network Automation with Go

Learn how to automate network operations and build applications using the Go programming language

Nicolas Leiva

Michael Kashin

BIRMINGHAM—MUMBAI

Network Automation with Go

Associate Group Product Manager: Mohd Riyan Khan

Publishing Product Manager: Mohd Riyan Khan

Content Development Editor: Nihar Kapadia

Technical Editor: Rajat Sharma

Copy Editor: Safis Editing

Project Coordinator: Manisha Singh

Proofreader: Safis Editing

Indexer: Hemangini Bari

Production Designer: Roshan Kawale

Marketing Coordinator: Nimisha Dua

First published: November 2022

Production reference: 1021222

Published by Packt Publishing Ltd.

Livery Place

35 Livery Street

Birmingham

B3 2PB, UK.

ISBN 978-1-80056-092-5

`www.packt.com`

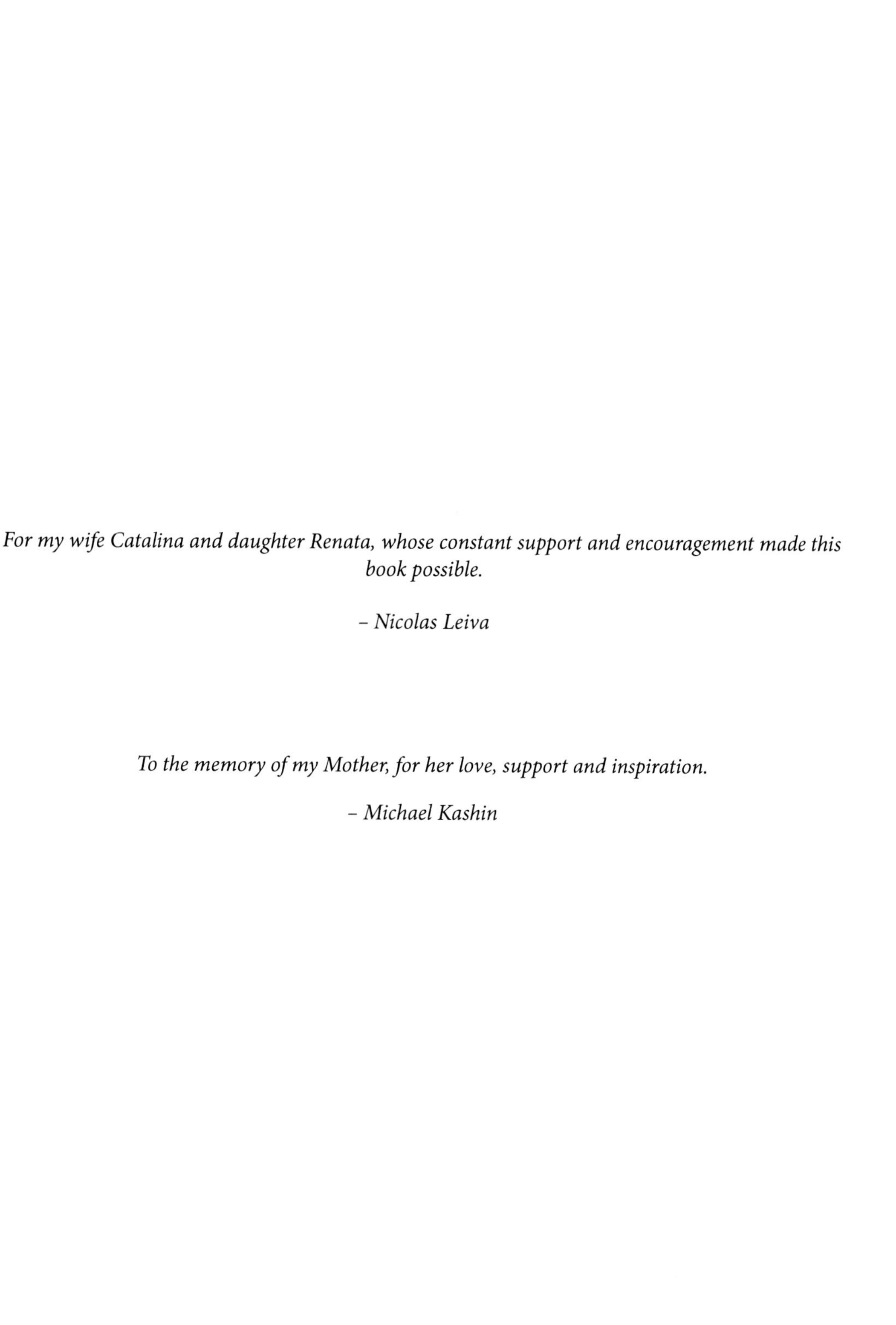

For my wife Catalina and daughter Renata, whose constant support and encouragement made this book possible.

– Nicolas Leiva

To the memory of my Mother, for her love, support and inspiration.

– Michael Kashin

Contributors

About the authors

Nicolas Leiva is a staff solutions architect at Red Hat. In his role, he helps customers of all business sizes to automate the provisioning and operation of IT infrastructure, services, and applications. Prior to that, he worked in the networking industry for 15 years, becoming a **Cisco Certified Design Expert** (CCDE) and **Cisco Certified Internetwork Expert** (CCIE). He is passionate about writing open source software in Go with a keen interest in cloud technologies.

I want to thank my parents, Rafael and Maria Estela, for guiding me in the right direction to get here and be the person I am today.

Michael Kashin is a cloud infrastructure solutions architect, currently working in the networking business unit of NVIDIA. Throughout his career, he held multiple roles ranging from network operations, through software development, to systems architecture and design. He enjoys breaking the boundaries between different disciplines and coming up with creative solutions to satisfy business needs and solve technical problems in the most optimal way. He is a prolific open source contributor and writer, with much of his work focused on cloud-native infrastructure, automation, and orchestration.

I want to thank my wife for putting up with me spending endless hours writing this book, and for looking after the kids all this time.

About the reviewers

John McGovern holds a first-class Honours Bachelor of Science degree (BSc Hons) in cybersecurity and networking from Glasgow Caledonian University. He is a technical instructor for CBT Nuggets and has developed a wide library of training around network automation, with a focus on Python programming, including Python-based libraries such as Nornir, Scrapli, and NAPALM. John is also a regular panelist on the *Network Automation Hangout* podcast and an active contributor to the Cisco DevNet Code Exchange program.

I would like to primarily thank the authors, Nicolas and Michael, for all of their great work in creating this fantastic learning resource. You both are incredible. I would also like to thank Stephen Hendry and Kamil Stachura for all of the help, guidance, and camaraderie over these last few years automating networks. And lastly, to Carl Montanari, Dmitry Figol, and Roman Dodin – you guys are the best; thank you for everything you do.

Chris Luke has been engineering networks since the early days of the dial-up internet, using home-grown software development as a tool to improve the reliability of those services. Chris is currently at Comcast, modernizing the configuration management and automation practices of the core network. He also leads a program teaching network engineers how to bring code to the day job.

Chris is currently a maintainer for the OpenConfig project and a committer for the FD.io VPP project. He has previously been the chairperson of the OpenDaylight Advisory Group and has contributed networking code to FreeBSD and Linux, as well as to the Bird and Quagga routing daemons and many other open source projects.

Table of Contents

3

Getting Started with Go 55

4

Networking (TCP/IP) with Go 135

Part 2: Common Tools and Frameworks

5

Network Automation 173

6

Configuration Management 189

7

Automation Frameworks 221

Part 3: Interacting with APIs

8

Network APIs 249

9

OpenConfig 293

10

Network Monitoring 327

11

12

Preface

This book explores network automation, a discipline that aims to generate consistent and repeatable processes to increase efficiency and reliability in network operations. As you progress through the chapters, you'll learn the Go language basics and put it into practice by coding common day-to-day network processes to jumpstart your network automation journey.

Who this book is for

This book is designed for all network engineers, administrators, and other network practitioners looking to understand what network automation is and how the Go programming language can help us develop network automation solutions. Since the first part of the book offers a comprehensive overview of Go's main features, this book is suitable for beginners with a solid grasp of programming basics.

What this book covers

Chapter 1, Introduction, explores networking and Go, the benefits of Go, and how it contrasts with Python.

Chapter 2, Go Basics, defines Go and talks about its guiding principles. It presents the Go source code file structure and shows how to compile Go programs.

Chapter 3, Getting Started with Go, covers different characteristics of Go that are relevant for network automation such as control flow, input and output operations, decoding and encoding, and concurrency.

Chapter 4, Networking (TCP/IP) with Go, focuses on practical use cases with Go for each layer of the TCP/IP model.

Chapter 5, Network Automation, discusses what network automation is, its impact on network operations, and its benefits for the business. It also talks about scaling individual use cases into a network automation system.

Chapter 6, Configuration Management, walks us through practical examples using Go to interact with network devices from different networking vendors via SSH and HTTP to configure and collect their operational state to verify any changes.

Chapter 7, Automation Frameworks, describes how some automation frameworks can integrate with Go with an emphasis on Ansible and Terraform.

Chapter 8, Network APIs, takes a look at machine-to-machine interfaces to manage network devices that enable network automation. From RESTCONF and OpenAPI to gRPC.

Chapter 9, OpenConfig, examines how to perform common operational tasks with OpenConfig gRPC services, such as provisioning a device, subscribing to a telemetry stream, and executing an action such as traceroute.

Chapter 10, Network Monitoring, dives into the world of network monitoring from different angles with Go; capturing network packets, processing data plane telemetry, running active probes to measure network performance, and visualizing metrics.

Chapter 11, Expert Insights, consists of people who have real-world hands-on experience with network automation and/or are using Go for network-related tasks and activities sharing their perspectives with us.

Chapter 12, Appendix: Building a Testing Environment, documents the process of building a testing environment that includes the compatible version of Containerlab and other related dependencies, to make sure you get a seamless experience running examples from any chapter of this book.

To get the most out of this book

This book assumes a basic understanding of networking and programming fundamentals. You need to be familiar with the Linux OS to be able to install software packages and run and interpret the results of provided commands. Most hands-on exercises are executed within a container environment, so a basic understanding of containers will help you explore and modify example programs.

Examples included in this book can be reproduced in most Linux environments. All software requirements and dependencies are covered in detail in the *Appendix*.

Software/hardware covered in the book	**Operating system requirements**
Go 1.18.1	Linux (Ubuntu 22.04, Fedora 35), Windows Subsystem for Linux (WSL2) or macOS
Containerlab 0.28.1	Linux (Ubuntu 22.04, Fedora 35), Windows Subsystem for Linux (WSL2) or macOS
Docker 20.10.14	Linux (Ubuntu 22.04, Fedora 35), Windows Subsystem for Linux (WSL2) or macOS

Download the example code files

You can download the example code files for this book from GitHub at `https://github.com/PacktPublishing/Network-Automation-with-Go`. If there's an update to the code, it will be updated in the GitHub repository.

We also have other code bundles from our rich catalog of books and videos available at `https://github.com/PacktPublishing/`. Check them out!

Download the color images

We also provide a PDF file that has color images of the screenshots and diagrams used in this book. You can download it here: `https://packt.link/hOgov`.

Conventions used

There are a number of text conventions used throughout this book.

`Code in text`: Indicates code words in text, database table names, folder names, filenames, file extensions, pathnames, dummy URLs, user input, and Twitter handles. Here is an example: "You can test this code from `ch03/type-definition/main.go`."

A block of code is set as follows:

```
func main() {
     a := -1

     var b uint32
     b = 4294967295

     var c float32 = 42.1
}
```

When we wish to draw your attention to a particular part of a code block, the relevant lines or items are set in bold:

```
func main() {
     a := 4294967295

     b := uint32(a)

     c := float32(b)
}
```

> **Tips or important notes**
> Appear like this.

Get in touch

Feedback from our readers is always welcome.

General feedback: If you have questions about any aspect of this book, email us at `customercare@packtpub.com` and mention the book title in the subject of your message.

Errata: Although we have taken every care to ensure the accuracy of our content, mistakes do happen. If you have found a mistake in this book, we would be grateful if you would report this to us. Please visit `www.packtpub.com/support/errata` and fill in the form.

Piracy: If you come across any illegal copies of our works in any form on the internet, we would be grateful if you would provide us with the location address or website name. Please contact us at `copyright@packt.com` with a link to the material.

If you are interested in becoming an author: If there is a topic that you have expertise in and you are interested in either writing or contributing to a book, please visit `authors.packtpub.com`.

Share Your Thoughts

Once you've read *Network Automation with Go*, we'd love to hear your thoughts! Scan the QR code below to go straight to the Amazon review page for this book and share your feedback.

https://packt.link/r/1-800-56092-3

Your review is important to us and the tech community and will help us make sure we're delivering excellent quality content.

Download a free PDF copy of this book

Thanks for purchasing this book!

Do you like to read on the go but are unable to carry your print books everywhere?

Is your eBook purchase not compatible with the device of your choice?

Don't worry, now with every Packt book you get a DRM-free PDF version of that book at no cost.

Read anywhere, any place, on any device. Search, copy, and paste code from your favorite technical books directly into your application.

The perks don't stop there, you can get exclusive access to discounts, newsletters, and great free content in your inbox daily

Follow these simple steps to get the benefits:

1. Scan the QR code or visit the link below

`https://packt.link/free-ebook/978-1-80056-092-5`

2. Submit your proof of purchase
3. That's it! We'll send your free PDF and other benefits to your email directly

Part 1: The Go Programming Language

This part provides an introduction to the book, the topics we will cover, and how to run the code examples provided throughout the course of the book. You can choose to use your personal computer or a virtual machine for this purpose.

Also, it provides a solid foundation for Go. By the end, you will be able to install and run Go programs. You will also learn how to manipulate network data with Go, such as IP addresses and XML/YAML/JSON documents, and use Go to run network transactions/protocols.

This part of the book comprises the following chapters:

- *Chapter 1, Introduction*
- *Chapter 2, Go Basics*
- *Chapter 3, Getting Started with Go*
- *Chapter 4, Networking (TCP/IP) with Go*

1
Introduction

Go has emerged as one of the top three most wanted programming languages according to the *Stack Overflow Developer Survey 2021* (*Further reading*), and it has become the preferred choice for writing cloud-native applications such as **Kubernetes**, **Docker**, **Istio**, **Prometheus**, and **Grafana**.

Despite this, we still don't see this trend manifest in the network engineering community, where fewer than 20% of network engineers saying they currently use Go for their network automation projects, according to the *NetDevOps* 2020 survey (*Further reading*), even though 41% of Go developers say they use Go for network programming in *Go Developer Survey 2020 Results* (*Further reading*).

This book strives to address this disparity by offering a practical introduction to Go and network automation for network engineers who want to evolve network management and operation using Go, and software engineers wanting to get into network infrastructure automation. We also hope that this book may be useful to network automation engineers who know and use Python today but want to expand their skill set with a different programming language.

We start by discussing the benefits of Go from different angles and how they apply to the networking field. By the end of this chapter, you should have a good understanding of the main aspects of Go and how to get Go installed on your computer to follow along with the code examples.

In this first chapter, we cover the following topics:

- Networking and Go
- Why Go?
- The future of Go
- Go versus Python
- Installing Go on your computer

Technical requirements

We assume basic familiarity with the command line, Git, and GitHub. You can find the code examples for this chapter in the book's GitHub repository (`https://github.com/PacktPublishing/Network-Automation-with-Go`), under the `ch01` folder.

To run the examples, proceed as follows:

1. Install Go 1.17 or later for your operating system. You can follow the instructions in the *Installing Go on your computer* section of this chapter or go to `https://go.dev/doc/install`.
2. Clone the book's GitHub repository with `git clone https://github.com/PacktPublishing/Network-Automation-with-Go.git`.
3. Change the directory to an example's folder with `cd Network-Automation-with-Go/ch01/concurrency`.
4. Execute `go run main.go`.

Networking and Go

Go is widely used in generic infrastructure software—from workload orchestration (Docker and Kubernetes), through telemetry and monitoring (Prometheus and Grafana), all the way to automation tooling (Terraform and Vagrant).

Networking is not the exception—some notable networking projects using Go include **Container Network Interface** (**CNI**) plugins such as **Cilium** or **Calico**, routing protocol daemons such as **GoBGP** and **Bio-RD**, **virtual private network** (**VPN**) software such as **Tailscale**, and most of **OpenConfig's** ecosystem, including projects such as **gRPC Network Management Interface** (**gNMI**) and **goyang**.

Other use cases include cloud and network services, **command-line interfaces** (**CLIs**), web development, **development-operations** (**DevOps**), and site reliability.

Go is a programming language the Go founders created to address modern challenges such as multi-core processing, distributed systems, and large-scale software development from day one.

Go's built-in first-class concurrency mechanisms make it an ideal choice for long-lived low-bandwidth **input/output** (**I/O**) operations, which are typical requirements of network automation and network operations applications.

What makes the Go language so appealing to software developers? Why, out of all the programming languages out there, should you invest time in learning Go? This is what we address in the next section.

Why Go?

When choosing which programming language to learn next, most people focus mainly on technical reasons. We believe that the choice can be a bit more nuanced, so we try to approach this question from different angles. We start with non-technical arguments, something that's often overlooked but that we believe is important and can have a major impact on both the learning process and day-to-day use. Following that, we cover generic technical arguments that help Go stand out in the very competitive landscape of modern programming languages. We close out this section by exploring different facets of Go that can benefit people, specifically in the fields of networking and network automation.

Non-technical reasons

Whether you are new to the language or have some experience with it, you can access more experienced Go developers in the community who are willing to help you learn more about the language. We include some pointers to community resources and go through the adoption and popularity of Go.

Last but not least, we want to address the maturity of the language, whether it's still in development, and where Go is headed in the future.

Community

A healthy community is almost always an attribute of a successful project. The Go programming language is no exception, with its welcoming and growing community of Go developers—Gophers, with about 2 million of them in the world, according to Russ Cox's article, *How Many Go Developers Are There?* (*Further reading*). You can see Renée French's *Go Gopher* mascot here:

Figure 1.1 – Go Gopher, by Renée French

The Go user community has several places where newcomers can ask questions and get help from more experienced Go developers, as listed here:

- *golang-nuts* mailing list (*Further reading*)—Google Groups mailing list for any generic language discussions
- *Go Forum* (*Further reading*)—a standalone forum for technical discussions, release announcements, and community updates
- *Go Language Collective* (*Further reading*)—the official **question-and-answer** (**Q&A**) channel on *Stack Overflow*
- *Gophers* Slack channel (*Further reading*)—a place for generic and topic-specific discussions, including a dedicated networking channel

If you want more live interactions, there are some options available as well, as outlined here:

- A good deal of in-person meetups are available via the **Go Developers Network** (**GDN**) (*Further reading*).
- One of the principal events in the Go community is *GopherCon*, held regularly in different parts of the world.
- The official Go wiki page hosted on GitHub keeps track of all future and past Go conferences and major events (*Further reading*).

Popularity

Ever since its foundation in the late 2000s, Go has gained a lot of interest from the developer community, not least because of who was behind it. Developed by a group of some of the best computer scientists employed by Google to solve the problems of C/C++, Go is a language that's both simple to understand and nearly as efficient as its predecessors. It took a few years to mature, but it had soon become the new hot start up language, and many up-and-coming software companies such as Docker and HashiCorp adopted it.

Most recently, the *Stack Overflow Developer Survey 2021* (*Further reading*) recognized Go as one of the top three most wanted programming languages by developers. Continuous support from its mothership, and the success of Kubernetes, have made it a de facto standard language to write cloud-native applications with such notable projects as Istio, CoreDNS, Prometheus, and Grafana. As more and more users adopt these applications, it's hard to imagine Go's popularity waning in the future.

Here are a few extra data points in support of Go's rising popularity that are worth mentioning:

- 225 out of 291 **Cloud Native Computing Foundation** (**CNCF**) projects use Go, as reported in the CNCF *DevStats* toolset (*Further reading*).

- Go ranks third as the language with the most stars on GitHub, according to GitHut 2.0 (`Further reading`).
- Go is behind three out of the four most popular development tools (Docker, Kubernetes, and Terraform) (*Further reading*).
- Go is in the top 10 of the *Stack Overflow Developer Survey 2021*'s top-paying technologies ranking (*Further reading*).

Maturity

While the Go team released Go (version 1) not too long ago (March 2012), Go has been getting minor changes ever since. The language designers assume a strict position against adding unnecessary features that may result in feature creep. At *GopherCon 2014*'s opening keynote, Rob Pike made this comment explicitly: "*The language is done.*" Russ Cox also mentioned this in his article *Go, Open Source, Community* (*Further reading*), referring to Go 1 specifically.

This doesn't mean Go does not have its fair share of pain points. For example, dependency management has been a problem the Go team addressed fairly recently with the introduction of **Go modules** to better group Go packages you release together. There was also a lack of **generics** support, a feature that the Go team is now introducing in **Go 1.18**, probably the most significant change since the release of Go (version 1). Now, users can represent functions and data structures with generic types, which enables code reuse. This addresses one of the primary requests from the community, as *Go Developer Survey 2020 Results* shows (*Further reading*).

Despite that, these few changes are very selective and designed to dramatically improve developer productivity. It's safe to assume that we won't see a situation where you have to learn new language concepts and idioms every year and have to rewrite your code to maintain forward compatibility. The Go 1 compatibility guarantee in *Go 1 and the Future of Go Programs* (*Further reading*) states the following:

> *It is intended that programs written to the Go 1 specification will continue to compile and run correctly, unchanged, over the lifetime of that specification. ...code that runs under Go 1.2 should be compatible with Go 1.2.1, Go 1.3, Go 1.4, and so on.*

Go benefits from the lessons learned from other programming languages. Pascal, Oberon, C, and Newsqueak are among the languages that influenced Go. We explore their impact in *Chapter 2, Go Basics*.

Go follows a 6-month release cycle (*Further reading*). In the Go release notes for each version (*Further reading*), there is a section at the top that describes changes to the language, which in general is very brief or empty. Over the last couple of years, they reported only four small enhancements to the language, which is a good sign of maturity.

How much Go will change in the future is something we discuss in the next section.

The future of Go

The success of Go version 1 has attracted a lot of developers, most of them with prior experience in other languages that helped shape their mindset and expectations of what a programming language should deliver. The Go team has defined a process to propose, document, and implement changes to Go (*Further reading*), to give a way for these new contributors to voice their opinions and influence the design of the language. They would label any proposals that break the language-compatibility guarantee, described in the preceding section, as Go 2.

The Go team announced the start of the process of developing Go version 2 at *GopherCon 2017* and with the blog post *Go 2, here we come!* (*Further reading*). The intention is to ensure the language continues to enable programmers to develop large-scale systems, and to scale to a sizable code base that big teams work on simultaneously. In *Toward Go 2* (*Further reading*), Russ Cox said the following:

> *Our goal for Go 2 is to fix the most significant ways Go fails to scale.*

Any language change proposal needs to follow the Go 2 language change template (*Further reading*). They are shipping all Go 2 features that are backward-compatible incrementally in Go 1. After that is complete, they can introduce backward-incompatible changes (see Go 2 proposals: *Further reading*), in case they offer a significant benefit, into Go 2.0.

Support for generic data types is part of the Go 2 draft designs document (*Further reading*), along with improved error handling, and error-value semantics. The first implementation of generics has already made it into Go 1. The other items in the list are still under evaluation, pushing the release of 2.0 further into the future.

Technical reasons

Go's build speed is a top-of-the-chart aspect of Go that Go developers are more satisfied with, according to *Go Developer Survey 2020 Results* (*Further reading*). It's followed very closely by Go's reliability, in second place.

The list of technical aspects we could highlight is large, but aside from build speed and reliability, we cover performance, cross-compiling, readability, and Go's tooling.

Type safety

Most programming languages can be broadly categorized as either statically typed when variable types are checked at compile time or dynamically typed when this check happens during the program execution (runtime). Go belongs to the first category and requires programs to declare all variable types explicitly. Some beginners or people with a background in dynamically typed languages might see this as a detractor.

Type declarations increase the amount of code that you need to write, but in return, you not only get performance benefits but also protection from type errors occurring at runtime, which can be a source of many subtle and hard-to-troubleshoot bugs. For example, consider the program in the next code example at https://github.com/PacktPublishing/Network-Automation-with-Go/blob/main/ch01/type-safety/main.go:

```
func process(s string) string {
    return "Hello " + s
}

func main() {
    result := process(42)
}
```

A process function takes a string data type as input and returns another string that concatenates Hello and the value of the input string. A dynamically typed program can crash if this function receives a value of a type different from string, such as an integer, for example.

These errors are very common, especially when dealing with complex data structures that can represent a network configuration or state. Go's static type checking prevents the compiler from producing a working binary generating the following error:

```
cannot use 42 (type untyped int) as type string in argument to
process
```

Readability also improves with Go's static typing. A developer might be able to keep the entire data model in mind when writing code from scratch, but as new users come into a project, code readability becomes critical to help them understand the logic to make their required code changes. No longer do they need to guess which value type a variable stores—everything is explicitly defined by the program. This feature is so valuable that some dynamically typed languages forgo the benefit of their brevity to introduce the support for type annotations (such as Python typing: *Further reading*), with the only goal to help **integrated development environments** (**IDEs**) and static linters catch obvious type errors.

Go builds are fast

Go is a compiled language that creates *small* binary files in seconds or a couple of minutes tops. Initial build time may be a bit longer, mostly because of the time it takes to download dependencies, generate extra code, and do other household activities. Subsequent builds run in a fraction of that time. For example, the next capture shows that it takes no more than 10 seconds to rebuild a 120-**megabytes** (**MB**) Kubernetes **application programming interface** (**API**) server binary:

```
$ time make kube-apiserver
+++ [0914 21:46:32] Building go targets for linux/amd64:
    cmd/kube-apiserver
```

```
> static build CGO_ENABLED=0: k8s.io/kubernetes/cmd/kube-
apiserver
make kube-apiserver  10.26s user 2.25s system 155% cpu 8.041
total
```

This allows you to iterate quickly through the development process and to keep focus, without spending minutes waiting for code to recompile. Some developer productivity tools, such as Tilt, take further actions to optimize the development workflow so that it takes seconds for changes to propagate from a developer's IDE to their local staging environment.

Reliability

Let's define this term as a set of properties of a programming language that help developers write programs that are less likely to fail because of bugs and other failure conditions, as Jiantao Pan from **Carnegie Mellon University** (**CMU**) describes in *Software Reliability* (*Further reading*). This is one of Go's core tenets, as its website (*Further reading*) highlights:

Build fast, reliable, and efficient software at scale.

Go developers also say reliability is the second aspect of Go they are most satisfied with, only behind build speed, based on *Go Developer Survey 2020 Results* (*Further reading*).

A more reliable software means less time spent chasing bugs and more time invested in the design and development of extra features. We've tried to put together a set of features that we think contribute to increased program reliability. This is not a definitive list, though, as interpretation and attribution of such features can be very subjective. Here are the features we've included:

- **Code complexity**—Go is a minimalistic language by design. This translates into simpler and less error-prone code.
- **Language stability**—Go comes with strong compatibility guarantees, and the design team tries to limit the number and impact of newly added features.
- **Memory safety**—Go prevents unsafe memory access, which is a common source of bugs and exploits in languages with pointer arithmetic, such as C and C++.
- **Static typing**—Compile-time type-safety checks catch many common bugs that would otherwise go unnoticed in dynamically typed languages.
- **Static analysis**—An automatic way to analyze and report several errors, such as unused variables or unreachable code paths, comes built into the language tooling with `go vet`.

Performance

Go is a highly performant language. The *Computer Language Benchmarks Game* (*Further reading*) shows that its performance is in the vein of languages with manual memory management, such as C/

C++ and Rust, and that it offers considerably better performance than dynamic type languages such as Python and Ruby.

It has native support for multi-core multithreaded **central processing unit** (**CPU**) architectures, allowing it to scale beyond a single thread and to optimize the use of CPU caches.

Go's built-in **garbage collector** helps you keep the memory footprint of your program low, and Go's explicit type declaration optimizes memory management and storage of values.

The Go runtime gives you profiling data, which you can visualize with `pprof` to help you hunt for memory leaks or spot bottlenecks in your program and fine-tune your code to achieve better performance and optimize resource utilization.

For more details on this subject, we recommend checking out Dave Cheney's *Five things that make Go fast* blog post (*Further reading*).

Cross-platform compiling

Go can natively produce binaries for different target architectures and operating systems. At the time of writing, the `go tool dist list` command returns 45 unique combinations with operating systems ranging from Android to Windows and instruction sets that go from `PowerPC` to `ARM`. You can change the default values inherited from the underlying operating system and architecture with GOOS and GOARCH environment variables.

You can build an operating system-native version of your favorite tool written in Go, regardless of which operating system you are currently on, as illustrated in the following code snippet:

```
ch01/hello-world$ GOOS=windows GOARCH=amd64 go build

ch01/hello-world$ ls hello-world*
hello-world.exe
```

The preceding output shows an example to create a Windows executable on a Linux machine.

Readability

This is, arguably, one of the best qualities of Go when compared to other high-performance languages such as C or C++. The Go programming language specification (*Further reading*) is relatively short, with around 90 pages (when other language specifications can span over 1,000 pages). It includes only 25 keywords, with only one for loop (`for`). The number of features is intentionally low to aid code clarity and to prevent people from developing too many language idioms or best practices.

Code formatting is an active battleground in other languages, while Go prevented this problem early on by shipping automatic opinionated formatting as part of the `go` command. A single run of `go fmt` on any unformatted (but syntactically correct) code updates the source file with the right amount of indentation and line breaks. This way, all Go programs have a similar look, which improves readability by reducing the number of personal style preferences in code.

Some might say that explicit type declarations alone improve code readability, but Go takes this a step further by making comments an integral part of the code documentation. All commented lines preceding any function, type, or variable declaration gets parsed by the `go doc` tool website (*Further reading*) or an IDE to autogenerate code documentation, as the following screenshot shows:

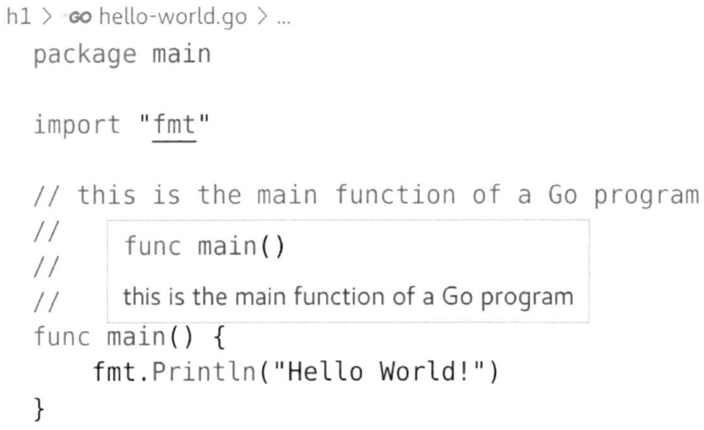

```
h1 > GO hello-world.go > ...
package main

import "fmt"

// this is the main function of a Go program
//        func main()
//
//        this is the main function of a Go program
func main() {
    fmt.Println("Hello World!")
}
```

Figure 1.2 – Automatic code documentation

Most modern IDEs have plugins that support not only documentation but automatic code formatting with `go fmt`, code linting and autocompletion, debugging, and a language server—a tool that allows developers to navigate through the code by going back and forth between type, variable, and function declarations and their references (`gopls`, the Go language server: *Further reading*). This last feature not only allows you to navigate code bases of any complexity without having to resolve import statements manually or search for string patterns in text, but also highlights any type inconsistencies on the fly before you compile a program.

Tooling

When setting up a new environment, one of the first things a typical developer would do is download and install a set of their favorite language tools and libraries to help with testing, formatting, dependency management, and so on. Go comes with all these utilities included by default, which are part of the `go` command. The following table summarizes some Go built-in tools and their purpose:

Tool	Purpose
doc	Display code documentation
fmt	Format a source code file
get	Download a Go package
mod	Work with program dependencies
test	Run tests
cover	Report code test coverage
vet	Perform code static analysis
pprof	Generate a code profiling report

Table 1.1 – Go tools

These are just a few of the most popular tools that get shipped together with the Go binary. This certainly reduces the room for creativity in the tooling ecosystem by giving developers a default choice that is good enough for most average use cases. Another benefit of this artificial scarcity is not having to reinstall and relearn a new set of tools every time you switch between different Go projects.

Go for networking

Some network automation processes can trigger hundreds—if not thousands—of simultaneous connections to network devices. Being able to orchestrate this at scale is one of the things that Go enables us to do.

You can see Egon Elbre's *Network Gopher* mascot in the following screenshot:

Figure 1.3 – Network Gopher, by Egon Elbre

Go comes with a strong networking package that offers you all the constructs to create network connections, packages to encode and decode data from popular formats, and primitives to work with bits and bytes.

Concurrency

Go has first-class support for concurrency with the help of lightweight threads managed by the Go runtime, called **goroutines**. This language construct makes it possible to embed asynchronous functions into an otherwise sequential program.

Any function call that you prepend with the `go` keyword runs in a separate goroutine—different from the main application goroutine—that does not block execution of the calling program.

Channels are another language feature that allows communication between goroutines. You can think of it as a **first-in, first-out** (**FIFO**) queue with sending and receiving ends existing in two different goroutines.

Together, these two powerful language constructs offer a way to write concurrent code in a safe and uniform way that allows you to connect to various networking devices simultaneously, without paying the tax of running an operating system thread for each one. For example, consider the following program in the next code example (`https://github.com/PacktPublishing/Network-Automation-with-Go/blob/main/ch01/concurrency/main.go`) that simulates interaction with remote network devices:

```
func main() {
    devices := []string{"leaf01", "leaf02", "spine01"}
    resultCh := make(chan string, len(devices))

    go connect(devices, resultCh)

    fmt.Println("Continuing execution")
    for msg := range resultCh {
        fmt.Println(msg)
    }
}
```

Connecting to remote devices can take a long time, and it would normally block the execution of the rest of the program. With the `connect` function running in a goroutine, as illustrated in the following code snippet, our program can continue its execution, and we can come back and collect the responses at any point in the future:

```
ch01/concurrency$  go run main.go
Continuing execution
```

```
Connected to device "leaf01"
Connected to device "spine01"
Connected to device "leaf02"
```

As the remote devices process the requests and return a response, our program starts printing the responses in the order it receives them.

Strong standard library

Go has a versatile standard library that covers different areas that may be applicable to networking—from cryptography to data encoding, from string manipulation to **regular expressions** (**regexes**) and templating. Standard library packages such as `net` and `encoding` offer interfaces for both client- and server-side network interactions, including the following:

- **Internet Protocol** (**IP**) prefix parsing and comparison functions
- Client and server implementations for IP, **Transmission Control Protocol/User Datagram Protocol** (**TCP/UDP**), and **HyperText Transfer Protocol** (**HTTP**) connections
- **Domain Name System** (**DNS**) lookup functions
- **Uniform Resource Locator** (**URL**) parsing and manipulations
- Serializing data formats such as **Extensible Markup Language** (**XML**), binary, and **JavaScript Object Notation** (**JSON**) for storage or transmission

Unless you have unique performance requirements, for example, most Go developers recommend against using external libraries for logic that can otherwise be implemented natively with the standard library. All standard packages are thoroughly tested with each release and used extensively in several large-scale projects. All this creates a better learning experience for newcomers because most-often-used data structures and functions are there already.

Data streaming

Network services are I/O-bound in general—they read or write bytes from or to the network. This mode of operation is how data streaming works in Go, which makes it appealing to network engineers who are familiar with byte processing for network protocol parsing, for example.

I/O operations in Go follow a model where a **Reader** reads data from a source, which can stream as an array of bytes to a **Writer** that writes that data to a destination. The following diagram should give you a clearer picture of what this means:

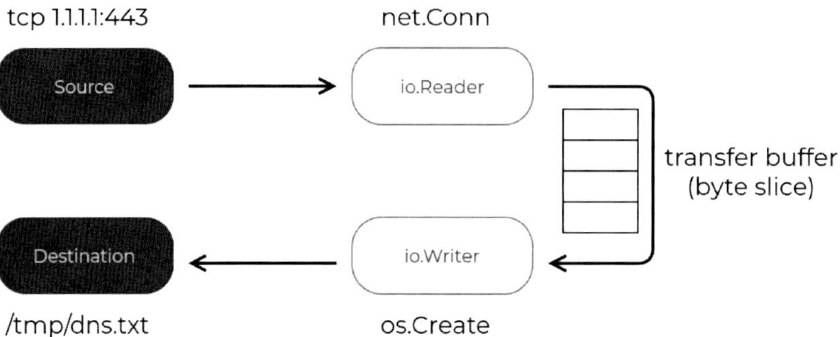

Figure 1.4 – Streaming from a network connection to a file example

A `Reader` is an interface that can read from a file, a cipher, a shell command, or a network connection, for example. You can then stream the data you capture to a `Writer` interface, which could also be a file or most of the other `Reader` examples.

The Go standard library offers these streaming interfaces, such as `net.Conn`, that, in this case, allow you to read and write from a network connection, transfer data between interfaces, and transform this data if needed. We cover this topic in much more detail in *Chapter 3, Getting Started with Go.*

While there are other variables to consider when selecting a programming language to work with, such as which one your company is currently using or which one you feel more comfortable with, our goal is to equip you with all the resources to understand what makes Go so appealing to large-scale system developers. If you want to begin in familiar territory, we compare and contrast Go with Python next. Python is the most popular programming language used for network automation today.

Go versus Python

The topic of comparing programming languages can very quickly turn into a heated debate. We believe all languages have their merits and we don't want to advocate for one being better than the other. Still, we do acknowledge that most people with a network automation background would know and use Python, so it would make sense to present some form of comparison between the two languages and highlight some of their most salient points.

Code execution

One of the biggest differences that affect the developer experience is how you distribute and execute your code.

Python programs require an interpreter to run on a target machine and access to all library dependencies. While there are projects such as Nuitka to compile Python, you need commercial support to obfuscate your source code, for example. Having all source code available allows you to make changes and iterate quickly when developing a feature or troubleshooting a bug.

Go programs do not require an interpreter, as you distribute them as a compiled binary file. Compiling to machine code may seem like an unnecessary hurdle, but compilation takes only a few seconds, and the resulting binary has all its required dependencies, so it's the only file that needs to exist on the target system.

Type system

Go requires all variable types to be statically defined, with type inference allowed only during initial variable declaration.

Although generics are making their way into Go, they do not allow the same amount of freedom as a Python type system. A lack of explicit type declaration makes Python a more approachable language for beginners and for use cases where development speed is more important than code robustness. However, as Python projects become more mature, they must make up for these initial gains by putting more focus on testing.

Performance

Go programs perform better when compared to Python across a wide range of use cases (see *The Computer Language Benchmarks Game*: *Further reading*). This is, in part, an outcome of the points we already mentioned in this section, but it's also the result of the effort the Go team has put into optimizing the language.

While things such as goroutines and type definition give Go developers enough tools to write high-performance code, each Go release brings new improvements in memory management and compiler optimizations that make code execution faster in the background.

Ease of use

Python is a language designed to be used for teaching and prototyping. At the same time, it's versatile and powerful enough to write complex programs such as web servers (Flask, Django), **machine learning** (**ML**) frameworks (PyTorch, TensorFlow), and infrastructure software (RabbitMQ, Ansible).

As the number of Python projects you work on grows, maintaining different virtual environments for dependency and environment management might become a hassle. This is an area where Go shines, with its self-hosted dependency manager and statically linked binaries.

Despite that, Python continues to hold its dominant position as the most approachable language with a large open source community and is unlikely to relinquish it any time soon.

Memory management

Both languages use dynamic memory management with automatic garbage collection. Most of the time, you wouldn't need to and are not advised to change any of the default settings, although both languages expose a few threshold variables that can be fine-tuned if needed.

The biggest difference comes from the fact that Go allocates memory based on a more precise set of data types and that it does static memory allocation at compile time in the stack for goroutines and functions, and only a subset of variables escape to the heap. In contrast, Python treats everything as an object, so even the most primitive types, such as `int` or `string`, are considerably larger, and they are dynamically allocated memory at runtime (in the heap).

Access to memory in the heap is not only slower but also needs to be garbage-collected, which adds an overhead to the program execution.

Syntax

Python has a very lightweight syntax and uses indentation to separate different blocks of code. The lack of trailing semicolons and excessive curly braces make it comprehensible, but writing it without an IDE—which would automatically manage the indentation—can be a challenge.

Go never considered white space for indentation, as the language designers don't believe having your semantics depend on invisible characters is a good idea. This, of course, comes down to personal preferences; formats such as **YAML Ain't Markup Language** (YAML), for example, also use spaces to structure data.

Go benefits from its built-in formatting tool that auto-indents the code and makes it look neat by automatically inserting blank lines in certain places. Also, Go developers use blank lines to split logically separate a set of lines in a function that makes the final program less dense and easier to read.

Failure handling

Another big difference is in error handling. Python uses implicit error handling as a convention by relying on exceptions that can be carefully caught in parts of code where you expect them to happen. This keeps in line with Python's readability and ease-of-use nature. Go uses explicit error checks, and most functions have errors as the last positional return value. This often results in the code looking like this:

```
config, err := buildConfig(deviceName)
if err != nil {
	return err
}
```

```
d, err := connect(deviceName)
if err != nil {
    return err
}

if err := configure(d, config); err != nil {
    return err
}
```

Although this makes a program more robust by forcing the developers to always think about the returned error and act on it as soon as it happens, this does create a lot of visual noise that human brains quickly learn to ignore. This is a recurrent topic in the Go community and one of the areas that Go version 2 is putting a focus on. The Go 2 draft design document for error handling covers the problem and proposal in detail (*Further reading*).

Concurrency

Concurrency has not only been a feature of Go since day one but also one of the key drivers behind the creation of Go in the first place. Go has enough first-class language constructs to deal with most common concurrency challenges, such as communication between processes and access to shared resources.

By contrast, you cannot run more than two or more Python threads at the same time because the **Global Interpreter Lock** (**GIL**) prevents it, which the Python language designers made part of the language early on. This is unless you architect your program to use the threading library. The GIL has performance benefits for single-threaded programs, and removing it from the language has been a recurrent topic in the Python community.

To implement concurrency, Python makes you run multiple processes to leverage all the CPUs that you have at your disposal (multiprocessing or concurrency pools). Over time, different libraries have attempted to improve the performance and **user experience** (**UX**) of concurrency in Python, with the most popular one being `asyncio`.

Despite that, better concurrency and parallelism are in the top three most desired features to add to Python, according to *Python Developers Survey 2020 Results* (*Further reading*). Most Python developers don't like the current implementation, as writing concurrent code in Python can be challenging and requires the use of compatible libraries.

Community

Being the more popular language of the two, Python has a larger community with a huge number of open source libraries and frameworks. Although its major use cases are data analysis, web development, and ML (*Python Developers Survey 2020 Results*: *Further reading*), today you can find libraries that deal with anything from game development to desktop plugins.

Most importantly, Python is the most popular language for network automation and has amassed many libraries and frameworks to work with network devices. Go has been more systems- and performance-centric, so we don't see as many network libraries and tools. Still, one heavy user of Go in the network engineering community has been the OpenConfig ecosystem, which today includes almost a dozen different projects written in Go.

Go is being rapidly adopted by web-scale companies, which means we are likely to see more network-related projects appearing in the future.

We hope this gives you a perspective and appreciation of the Go language features. The next step is to install Go on your computer.

Installing Go on your computer

The Go download and install instructions (`https://golang.org/doc/install#install`) require you to download a file from `https://go.dev/` and follow a couple of instructions. We include here the steps for **Go version 17.7**, which is the latest version available at the time of writing. Newer versions of Go 1 should continue to work.

Windows

To install Go on Windows, follow these steps:

1. Download `https://golang.org/dl/go1.17.7.windows-amd64.msi`.
2. Execute the `go1.17.7.windows-amd64.msi` file and follow the instructions.
3. Open the **Command Prompt** window (`cmd`) and run `go version` to verify the installation.

Mac

If you have Homebrew installed, you can run `brew install go`. Otherwise, you can follow these steps:

1. Download `https://golang.org/dl/go1.17.7.darwin-amd64.pkg`.
2. Execute the `go1.17.7.darwin-amd64.pkg` file and follow the instructions.
3. Open a Terminal and run `go version` to verify the installation.

Linux

Go is typically available as a system package in a Linux distribution, but is often an older version. Follow these steps to install a more recent release:

1. Download `https://golang.org/dl/go1.17.7.linux-amd64.tar.gz`.
2. Remove any existing Go installation with `rm -rf /usr/local/go`.
3. Extract the archive you downloaded into `/usr/local` with `tar -C /usr/local -xzf go1.17.7.linux-amd64.tar.gz`.
4. Add `/usr/local/go/bin` to the `PATH` environment variable with `export PATH=$PATH:/usr/local/go/bin`. To make this persistent, add this line as well in `$HOME/.bash_profile`. This last part is valid for `bash`, but you might want to do something similar if you use a different shell.
5. Run `go version` to verify the installation

There you go! You can now download and install Go in your system without any hassle. To install a different version, just replace `17.7` in the instructions with a target version of your choice.

Summary

In this chapter, we reviewed why Go is relevant for networking and network automation. We looked at the various aspects of Go that make it the preferred choice for millions of developers. We also explored how you can install it on your computer. In the next chapter, we will dive deeper into the Go programming language, its source files, and its tools.

Further reading

You can refer to these resources for further reading:

- *Stack Overflow Developer Survey 2021*: `https://insights.stackoverflow.com/survey/2021#most-loved-dreaded-and-wanted-language-want`
- *NetDevOps* 2020 survey: `https://dgarros.github.io/netdevops-survey/reports/2020`
- *Go Developer Survey 2020 Results*: `https://go.dev/blog/survey2020-results`
- *How Many Go Developers Are There?*: `https://research.swtch.com/gophercount`
- *golang-nuts*: `https://groups.google.com/forum/#!forum/golang-nuts`
- *Go Forum*: `https://forum.golangbridge.org/`
- *Go Language Collective*: `https://stackoverflow.com/collectives/go`

- *Gophers Slack channel*: `https://invite.slack.golangbridge.org/`
- **Go Developers Network** (**GDN**): `https://www.meetup.com/pro/go`
- CNCF DevStats toolset: `https://k8s.devstats.cncf.io/d/67/licenses-and-programming-languages?orgId=1`
- `https://madnight.github.io/githut/#/stars/2021/2`
- Go 6-month release cycle: `https://github.com/golang/go/wiki/Go-Release-Cycle`
- Go release notes: `https://golang.org/doc/devel/release`
- `https://github.com/golang/proposal#proposing-changes-to-go`
- Toward Go 2: `https://go.dev/blog/toward-go2`
- Go 2 language change template: `https://github.com/golang/proposal/blob/master/go2-language-changes.md`
- Go 2 proposals: `https://github.com/golang/go/issues?utf8=%E2%9C%93&q=is%3Aissue+is%3Aopen+label%3AGo2+label%3AProposal`
- Go 2 draft design document: `https://go.googlesource.com/proposal/+/master/design/go2draft.md`
- Python typing: `https://docs.python.org/3/library/typing.html`
- `go doc` tool website: `https://pkg.go.dev/`
- Go language server: `https://go.googlesource.com/tools/+/refs/heads/master/gopls/README.md#editors`
- Go 2 draft design document: `https://go.googlesource.com/proposal/+/master/design/go2draft-error-handling-overview.md`
- *Go Conferences and Major Events*: `https://github.com/golang/go/wiki/Conferences#go-conferences-and-major-events`
- Popular development tools: `https://insights.stackoverflow.com/survey/2021#most-loved-dreaded-and-wanted-tools-tech-love-dread`
- Top-paying technologies ranking: `https://insights.stackoverflow.com/survey/2021#technology-top-paying-technologieshttps://insights.stackoverflow.com/survey/2021#technology-top-paying-technologies`
- Go version 1: `https://go.dev/blog/go1`
- *Why does Go not have feature X?*: `https://golang.org/doc/faq#Why_doesnt_Go_have_feature_Xhttps://golang.org/doc/faq#Why_doesnt_Go_have_feature_X`

- *Go, Open Source, Community*: `https://go.dev/blog/open-source`
- *Go 1 and the Future of Go Programs*: `https://golang.org/doc/go1compat`
- *Go 2, here we come!*: `https://go.dev/blog/go2-here-we-come`
- *Software Reliability*: `https://users.ece.cmu.edu/~koopman/des_s99/sw_reliability/`
- *The Computer Language Benchmarks Game*: `https://benchmarksgame-team.pages.debian.net/benchmarksgame/fastest/go-gpp.html`
- *Five things that make Go fast*: `https://dave.cheney.net/2014/06/07/five-things-that-make-go-fast`
- *The Go Programming Language Specification*: `https://golang.org/ref/spec`
- *Python Developers Survey 2020 Results*: `https://www.jetbrains.com/lp/python-developers-survey-2020/`

2
Go Basics

With so many programming languages out there, it's fair to wonder why anyone would have to invent yet another one. What the background is of the people behind Go and what the problems are they are trying to solve with this new language are some of the items we will address in this chapter.

These topics give us some perspective on the challenges large-scale software development presents to software developers today and why modern technologies such as programming languages are constantly evolving.

By the end of this chapter, you should have a better understanding of where Go comes from and its role in developing distributed systems running on multi-core processors, as well as be familiar with Go's source code structure as we go through the following areas:

- What is Go?
- Go's guiding principles
- Go source code file structure
- Go packages and modules
- Compiling Go programs
- Running Go programs online
- Exploring the Go tool to manage Go source code

Technical requirements

We assume that you have basic familiarity with the command line, Git, and GitHub. You can find the code examples for this chapter in the book's GitHub repository, `https://github.com/PacktPublishing/Network-Automation-with-Go`, in the `ch02` folder.

To run the examples, follow these steps:

1. Install Go 1.17 or later for your operating system. You can follow the instructions in *Chapter 1, Introduction*, in the *Installing Go* on your computer section, or go to `https://go.dev/doc/install`.
2. Clone the book's GitHub repository with `git clone` at `https://github.com/PacktPublishing/Network-Automation-with-Go.git`.
3. Change the directory to an example's folder – `cd Network-Automation-with-Go/ch02/pong`.
4. Execute `go run main.go`.

What is Go?

During the second half of 2007, *Robert Griesemer*, *Rob Pike*, and *Ken Thompson* started discussing the design of a new programming language that would solve some problems they were experiencing when writing software at Google, such as the increased complexity to use some languages, long code compilation times, and not being able to program efficiently on multiprocessor computers.

Rob Pike was trying to take some concurrency and communicating channels ideas into C++, based on his earlier work on the Newsqueak language in 1988, as he describes in *Go: Ten years and climbing* (*Further reading*) and *Less is exponentially more* (*Further reading*). This turned out to be too hard to implement. He would work out of the same office with *Robert Griesemer* and *Ken Thompson*. Ken had worked together with Rob Pike in the past to create the character-encoding UTF-8, while *Ken Thompson* had designed and implemented the Unix operating system and invented the B programming language (the predecessor to the C programming language).

They chose the name **Go** for this new programming language because it's short, but the DNS entry for `go.com` wasn't available, so Go's website ended up at `golang.org`. And so, **golang** became a nickname for Go. While golang is convenient for search queries, it's not the name of the language (which is Go):

```
Subject: Re: prog lang discussion
From: Rob 'Commander' Pike
Date: Tue, Sep 25, 2007 at 3:12 PM
To: Robert Griesemer, Ken Thompson

i had a couple of thoughts on the drive home.

1. name

'go'. you can invent reasons for this name but it has nice properties.
it's short, easy to type. tools: goc, gol, goa. if there's an interactive
debugger/interpreter it could just be called 'go'. the suffix is .go
...
```

Figure 2.1 – The initial Go discussion email thread

Though they initially thought of C/C++ to be the starting point, they ended up starting from scratch to define a more expressive language, despite a large number of simplifications when compared to its predecessors. Go inherits some things from C, such as, but not limited to, basic data types, expression syntax, pointers, and compilation to machine code, but it doesn't have things such as the following:

- Header files
- Exceptions
- Pointer arithmetic
- Subtype inheritance (no subclasses)
- `this` in methods
- Promotion to a superclass (it uses embedding instead)
- Circular dependencies

Pascal, Oberon, and Newsqueak are among the programming languages that have influenced Go. In particular, its concurrency model comes from *Tony Hoare*'s **Communicating Sequential Processes (CSPs)** (*Further reading*) white paper, and CSP's implementations in *Rob Pike*'s interpreted language Newsqueak and, later, Phil Winterbottom's C-like compiled version, Alef. The next figure shows Go's family tree:

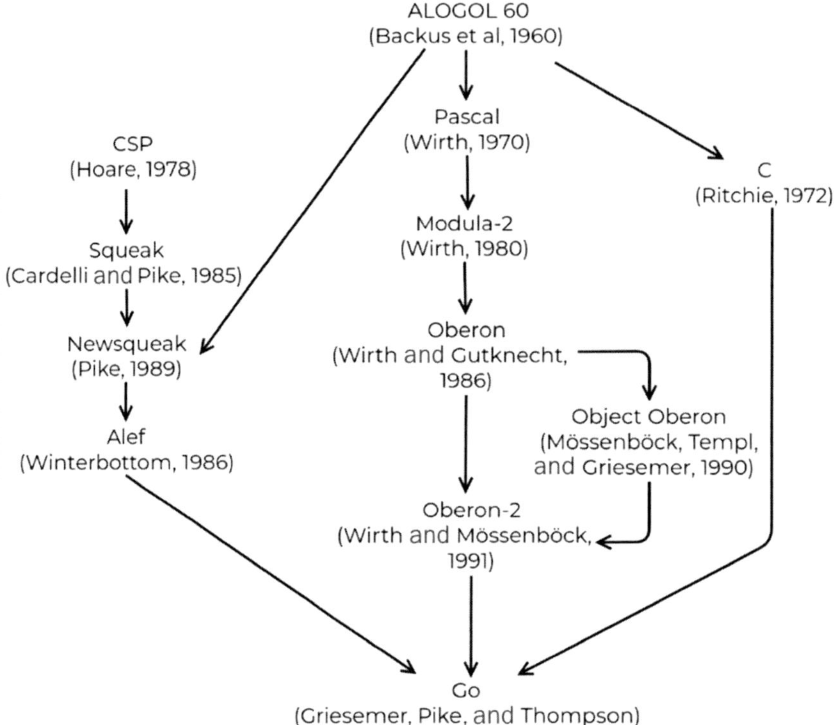

Figure 2.2 – The Go ancestors

The number of C++ programmers that come to Go is just a few compared to what the Go founders expected. Most Go programmers actually come from languages such as Python and Ruby.

Go became an open source project on November 10, 2009. They host Go's source code at `https://go.googlesource.com/go` and keep a mirror of the code at `https://github.com/golang/go` where you can submit pull requests. While Go is an open source programming language, it's actually supported by Google.

They wrote the first Go compiler in C, but they later converted it to Go. Russ Cox describes this in detail in Go 1.3+ Compiler Overhaul (*Further reading*). As mind-blowing as it may sound, the Go source code of today is written in Go.

They released Go 1 on March 28, 2012. We highlight some notable changes to the language since then in the summarized version of Go's timeline in the next figure:

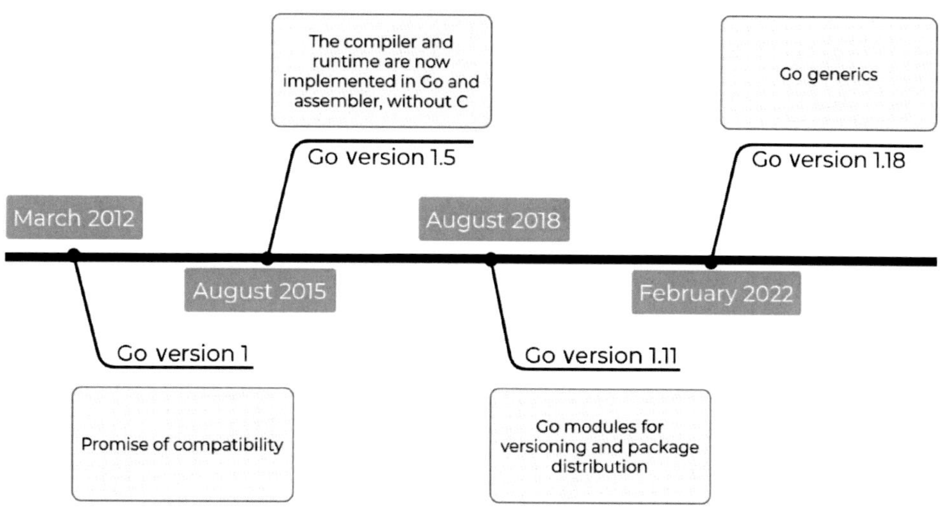

Figure 2.3 – Go's brief timeline

Go is a stable language, and the semantics should not change unless Go 2 happens. The only change that the Go team has confirmed at this point is the addition of generic programming using type parameters in early 2022 (Go 1.18), as described in the Type Parameters Proposal (*Further reading*).

Go is a programming language that attempts to combine the ease of programming of a dynamically typed language with the efficiency and safety of a statically typed language. It builds executable files in seconds, and with Go's first-class support for concurrency, we can take full advantage of multi-core CPUs.

Before we dive into Go code, we cover some guiding principles that make Go unique through the Go proverbs.

Go Proverbs

Rob Pike introduced the Go language proverbs at *Gopherfest* in *2015* to explain or teach Go philosophically. These are general guidelines that Go developers tend to adhere to. Most of these proverbs are good practices – but optional – that convey the spirit of the language.

We only include our favorite proverbs here. You can check out the full list at *Go Proverbs* (*Further reading*):

- Gofmt's style is no one's favorite, yet gofmt is everyone's favorite. When you write code in Go, you don't have to worry about the debate of white spaces versus tabs, or where you put braces or curly brackets. Gofmt (`gofmt`) formats your code with a prescriptive style guide, so all Go code looks the same. This way, you don't have to think about it when you write or read Go code:

- **Clear is better than clever**: Go favors clear code over clever code that is difficult to analyze or describe. Write code other people can read and with behavior they can understand.
- **Errors are values**: An error in Go is not an exception. It's a value you can use in your program logic – as a variable, for example.
- **Don't just check errors; handle them gracefully**: Go encourages you to think about whether you should do something with an error, instead of just returning it and forgetting about it. Depending on the error, maybe you can trigger a different execution path, add more info to it, or save it for later.
- **A little copying is better than a little dependency**: If you only need a few lines from a library, maybe you can just copy those lines instead of importing the entire library to keep your dependency tree under control and make your code more compact. This way, your program not only compiles faster but is also more manageable and simpler to understand.
- **Don't communicate by sharing memory; share memory by communicating**: This describes how concurrent processes in Go can coordinate between each other. In other languages, concurrent processes communicate by sharing memory, which you have to protect with locks to prevent a data race condition when these processes try to access a memory location concurrently. Go, in contrast, uses channels instead to pass references to data between processes, so only one process has access to the data at a time.
- **Concurrency is not parallelism**: Concurrency is structuring the execution of independent processes, whose instructions are not necessarily executed in sequence. Whether these instructions run in parallel depends on the availability of different CPU cores or hardware threads. *Rob Pike*'s *Concurrency is not Parallelism* (*Further reading*) talk is a must for Go developers.

The Go proverbs cover different aspects of Go, from formatting your Go code to how Go achieves concurrency.

Now, it's time to roll up our sleeves as we start looking into Go source code files.

Go source code files

While there isn't a filename convention for Go source code files, their filenames are typically one-word, all lowercase, and include an underscore if it has more than one word. It ends with the `.go` suffix.

Each file has three parts:

- **Package clause**: This defines the name of the package a file belongs to.
- **Import declaration**: This is a list of packages that you need to import.

- **Top-level declaration**: This is constant, variable, type, function, and method declarations with a package scope. Every declaration here starts with a keyword (`const`, `var`, `type`, or `func`):

```
// package clause
package main

// import declaration
import "fmt"

// top level declaration
const s = "Hello, 世界"
func main() {
    fmt.Println(s)
}
```

The code example shows the package declaration for the `main` package at the top. It follows the import declaration, where we specify that we use the `fmt` package in this file. Then, we include all declarations in the code – in this case, an `s` constant and the `main` function.

Packages

A package is one or more `.go` files in the same folder that declares the related constants, types, variables, and functions. These declarations are accessible to every file in the same package, so breaking down the code into different files is optional. It's more of a personal preference on how to better organize code.

In the standard library, they divide the code into separate files for larger packages. The `encoding/base64` package has one `.go` file (other than the test and example files), such as the following:

```
$ ls -1 /usr/local/go/src/encoding/base64/ | grep -v _test.go
base64.go
```

By contrast, the `encoding/json` package has nine `.go` source code files:

```
$ ls -1 /usr/local/go/src/encoding/json/ | grep -v _test.go
decode.go
encode.go
fold.go
fuzz.go
indent.go
scanner.go
```

```
stream.go
tables.go
tags.go
```

Package names are short and meaningful (no underscore). Users of a package refer to the package name when importing something from it – for example, the `Decode` method exists in the `json` and `xml` packages. Users can call these methods with `json.Decode` and `xml.Decode`, respectively.

One special package is `main`. This is the entry point for any program that imports other packages. This package must have a `main` function that takes no arguments and returns no value, such as the code example at the beginning of this section.

Go modules

Go modules became the default way to release packages in Go 1.16. They were first introduced in Go 1.11, back in 2018, to improve dependency management in Go. It allows you to define an import path and the dependencies for a package or collection of packages.

Let's define a small package called `ping`, with a `Send` function that returns a string with the word `pong`:

```
package ping

func Send() string {
    return "pong"
}
```

This is the `https://github.com/PacktPublishing/Network-Automation-with-Go/blob/main/ch02/ping/code.go` file in the book's GitHub repository. You can create a module for this package with the `go mod init` command at the root folder of this example (`ch02/ping`). The argument for this command should be the module location, where users can get access to it. The result is a `go.mod` file with the import path and a list of external package dependencies in it:

```
ch02/ping$ go mod init github.com/PacktPublishing/Network-
Automation-with-Go/ch02/ping
go: creating new go.mod: module github.com/PacktPublishing/
Network-Automation-with-Go/ch02/ping
```

With this, anyone can now import this package. The following program imports this package to the `pong` output:

```
package main

import (
```

```
    "fmt"
    "github.com/PacktPublishing/Network-Automation-with-Go/
ch02/ping"
)

func main() {
    s := ping.Send()
    fmt.Println(s)
}
```

You can run this program from the Go Playground (*Further reading*), which imports the module we just created. This is also a great segue into the next section on packet importing and a sneak peek into the Go Playground section that we will cover in just a few more pages.

Importing packages

The `import` keyword lists the packages to import in a source file. The import path is the module path, followed by the folder where the package is within the module, unless the package is in the standard library, in which case you only need to reference the directory. Let's examine an example of each scenario.

To give an example, the `google.golang.org/grpc` module has a package in the `credentials` folder. You would import it with `google.golang.org/grpc/credentials`. The last part of the path is how you prefix the package types and functions, `credentials.TransportCredentials` and `credentials.NewClientTLSFromFile`, respectively, in the next code sample.

Go's standard library (*Further reading*) at `go/src` is a collection of packages of the `std` module. The `fmt` folder hosts the package that implements functions to format input and output. The path to import this package is just `fmt`:

```
package xrgrpc

import (
    "fmt"
    /* ... <omitted for brevity > ... */
    "google.golang.org/grpc/credentials"
)

func newClientTLS(c client) (credentials.TransportCredentials,
error) {
    if c.Cert != "" {
```

```
            return credentials.NewClientTLSFromFile(...)
        }
        /* ... <omitted for brevity > ... */
        fmt.Printf("%s", 'test')
        /* ... <omitted for brevity > ... */
}
```

Packages do not live in a central repository such as `maven`, `pip`, or `npm`. You can share your code by upstreaming it to a version control system and distribute it by sharing its location. Users can download it with the `go` command (`go install` or `go get`).

For developing and testing purposes, you can reference local packages by pointing to their local path in the `go.mod` file:

```
module github.com/PacktPublishing/Network-Automation-with-Go/
ch02/pong

go 1.17

require github.com/PacktPublishing/Network-Automation-with-Go/
ch02/ping v0.0.0-20220223180011-2e4e63479343

replace github.com/PacktPublishing/Network-Automation-with-Go/
ch02/ping v1.0.0 => ../ping
```

In the `ch02/pong` example, the Go tool automatically created the first three lines of the `go.mod` file for us, referencing the ping module from the book's GitHub repository (*Further reading*). We later added a fourth line to replace that module, with the contents of the local version of it (`../ping`).

Comments

Code comments in Go play a key role, as they become your package documentation. The `go doc` tool takes the comments preceding a type, constant, function, or method that you export in a package as a document string for that declaration, producing an HTML file that the tool presents as a web page.

To give an example, all public Go packages (*Further reading*) display this autogenerated documentation.

Go offers two ways to create comments:

- C++-style `//` line comments, which is the most common form:

```
// IsPrivate reports whether ip is a private address,
according to
// RFC 1918 (IPv4 addresses) and RFC 4193 (IPv6
addresses).
func (ip IP) IsPrivate() bool {
    if ip4 := ip.To4(); ip4 != nil {
        return ip4[0] == 10 ||
            (ip4[0] == 172 && ip4[1]&0xf0 == 16) ||
            (ip4[0] == 192 && ip4[1] == 168)
    }
    return len(ip) == IPv6len && ip[0]&0xfe == 0xfc
}
```

- C-style `/* */` block comments, which are primarily for package descriptions or large blocks of formatted/indented code:

```
/*
Copyright 2014 The Kubernetes Authors.
Licensed under the Apache License, Version 2.0 (the
"License");
...
See the License for the specific language governing
permissions and
limitations under the License.
*/
package kubectl
```

Dave Cheney in *Practical Go: Real-world advice for writing maintainable Go programs* (*Further reading*) suggests that a code comment should explain one – and only one – of these three things:

- What it does
- How something does what it does
- Why something is why it is

A good practice is to make comments on variables that describe their contents, rather than their purpose. You could use the name of the variable to describe its purpose. This brings us to the naming style.

Names

The convention for declaring names in Go is to use camel case (MixedCaps or mixedCaps) instead of, for example, dashes or underscores when you use more than one word for the name of a function or variable. The exception to the rule are acronyms that have a consistent case, such as `ServeHTTP` and not `ServeHttp`:

```
package net

// IsMulticast reports whether ip is a multicast address.
func (ip IP) IsMulticast() bool {
	if ip4 := ip.To4(); ip4 != nil {
		return ip4[0]&0xf0 == 0xe0
	}
	return len(ip) == IPv6len && ip[0] == 0xff
}
```

The first letter of the name determines whether the package exports this top-level declaration. Packages export names that start with a capital letter. These names are the only ones an external user of the package can reference when importing the package – for example, you can reference `IsMulticast` in the preceding code sample from another package as `net.IsMulticast`:

```
package net

func allFF(b []byte) bool {
	for _, c := range b {
		if c != 0xff {
			return false
		}
	}
	return true
}
```

If the first letter is lowercase, no other package has access to this resource. Packages can have declarations that are only for internal consumption. The `allFF` function in the last code example comes from the `net` package. This means only functions in the `net` package can call the `allFF` function.

Languages such as Java and C++ have explicit keywords such as `public` and `private` to control access to types and methods. Python follows the convention of naming variables or methods for internal use with a single underscore prefix. In Go, you can access any variable or method that starts with a lowercase letter from any source code file within the package, but not from another package.

Executing your Go code

The Go compiler translates Go programs into machine code, producing a binary file. Aside from your program, the binary includes the Go runtime, which offers services such as garbage collection and concurrency. Having access to binary files that work for different platforms makes Go programs very portable.

Let's compile the `https://github.com/PacktPublishing/Network-Automation-with-Go/blob/main/ch02/pong/code.go` file of the book's GitHub repository with the `go build` command. You can also time this operation with the `time` command to see how fast Go builds really are:

```
ch02/pong$ time go build

real   0m0.154s
user   0m0.190s
sys    0m0.070s
```

Now, you can execute the binary file. The default filename is the package name, pong. You can change the filename with the `-o` option of the `go build` command. There will be more on this in the *Go tool* section:

```
ch02/pong$ ./pong
pong
```

If you don't want to generate a binary or executable file and only run the code, you can use the `go run` command instead:

```
ch02/pong$ go run main.go
pong
```

Either option is fine, and it probably comes down to a matter of personal preference or whether you intend to share the compiled artifact with others or deploy it to servers.

Go files have three main parts and they are organized into packages and modules.

You can run all the examples on your computer after installing Go, or you can run them online, as we discuss in the next section.

Running Go programs online

Sometimes, you need to test some code quickly or just want to share a code example with someone who might not have Go installed on their computer. In those situations, there are at least three websites where you can run and share Go code for free:

- The Go Playground
- The Go Play Space
- The Gotip Playground

They all share the backend infrastructure, but with subtle differences.

The Go Playground

The Go team runs the Go Playground (`https://play.golang.org/`) on golang.org's servers. They shared some insights and its architecture in the article *Inside the Go Playground* (*Further reading*), but more recently, *Brad Fitzpatrick* shared the history and the implementation details of the latest incarnation of the Go Playground (*Further reading*).

This service receives your program, runs it on a sandbox, and returns its output. This is very convenient if you are on your mobile phone, for example, and you want to verify the syntax of a function or something else.

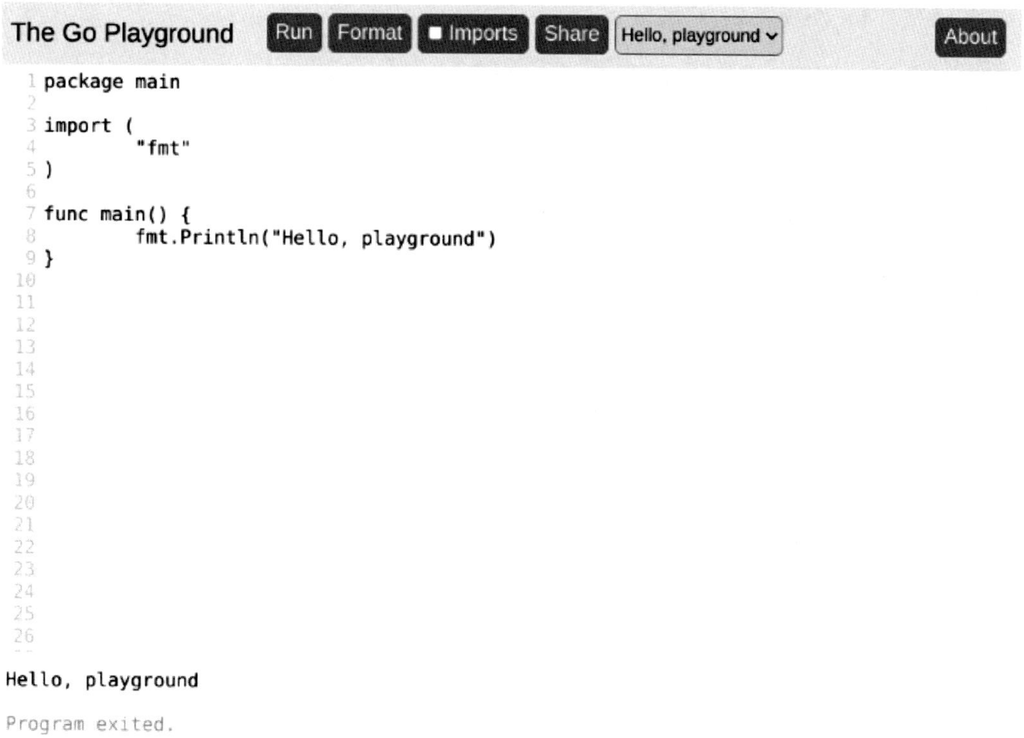

The Go Playground Run Format Imports Share Hello, playground About

```
package main

import (
	"fmt"
)

func main() {
	fmt.Println("Hello, playground")
}
```

```
Hello, playground

Program exited.
```

Figure 2.4 – The Go Playground

If you are curious about how they built this service or you want to run it locally in your environment, make sure you check out the Playground source code (*Further reading*).

The Go Play Space

If you can't live without syntax highlighting, go to the Go Play Space (*Further reading*). This is an experimental alternative Go Playground frontend. They proxy the code execution to the official Go Playground so that programs work the same. They also store shared snippets on the `golang.org` servers:

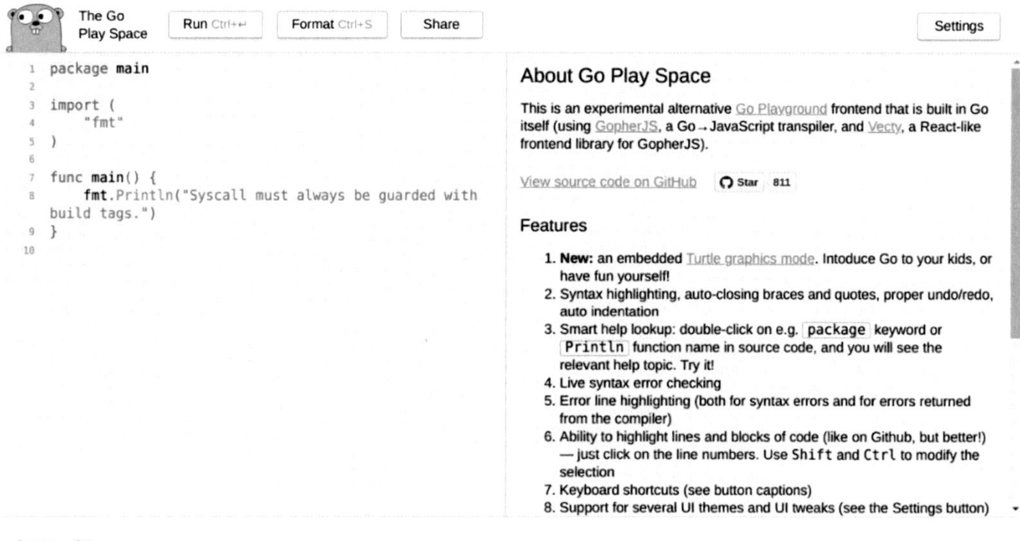

Figure 2.5 – The Go Play Space

Figure 2.5 shows some extra features that the Go Play Space includes besides syntax highlighting, such as auto-closing braces, access to documentation, and different UI themes.

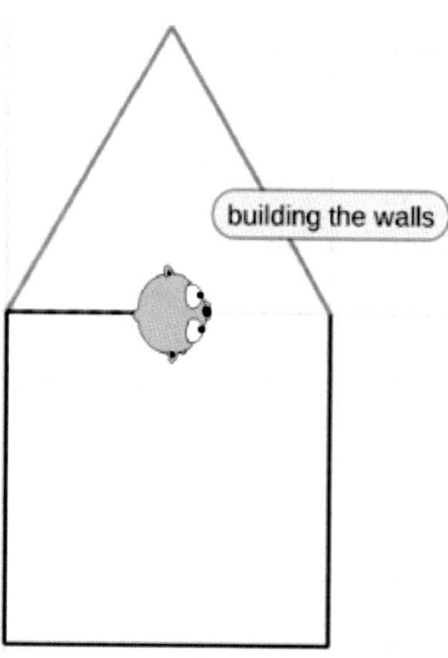

Figure 2.6 – Building a house in the Go Play Space

We could not pass over the fact that it also has a Turtle graphics mode to help you visualize algorithms for fun, such as having a gopher build a house, as shown in *Figure 2.6*.

A look into the Future

The Gotip Playground runs on golang.org's servers as well. This instance of the Go playground runs the latest development branch of Go. You can use it to test upcoming features that are in active development, such as the syntax described in the Type Parameters Proposal (*Further reading*) or the new `net/netip` package, without having to install more than one Go version on your system if you don't want to.

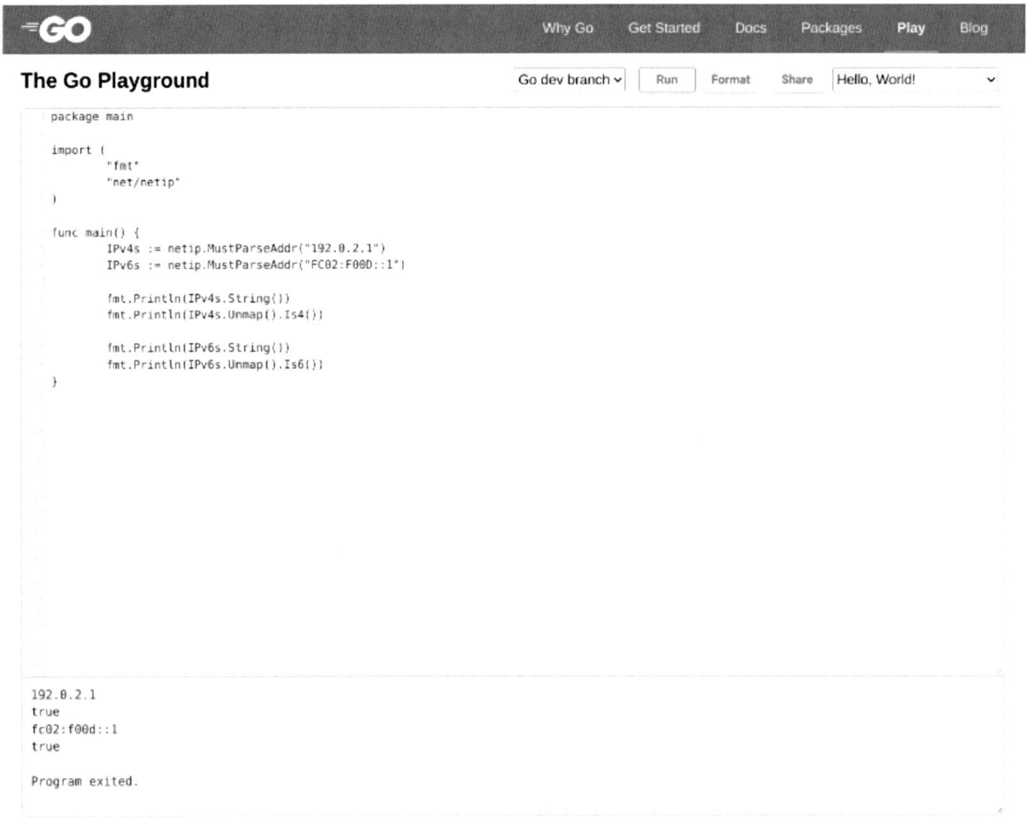

Figure 2.7 – The Gotip Playground

You can access the Gotip Playground via `https://gotipplay.golang.org/` or by selecting the **Go dev branch** dropdown at `https://go.dev/play/`.

These are all great options to run Go programs online that are available to you at no cost. In the next section, we go back to working on the command line as we explore the Go tool to manage Go source code.

The Go tool

One of the convenient things about Go – as a programming language – is that a single tool handles all interactions with, and operations on, the source code. When installing Go, make sure that the go tool is in the searchable OS path so that you can invoke it from any command-line terminal. The user experience, regardless of the OS or platform architecture, is uniform and doesn't require any customization when moving from one machine to another.

IDEs also use the go tool to build and run code, report errors, and automatically format Go source code. The go executable accepts a *verb* as the first argument that determines what go tool function to apply to Go source files:

```
$ go
Go is a tool for managing Go source code.

Usage:

     go <command> [arguments]

The commands are:

     bug          start a bug report
     build        compile packages and dependencies
     ...
     mod          module maintenance
     run          compile and run Go program
     test         test packages
     tool         run specified go tool
     version      print Go version
     vet          report likely mistakes in packages
```

We're only exploring a subset of the functions of the Go tool in this section. You can find the full list and every detail of each one in the Go cmd documentation (*Further reading*). The commands we're covering are as follows:

- build
- run
- mod

- `get`
- `install`
- `fmt`
- `test`
- `env`

These help you build and run your Go programs, manage their dependencies, and format and test your code.

Build

We use the `go build` command to compile a Go program and generate an executable binary. If you are not using Go modules yet, the command expects a list of Go source files to compile as an argument. It generates a binary file as a result, with the same name as the first source file (without the `.go` suffix). In the `ch02/hello` folder of the book's GitHub repository (*Further reading*), we have the `main.go` and `vars.go` files.

You can build an executable file for the program in these files with the `go build` command:

```
ch02/hello$ go build *.go

ch02/hello$ ./main
Hello World
```

Packaging compiled binaries is a common way of distributing Go programs, since it allows users of a program to skip the compilation stage and reduce the installation procedure to just a few commands (`download` and `unzip`). But you can only run this binary file on a machine with the same architecture and OS. To produce binary files for other systems, you can cross-compile to a wide range of OSs and CPU architectures. For example, the following table shows some target CPU instruction sets that are supported:

Value	Architecture
`amd64,386`	The x86 instruction set, 64-bit and 32-bit
`arm64,arm`	The ARM instruction set, 64-bit (AArch64) and 32-bit
`ppc64,ppc64le`	The 64-bit PowerPC instruction set, big-endian and little-endian
`riscv64`	The 64-bit RISC-V instruction set

Table 2.1 – Some supported CPU architectures

Out of a long list of supported operating systems, the next table shows the most popular options:

Value	OS
darwin	Linux
linux	macOS/iOS (Darwin)
windows	Windows

Table 2.2 – Some supported OSs

The GOOS and GOARCH environment variables allow you to generate cross-compiled binaries for any other supported system. If you are on a Windows machine, you can generate a binary for macOS running on a 64-bit Intel processor with the following command:

```
ch02/hello$ GOOS=darwin GOARCH=amd64 go build *.go
```

The go tool dist list command shows a complete set of unique combinations of OSs and architectures that the Go compiler supports:

```
$ go tool dist list
...
darwin/amd64
darwin/arm64
...
linux/386
linux/amd64
linux/arm
linux/arm64
...
windows/386
windows/amd64
```

The go build command supports different flags to change its default behavior. Two of the most popular flags are -o and -ldflags.

You can use -o to override the default binary name with a name of your preference. In the example, we've selected another_name:

```
ch02/hello$ go build -o another_name *.go

ch02/hello$ ./another_name
Hello World
```

To inject environment data at compile time into your program, use `-ldflags` with a reference to a variable and its value. This way, you can have access to build information during the program execution, such as the date you compiled the program or the version of the source code (`git commit`) you compiled it from:

```
ch02/hello$ go build -ldflags='-X main.Version=1.0 -X main.
GitCommit=600a82c442' *.go

ch02/hello$ ./main
Version: "1.0"
Git Commit: "600a82c442"
Hello World
```

The last example is a very common way of version-tagging a Go binary. The benefit of this approach is that it doesn't require any changes to the source code, and you can automate the entire process in a continuous delivery pipeline.

Run

Another way to run a Go program is by using the `go run` command. It accepts the same flags as `go build` with two differences:

- It doesn't produce a binary.
- It runs the program right after compilation.

The most common use case for `go run` is local debugging and troubleshooting, where a single command combines the processes of compilation and execution:

```
ch02/hello$ go run {main,vars}.go
Hello World
```

In the example, we run the program in the `main.go` and `vars.go` files, which produces the `Hello World` output.

Mod

With the introduction of Go modules, the `go` tool got an extra command to work with them – `go mod`. To describe its functionally, let's review a typical Go program development workflow:

1. You create a new project in a folder and initialize Go modules with the `go mod init` command, with a reference to the module name – `go mod init example.com/my-project`. This creates a pair of files, `go.mod` and `go.sum`, that keep track of your project's dependencies.

The next output shows the size of these two files of a real-life project. `go.mod` lists all the dependencies and is relatively small in size compared to `go.sum`, which has the checksum for all the dependencies:

```
$ ls -lhs go.*
4.0K go.mod
 92K go.sum
```

If you plan to share this project with others, the name of the module should be a path that is reachable on the internet. It normally points to your source code repository – for example, `github.com/username/my-project`. A real-life example is `github.com/gohugoio/hugo/`.

2. As you develop your code and add more and more dependencies, the go tool updates the `go.mod` and `go.sum` files automatically whenever you run the `go build` or `go run` commands.
3. When you add a dependency, the `go` tool locks its version in the `go.mod` file to prevent accidental code breakages. If you decide you want to update to a newer minor version, you can use the `go get -u package@version` command.
4. If you remove a dependency, you can run `go mod tidy` to clean up the `go.mod` file.
5. The two `go.*` files contain a full list of dependencies, including the ones that are not directly referenced in your code, that are indirect or chained/transitive dependencies. If you want to find out why a particular dependency is present in your `go.mod` file, you can use the `go mod why package` or `go mod graph` commands to print the dependency tree on the screen:

```
hugo$ go mod why go.opencensus.io/internal
# go.opencensus.io/internal
github.com/gohugoio/hugo/deploy
gocloud.dev/blob
gocloud.dev/internal/oc
go.opencensus.io/trace
go.opencensus.io/internal
```

The `go list` command can also be of help. It lists all the module dependencies:

```
hugo$ go list -m all | grep ^go.opencensus.io
go.opencensus.io v0.23.0
```

It also lists the actual package dependencies:

```
hugo$ go list all | grep ^go.opencensus.io
go.opencensus.io
```

```
go.opencensus.io/internal
go.opencensus.io/internal/tagencoding
go.opencensus.io/metric/metricdata
go.opencensus.io/metric/metricproducer
go.opencensus.io/plugin/ocgrpc
...
go.opencensus.io/trace/propagation
go.opencensus.io/trace/tracestate
```

If you prefer a visual representation, there are projects such as Spaghetti (*Further reading*), a dependency analysis tool for Go packages, that can present this information with a user-friendly interface, as shown in *Figure 2.8*:

github.com/gohugoio/hugo

Click on a package in the tree view to display information about it, including a path by which it is reached from one of the initial packages. Use the *break* button to remove an edge from the graph, so that you can assess what edges need to be broken to eliminate an unwanted dependency.

Packages

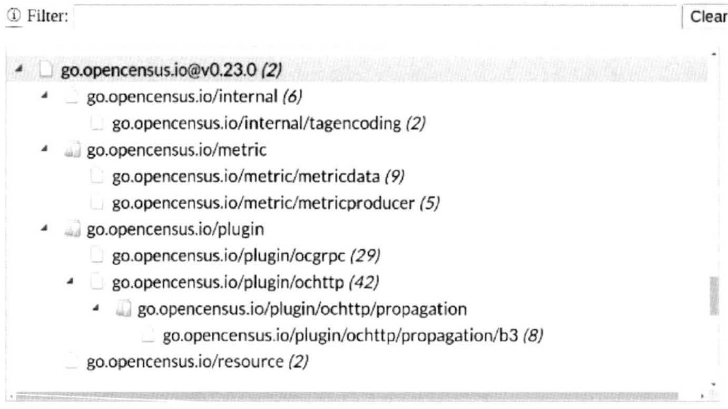

Selected package: go.opencensus.io

Imports: ...

Imported by: ...

Path from initial package:

github.com/gohugoio/hugo
break | break all → **github.com/gohugoio/hugo/commands**
break | break all → **github.com/gohugoio/hugo/deploy**
break | break all → gocloud.dev/blob
break | break all → gocloud.dev/internal/oc
break | break all → go.opencensus.io/plugin/ocgrpc
break | break all → **go.opencensus.io/trace**
break | break all → **go.opencensus.io/internal**
break | break all → go.opencensus.io

Figure 2.8 – Hugo dependency analysis

One thing that is important to mention is that Go modules use semantic versioning. If you need to import a package that is part of a module at major version 2 or higher, you need to include that major version suffix in their import path (`github.com/username/my-project/v2 v2.0.0`, for example).

Before we move to the next command, let's create a `go.mod` file for the example in the `ch02/hello` folder of the book's GitHub repository (*Further reading*):

```
ch02/hello$ go mod init hello
go: creating new go.mod: module hello
go: to add module requirements and sums:
go mod tidy

ch02/hello$ go mod tidy

ch02/hello$ go build

ch02/hello$ ./hello
Hello World
```

Now, you can build a binary file for the program with `go build` without having to reference all the Go files in the folder (`*.go`).

Get

Before the Go 1.11 release, you could use the `go get` command to download and install Go programs. This legacy behavior is being completely deprecated, starting from Go 1.17, so we won't cover it here. From now on, the sole role of this command is the management of dependencies in the `go.mod` file to update them to a newer minor version.

Install

The easiest way to compile and install a Go binary without explicitly downloading the source code is to use the `go install [packages]` command. In the background, the go tool still downloads the code if necessary, runs `go build`, and copies the binary into the `GOBIN` directory, but the go tool hides all this from the end user:

```
$ go install example.com/cmd@v1.2.3

$ go install example.com/cmd@latest
```

The `go install` command accepts an optional version suffix – for example, `@latest` – and falls back to the local `go.mod` file if the version is missing. Thus, when running `go install`, it's recommended to always specify a version tag to avoid errors if the `go` tool cannot find a local `go.mod` file.

Fmt

Go takes much of the code formatting out of developers' hands by shipping an opinionated formatting tool that you can invoke with the `go fmt` command pointing to your Go source code – for example, `go fmt source.go`.

Chapter 1, Introduction, covers how this improves code readability by making all Go code look similar. Most IDEs with plugins for Go automatically format your code every time you save it, making it one less problem to worry about for developers.

Test

Go is also opinionated when it comes to testing. It makes a few decisions on behalf of developers about the best way to organize code testing to unify the user experience and discourage the use of third-party frameworks:

1. It automatically executes all files with the `_test.go` suffix in their filenames when you run the `go test` command. This command accepts an optional argument that specifies which package, path, or source file to test.
2. The Go standard library includes a special `testing` package that works with the `go test` command. Aside from unit test support, this package offers comprehensive coverage reports and benchmarks.

To put this into practice, we include a test program for the `ping` package that we described in the Go modules section. The `ping` package has a `Send` function, which returns the `pong` string when called. The test we perform should verify this. In the test program, we start by defining a string with the value we expect (`pong`) and then compare it to the result of the `ping` function. The `code_test.go` file (`https://github.com/PacktPublishing/Network-Automation-with-Go/blob/main/ch02/ping/code_test.go`) in the same folder as `ping` represents this in Go code:

```
package ping_test

import (
    "github.com/PacktPublishing/Network-Automation-with-Go/
ch02/ping"
    "testing"
)
```

```
func TestSend(t *testing.T) {
    want := "pong"
    result := ping.Send()
    if result != want {
        t.Fatalf("[%s] is incorrect, we want [%s]", result, 
want)
    }
}
```

All test functions have a `TestXxx(t *testing.T)` signature, and whether they have access to any other functions and variables defined in the same package depends on how you name the package:

- **ping**: This gives you access to everything in the package.
- **ping_test**: This is a package type (the `_test` suffix) that can live in the same folder as the package you are testing, but it does not have access to the original package variables and methods, so you must import it as any other user would do it. It's an effective way to document how to use the package while testing it. In the example, we use the `ping.Send` function instead of `Send` directly, as we are importing the package.

This is an assurance that the `Send` function always does the same even if they must optimize the code later. Now, every time you change the code, you can run the `go test` command to verify that the code still behaves the way you expect. By default, when you run `go test`, it prints the results of every test function it finds along with the time to execute them:

```
ch02/ping$ go test
PASS
ok github.com/PacktPublishing/Network-Automation-with-Go/ch02/
ping 0.001s
```

If someone makes a change in the code that modifies the behavior of the program so that it can no longer pass the test cases, we are in the presence of a potential bug. You can proactively identify software issues with the `go test` command. Let's say they change the return value of the `Send` function to `p1ong`:

```
func Send() string {
    return "p1ong"
}
```

The `go test` command then generates an error the next time your continuous integration pipeline runs the test cases:

```
ch02/ping$ go test
--- FAIL: TestSend (0.00s)
  code_test.go:12: [plong] is incorrect, we want [pong]
FAIL
exit status 1
FAIL github.com/PacktPublishing/Network-Automation-with-Go/
ch02/ping 0.001s
```

Now, you know you can't promote this code to production. The benefit of testing is that you reduce the number of software bugs your users might run into, as you can catch them beforehand.

Env

The `go env` command displays the environment variables that the `go` command uses for configuration. The `go` tool can print these variables as flat text or in the JSON format with the `-json` flag:

```
$ go env -json
{
    ...
    "GOPROXY": "https://proxy.golang.org,direct",
    "GOROOT": "/usr/local/go",
    ...
    "GOVERSION": "go1.17",
    "PKG_CONFIG": "pkg-config"
}
```

You can change the value of a variable with `go env -w <NAME>=<VALUE>`. The next table describes some of these configuration environment variables:

Name	Description
GOARCH	The architecture or processor for which to compile code
GOBIN	The directory where `go install` installs a command
GOMODCACHE	The directory where the go command stores downloaded modules
GOOS	The OS for which to compile code
GOPROXY	The URL of the Go module proxy
GOROOT	The root of the go tree

Table 2.3 – Some configuration environment variables

When you change a variable, the `go` tool stores its new value in the path specified by the `GOENV` variable, which defaults to `~/.config/go`:

```
$ go env -w GOBIN=$(go env GOPATH)/bin

$ cat ~/.config/go/env
GOBIN=/home/username/go/bin
```

The preceding output example shows how to set the `GOBIN` directory explicitly and how to verify it.

Go offers a command-line utility that helps you manage your source code, from formatting your code to performing dependency management.

Summary

In this chapter, we reviewed Go's origins and its guiding principles, and how you should structure Go source code files and work with dependencies to run your Go programs.

In the next chapter, we will drill down into the semantics of the Go language, the variable types, math logic, control flow, functions, and, of course, concurrency.

Further reading

- *Less is exponentially more*: `https://commandcenter.blogspot.com/2012/06/less-is-exponentially-more.html?m=1`
- *Go: Ten years and climbing*: `https://commandcenter.blogspot.com/2017/09/go-ten-years-and-climbing.html`
- *Communicating Sequential Processes*: `https://www.cs.cmu.edu/~crary/819-f09/Hoare78.pdf`
- *Go 1.3+ Compiler Overhaul*: `https://golang.org/s/go13compiler`
- *Type Parameters Proposal*: `https://go.googlesource.com/proposal/+/refs/heads/master/design/43651-type-parameters.md`
- *Go Proverbs*: `https://go-proverbs.github.io/`
- *Concurrency is not Parallelism*: `https://www.youtube.com/watch?v=oV9rvDllKEg`
- The book's GitHub repository: `https://github.com/PacktPublishing/Network-Automation-with-Go`
- Go Playground: `https://go.dev/play/p/ndfJcayqaGV`
- Playground source code: `https://go.googlesource.com/playground`

- Go Play Space: `https://goplay.space/`
- Go's standard library: `https://github.com/golang/go/tree/master/src`
- *Practical Go: Real-world advice for writing maintainable Go programs*: `https://dave.cheney.net/practical-go/presentations/qcon-china.html#_comments`
- The latest incarnation of the Go Playground: `https://talks.golang.org/2019/playground-v3/playground-v3.slide#1`
- *Inside the Go Playground*: `https://go.dev/blog/playground`
- Cmd documentation: `https://pkg.go.dev/cmd/go#pkg-overview`
- Spaghetti: `https://github.com/adonovan/spaghetti`
- *Deprecation of 'go get' for installing executables*: `https://golang.org/doc/go-get-install-deprecation`

3
Getting Started with Go

In this chapter, we dive into the Go basics and the characteristics that make it comparable to a dynamically typed language, but with the efficiency and safety of a statically typed, compiled language.

We also explore different Go packages to manipulate data in different formats and how to scale programs with Go's concurrency model. Being able to manipulate data effectively and take advantage of all the resources of systems running multi-core processors are key elements to keep in mind when automating networks.

During this chapter, we cover the following key topics:

- Go variable types
- Go's arithmetic, comparison, and logical operators
- Control flow
- Functions in Go
- Interfaces in Go
- Input and output operations
- Decoding and encoding with Go
- Concurrency

Technical requirements

We assume basic familiarity with the command line, Git, and GitHub. You can find the code examples for this chapter in the book's GitHub repository at `https://github.com/PacktPublishing/Network-Automation-with-Go`, under the `ch03` folder.

To run the examples, perform the following steps:

1. Install Go 1.17 or later for your operating system. You can follow the instructions in *Chapter 1, Introduction*, in the *Installing Go* section, or go to `https://go.dev/doc/install`.
2. Clone the book's GitHub repository with `git clone https://github.com/PacktPublishing/Network-Automation-with-Go.git`.
3. Change the directory to an example folder:

   ```
   cd Network-Automation-with-Go/ch03/json.
   ```

4. Execute `go run main.go`.

Go's type system

Go is a statically typed language, which means the compiler must know the types of all variables to build a program. The compiler looks for a special variable declaration signature and allocates enough memory to store its value:

```
func main() {
    var n int
    n = 42
}
```

By default, Go initializes the memory with the zero value corresponding to its type. In the preceding example, we declare `n`, which has an initial value of `0`. We later assign a new value of `42`:

Type	Zero Value
Integer	0
String	""
Boolean	false
Pointer	nil

Table 3.1 – Zero values

As its name suggests, a variable can change its value, but only as long as its type remains the same. If you try to assign a value with a different type or redeclare a variable, the compiler complains with an appropriate error message.

If we append a line with `n = "Hello"` to the last code example, the program wouldn't compile, and it would return the following error message: `cannot use "Hello" (type untyped string) as type int in assignment`.

You can use type inference as a shortcut for variable declarations. In that case, you omit an explicit type argument in your declaration. Just keep in mind that Go has limited support for type inference inside of a function.

Instead of explicitly defining a type for each variable, you can use a special short assignment symbol, `:=`, and let the compiler guess the variable type based on its value, as in the next example, where the compiler assumes the variable `n` is of type `int`:

```
func main() {
    n := 42
}
```

Just like with variables, the compiler can also infer a constant type. The value of constants cannot change throughout the program and we generally use them to represent real-world values such as the number π (**Pi**), static names of objects or places, and so on:

```
const Book = "Network Automation with Go"
```

Now, let's have a closer look at the different types available in Go and their common use cases.

Basic types

According to Go's language specification, there are four groups of basic or primitive types predeclared globally and available to all Go programs by default:

- Numeric
- Strings
- Boolean
- Error

Numeric

Go defines several numeric types to store integers and real numbers of different sizes. Type names normally contain information about their sign and the size of the value (in bits). The only notable exceptions are `int` and `uint` types, whose values depend on the machine and normally default to 32 bits for 32-bit CPUs, or 64 bits for 64-bit CPU architectures:

Type	Values	Size
int8	-128 to 127	1 byte
uint8	0 to 255	1 byte
int16	-32768 to 32767	2 bytes
uint16	0 to 65535	2 bytes
int32	-2^31 to 2^31 - 1	4 bytes
uint32	0 to 2^32 - 1	4 bytes
int64	-2^64 to 2^64 - 1	8 bytes
uint64	0 to 2^64-1	8 bytes
float32	real numbers	4 bytes
float64	real numbers	8 bytes

Table 3.2 – Numeric type variables

Here are some examples of how to instantiate variables of numeric types. These are all valid options, and you can use whichever is most appropriate for the range of values you need to store or produce. You can test this code from `ch03/type-definition/main.go` (in the *Further reading* section). Notice we use type inference for `a`, so its type is `int` and its size is 8 bytes on a 64-bit machine. The second variable (`b`) is an unsigned 32-bit integer (4 bytes). The last variable (`c`) is a floating-point number (4 bytes):

```
func main() {
    a := -1

    var b uint32
    b = 4294967295

    var c float32 = 42.1
}
```

You can also convert a `v` value to the `T` type with the expression `T(v)`, as in the next example. Here, `b` results from converting `a`, an integer, to an unsigned 32-bit integer, and finally, `c` is a floating-point number from converting `b`:

```
func main() {
    a := 4294967295
```

```
    b := uint32(a)

    c := float32(b)
}
```

Once you have defined a type for a variable, any new operation has to match this type on both sides of the assignment operator (=). You could not append `b = int64(c)` at the end of the preceding example, as `b` would be of the `uint32` type.

Type conversion is always explicit in Go, unlike other programming languages that may do this implicitly and sometimes call this type casting.

Strings

Go supports two styles of string literals: you can enclose the characters with double-quotes to make it an interpreted literal, or use back-quotes for raw string literals, as in the next example:

```
func main() {
    d := "interpreted\nliteral"

    e := `raw
literal`

    fmt.Println(d)
    fmt.Println(e)
}
```

Notice the escape sequence in `d`. Go interprets this to generate a new line character within the string. The following is the output of this program, which you can find at `ch03/string-literals/main.go` (in the *Further reading* section):

```
ch03/string-literals$ go run main.go
interpreted
literal
raw
literal
```

You can compare strings with the == and != operators. You can concatenate strings with the + and += operators. The example at `ch03/string-concatenate/main.go` (in the *Further reading* section) shows these operators in action:

```
func main() {
	s1 := "Net"
	s2 := `work`

	if s1 != s2 {
		fmt.Println(s1 + s2 + " Automation")
	}
}
```

Until this point, nothing seems to be too different from other programing languages. But in Go, a string is actually a slice of bytes, or to be more precise, a sequence of UTF-8 Unicode points. In memory, Go represents this as a two-word structure containing a pointer to the string data and its length.

Let's define a new string, `n`, with the `Network Automation` string literal in `ch03/string-memory/main.go` (in the *Further reading* section). We can store each character as one or more bytes using the variable-width character encoding UTF-8. For English, we use one byte per character, so the string literal in this case is 18 bytes long:

```
func main() {
	n := "Network Automation"
	fmt.Println(len(n))

	w := n[3:7]
	fmt.Println(w)
}
```

We can define another string as a subset of another. For this, we specify the lower bound in the original string and the upper bound. The index count starts at zero and the resulting string doesn't include the character in the upper bound index. For `n[3:7]`, we set the boundaries at characters "w" and " ". The program prints the following:

```
ch03/string-memory$ go run main.go
18
work
```

While the `n` and `w` variables reference strings of different lengths, the variable size of both is the same, just like for any other string variable. A string variable is a two-word structure. A word is usually 32 or

64 bits depending on the CPU architecture. Two 64-bit words are 16 bytes (2 x 8-byte), so for 64-bit platforms, a string is a 16-byte data structure. Out of those 16 bytes, 8 bytes are a pointer to the actual string data (a slice), and the remaining 8 bytes are to store the length of the string slice. *Figure 3.1* shows what this looks like in memory:

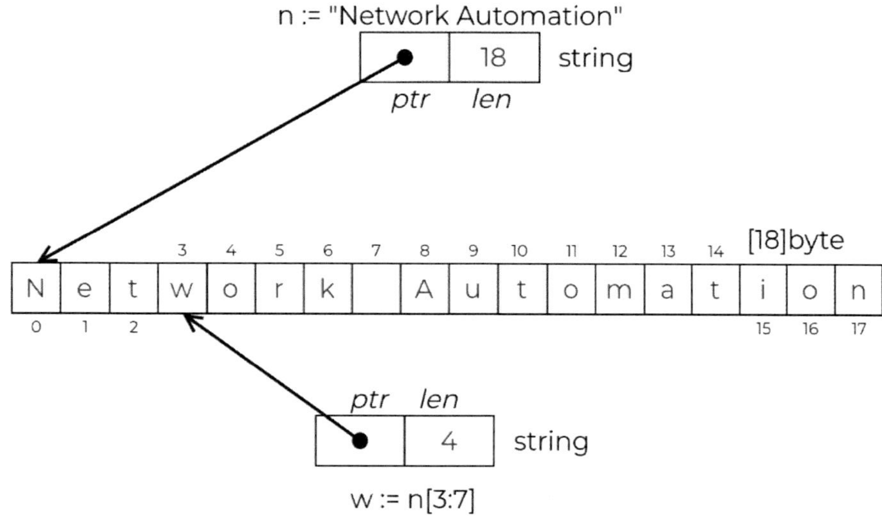

Figure 3.1 – What a string looks like in memory

It's OK that more than one string references the same underlying slice, as this slice is immutable, meaning that you can't change its contents. While the slice stores the string data, you can't change a character of the string by referencing an index of the slice, because it's immutable.

By contrast, if you want to change the value of a string variable, let's say you need to assign a different text to it, Go points the string data structure to a new underlying slice with the new string content you supply. All this happens behind the scenes, so you don't need to worry about this.

Boolean

The `bool` data type uses one byte of memory, and it stores a value of either `true` or `false`. As in other programming languages, you can use variables of the `bool` type in conditional statements to change the control flow of a program. The `if` conditional explicitly requires a `bool` type:

```
func main() {
    condition := true

    if condition {
        fmt.Printf("Type: %T, Value: %t \n",
```

```
                                   condition, condition)
        }
    }
```

If you run this program at ch03/boolean/main.go (in the *Further reading* section), you get the following output:

```
ch03/boolean$ go run main.go
Type: bool, Value: true
```

Because the condition is true, we print the condition variable type and value.

Error

Go has a unique approach to error handling and defines a special error type to represent a failure condition. You can generate errors, change them, print them on a screen, or use them to change the control flow of a program. The next code sample shows the two most common ways of generating a new variable of the Error type:

```
func main() {
    // Creates a variable of 'error' type
    err1 := errors.New("This is a new error")

    // string formatting when building an error message
    msg := "another error message"
    err2 := fmt.Errorf("This is %s", msg)
}
```

You can make any user-defined type an error, as long as it implements a special Error() method that returns a string. We talk more about implementing methods in the *Interfaces* section later in this chapter.

One common way of error handling is to allow it to bubble up until a point in a program where you can decide how to react to it — whether to fail and stop the execution or log and retry. Regardless of that, the use of errors is pervasive in Go, and all functions that can fail return an error as their last argument, so the following pattern is very common in Go programs:

```
func main() {
    result, err := myFunction()

    if err != nil {
        fmt.Printf("Received an error: %s", err)
```

```
        return err
    }
}
```

The `myFunction` function returns two values. In the outer function in the preceding example, we store the first return value of `myFunction` in a variable named `result`, and the second return value in the `err` variable, to store the value of any potential error inside `myFunction`, which now surfaces to the calling function.

Depending on the logic of the program, you need to decide how to handle the error. Here, if the error isn't null (`nil`), we print the error message and finish the execution of the function (`return`). We could also have just logged it and allowed the program to continue.

Container types

The next level up from the primitive types is a container type. These are still standard types that are available to any Go program without any explicit import statement. But, they represent more than just a single value. We use container types in Go to store different values of the same type; these include the following:

- Arrays
- Slices
- Maps

In the following sections, we discuss the use cases and implementation details of these three types.

Arrays

One of the first things any programmer needs, after they've gained the ability to deal with primitive types, is the ability to store collections of values of these types. For example, a network inventory may store a list of device hostnames or IP addresses. The most common solution for this problem is a data structure called an `array`. Go's `array` types have the `[n]T` signature, where `n` is the length of the array and `T` is the value type you store in the array.

Here is an example of how you can use arrays in Go with strings. We purposely mix different semantic ways you can define an array, so you can choose the style you prefer. We first define the `hostnames` array on a single line and then the `ips` array on a multiline statement:

```
func main() {
    hostnames := [2]string{"router1.example.com",
                           "router2.example.com"}
```

```
    ips := [3]string{
        "192.0.2.1/32",
        "198.51.100.1/32",
        "203.0.113.1/32",
    }

    // Prints router2.example.com
    fmt.Println(hostnames[1])

    // Prints 203.0.113.1/32
    fmt.Println(ips[2])
}
```

This gets even more interesting for network engineers when working with arrays of bytes. Look at the next example of how Go reads the input decimal number (`127` for example), and the binary data is at your fingertips. Both array examples are available at `ch03/arrays/main.go` (see the *Further reading* section):

```
func main() {
    // ipv4 is [0000 0000, 0000 0000, 0000 0000, 0000 0000]
    var ipAddr [4]byte

    // ipv4 is [1111 1111, 0000 0000, 0000 0000, 0000 0001]
    var localhost = [4]byte{127, 0, 0, 1}

    // prints 4
    fmt.Println(len(localhost))

    // prints [1111111 0 0 1]
    fmt.Printf("%b\n", localhost)

    // prints false
    fmt.Println(ipAddr == localhost)
}
```

Go arrays have many benefits. They are very memory efficient, as they store values sequentially and don't have any extra metadata overhead. They are also comparable, meaning you can check whether two arrays are equal, assuming their values have comparable types.

But, because of their fixed size, we rarely use arrays directly in Go. The only exception is when you know the size of your dataset ahead of time. With that in mind, in networking, we deal with a lot of fixed-sized datasets; they make up most of the network protocol headers, so arrays can be convenient for that and things such as IP and MAC addresses, port or sequence numbers, and various VPN labels.

Slices

Arrays have an immutable structure by definition (fixed-size). While you can alter the value within an array, they cannot grow and shrink as the size of the stored data changes. But, implementation-wise, this has never been a problem. Many languages implement arrays as dynamic data structures that change their size behind the scenes.

Of course, there is some performance penalty involved when growing an array, but with some clever algorithms, it's possible to reduce the number of changes and make the end user experience as frictionless as possible. Slices play this role in Go; they are the most widely used array-like data structure in Go.

Providing the length of the slice when creating it is optional. Behind the scenes, Go creates a backing array that defines the upper bound to what size the slice can grow to. That upper bound is what we know as the **capacity** of the slice. In general, the capacity is equal to the length of the slice, but that is not always the case. If the slice needs to grow beyond its capacity, Go creates a new larger backing array and copies over the contents of the original array. The next example shows three ways to create a slice and the values for capacity and length for each slice:

```
func main() {
    empty := []string{}
    words := []string{"zero", "one", "two", "three",
                      "four", "five", "six"}
    three := make([]string, 3)

    fmt.Printf("empty: length: %d, capacity: %d, %v\n",
                        len(empty), cap(empty), empty)
    fmt.Printf("words: length: %d, capacity: %d, %v\n",
                      len(words), cap(words), words)
    fmt.Printf("three: length: %d, capacity: %d, %v\n",
                      len(three), cap(three), three)
    /* ... <continues next > ... */
}
```

This program, which you can find at `ch03/slices/main.go` (see the *Further reading* section), prints the following:

```
ch03/slices$ go run main.go
empty: length: 0, capacity: 0, []
words: length: 7, capacity: 7, [zero one two three four five
six]
three: length: 3, capacity: 3, [  ]
```

Just like with strings, you can slice a slice, which creates a new reference to a section of the same backing array. For example, if you create a new slice based on the slice words from the preceding example with `words[1:3]`, you end up with a slice that has `one` and `two` elements, so the length of this slice is two. Its capacity is six, though. Why six? The backing array is the same, but the new slice starts at index one, and the last index of the backing array is seven. *Figure 3.2* shows what this looks like in memory:

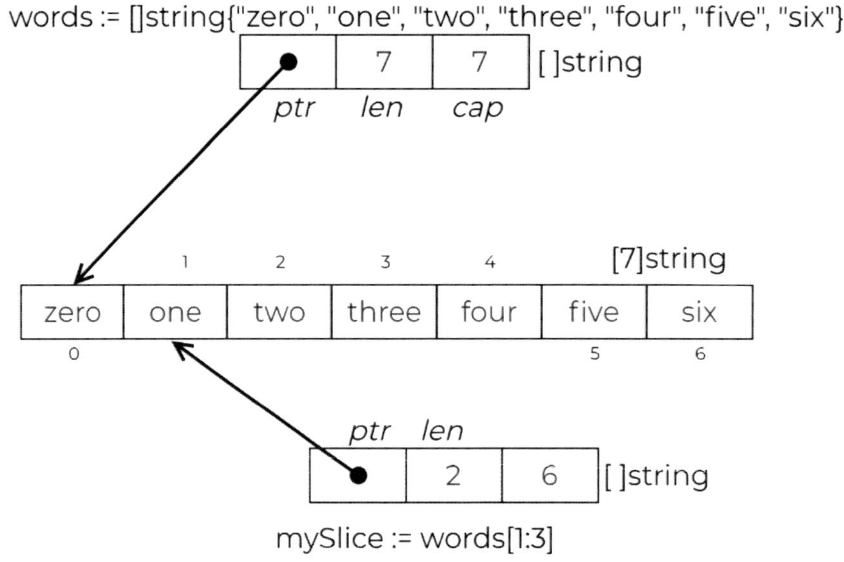

Figure 3.2 – What slices look like in memory

To add elements to the end of slice, you can use the built-in `append` function. Let's start from the slice we were just referencing and call it `mySlice`:

```
func main() {
    /* ... <continues from before > ... */
```

```
    mySlice := words[1:3]
    fmt.Printf(" mySlice: length: %d, capacity: %d, %v\n",
            len(mySlice), cap(mySlice), mySlice)

    mySlice = append(mySlice, "seven")
    fmt.Printf(" mySlice: length: %d, capacity: %d, %v\n",
            len(mySlice), cap(mySlice), mySlice)

    mySlice = append(mySlice, "eight", "nine", "ten",
                    "eleven")
    fmt.Printf(" mySlice: length: %d, capacity: %d, %v\n",
            len(mySlice), cap(mySlice), mySlice)
}
```

If we run this program from `ch03/slices/main.go` (see the *Further reading* section), we can see how Go allocates a new backing array when it needs extra capacity. When it had three elements already, and we asked to add another four to a slice with a capacity of six, Go automatically allocated a new backing array with a capacity of 12 to support the extra elements and future growth:

```
ch03/slices$ go run main.go
...
 mySlice: length: 2, capacity: 6, [one two]
 mySlice: length: 3, capacity: 6, [one two seven]
 mySlice: length: 7, capacity: 12, [one two seven eight nine
ten eleven]
```

The bottom line is that while this might sound hard to grasp, it all happens behind the scenes. What we want to leave you with about slices is that they are a three-word data structure, and are 24 bytes on most computers nowadays.

Maps

Maps are a container type that makes it possible to store a mapping between one type, for example, a string or an integer, as the key to another type stored as the value. A map is of the `map[KeyType]ValueType` form, where `KeyType` is any type that is comparable and `ValueType` may be any type at all. One example would be `map[int]string`.

One way to initialize a map is with the built-in `make` function as in the next example, where we create a map of `string` as key and also with `string` as value. You can add new values to the map, referencing the key you want to associate that value with. In the example, we map `spine` to `192.168.100.1`:

```
func main() {
    dc := make(map[string]string)

    dc["spine"] = "192.168.100.1"

    ip := dc["spine"]
    ip, exists := dc["spine"]

    if exists {
        fmt.Println(ip)
    }
}
```

To retrieve a value and assign it to a variable, you can reference the key just like when adding values, but this time, on the right side of the equals sign, as in the preceding example, where we assigned the value of `dc["spine"]` to the `ip` variable.

You can also do membership testing, to check whether a certain key is on the map. A two-value assignment tests for the existence of a key, as in `ip, exists := dc["spine"]`, where `exists` is a Boolean value that is only `true` if `dc["spine"]` exists.

Another way to initialize a map is with data, as in the next example. To delete elements, you can use the built-in `delete` function:

```
func main() {
    inv := map[string]string{
        "router1.example.com": "192.0.2.1/32",
        "router2.example.com": "198.51.100.1/32",
    }

    fmt.Printf("inventory: length: %d, %v\n", len(inv),
              inv)

    delete(inv, "router1.example.com")

    fmt.Printf("inventory: length: %d, %v\n", len(inv),
```

```
                    inv)
}
```

This program prints the following:

```
ch03/maps$ go run main.go
inventory: length: 2, map[router1.example.com:192.0.2.1/32
router2.example.com:198.51.100.1/32]
inventory: length: 1, map[router2.example.com:198.51.100.1/32]
```

The full code for this section is available at `ch03/maps/main.go` (see the *Further reading* section).

User-defined types

Unlike the types we discussed before, user-defined types, as the name suggests, are types that you define. In this category we have the following:

- Structs
- Interfaces

Interfaces are the only abstract type in Go and define a contract for concrete types, such as structs. They describe behavior, not implementation details, which helps us break the business logic of our programs into building blocks with interfaces between them. We cover them in detail in a dedicated section for interfaces later in this chapter.

Structs

A struct is a data structure that represents a collection of fields with their data types. Structs look a bit like mappings, except the keys in this case are fixed. They become an extension of the variable name.

Let's define a router (`Router`) that has four `string` fields and one `bool` field:

```
type Router struct {
    Hostname  string
    Platform  string
    Username  string
    Password  string
    StrictKey bool
}
```

Now, this new type can also be part of another user-defined type, as in the following `Inventory` type, which has a slice of these routers we just defined:

```
type Inventory struct {
    Routers []Router
}
```

Here are a few examples of how to create an instance of a struct and assign values to its fields:

```
func main() {
    var r1 Router
    r1.Hostname = "router1.example.com"

    r2 := new(Router)
    r2.Hostname = "router2.example.com"

    r3 := Router{
        Hostname:  "router3.example.com",
        Platform:  "cisco_iosxr",
        Username:  "user",
        Password:  "secret",
        StrictKey: false,
    }
    /* ... <continues next > ... */
}
```

The caveat is that `r2` is now actually a pointer to `Router` (that's how `new` works), but it's not something we need to worry about right now. Let's put all the routers in an `Inventory` type variable:

```
func main() {
    /* ... <continues from before > ... */
    inv := Inventory{
        Routers: []Router{r1, *r2, r3},
    }

    fmt.Printf("Inventory: %+v\n", inv)
}
```

Now, we have all our routers conveniently in a variable we can use. All the fields we haven't assigned a value yet are zero value ("", or empty for strings):

```
ch03/structs$ go run main.go
Inventory: {Routers:[{Hostname:router1.example.com Platform:
Username: Password: StrictKey:false} {Hostname:router2.
example.com Platform: Username: Password: StrictKey:false}
{Hostname:router3.example.com Platform:cisco_iosxr
Username:user Password:secret StrictKey:false}]}
```

The code in this example is available at `ch03/structs/main.go` (see the *Further reading* section).

Until this point, we have not talked about other variable types such as pointers, channels, and functions. We cover these in other sections of this chapter. Please bear with us. In the next section, we introduce some math and logical operators that allow us to execute different actions in our programs.

Arithmetic, comparison, and logical operators

Operators are special symbols that perform specific mathematical, logical, or relational computations on variables of different types. We cover the following three types of operators in this section:

- Arithmetic operators
- Logical operators
- Comparison operators

While we don't cover all corner cases and permutations of types, we'd like to focus on a few operators that might be interesting in the network automation context.

Arithmetic operators

These operators perform mathematical calculations with numeric values. The resulting value depends on the order and type of the operands:

Symbol	Name	Applies to
+	sum	integers, floats, complex values, strings
-	difference	integers, floats, complex values
*	product	integers, floats, complex values
/	quotient	integers, floats, complex values
%	remainder	integers
&	bitwise AND	integers
|	bitwise OR	integers
^	bitwise XOR	integers
&^	bit clear (AND NOT)	integers
<<	left shift	integer << integer >= 0
>>	right shift	integer >> integer >= 0

Table 3.3 – Arithmetic operators

They follow the standard mathematical logic implemented in most programming languages:

```
func main() {
    // sum s == 42
    s := 40 + 2

    // difference d == 0.14
    d := 3.14 - 3

    // product p == 9.42
    p := 3 * 3.14

    // quotient q == 0
    q := 3.0 / 5

    // remainder r == 2
    r :=  5 % 3
}
```

Strings are the only non-numeric type that can make use of an arithmetic operator. You can use + for string concatenation, to link together two or more text strings into one string:

```
func main() {
    // s == "Hello, World"
    s := "Hello" + ", " + "World"
}
```

One of the most interesting applications of arithmetic operations is interacting with binary data, something that many network engineers are familiar with.

Network protocols have deterministic structures expressed in a set of headers that contain forwarding information and facts of the encapsulated payload.

You can use the arithmetic operators bit shift and bitwise (`OR`, `AND`, and `XOR`) to create or extract data from network headers.

To see this in action, let's work with a 20-byte long **Transmission Control Protocol** (**TCP**) header that has the following information:

- Source port address – 2 bytes
- Destination port address – 2 bytes
- Sequence number – 4 bytes
- Acknowledgment number – 4 bytes
- Header length and reserved – 1 byte
- Control flags – 1 byte:
    - `CWR`: **Congestion Window Reduced** flag
    - `ECE`: **Explicit Congestion Notification** (**ECN**)-echo flag
    - `URG`: Urgent pointer
    - `ACK`: Acknowledgment number is valid
    - `PSH`: Request for push
    - `RST`: Reset the connection
    - `SYN`: Synchronize sequence numbers
    - `FIN`: Terminate the connection
- Window size – 2 bytes
- Checksum – 2 bytes
- Urgent pointer – 2 bytes

Figure 3.3 shows the TCP header structure including all the mandatory fields we just listed:

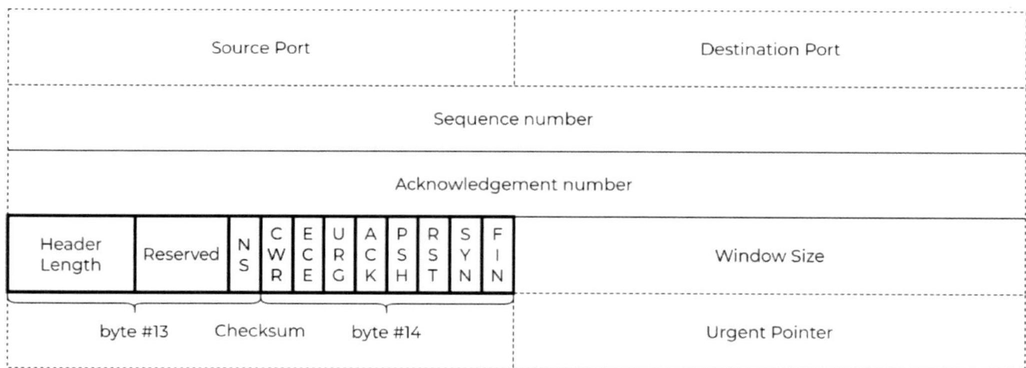

Figure 3.3 – TCP header structure

In the next code example, we build a TCP header from an empty slice of bytes. We write its length in the first four bits of byte 13 and then set the `SYN` flag in byte 14 of the TCP header.

The header length field of the TCP header represents the number of 32-bit words the TCP header has. You can see it as the number of rows in it, as *Figure 3.3* shows. Here, the length is five words.

The following code snippet (the full version is at `ch03/tcp-header/main.go` (see the *Further reading* section)) shows how to set this length on a TCP header using arithmetic operations:

```
func main() {
    // Header length (measured in 32-bit words) is 5
    var headerWords uint8 = 5

    // Header length in bytes is 20
    headerLen := headerWords * 32 / 8

    // Build a slice of 20 bytes to store the TCP header
    b := make([]byte, headerLen)

    // Shift header words bits to the left to fit
    // the Header Length field of the TCP header
    s := headerWords << 4

    // OR operation on byte 13 and the store new value
    b[13] = b[13] | s
```

```
    // Print the 13 byte of the TCP header -> [01010000]
    fmt.Printf("%08b\n", b[13])
    /* ... <continues next > ... */
}
```

Figure 3.4 shows how the `headerWords` 8-bit unsigned integer variable, which is compatible with the size of a single byte, got bit-shifted left to fit into its appropriate positions in the header's field.

The left shift operation moves the original bits, dropping the overflowing bits on the right and replacing the bits on the left with zeros. The bitwise `OR` operator combines the resulting value with the existing byte. This is a common pattern to make sure that none of the bits you configured before get lost since the bitwise `OR` operator always keeps the `1` bits if they are present in any of the operands:

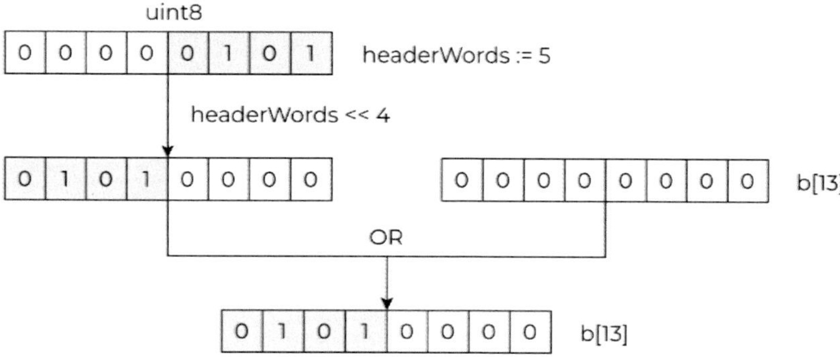

Figure 3.4 – Building a TCP header, part one

To set a flag, we can do something similar, where we set one bit and shift it to the left to leave it in the second position to signal `SYN`:

```
func main() {
    /* ... <continues from before > ... */
    // assume that this is the initial TCP SYN message
    var tcpSyn uint8 = 1

    // SYN flag is the second bit from the right so
    // we shift it by 1 position
    f := tcpSyn << 1

    // OR operation on byte 14 and store the new value
    b[14] = b[14] | f
```

```
    // Print the 14 byte of the TCP header -> [00000010]
    fmt.Printf("%08b\n", b[14])
    /* ... <continues next > ... */
}
```

Figure 3.5 depicts the bit operations in the preceding code example:

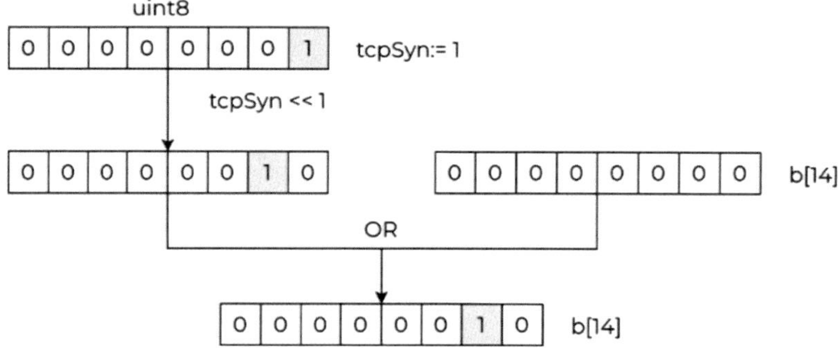

Figure 3.5 – Building a TCP header, part two

Now, let's see how the reverse process of parsing those two bytes on the receiving side can look:

```
func main() {
    /* ... <continues from before > ... */
    // only interested if a TCP SYN flag has been set
    tcpSynFlag := (b[14] & 0x02) != 0

    // Shift header length right, drop any low-order bits
    parsedHeaderWords := b[13] >> 4

    // prints "TCP Flag is set: true"
    fmt.Printf("TCP Flag is set: %t\n", tcpSynFlag)

    // prints "TCP header words: 5"
    fmt.Printf("TCP header words: %d\n", parsedHeaderWords)
}
```

This time, we're using the opposite set of bit operations. The right shift moves all bits from left to right, dropping the bits on the right and adding zeros to the left:

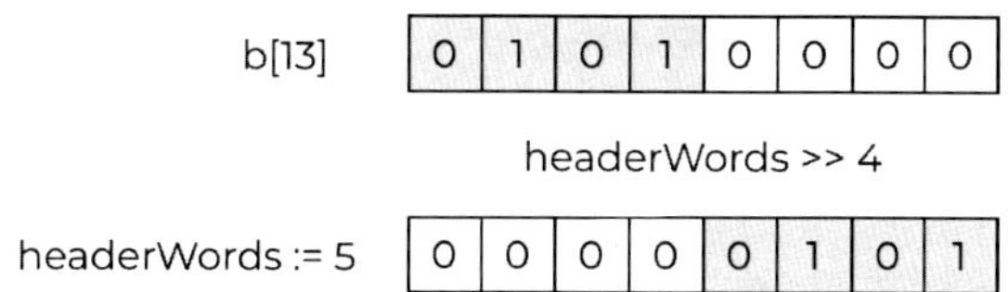

Figure 3.6 – Parsing a TCP header, part one

The bitwise `AND` operator has the same behavior as a network mask. It keeps the bits that are set to `1` and resets everything else to zero, effectively hiding the non-important bits. In our case, we're using the `0x02` mask value or `0000 0010` in binary, which hides everything else and only leaves us with the second bit from the right. We can then shift that bit to the right and check its value:

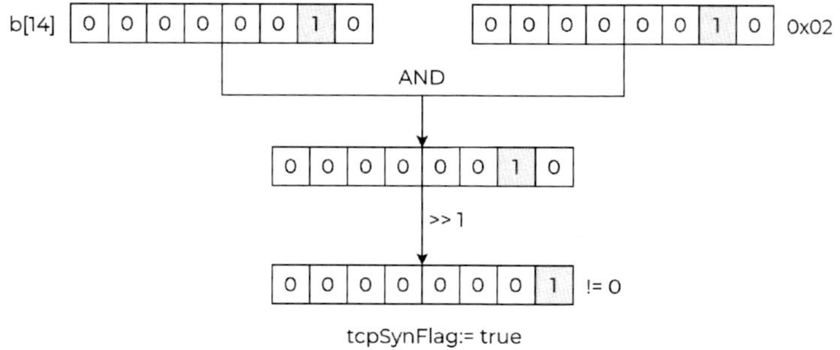

Figure 3.7 – Parsing a TCP header, part two

Being able to work at the bit and byte level is a powerful programming capability.

Logical operators

Logical operators are a basic set of Boolean operations that follow the rules of Boolean algebra — conjunction, disjunction, and negation:

x	y	AND	OR	NOT(x)
0	0	0	0	1
0	1	0	1	1
1	0	0	1	0
1	1	1	1	0

Table 3.4 – Logical operators

There is nothing surprising in Go's implementation of these logical operators, the only thing worth remembering is that there is no syntactic sugar for them, so the only acceptable values are `&&` for `AND` , `||` for `OR`, and `!` for `NOT`.

Comparison operators

We use the equal and not equal (== and !=) operators to compare a pair of comparable values and return a Boolean (`true|false`). You can apply greater than and less than operators (<, <=, >, and >=) to ordered values:

Symbol	Name
==	equal
!=	not equal
<	less
<=	less or equal
>	greater
>=	greater or equal

Table 3.5 – Comparison operators

Here's a brief example of comparison operators in action, with their most common types:

```
func main() {
    // all strings are comparable
    fmt.Println("hello" == "hello")

    // strings are ordered alphabetically
    fmt.Println("hello" < "world")

    // integers are comparable and ordered
    fmt.Println(1 < 10)

    // floating point numbers are also comparable
```

```
    fmt.Println(10.0 >= 1.1)
}
```

In the preceding example, all statements evaluate and print `true`. You can find the complete list of comparable and ordered properties of other Go types, such as pointers, channels, and arrays, in the *Comparison operators* section of the Go language specification (see *Further reading*).

This concludes this introduction to the Go data types and different operators used to perform day-to-day operations. Now, it's time to put together the first building blocks of our programs as we dive into Go's control flow and functions.

Control flow

Control flow constructs are a key building block of any computer program, as they allow you to express complex behaviors with conditions and iteration. Go's support for control flow reflects its minimalistic design, which is why you'd mostly see a couple of variations of conditional statements and one version of loop in the entire language specification. It may seem surprising, but this makes Go easier to read, as it forces the same design patterns on all programs. Let's start with the simplest and the most common control flow blocks.

for loops

In its simplest form, the `for` loop allows you to iterate over a range of integers while doing some work in each iteration. For example, this is how you would print all numbers from `0` to `4`:

```
func main() {
    for i := 0; i < 5; i++ {
        fmt.Println(i)
    }
}
```

The first line has the `init` statement, `i := 0`, the condition statement, `i < 5`, and the `post` (each iteration) statement, `i++`, separated by semicolons (`;`). The code continues to evaluate the condition statement and the post statement of the `for` loop until the condition is no longer `true`, that is, until `i >= 5`.

This loop type (`for`) has many variations and one of the most common ones is the iteration over a container type. Here are two examples:

- This is an example of iterating over a slice:

  ```
  func main() {
      slice := []string{"r1", "r2", "r3"}
  ```

```
    for i, v := range slice {
        fmt.Printf("index %d: value: %s\n", i, v)
    }
}
```

- This is an example of iterating over a map:

```
func main() {
    hashMap := map[int]string{
        1: "r1",
        2: "r2",
        3: "r3",
    }

    for i, v := range hashMap {
        fmt.Printf("key %d: value: %s\n", i, v)
    }
}
```

The special `range` keyword loops through all values of a slice or a map, creating a copy of the current item on a new pair of key/value variables for each iteration (`i` and `v` in the examples). You can also use `range` to iterate over arrays and strings. This keyword has special behavior for channels, which we cover later in the *Concurrency* section.

Another common variation of this loop construct is the infinite loop. You can use this when you don't know the number of iterations ahead of time, but you know when to stop:

```
func main() {
    for {
        time.Sleep(time.Second)
        break
    }
}
```

The key distinction here is the absence of any conditions in the loop definition, which is a shorthand for `true`; that is, the condition statement always evaluates to `true` and the loop iterates infinitely. The only way to stop this kind of loop is to use the `break` keyword.

Go doesn't have a `while` keyword for loops, which you can find in many other programming languages. But, you can make Go's `for` loop act in the same way as `while`, by dropping the `init` and `post` statements as the next code example shows:

```
func main() {
	i := 0
	for i < 5 {
		fmt.Println(i)
		i++
	}
}
```

Another special keyword worth mentioning in this context is `continue`, which skips the remainder of the current iteration of a loop. The following example prints all numbers from `0` to `4`, but only if they are even:

```
func main() {
	// prints 0 2 4
	for i := 0; i < 5; i++ {
		if i % 2 != 0 {
			continue
		}
		fmt.Println(i)
	}
}
```

In this example, we skip numbers that have a non-zero remainder when divided by two with the `if i % 2 != 0` clause. This is a conditional statement, which is the topic of the next section.

Conditional statements

Control structures help you define the behavior or direction to follow when a program can follow different execution paths.

Let's start with a two-way conditional statement. We try to connect to a website (`https://www.tkng.io/`) and then print the response we receive if the connection is successful, or we return the error message if the `HTTP GET` operation fails. If the error is not null (`err != nil`), we return. Otherwise (`else`), we print the information (`fmt.Printf`):

```
func main() {
	resp, err := http.Get("https://www.tkng.io/")
```

```
    if err != nil {
            log.Fatalf("Could not connect: %v", err)
    } else {
            fmt.Printf("Received response: %v",
                        resp.Status)
    }
}
```

One way to improve the readability of the preceding example is to left-align the successful execution path of the program, meaning that if one of the branches of the `if` condition ends in a terminating statement, as in our case with `return`, you can drop the entire `else` clause and rewrite the code as follows:

```
func main() {
    resp, err := http.Get("https://www.tkng.io/")
    if err != nil {
            log.Fatalf("Could not connect: %v", err)
    }

    fmt.Printf("Received response: %v", resp.Status)
}
```

Like any typical `if-then-else` construct, Go's conditional statements can encode multi-way conditions with many `if-else` statements. But, Go developers usually prefer to use a `switch` statement in this scenario, because it's a more concise and readable form of the multi-stage `if-then-else`.

Consider the following example, which sends an `HTTP GET` request and prints a message based on the returned status code. The full code is at `ch03/switch/main.go` (see *Further reading*):

```
func main() {
    resp, err := http.Get("http://httpstat.us/304")
    if err != nil {
        log.Fatalf("Could not connect: %v", err)
    }

    switch {
    case resp.StatusCode >= 600:
        fmt.Println("Unknown")
```

```
        case resp.StatusCode >= 500:
            fmt.Println("Server Error")
        case resp.StatusCode >= 400:
            fmt.Println("Client Error")
        case resp.StatusCode >= 300:
            fmt.Println("Redirect")
        case resp.StatusCode >= 200:
            fmt.Println("Success")
        case resp.StatusCode >= 100:
            fmt.Println("Informational")
        default:
            fmt.Println("Incorrect")
        }
    }
```

You can write this example as a chain of `if-then-else` statements as well, but using `switch` makes your code cleaner, and many Go developers consider it good practice for these situations.

goto statements

Another way you can transfer the control from one part of a program to another is by using a `goto` statement.

You can use `goto` statements to break out of a nested or infinite loop or to implement logic.

Building upon the preceding code example, let's see how we can use `goto` statements to implement various exit points from a function. You can find the full code of the example at `ch03/goto/main.go` (see *Further reading*):

```
func main() {
    resp, err := http.Get("http://httpstat.us/304")
    if err != nil {
        log.Fatalf("Could not connect: %v", err)
    }

    switch {
    case resp.StatusCode >= 600:
        fmt.Println("Unknown")
        goto exception
    case resp.StatusCode >= 500:
```

```
            fmt.Println("Server Error")
            goto failure
        case resp.StatusCode >= 400:
            fmt.Println("Client Error")
            goto failure
        case resp.StatusCode >= 300:
            fmt.Println("Redirect")
            goto exit
        case resp.StatusCode >= 200:
            fmt.Println("Success")
            goto exit
        case resp.StatusCode >= 100:
            fmt.Println("Informational")
            goto exit
        default:
            fmt.Println("Incorrect")
            goto exception
        }

    exception:
        panic("Unexpected response")

    failure:
        log.Fatalf("Failed to connect: %v", err)

    exit:
        fmt.Println("Connection successful")
}
```

The `goto` statements have a somewhat evil reputation in most programming languages because of their power to break the flow of a program, often making it harder to read, with many prominent computer scientists warning against their inconsiderate use. Still, these statements do have their place and you can find them in many projects and even in the Go standard library.

Loops, conditional statements, and things like `goto` help you define the control flow of your Go programs. We still haven't covered some extra control flow constructs and corner cases used together with channel types. We cover them later in the *Concurrency* section of this chapter, but before we get there, we first need to talk about another important area of code organization: functions.

Functions

On the surface, a Go function is exactly the same as in any other programming language: a section of code designed to perform a certain task grouped into a reusable container. Thanks to the static nature of the language, all functions have a signature that defines the number and types of acceptable input arguments and output values.

Consider the following function (`generateName`), which generates a new name based on a pair of input strings (`base` and `suffix`). You can find the full code of the next example at `ch03/functions1/main.go` (see *Further reading*):

```
func generateName(base string, suffix string) string {
    parts := []string{base, suffix}
    return strings.Join(parts, "-")
}

func main() {
    s := generateName("device", "01")

    // prints "device-01"
    fmt.Println(s)
}
```

This function's signature is `func (string, string) string`, meaning that it accepts two arguments of the `string` type and returns another string. You can assign the returned value to a variable or pass it as an argument directly to another function.

Go's functions are values, which means you can pass them as an input argument and even return them as the output from another function.

To illustrate this, we define a new function named `processDevice`, which takes two parameters, a function with a `func (string, string) string` signature, and a `string`. In the body of this function, two relevant strings are in play: `base`, which is statically set to `device`, and `ip`, which is the string the function receives as the second argument:

```
func processDevice(getName func (string, string) string, ip
string) {
    base := "device"
    name := getName(base, ip)
    fmt.Println(name)
}
```

The most interesting part of this function is on the second line of its body, where it calls the `getName` function. This function is what `processDevice` received as an argument, which could be any function as long as it takes two strings as arguments and returns just one string. That's the case with the `generateName` function we defined for an earlier example, which means we can pass `generateName` as an argument to `processDevice` to build a unique device name. Let's see what this would look like. The code of this example is available at `ch03/functions1/main.go` (see *Further reading*):

```
func main() {
    // prints "device-192.0.2.1"
    processDevice(generateName, "192.0.2.1")
}
```

The benefit of this approach is the pluggable nature of the first argument. If we decide at any point that another function (for example, `generateName2`) is a better fit because it uses a different format to join the strings or something else, or maybe you want to make a change to create the device names differently but don't want to alter the `generateName` function in case you need to roll back your changes quickly, then you can use a temporary `clone` function with a different name where you make the adjustments.

Function arguments

In Go, we pass the function arguments by value, meaning that Go creates a copy of every input variable and passes that copy to the called function. Go saves the new function-scoped variables in the stack memory, as long as the compiler knows their lifetime and memory footprint at compile time. The stack is a very efficient region in memory designed to store variables that don't need to be garbage collected, as it allocates or de-allocates memory automatically when the function returns. Memory that needs to be garbage collected goes to another location in memory known as the heap.

Consider the following example of a function attempting to mutate an input string. You can access the code for the next example at `ch03/functions2/main.go` (see *Further reading*):

```
type Device struct {
    name string
}

func mutate(input Device) {
    input.name += "-suffix"
}

func main() {
```

```
    d := Device{name: "myname"}
    mutate(d)

    // prints "myname"
    fmt.Println(d.name)
}
```

Since Go creates a copy of the input `Device` when passing it as a value to the `mutate` function, any changes that happen to that `Device` inside the body of this function are not visible outside of it, hence it doesn't affect the original variable, `d`. That is why `d.name` prints `myname` and not `myname-suffix`.

In Go, we have two types of data we can work with: values and the memory addresses of those values (pointers). With this in mind, there are two ways to implement the desired (mutating) behavior when passing values to a function:

- Change the function to return the mutated value and assign it to a variable. Still, this does not really mutate the original value but actually generates a new one instead.

  Change the function to accept a pointer to a variable that stores a `Device`. This is what our program would look like in this case:

  ```
  type Device struct {
      name string
  }

  func mutate(input *Device) {
      input.name += "-suffix"
  }

  func main() {
      d := Device{name: "myname"}
      mutate(&d)

      // prints "myname-suffix"
      fmt.Println(d.name)
  }
  ```

Pointers are a common way of sharing data across program boundaries in Go, such as function calls. In this case, we still pass the input argument by value (`&d`), but this time, the value we copy and pass is a pointer to a memory address, instead of the actual content of the `d` variable. Now, when you change what that memory address is pointing to, you are mutating the value of the original `d` variable:

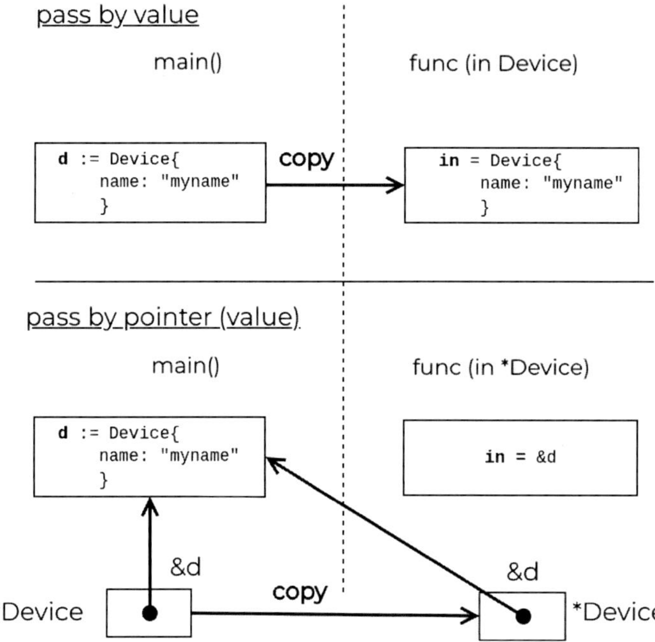

Figure 3.8 – Values and pointers

Go pointers are a powerful idea. The key operations you need to be aware of are as follows:

- Taking an address of a variable using the `&` operator
- Dereferencing a pointer, that is, getting the address of the referenced value using the `*` operator

Whenever you need to change the value of a variable, or when a variable is big enough to make copying it inefficient, you need to make sure that you pass it by a pointer. This rule applies to all the primitive types — `integer`, `string`, `boolean`, and so on.

A couple of types in Go do not hold the actual value but point to its memory address instead. While these are internal implementation details, it's something worth keeping in mind. For example, channels and maps are two types that are actually pointers to internal data structures (runtime types). This means that even if you pass them around by value, you end up mutating the contents of the channel or map. The same, by the way, applies to functions.

See the following example where we pass a map (`m`) by value to a function (`fn`). This function adds a new key-value pair to the map, a value that the outer function (`main`) can access as well:

```
func fn(m map[int]int) {
    m[1] = 11
}

func main() {
    m := make(map[int]int)
    fn(m)

    // prints 11
    fmt.Println(m[1])
}
```

In the *Go's type system* section in this chapter, we learned that a slice is a type in Go that stores metadata about the underlying data along with a pointer to it. It may be tempting to assume that you can pass around this data type as a value and be able to mutate it. But, while this data structure has a pointer in it, you also create a copy of the rest of the metadata values (length and capacity), creating a disconnection between the slice in the called and calling functions.

For this reason, mutations in slices may have an unpredictable result. In-place changes may be visible but appends may not. This is why they always recommend passing them as pointers to avoid subtle bugs such as the following one:

```
func mutateV(input []string) {
    input [0] = "r03"
    input  = append(input , "r04")
}

func main() {
    d1 := []string{"r01", "r02"}
    mutateV(d1)
```

```
    // prints "[r03 r02]"
    fmt.Printf("%v\n", d1)
}
```

You can avoid this bug if you use a pointer instead, in which case, all changes to the underlying slice are reflected in the outer context:

```
func mutateP(input *[]string) {
    (*input)[0] = "r03"
    *input = append(*input, "r04")
}

func main() {
    d2 := []string{"r01", "r02"}
    mutateP(&d2)

    // prints "[r03 r02 r04]"
    fmt.Printf("%v\n", d2)
}
```

The full code for both of these examples is at `ch03/mutate-slice/main.go` (see *Further reading*).

Error handling

In Go, errors are not exceptions that you have to handle somewhere else in the code. We handle them as they come along. An error might require you to immediately stop the execution of a program, or maybe you could continue to run the program and propagate the error to another part of the program or the user so they can make an informed decision about what to do with this error. Remember, *don't just check errors, handle them gracefully*.

When it comes to writing functions, the rule of thumb is that if a function is likely to run into an error, it must return it to the caller:

```
func makeCall(url string) (*http.Response, error) {
    resp, err := http.Get("example.com")
    if err != nil {
        return nil, fmt.Errorf("error in makeCall: %w",
                                          err)
    }
```

```
    return resp, nil
}
```

The error message should be meaningful and offer enough context to the user to be able to identify the cause of the error and the place in the code where it happened. It's up to the caller of this function to decide what to do with this error from the following possible actions:

- Log it and continue.
- Ignore it.
- Interrupt execution and panic.
- Pass it up to the outer function.

Methods

Methods are a way of adding behavior to user-defined types, which, by default, can only store values. If you want those types to act, you can add a special function that would contain the name of the associated data type (method receiver) between the `func` keyword and the function name, such as `GetFullName` in the next example:

```
type Device struct {
    name string
}

func (d Device) GetFullName() string {
    return d.name
}

func main() {
    d1 := Device{name: "r1"}

    // prints "r1"
    fmt.Println(d1.GetFullName())
}
```

In all aspects, methods are just like functions — they accept zero or more arguments and return zero or more values. The biggest difference is that methods also have access to their receiver and can at the very least read its fields, as you've seen in the preceding example.

It's also possible to create a method that mutates the receiving type by defining it on a pointer:

```
type Device struct {
    name string
}

func (d *Device) GenerateName() {
    d.name = "device-" + d.name
}

func (d Device) GetFullName() string {
    return d.name
}

func main() {
    d2 := Device{name: "r2"}
    d2.GenerateName()

    // prints "device-r2"
    fmt.Println(d2.GetFullName())
}
```

In this case, we define the `GenerateName` method on a pointer receiver and, thus, can safely set, delete or change its values — all these changes are visible in the outer scope.

The full code for the method code examples is available at `ch03/methods/main.go` (see *Further reading*).

Variadic functions

So far, we've only seen examples with functions that take a strictly pre-defined number of arguments. But, that's not the only option in Go; you can actually pass an arbitrary number of arguments to a function as long as you meet the following conditions:

- All extra arguments are of the same type.
- They are always the last arguments to a function.

The function signature looks slightly different. All extra arguments are automatically grouped into a slice and you denote them with three dots (`...`) before their type:

```
func printOctets(octets ...string) {
    fmt.Println(strings.Join(octets, "."))
}

func main() {
    // prints "127.1"
    printOctets("127", "1")

    ip := []string{"192", "0", "2", "1"}

    // prints "192.0.2.1"
    printOctets(ip...)
}
```

One benefit of variadic arguments, compared to declaring them as a slice argument instead, is the flexibility; you don't have to create a slice before calling a function, and you can completely omit any trailing arguments if they are not needed and still satisfy the function's signature.

The full code for the variadic code example is available at `ch03/variadic/main.go` (see *Further reading*).

Closures

Functions in Go have different properties. They are values, so a function can accept another one as its argument.

Another interesting property is that when one function (outer) returns another function (inner), the inner function remembers and it has complete access to all variables that you defined in the scope of the outer function.

This is what's called a **function closure**, and here's a canonical example of how you can use it to generate a sequence of numbers. Here, the inner anonymous function with the `func() string` signature mutates the `i` variable defined in the `suffixGenerator` outer function every time it's called:

```
func suffixGenerator() func() string {
    i := 0
    return func() string {
        i++
```

```
        return fmt.Sprintf("%02d", i)
    }
}

func main() {
    generator1 := suffixGenerator()

    // prints "device-01"
    fmt.Printf("%s-%s\n", "device", generator1())

    // prints "device-02"
    fmt.Printf("%s-%s\n", "device", generator1())

    generator2 := suffixGenerator()

    // prints "device-01"
    fmt.Printf("%s-%s\n", "device", generator2())
}
```

Every time we call `suffixGenerator`, we assign a new instance of the anonymous function it returns to a variable. `generator1` and `generator2` are now functions that keep track of the number of times we call each one.

Closures are a popular technique to create a surrounding context (environment). For example, API call functions in middleware software use closures to perform logging and telemetry data collection on every call, without the API caller needing to care about those details.

Defer

When writing a program that opens remote network connections or local files, it's important to promptly close these as soon as you no longer need them to prevent resource leaks — all operating systems have limitations on the number of open files or connections.

Go's idiomatic way of dealing with this class of problems is to address them as early in the code as possible with the help of the `defer` statement. You should place this statement right next to the `open`/`connect` function call. Go only evaluates this statement when the function returns.

In the following example, the two `defer` statements run only *after* the final statement of the function:

```
func main() {
    resp, err := http.Get("http://example.com")
    if err != nil {
        panic(err)
    }
    defer resp.Body.Close()
    defer fmt.Println("Deferred cleanup")

    fmt.Println("Response status:", resp.Status)
}
```

You can stack together many `defer` statements to perform staged cleanup. They execute in last-in-first-out order – `Println("Deferred cleanup")` runs before `resp.Body.Close()`. This is what you see when you run this program:

```
ch03/defer$ go run main.go
Response status: 200 OK
Deferred cleanup
```

The full code for this code example is available at `ch03/defer/main.go` (see *Further reading*).

Now that we've covered the Go functions fundamentals, it's time to move onto the next level of abstraction that describes object behaviors through a unique set of methods: interfaces.

Interfaces

Interfaces are one of the most powerful constructs in Go, so it's very important to understand what they do and when you can use them. From a purely theoretical point of view, interfaces are an abstract type. They do not contain implementation details but define a set of behaviors through method signatures.

If a Go type defines all method signatures declared by an interface, this Go type *implements* that interface implicitly, with no explicit declaration. This is how Go deals with common behaviors exhibited by more than one type, and what other languages often express through object inheritance.

Network automation example

To introduce the idea, we use a contrived network automation example. Let's say we are developing a Go package to deal with common tasks across different network devices. We model a Cisco IOS XE device as a `CiscoIOS` type with two fields — one that identifies the hostname of a device (`Hostname`) and another that identifies the underlying hardware platform (`Platform`). For this `CiscoIOS` type, we define a method that gets us the uptime of a device (`getUptime`) as an integer. Finally, we define a function to compare two devices and find out which one has been running longer without a reboot:

```
type CiscoIOS struct {
    Hostname string
    Platform string
}

func (r CiscoIOS) getUptime() int {
    /* ... <omitted for brevity > ... */
}

func LastToReboot(r1, r2 CiscoIOS) bool {
    return r1.getUptime() < r2.getUptime()
}
```

Everything works fine until we add another platform to the mix. Let's say we now also have a `CiscoNXOS` type and it has `Hostname` and `Platform` fields, but it also has a Boolean `ACI` field to show whether this switch is ACI-enabled. As with the `CiscoIOS` type, we define a method that returns the uptime of a `CiscoNXOS` device:

```
type CiscoNXOS struct {
    Hostname string
    Platform string
    ACI      bool
}

func (s CiscoNXOS) getUptime() int {
    /* ... <omitted for brevity > ... */
}
```

The challenge now is to compare the uptime of a `CiscoNXOS` device type with the uptime of a `CiscoIOS` device type. The `LastToReboot` function signature tells us it only accepts variables of a `CiscoIOS` type as an argument, so we cannot pass an element of a `CiscoNXOS` type to it.

You can fix this by creating an interface. By doing this, you abstract away the implementation details of the device and only focus on the need to present the device uptime as an integer via the `getUptime` function. Let's call this interface `NetworkDevice`:

```
type NetworkDevice interface {
    getUptime() int
}
```

The next step is to change the `LastToReboot` function to accept a `NetworkDevice` type instead of `CiscoIOS`, as in the next code snippet:

```
func LastToReboot(r1, r2 NetworkDevice) bool {
    return r1.getUptime() < r2.getUptime()
}
```

Because both `CiscoIOS` and `CiscoNXOS` have a `getUptime() int` method, they implicitly satisfy the `NetworkDevice` interface, hence you can pass either one of them as a parameter to the `LastToReboot` function. A **sample program** (see *Further reading*) that uses these definitions to compare the uptime of these two device types would look as follows:

```
func main() {
    ios := CiscoIOS{}
    nexus := CiscoNXOS{}

    if LastToReboot(ios, nexus) {
        fmt.Println("IOS-XE has been running for less time, so
it was the last to be rebooted")
        os.Exit(0)
    }
    fmt.Println("NXOS was the last one to reboot")
}
```

Interfaces can help you scale your programs. The interface `NetworkDevice` enables us to add any number of device types. It's not only a great resource for good code design but also to set clear expectations of what the data should do in an API, regardless of what the data is. In the example, we don't care what operating system the device is running, only that we have a method available to get its uptime as an integer.

Standard library example

For a more real-world example, let's turn our attention to the `net` package in the standard library, which has an interface that represents a network connection (`Conn`). Interface fields are often verbs that describe behavior and not state (for example, `SetDeadline` for the `Conn` interface). By contrast, a more descriptive name for the `RemoteAddr` method might have been `getRemoteAddr`:

```
// src/net/net.go
// Conn is a generic stream-oriented network connection.
type Conn interface {
    /* ... <omitted for brevity > ... */

    // LocalAddr returns the local network address.
    LocalAddr() Addr

    // RemoteAddr returns the remote network address.
    RemoteAddr() Addr

    SetDeadline(t time.Time) error
    SetReadDeadline(t time.Time) error
    SetWriteDeadline(t time.Time) error
}
```

The standard library includes several implementations of this interface. One of them is in the `crypto/ssh` library, through the `chanConn` concrete type. A concrete type is any non-interface type that stores its own data and, in this case, `chanConn` stores values for local (`laddr`) and remote (`raddr`) addresses of a **Secure Shell Protocol (SSH)** connection.

This type also defines methods, such as `LocalAddr() net.Addr` and `SetReadDeadline(deadline time.Time) error`. In fact, it has all methods of the `net.Conn` interface, hence it satisfies the interface:

```
// ssh/tcpip.go
// chanConn fulfills the net.Conn interface without
// the tcpChan having to hold laddr or raddr directly.
type chanConn struct {
    /* ... <omitted for brevity > ... */
    laddr, raddr net.Addr
}
```

```
// LocalAddr returns the local network address.
func (t *chanConn) LocalAddr() net.Addr {
    return t.laddr
}

// RemoteAddr returns the remote network address.
func (t *chanConn) RemoteAddr() net.Addr {
    return t.raddr
}

func (t *chanConn) SetDeadline(deadline time.Time) error {
    if err := t.SetReadDeadline(deadline); err != nil {
        return err
    }
    return t.SetWriteDeadline(deadline)
}

func (t *chanConn) SetReadDeadline(deadline time.Time) error {
    return errors.New("ssh: tcpChan: deadline not supported")
}

func (t *chanConn) SetWriteDeadline(deadline time.Time) error {
    return errors.New("ssh: tcpChan: deadline not supported")
}
```

Now, any function that accepts `net.Conn` as input can take `chanConn` as well. Or vice versa, if a function returns `net.Conn`, it can also return `chanConn`, as in the next example from the same source code file:

```
// ssh/tcpip.go
// Dial initiates a conn to the addr from remote host.
// Resulting conn has a zero LocalAddr() and RemoteAddr().
func (c *Client) Dial(n, addr string) (net.Conn, error) {
    var ch Channel
    switch n {
    case "tcp", "tcp4", "tcp6":
    // Parse the address into host and numeric port.
```

```
    host, portString, err := net.SplitHostPort(addr)
    if err != nil {
        return nil, err
    }

    /* ... <omitted for brevity > ... */

    return &chanConn{
        Channel: ch,
        laddr:   zeroAddr,
        raddr:   zeroAddr,
    }, nil

    /* ... <omitted for brevity > ... */
}
```

Don't worry if these code snippets look daunting to you. These come from the actual SSH package of the Go standard library, so this is as complex as it gets.

Interfaces as contracts

Interfaces are a valueless type; they only define method signatures. You can define a variable of an interface type, but you can only assign a concrete implementation of this interface as the value of this variable.

In the next code example, the `r` variable is of the `io.Reader` type, which is an interface. At that point, we know nothing about this variable but we do know that whatever value we assign to this variable must satisfy the `io.Reader` interface in order for the compiler to accept it.

In this case, we're using `strings.NewReader("text")`, which implements the `io.Reader` interface to read from a `string` value that gets passed as an argument:

```
func main() {
    var r io.Reader
    r = strings.NewReader("a random text")
    io.Copy(os.Stdout, r)
}
```

The last line of code copies what we read to standard output (`Stdout`) or the user's screen. The `io.Copy` function copies from `io.Reader` (`r`) to `io.Writer` (`os.Stdout` satisfies this interface), so we can copy from the string to the terminal.

While this looks a bit more complicated than just printing the string with `fmt.Println`, interfaces make our code more versatile, allowing you to replace either the source or destination of the data in the example without too much effort. This is possible because the `io.Reader` and `io.Writer` interfaces serve as a contract between both the `io.Copy()` consumer and the `strings.NewReader` and `os.Stdout` providers, ensuring they both conform to the rules defined by this interface.

Interfaces allow you to define a clear division between different modules of a program and offer an API where users can define the implementation details. In the next section, we examine in detail the `io.Reader` and `io.Writer` interfaces and their role in **input/output** (**I/O**) operations.

Input and output operations

A common operation in a program is to move data around and reformat it. For example, you can open a file, load its content in memory, encode it to a different format, maybe `jpeg`, and then write it to a file on the disk. This is where the `io.Reader` and `io.Writer` interfaces play a key role in Go's I/O model, as they allow you to stream data from a source to a destination via a transfer buffer. This means you don't need to load the entire file in memory to encode it and write it to the destination, making the process more efficient.

The io.Reader interface

The `io` package in the standard library defines one of the most popular interfaces in Go, the `io.Reader` interface, which can read a stream of bytes (`p`). It returns the number of bytes read (`n`) and any error encountered (`err`):

```
type Reader interface {
    Read(p []byte) (n int, err error)
}
```

Any concrete type that has a `Read` with this signature implements the `io.Reader` interface. You don't need to do anything else:

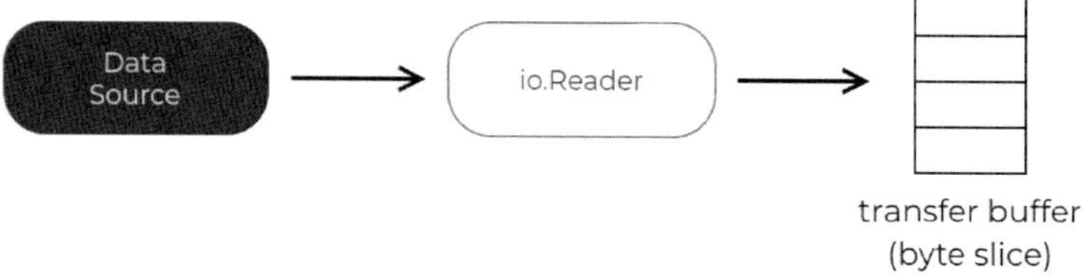

Figure 3.9 – The io.Reader interface

The `strings.Reader` type (in the `strings` package of the standard library) has a method with the `Read(p []byte) (n int, err error)` signature, hence it satisfies the `io.Reader` interface. The strings package also provides a convenient NewReader function that returns a pointer to a new instance of the strings.Reader type. The following is an actual snippet from the strings package source code:

```
// src/strings/reader.go
// A Reader implements the io.Reader, ...
// from a string.
type Reader struct {
    s        string
    i        int64 // current reading index
    prevRune int   // index of previous rune; or < 0
}

// Read implements the io.Reader interface.
func (r *Reader) Read(b []byte) (n int, err error) {
    if r.i >= int64(len(r.s)) {
        return 0, io.EOF
    }
    r.prevRune = -1
    n = copy(b, r.s[r.i:])
    r.i += int64(n)
    return
}

// NewReader returns a new Reader reading from s.
func NewReader(s string) *Reader { return &Reader{s, 0, -1} }
```

The preceding code also shows a concrete Reader implementation (with data fields) that has a Read method.

The io.Writer interface

The io package also specifies the io.Reader interface, which can write len(p) bytes to the underlying data stream. It returns the number of bytes written (n) and any error encountered that caused the write to stop early (err):

```
type Writer interface {
    Write(p []byte) (n int, err error)
}
```

Any concrete type that has a `Write` method with this signature implements the `io.Writer` interface:

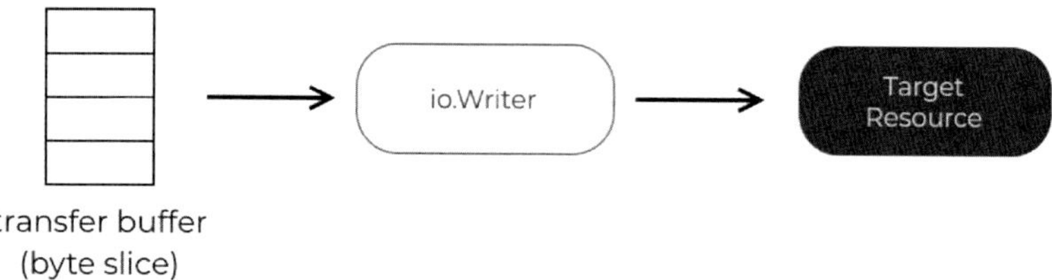

Figure 3.10 – The io.Writer interface

One example is `os.File` in the `os` package of the standard library. It has a method with the `Write(p []byte) (n int, err error)` signature, hence it satisfies the `io.Writer` interface:

```
// src/os/types.go
// File represents an open file descriptor.
type File struct {
    *file // os specific
}

// Read reads up to len(b) bytes from the File.
// It returns the number of bytes read and any error.
// At end of file, Read returns 0, io.EOF.
func (f *File) Read(b []byte) (n int, err error) {
    if err := f.checkValid("read"); err != nil {
        return 0, err
    }
    n, e := f.read(b)
    return n, f.wrapErr("read", e)
}

func Create(name string) (*File, error) {
    return OpenFile(name, O_RDWR|O_CREATE|O_TRUNC, 0666)
}
```

The `os` package also offers a convenient `Create` function that returns a pointer to an `os.File` from a file location. The preceding is an actual snippet from the `os` package source code.

The io.Copy function

The `io.Copy` function allows you to copy data from a source to a destination, as we discussed at the end of the *Interfaces* section. Even though you pass concrete type data to this function, `io.Copy` actually doesn't care what the data is, as it takes interface types as an argument, so it's interested in what the data can do instead. It needs a readable source and a writable destination:

```
// src/io/io.go
// Copy copies from src to dst until either EOF is reached
// on src or an error occurs.
func Copy(dst Writer, src Reader) (written int64, err error) {
    return copyBuffer(dst, src, nil)
}
```

As *Figure 3.11* shows, `io.Copy` uses a 32 KB transfer buffer to stream the data from the source to the destination:

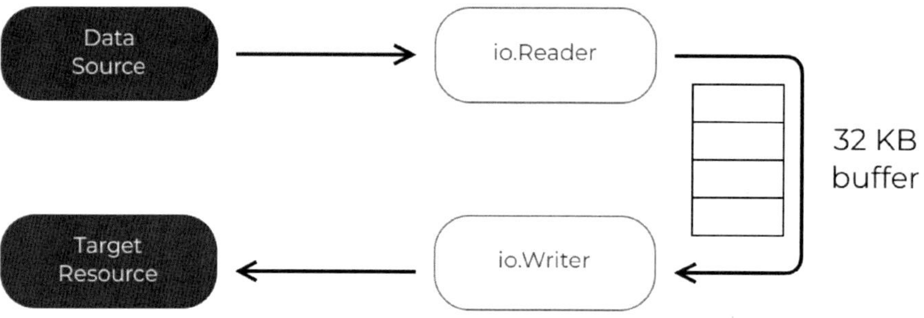

Figure 3.11 – The io.Copy function

Let's test this. We can get an `io.Reader` from a string built with `strings.NewReader`, and `os.Create` gives us an `io.Writer`, which writes to a file on the disk. You can follow along with the code at `ch03/io-interface1/main.go` (see *Further reading*):

```
func main() {
    src := strings.NewReader("The text")
    dst, err := os.Create("./file.txt")
    if err != nil {
        panic(err)
    }
    defer dst.Close()
```

```
    io.Copy(dst, src)
}
```

While, in this case, we select a string and a file combination, you can use the same `io.Copy` function to read from the network and print to the terminal, for example. For now, let's inspect the file we just produced:

```
ch03/io-interface1$ go run main.go

ch03/io-interface1$ cat file.txt
The text
```

Let's examine a network-related example. The `net/http` package has the `Get` function that takes a URL (`string`) and returns a pointer to a `http.Response`, which has a field (`Body`) that satisfies the `io.Reader` interface, and the `os.Stdout` terminal satisfies the `io.Writer` interface. This gives us another combination to try out. Let's see it in action. The code is very close to what we ran before, and is available at `ch03/io-interface2/main.go` (see *Further reading*):

```
func main() {
    res, err := http.Get("https://www.tkng.io/")
    if err != nil {
        panic(err)
    }
    src := res.Body
    defer src.Close()
    dst := os.Stdout
    io.Copy(dst, src)
}
```

The same `io.Copy` function now allows us to take the content from a URL and print it to the terminal:

```
ch03/io-interface2$ go run main.go
<!doctype html><html lang=en class="js
csstransforms3d"><head><meta charset=utf-8><meta name=viewport
content="width=device-width,initial-scale=1"><meta
name=generator content="Hugo 0.74.3"><meta name=description
content="The Kubernetes Networking Guide">...
```

With `io.Copy`, we move data from one point to another. Now, we need to add another piece to the puzzle to transform the data as we stream it.

Composition

One way to transform the data as we stream it is by embedding one struct type into another, which we know as **composition**. This way, we can chain together several `io.Reader` or `io.Writer` interfaces to perform one or more operations and not just copy the data from source to destination.

The benefit of following this pattern is to write reusable segments of code, which you can use for any `io.Reader` or `io.Writer` interface in this case. Let's look at the example at `ch03/reader/main.go` (see *Further reading*):

```
type myReader struct {
    src io.Reader
}

func (r *myReader) Read(buf []byte) (int, error) {
    tmp := make([]byte, len(buf))
    n, err := r.src.Read(tmp)
    copy(buf[:n], bytes.Title(tmp[:n]))
    return n, err
}

func NewMyReader(r io.Reader) io.Reader {
    return &myReader{src: r}
}
```

We define a new `myReader` type with a single `src` field of the `io.Reader` type. In Go, when we embed a type, the methods of that type become methods of the outer type, so `myReader` has a `Read` method from `src` now.

But, we want to change the behavior and do something with the data. Hence, we define a new `Read` method that takes precedence over any other more deeply nested method part of the type.

In this `Read` method, we read from the buffer and convert it to title case with `bytes.Title`, assuming we are working with strings. Last but not least, `NewMyReader` is what glues together an existing reader with this new one, connecting the dots between two pieces of code. Let's see it in action:

```
func main() {
    r1 := strings.NewReader("network automation with go")
    r2 := NewMyReader(r1)
```

```
    io.Copy(os.Stdout, r2)
}
```

We create a reader from a string in `r1` and then use that as the input for `myReader` in `r2`:

```
ch03/reader$ go run main.go
Network Automation With Go
```

When we now copy from `r2` to `os.Stdout`, we read from the string and also change the content to title case before writing it to the terminal.

Input and output primitives are present in almost every Go library. The next section is no exception. Encoding and decoding in Go take full advantage of the `io.Reader` and `io.Writer` interfaces.

Decoding and encoding

One of the most common network automation tasks is the ingesting and processing of structured data. You can retrieve data from or send it to a remote location or even store it on a local disk. Regardless of its location, you have to convert this data into an appropriate format. Encoding, or marshaling, is the process of transforming bytes from a Go data structure into a structured textual representation. Decoding, or unmarshalling, is the reverse process of populating Go values with externally sourced data.

Some examples of structured data encoding schemes are YAML, JSON, XML, and Protocol Buffers. Go's standard library includes packages that implement encoding and decoding for most of these popular formats, and they all leverage the `io.Reader` and `io.Writer` interface primitives that we learned about in the last section.

In this section, we go through how Go deals with the following tasks:

- Using tags to annotate Go structs to help libraries encode and decode structured data
- Parsing of structured data using the empty interface
- Performing deeply nested set and lookup operations using third-party libraries

Decoding

We start our overview with decoding, as this is usually one of the first steps in a network automation pipeline. Let's assume that we're building a program that needs to interact with various remote network devices. We store the information of these devices in an inventory file we save on a local disk.

Decoding JSON

In the first example, we see how to deal with a JSON inventory (`input.json`). All outputs of this part are available in the `ch03/json` folder of the book's repository (see *Further reading*):

```
{
  "router": [
    {
      "hostname": "router1.example.com",
      "ip": "192.0.2.1",
      "asn": 64512
    },
    {
      "hostname": "router2.example.com",
      "ip": "198.51.100.1",
      "asn": 65535
    }
  ]
}
```

In the first code example in `ch03/json/main.go` (see *Further reading*), we define a couple of Go structs that can hold the JSON input data from the preceding output in memory. We call the first type `Router`, which has `Hostname`, `IP`, and `ASN` fields. The other type is `Inventory`, which stores a list of routers. The fields in the `Router` type have optional tags such as `json:"key"` to denote alternative key names in the original JSON structure:

```
type Router struct {
    Hostname string `json:"hostname"`
    IP       string `json:"ip"`
    ASN      uint16 `json:"asn"`
}

type Inventory struct {
    Routers []Router `json:"router"`
}
```

To read from a file, we create an `io.Reader` type (`file`) from the input file with `os.Open`:

```
func main() {
    file, err := os.Open("input.json")
```

```
    // process error

    defer file.Close()
    /* ... <continues next > ... */
}
```

Now, the `json` library, as well as any other encoding library, has a function that allows you to pass an `io.Reader` type as an argument to extract data from it. This means it can decode from a file, a string, a network connection, or anything else that implements the `io.Reader` interface with the same function call:

```
func main() {
    /* ... <continues from before > ... */
    d := json.NewDecoder(file)
    /* ... <continues next > ... */
}
```

Once you've created a decoder, you can use the `Decode` method to read and parse the contents of the JSON file into a variable (`inv`) of the `Inventory` type. Remember, to mutate the data struct, you need to pass it as a pointer:

```
func main() {
    /* ... <continues from before > ... */
    var inv Inventory

    err = d.Decode(&inv)
    // process error
    fmt.Printf("%+v\n", inv)
}
```

If you print the `inv` variable now, you would see it populate with data from the inventory JSON file:

```
ch03/json$ go run main.go
{Routers:[{Hostname:router1.example.com IP:192.0.2.1 ASN:64512}
{Hostname:router2.example.com IP:198.51.100.1 ASN:65535}]}
```

Decoding into an empty interface

The field tags we've just seen are a very convenient way to map data during encoding and decoding. The condition to have all Go types predefined ahead of time offers type safety, but at the same time, you can see it as a major detractor if you are coming from another language where the decoding process does not need this.

But, you can also skip this in Go, with a few caveats that we discuss later. To show you how it works, we use a slightly different version of an earlier example. This new version is available in the `ch03/json-interface` folder (see *Further reading*). Instead of defining all Go structs, we use a special variable of the `map[string]interface{}` type and pass it as an argument to the `Decode` method call:

```
func main() {
    /* ... <omitted for brevity > ... */
    var empty map[string]interface{}

    err = d.Decode(&empty)
    // process error

    // prints map[router:[map[asn:64512 hostname:router1.
example.com
    // ip:192.0.2.1] map[asn:65535 hostname:router2.example.com
    // ip:198.51.100.1]]]
    fmt.Printf("%v\n", empty)
    /* ... <continues next > ... */
}
```

An *empty interface*, or `interface{}`, doesn't define any methods, which means it can hold any value — `integer`, `string`, `float`, or user-defined. The only caveat is that, since Go is a statically typed language, those values remain an empty interface until we do an explicit type conversion, that is, until we tell Go what type we expect to see.

From the output of the empty variable of the `map[string]interface{}` type, where we decoded the JSON content in the preceding example, we see that the value of the map we print is an array. To parse these values and print them individually, we'd have to tell Go to treat them as a slice of unknown values, which you can express as `[]interface{}`:

```
func main() {
    /* ... <continues from before > ... */
    for _, r := range empty["router"].([]interface{}) {
        fmt.Printf("%v\n", r)
    }
}
```

The output of these print statements is the string representation of two `map[string]interface{}` maps, which means we've only parsed the keys (as strings), but the values are still undefined:

```
ch03/json-interface $ go run main.go
...
map[asn:64512 hostname:router1.example.com ip:192.0.2.1]
map[asn:65535 hostname:router2.example.com ip:198.51.100.1]
```

We could continue this process until we find the right type for all values of this object, but this process is obviously quite tedious. This is why we mainly see this approach in encoding libraries or as a troubleshooting step to take a quick glance at the structure of the potentially unknown input data.

Another option for quick operations with JSON data is external Go packages, which you can use to perform deep JSON lookup (**GJSON**) and set (**SJSON**) operations without having to build structs for the entire object. In both cases, the parsing still happens behind the scenes, but the user is only presented with their data or an error if the key doesn't exist. We use GJSON (see *Further reading*) in a gRPC example in *Chapter 8, Network APIs*.

Decoding XML

While the XML input file looks different, the data is the same and the Go program doesn't change much. The next example is in the `ch03/xml` folder of the book's repository (see *Further reading*):

```
<?xml version="1.0" encoding="UTF-8" ?>
<routers>
  <router>
    <hostname>router1.example.com</hostname>
    <ip>192.0.2.1</ip>
    <asn>64512</asn>
  </router>
  <router>
    <hostname>router2.example.com</hostname>
    <ip>198.51.100.1</ip>
    <asn>65535</asn>
  </router>
</routers>
```

If we compared the final program with the one we did for JSON, we would notice four changes:

- We import `encoding/xml` instead of `encoding/json`.
- We use XML tags `xml:"hostname"` instead of the JSON equivalents for struct fields.

- The input file is a `.xml` file.
- We use the `NewDecoder` function from the `xml` library instead.

The rest of the code remains exactly the same. The next code output highlights the actual lines that change; we omitted the rest of the lines as they are the same as in the JSON example:

```
package main

import (
    "os"
    "encoding/xml"
)

type Router struct {
    Hostname string `xml:"hostname"`
    IP       string `xml:"ip"`
    ASN      uint16 `xml:"asn"`
}

type Inventory struct {
    Routers []Router `xml:"router"`
}

func main() {
    file, err := os.Open("input.xml")
    /* ... <omitted for brevity > ... */
    d := xml.NewDecoder(file)
    /* ... <omitted for brevity > ... */
}
```

Just like JSON, XML has its own external libraries that can help you deal with complex input data without having to build the hierarchy of Go types. One of them is the `xmlquery` package (see *Further reading*), which lets you make XML Path Language (XPath) queries from Go.

YAML

Now, let's look at how we would parse a YAML inventory. You can find this example in the `ch03/yaml` directory of the book's repository (see *Further reading*):


```
router:
  - hostname: "router1.example.com"
    ip: "192.0.2.1"
    asn: 64512
  - hostname: "router2.example.com"
    ip: "198.51.100.1"
    asn: 65535
```


By now, you would probably already have guessed that the number and nature of things that change from the JSON example are the same as for XML, which is to say, not much. The following code snippet highlights only the changed lines of code, and you can find the full code example at `ch03/yaml/main.go` (see *Further reading*):

```
package main

import (
    "os"
    "gopkg.in/yaml.v2"
)

type Router struct {
    Hostname string `yaml:"hostname"`
    IP       string `yaml:"ip"`
    ASN      uint16 `yaml:"asn"`
}
type Inventory struct {
    Routers []Router `yaml:"router"`
}

func main() {
    /* ... <omitted for brevity > ... */
    d := yaml.NewDecoder(file)
    /* ... <omitted for brevity > ... */
}
```

This Go program produces the same result as both the JSON and XML examples, but before we can run it, we need to go get the external YAML library dependency first (`gopkg.in/yaml.v2`):

```
ch03/yaml$ go get gopkg.in/yaml.v2
go get: added gopkg.in/yaml.v2 v2.4.0

ch03/yaml$ go run main.go
{Routers:[{Hostname:router1.example.com IP:192.0.2.1 ASN:64512}
{Hostname:router2.example.com IP:198.51.100.1 ASN:65535}]}
```

It's also possible to parse and query YAML documents without having to predefine data structures. One tool that does that is `yq` (see *Further reading*), which implements a shell CLI tool in Go in the style of `jq` (the `sed` for JSON data). You can use `yq` in your Go program via its built-in `yqlib` package.

Encoding

Just as important as being able to decode data from a source is processing the data in the opposite direction, producing a structured data document based on an in-memory data model. In the next example, we pick up where we left off in the *Decoding* section and take the in-memory data we got from a JSON input file to output a corresponding XML document.

One of the first things we have to do in the code is to update the struct tags with an extra key-value pair for XML. Although this is not strictly necessary, as the XML library can fall back to using field names instead, it's generally considered a best practice to annotate explicitly all relevant fields that you encode:

```
type Router struct {
    Hostname string `json:"hostname" xml:"hostname"`
    IP       string `json:"ip" xml:"ip"`
    ASN      uint16 `json:"asn" xml:"asn"`
}

type Inventory struct {
    Routers []Router `json:"router" xml:"router"`
}
```

The full code of this example is available in the `ch03/json-xml` directory (see *Further reading*) of the book's repository, so for the sake of brevity, we only include the extra code that we add to encode the `inv` variable into an XML document:

```
func main() {
    /* ... <omitted for brevity > ... */
```

```
    var dest strings.Builder

    e := xml.NewEncoder(&dest)

    err = e.Encode(&inv)
    // process error

    fmt.Printf("%+v\n", dest.String())
}
```

To produce a string output, we're using the `strings.Builder` type, which implements the `io.Writer` interface required by the `Encode` method. This highlights the power of interfaces, as we could have passed in a network connection and sent the XML data to a remote host instead, with almost the same program. The next snippet shows the output of the program:

```
ch03/json-xml$ go run main.go
<Inventory><router><hostname>router1.example.com</
hostname><ip>192.0.2.1</ip><asn>64512</asn></
router><router><hostname>router2.example.com</
hostname><ip>198.51.100.1</ip><asn>65535</asn></router></
Inventory>
```

One encoding format we haven't covered yet is Protocol Buffers, which is part of the gRPC section of *Chapter 8*.

At this point, we've covered enough Go language theory to write effective programs to interact with and automate a network device. The only bit that we have left, which is also one of the most salient features of the language, is concurrency.

Concurrency

If there was one feature that would characterize Go amongst other popular programming languages, it would be concurrency. Go's built-in concurrency primitives (goroutines and channels) are one of the best abstractions we know for writing efficient code that can run more than one task simultaneously.

Your program starts in the main goroutine, but at any point, you can spawn other concurrent goroutines and create communication channels between them. You can do this with considerably less effort and less code compared to other programming languages, which improves the developing experience and your code's support:

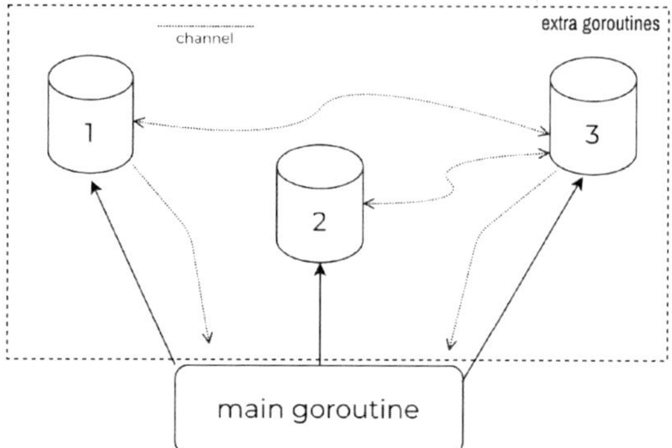

Figure 3.12 – Go's concurrency

In this section, we cover the following concurrency primitives:

- Goroutines and the use of the `sync` package for their coordination
- How we use channels to send and receive data between goroutines
- The use of mutexes with data shared between different goroutines

Goroutines

One way to think of Goroutines is as user-space threads that the Go runtime manages. They are computationally cheap to spawn and manage, so they can scale to hundreds of thousands, even on an average machine, with memory being the primary limiting factor.

It's typical to create goroutines for tasks that may block the execution of the main function. You can imagine why this would be particularly helpful in a network automation context, where we have to deal with remote network calls and wait for network devices to execute the commands.

We introduce the basic goroutine theory by building another network automation example. In the preceding section, we learned how to load and parse a device inventory. In this section, we pick up where we left off and see how to interact with these network devices.

To start off, we use an inventory file (`input.yml`) with a single device. This file is in the `ch03/single` folder (see *Further reading*) of the book's repository:

```
router:
- hostname: sandbox-iosxe-latest-1.cisco.com
  platform: cisco_iosxe
  strictkey: false
  username: developer
  password: C1sco12345
```

To store this inventory, we define a type hierarchy like the one we had in the encoding/decoding section. The code example output only shows some fields for brevity:

```
type Router struct {
    Hostname  string `yaml:"hostname"`
    /* ... <omitted for brevity > ... */
}

type Inventory struct {
    Routers []Router `yaml:"router"`
}
```

We define another function called `getVersion` that accepts an argument of the `Router` type, connects and retrieves the software and hardware version information, and prints it on a screen. The exact implementation of this function is not important and we don't focus on it in this chapter yet, but you can see the full code example at `ch03/single/main.go` (see *Further reading*):

```
func getVersion(r Router) {
    /* ... <omitted for brevity > ... */
}

func main() {
    src, err := os.Open("input.yml")
    //process error
    defer src.Close()

    d := yaml.NewDecoder(src)

    var inv Inventory
    err = d.Decode(&inv)
    // process error

    getVersion(inv.Routers[0])
}
```

Since we only have one device in the inventory, we can access it directly using a slice index. The execution of this program takes a little under 2 seconds:

```
ch03/single$ go run main.go
Hostname: sandbox-iosxe-latest-1.cisco.com
Hardware: [CSR1000V]
SW Version: 17.3.1a
Uptime: 5 hours, 1 minute

This process took 1.779684183s
```

Now, let's look at a similar example, stored in the `ch03/sequential` directory (see *Further reading*), where we've added two extra devices to the inventory:

```
router:
- hostname: sandbox-iosxe-latest-1.cisco.com
  platform: cisco_iosxe
  ...

- hostname: sandbox-nxos-1.cisco.com
  platform: cisco_nxos
  ...

- hostname: sandbox-iosxr-1.cisco.com
  platform: cisco_iosxr
  ...
```

As we discussed in the *Control flow* section, we can iterate over arrays and slices with the `range` form of a `for` loop. Here, we iterate over each `Router` in `inv.Routers`, assigning it to the `v` variable in each iteration. We ignore the value of the index by assigning it to the blank identifier written as _ (underscore). Finally, we call the `getVersion` function for the `v` router:

```
func main() {
    /* ... <omitted for brevity > ... */
    for _, r := range inv.Routers {
        getVersion(v)
    }
}
```

It takes around 7 seconds to execute as it connects to one device after another:

```
ch03/sequential$ go run main.go
Hostname: sandbox-iosxe-latest-1.cisco.com
Hardware: [CSR1000V]
SW Version: 17.3.1a
Uptime: 5 hours, 25 minutes

Hostname: sandbox-nxos-1.cisco.com
Hardware: C9300v
SW Version: 9.3(3)
Uptime: 0 day(s), 3 hour(s), 2 minute(s), 18 second(s)

Hostname: sandbox-iosxr-1.cisco.com
Hardware: IOS-XRv 9000
SW Version: 6.5.3
Uptime: 2 weeks 8 hours 23 minutes

This process took 6.984502353s
```

This is a prime example of code that we could optimize through the use of goroutines. All we need to do initially is to add a `go` keyword before the statement that we need to run in a goroutine:

```
func main() {
    /* ... <omitted for brevity > ... */
    for _, r := range inv.Routers {
        go getVersion(v)
    }
}
```

In the code example, we spawn a separate goroutine for each invocation of the `getVersion(v)` statement. Everything happens in the background; any blocking statement inside a spawned goroutine does not affect the other goroutines, so all three function calls, plus the main goroutine, now run concurrently.

The default behavior of these spawned goroutines is to release control immediately, so in this example, the code iterates over all three devices and then returns. It doesn't actually wait for the spawned goroutines to complete.

But, in our case, we'd like to see the result of all three function calls before we exit the program. This is where we can use a special `sync.WaitGroup` type, which blocks the main goroutine until all spawned goroutines complete. It does this by keeping a counter that tracks all currently active goroutines and blocks until that counter goes down to zero.

This is what we do to introduce this idea in the code example we are working with:

- We create a new `wg` variable of the `sync.WaitGroup` type.
- While iterating through our inventory, we increase the `WaitGroup` counter by one with `wg.Add(1)`.
- Each spawned goroutine consists of an anonymous function that runs `getVersion`, but also calls `wg.Done` at the very end to decrement the `WaitGroup` counter by one with a `defer` statement.
- The main goroutine blocks on `wg.Wait` until the `WaitGroup` counter becomes zero. This happens after all the spawned instances of the `getVersion` functions return.

You can find the full code of this example at `ch03/concurrency/main.go` (see *Further reading*):

```
func main() {
    /* ... <omitted for brevity > ... */
    var wg sync.WaitGroup

    for _, v := range inv.Routers {
        wg.Add(1)

        go func(r Router) {
            defer wg.Done()
            getVersion(r)
        }(v)

    }
    wg.Wait()
}
```

Now, let's see what effect these changes have on the execution time of the program:

```
ch03/concurrency$ go run main.go
Hostname: sandbox-iosxe-latest-1.cisco.com
Hardware: [CSR1000V]
```

```
SW Version: 17.3.1a
Uptime: 5 hours, 26 minutes

Hostname: sandbox-iosxr-1.cisco.com
Hardware: IOS-XRv 9000
SW Version: 6.5.3
Uptime: 2 weeks 8 hours 25 minutes

Hostname: sandbox-nxos-1.cisco.com
Hardware: C9300v
SW Version: 9.3(3)
Uptime: 0 day(s), 3 hour(s), 4 minute(s), 11 second(s)

This process took 2.746996304s
```

We've gone down to roughly 3 seconds, which is how long it took to communicate with the slowest device in the inventory. This is a pretty significant win, considering we didn't have to change any of the *worker* functions (`getVersion` in this case). You might apply the same refactoring to many other similar programs with minimal changes to their existing code bases.

This approach works well with natively synchronous functions that you can run with or without a goroutine. But, if we know that a certain function always runs in a goroutine, it's totally possible to make it goroutine-aware from the very beginning. For example, this is how we could have refactored the `getVersion` function to accept an extra `WaitGroup` argument and make the `wg.Done` call part of the function:

```
func getVersion(r Router, wg *sync.WaitGroup) {
    defer wg.Done()
    /* ... <omitted for brevity > ... */
}
```

Having a function like that would simplify the code of the main function since we no longer need to wrap everything in an anonymous function just to make the `wg.Done` call:

```
func main() {
    /* ... <omitted for brevity > ... */
    for _, v := range inv.Routers {
        wg.Add(1)
        go getVersion(v, &wg)
    }
```

```
    wg.Wait()
}
```

The complete code for this example is available in the `ch03/concurrency2` directory (see *Further reading*).

Channels

As soon as anyone becomes familiar with goroutines, the next thing they normally want to do is exchange data between them. Go channels allow goroutines to communicate with each other. A real-world analogy to describe Go channels are first-in-first-out pipes – they have fixed throughput and allow you to send data in both directions.

You can use channels for both goroutine synchronization (a form of signaling used for work coordination) and general-purpose data exchange.

We create channels with the `make` keyword, which initializes them and makes them ready to use. The two arguments that `make` accepts are the channel type, which defines the data type you can exchange over the channel, and an optional capacity. The channel capacity determines how many unreceived values it can store before it starts blocking a sender, acting then as a buffer.

The following code snippet shows how we send and receive an integer over a channel. Here, `send` is the value we want to send to the `ch` channel we created. The `<-` operator lets us send data to a channel. Next, we declare a `receive` variable, whose value comes from the `ch` channel:

```
func main() {
    ch := make(chan int, 1)

    send := 1
    ch <- send
    receive := <-ch

    // prints 1
    fmt.Println(receive)
}
```

But, sending and receiving data in a single goroutine is not the goal here. Let's examine another example of using channels for communication between different goroutines. We pick up the example we've used in this section so far and introduce another *worker* function whose job is to print the results produced by the `getVersion` function.

The new `printer` function uses a `for` loop to receive values from an `in` channel and it prints them on the terminal:

```
func printer(in chan data {
    for out := range in {
        fmt.Printf("Hostname: %s\nHW: %s\nSW Version: %s\
nUptime: %s\n\n", out.host, out.hw, out.version, out.uptime)
    }
}
```

We create the `ch` channel in the main goroutine before we spawn any of the goroutines. We pass it as an argument to both `getVersion` and `printer` functions. The first extra goroutine we start is an instance of the `printer` function that listens for messages coming from the device over the `ch` channel:

```
func main() {
    /* ... <omitted for brevity > ... */
    ch := make(chan data)

    go printer(ch)

    var wg sync.WaitGroup
    for _, v := range inv.Routers {
        wg.Add(1)
        go getVersion(v, ch, &wg)
    }
    wg.Wait()
    close(ch)
}
```

The next step is to start a goroutine for each network device in the inventory to capture the output we need and send it over the channel with the `getVersion` function. After we collect and print the data, we close the channel and end the program:

```
ch03/concurrency3$ go run main.go
Hostname: sandbox-iosxe-latest-1.cisco.com
HW: [CSR1000V]
SW Version: 17.3.1a
Uptime: 1 day, 12 hours, 42 minutes
```

```
Hostname: sandbox-iosxr-1.cisco.com
HW: IOS-XRv 9000
SW Version: 7.3.2
Uptime: 1 day 2 hours 57 minutes

Hostname: sandbox-nxos-1.cisco.com
HW: C9300v
SW Version: 9.3(3)
Uptime: 5 day(s), 6 hour(s), 25 minute(s), 44 second(s)
```

The complete code for this example is available in the `ch03/concurrency3` (*Further reading*) directory.

Channels and Timers

One thing we didn't consider in the last couple of examples was the scenario where a network device is not reachable, or the connection to it hangs, or maybe a device takes forever to return the output we need. In these cases, we need to set up a timeout so we don't wait forever and we can end the program gracefully.

You can handle this at the connection level, but also, channels offer you a couple of resources to keep track of time via these timer types:

- **Timer** — To wait for a certain amount of time
- **Ticker** — To perform an action repeatedly at some interval

Timer

`Timer` can help you define a timeout for your program. To illustrate this, we can rewrite the example we have been working with to print all the messages from the `ch` channel in the main function, instead of calling a separate function (`printer`).

A `select` statement inside an infinite loop handles this as follows. Unlike a `switch` statement, we use `select` with channels when we don't have to choose an option in order. For each iteration, we either wait for a message from the `ch` channel or if 5 seconds have elapsed (`time.After(5 * time.Second)`), we close the channel and exit the program:

```
func main() {
    /* ... <omitted for brevity > ... */
    for {
        select {
```

```
        case out := <-ch:
            fmt.Printf(
    "Hostname: %s\nHW: %s\nSW Version: %s\nUptime:%s\n\n",
            out.host, out.hw, out.version, out.uptime)
        case <-time.After(5 * time.Second):
            close(ch)
            fmt.Println("Timeout: 5 seconds")
            return
        }
    }
}
```

This forces the runtime to always be 5 seconds, even if not all the tasks have been completed. This is not the most efficient way to solve this problem, but it shows how to timeout without introducing the `context` package from the standard library that you could also use in this scenario.

The complete code for this example is available in the `ch03/concurrency5` directory of the book's repository (see *Further reading*).

Ticker

A common use for a ticker is in cases where you want to execute periodic tasks. In the next code example, we create a `ticker` that runs every half second, which we use as a trigger to print out a message to the terminal. We also create a `done` channel, just to signal that we want to stop the execution of the program after 2 seconds and 100 milliseconds:

```
func main() {
    ticker := time.NewTicker(500 * time.Millisecond)
    done := make(chan bool)

    go repeat(done, ticker.C)

    time.Sleep(2100 * time.Millisecond)
    ticker.Stop()
    done <- true
}
```

Tickers from the `time` package have a `C` channel that they use to signal every interval. We pass this channel and the `done` channel to the `repeat` function that we execute in a goroutine:

```
func repeat(d chan bool, c <-chan time.Time) {
    for {
        select {
        case <-d:
            return
        case t := <-c:
            fmt.Println("Run at", t.Local())
        }
    }
}
```

This function runs an infinite loop that waits for a signal from the `ticker` or the `done` channel to end the execution. This is what the output looks like:

```
ch03/ticker$ go run main.go
Tick at 2021-11-17 23:19:33.914906389 -0500 EST
Tick at 2021-11-17 23:19:34.414279709 -0500 EST
Tick at 2021-11-17 23:19:34.915058301 -0500 EST
```

The complete code for this example is available in the `ch03/ticker` directory (see *Further reading*).

Shared data access

Channels are thread-safe, so it's always a good idea to use them as the default option for data communication between goroutines. But sometimes, you may still need to access and change data that more than just one goroutine has access to.

The problem with concurrent data access is that it may cause data corruption when many goroutines try to change the same field or read from a field that someone else might be changing. Go's `sync` package includes three helper types you can use to serialize these kinds of operations:

- The `sync.Mutex` type is a general-purpose mutual exclusion lock that has two states — locked and unlocked.
- The `sync.RWMutex` type is a special mutex for read-write operations where only write operations are mutually exclusive but simultaneous read operations are safe.
- The `sync.Map` mutex covers a couple of map corner case scenarios that we don't delve into in this book. The **sync.Map documentation** talks about them (see *Further reading*).

Now, let's see an example of how you can use `sync.RWMutexto` to safeguard concurrent map access. Using the example theme we have used through this section as the baseline, let's add another variable that records whether we are able to connect successfully to a remote device. We call this variable `isAlive` and pass it to the `getVersion` function as an argument:

```
func main() {
    /* ... <omitted for brevity > ... */
    isAlive := make(map[string]bool)

    /* ... <omitted for brevity > ... */
    for _, v := range inv.Routers {
        wg.Add(1)
        go getVersion(v, ch, &wg, isAlive)
    }
    /* ... <omitted for brevity > ... */
}
```

We define the `m` mutex as a package-level global variable to make sure all functions are using the same mutex for synchronization. We lock this mutex just before we change the `isAlive` map and unlock it right after we make the change in the `getVersion` function:

```
var m sync.RWMutex = sync.RWMutex{}

func getVersion(r Router, out chan data, wg *sync.WaitGroup,
isAlive map[string]bool) {
    defer wg.Done()
    /* ... <omitted for brevity > ... */

    rs, err := d.SendCommand("show version")
    if err != nil {
        fmt.Printf("fail to send cmd for %s: %+v\n",
                    r.Hostname, err)
        m.Lock()
        isAlive[r.Hostname] = false
        m.Unlock()
        return
    }
```

```
        m.Lock()
        isAlive[r.Hostname] = true
        m.Unlock()
    }
```

Finally, we add another mutex for a loop in the main function that uses a read-specific lock while iterating over a map to prevent it from being accidentally modified in the process:

```
func main() {
    /* ... <omitted for brevity > ... */
    m.RLock()
    for name, v := range isAlive {
        fmt.Printf("Router %s is alive: %t\n", name, v)
    }
    m.RUnlock()
    /* ... <omitted for brevity > ... */
}
```

You can check the full code in the `ch03/concurrency4` directory (see *Further reading*). The next output shows what this program produces:

```
ch03/concurrency4$ go run main.go
Hostname: sandbox-iosxe-latest-1.cisco.com
Hardware: [CSR1000V]
SW Version: 17.3.1a
Uptime: 8 hours, 27 minutes

Hostname: sandbox-iosxr-1.cisco.com
Hardware: IOS-XRv 9000
SW Version: 7.3.2
Uptime: 1 day 11 hours 43 minutes

Hostname: sandbox-nxos-1.cisco.com
Hardware: C9300v
SW Version: 9.3(3)
Uptime: 5 day(s), 15 hour(s), 11 minute(s), 42 second(s)

Router sandbox-iosxe-latest-1.cisco.com is alive: true
```

```
Router sandbox-iosxr-1.cisco.com is alive: true
Router sandbox-nxos-1.cisco.com is alive: true
This process took 3.129440011s
```

Sometimes, you might forget to use mutexes, especially for non-trivial user-defined data types, or when you accidentally leak a variable between goroutines. In these cases, you can use the data race detector built into the go tool. Add the `-race` flag to any of the go `test/run/build` commands to check and get a report of any unprotected access requests to shared memory.

To see how it works, let's focus on the `isAlive` map we manipulate concurrently on different instances of the `getVersion` function. Earlier, we surrounded this with a mutex, which we now remove in `ch03/race/main.go` (see *Further reading*):

```
func getVersion(r Router, out chan map[string]interface{}, wg
*sync.WaitGroup, isAlive map[string]bool) {
    defer wg.Done()
    /* ... <omitted for brevity > ... */

    // m.Lock()
    isAlive[r.Hostname] = true
    // m.Unlock()
    out <- "test"
}
```

When you run the program with the extra `-race` flag, Go highlights the data race condition it detects:

```
ch03/race$ go run -race main.go
MESSAGE: test
MESSAGE: test
==================
WARNING: DATA RACE
Write at 0x00c00011c6f0 by goroutine 9:
  runtime.mapassign_faststr()
      /usr/local/go/src/runtime/map_faststr.go:202 +0x0
  main.getVersion()
      ~/Network-Automation-with-Go/ch03/race/main.go:35 +0xeb
  main.main·dwrap·5()
      ~/Network-Automation-with-Go/ch03/race/main.go:74 +0x110
```

```
...
==================
MESSAGE: test
Router sandbox-iosxe-latest-1.cisco.com is alive: true
Router sandbox-iosxr-1.cisco.com is alive: true
Router sandbox-nxos-1.cisco.com is alive: true
This process took 1.918348ms
Found 1 data race(s)
exit status 66
```

Go's built-in data race detector alleviates the task of debugging data races, which are among the hardest bugs to debug in concurrent systems.

Concurrency caveats

Concurrency is a powerful tool. You could even envision using goroutines everywhere in your code and following design patterns such as worker pools to split up your work between different goroutines to get the initial speed gains for a relatively small price of increased complexity.

But, it's important to consider that *concurrency is not parallelism* (see *Further reading*) and there is always some overhead involved in the coordination of goroutines and mapping them to OS threads. We also shouldn't forget that the underlying hardware resources are finite and so are the concurrency performance gains, as they inevitably flatten out at a certain point (see *Simulating a real-world system in Go* in the *Further reading* section).

Finally, concurrent programming is hard; it's hard to write code that's safe, and hard to reason about and debug when it breaks. It's important not to over-engineer your code with goroutines and use them when and where you truly need them, measure your gains and detect race conditions, avoid memory sharing if possible, and opt for communicating via channels.

Summary

This chapter concludes the theoretical introduction to Go as a programming language. We went from Go variable types and performing operations with them, to reviewing the key building blocks of Go programs, and how to take advantage of some of Go's most notable packages from its standard library to help you build scalable applications.

Starting from the next chapter, we turn our attention to network-specific tasks that are more applicable to real-world scenarios. We still continue introducing some theoretical concepts throughout the book, but most content is on concrete use cases rather than abstract theory.

Further reading

- ch03/type-definition/main.go: https://github.com/PacktPublishing/Network-Automation-with-Go/blob/main/ch03/type-definition/main.go
- ch03/string-literals/main.go: https://github.com/PacktPublishing/Network-Automation-with-Go/blob/main/ch03/string-literals/main.go
- ch03/string-concatenate/main.go: https://github.com/PacktPublishing/Network-Automation-with-Go/blob/main/ch03/string-concatenate/main.go
- ch03/string-memory/main.go: https://github.com/PacktPublishing/Network-Automation-with-Go/blob/main/ch03/string-memory/main.go
- ch03/boolean/main.go: https://github.com/PacktPublishing/Network-Automation-with-Go/blob/main/ch03/boolean/main.go
- ch03/arrays/main.go: https://github.com/PacktPublishing/Network-Automation-with-Go/blob/main/ch03/arrays/main.go
- ch03/slices/main.go: https://github.com/PacktPublishing/Network-Automation-with-Go/blob/main/ch03/slices/main.go
- ch03/maps/main.go: https://github.com/PacktPublishing/Network-Automation-with-Go/blob/main/ch03/maps/main.go
- ch03/structs/main.go: https://github.com/PacktPublishing/Network-Automation-with-Go/blob/main/ch03/structs/main.go
- ch03/tcp-header/main.go: https://github.com/PacktPublishing/Network-Automation-with-Go/blob/main/ch03/tcp-header/main.go
- *Comparison operators*: https://golang.org/ref/spec#Comparison_operators
- ch03/switch/main.go: https://github.com/PacktPublishing/Network-Automation-with-Go/blob/main/ch03/switch/main.go
- ch03/goto/main.go: https://github.com/PacktPublishing/Network-Automation-with-Go/blob/main/ch03/goto/main.go
- ch03/functions1/main.go: https://github.com/PacktPublishing/Network-Automation-with-Go/blob/main/ch03/functions1/main.go
- ch03/functions2/main.go: https://github.com/PacktPublishing/Network-Automation-with-Go/blob/main/ch03/functions2/main.go
- ch03/mutate-slice/main.go: https://github.com/PacktPublishing/Network-Automation-with-Go/blob/main/ch03/mutate-slice/main.go

- `ch03/methods/main.go`: `https://github.com/PacktPublishing/Network-Automation-with-Go/blob/main/ch03/methods/main.go`
- `ch03/variadic/main.go`: `https://github.com/PacktPublishing/Network-Automation-with-Go/blob/main/ch03/variadic/main.go`
- `ch03/defer/main.go`: `https://github.com/PacktPublishing/Network-Automation-with-Go/blob/main/ch03/defer/main.go`
- *Sample program*: `https://github.com/PacktPublishing/Network-Automation-with-Go/blob/main/ch03/interfaces-sample/main.go`
- `ch03/io-interface1/main.go`: `https://github.com/PacktPublishing/Network-Automation-with-Go/blob/main/ch03/io-interface1/main.go`
- `ch03/io-interface2/main.go`: `https://github.com/PacktPublishing/Network-Automation-with-Go/blob/main/ch03/io-interface2/main.go`
- `ch03/reader/main.go`: `https://github.com/PacktPublishing/Network-Automation-with-Go/blob/main/ch03/reader/main.go`
- `ch03/json`: `https://github.com/PacktPublishing/Network-Automation-with-Go/tree/main/ch03/json`
- Book's GitHub repository: `https://github.com/PacktPublishing/Network-Automation-with-Go`
- `ch03/json/main.go`: `https://github.com/PacktPublishing/Network-Automation-with-Go/blob/main/ch03/json/main.go`
- `ch03/json-interface`: `https://github.com/PacktPublishing/Network-Automation-with-Go/tree/main/ch03/json-interface`
- *GJSON*: `https://github.com/tidwall/gjson`
- *SJSON*: `https://github.com/tidwall/sjson`
- `ch03/xml`: `https://github.com/PacktPublishing/Network-Automation-with-Go/tree/main/ch03/xml`
- `xmlquery`: `https://github.com/antchfx/xmlquery`
- `ch03/yaml`: `https://github.com/PacktPublishing/Network-Automation-with-Go/tree/main/ch03/yaml`
- `ch03/yaml/main.go`: `https://github.com/PacktPublishing/Network-Automation-with-Go/blob/main/ch03/yaml/main.go`
- *yq*: `https://github.com/mikefarah/yq`
- `ch03/json-xml`: `https://github.com/PacktPublishing/Network-Automation-with-Go/tree/main/ch03/json-xml`

- ch03/single: https://github.com/PacktPublishing/Network-Automation-with-Go/tree/main/ch03/single
- ch03/single/main.go: https://github.com/PacktPublishing/Network-Automation-with-Go/blob/main/ch03/single/main.go
- ch03/sequential: https://github.com/PacktPublishing/Network-Automation-with-Go/tree/main/ch03/sequentia
- ch03/concurrency/main.go: https://github.com/PacktPublishing/Network-Automation-with-Go/blob/main/ch03/concurrency/main.go
- ch03/concurrency2: https://github.com/PacktPublishing/Network-Automation-with-Go/tree/main/ch03/concurrency2
- ch03/concurrency3: https://github.com/PacktPublishing/Network-Automation-with-Go/tree/main/ch03/concurrency3
- ch03/concurrency5: https://github.com/PacktPublishing/Network-Automation-with-Go/tree/main/ch03/concurrency5
- ch03/ticker: https://github.com/PacktPublishing/Network-Automation-with-Go/tree/main/ch03/ticker
- *sync.Map documentation*: https://pkg.go.dev/sync#Map
- ch03/concurrency4: https://github.com/PacktPublishing/Network-Automation-with-Go/tree/main/ch03/concurrency4
- ch03/race/main.go: https://github.com/PacktPublishing/Network-Automation-with-Go/blob/main/ch03/race/main.go
- *Simulating a real-world system in Go*: https://www.youtube.com/watch?v=_YK0viplIl4
- *Concurrency is not parallelism*: https://blog.golang.org/waza-talk

4
Networking (TCP/IP) with Go

Every network engineer has at some point learned about the seven layers of the **Open Systems Interconnection** (**OSI**) model. A more concise version of it, with only four layers, is the TCP/IP model, which is the architectural model that governs communications over the internet.

Each layer defines a function, which one data communication protocol per layer performs. These layers pile one upon another, so we often call this collection of protocols a protocol stack. A data packet has to go through each of the four layers of the protocol stack before it gets to the destination host.

Go has several packages to work with protocols at each layer of the TCP/IP model. This enables us to build solutions for an array of use cases – from IP address management to running application transactions through the network or even implementing network protocols:

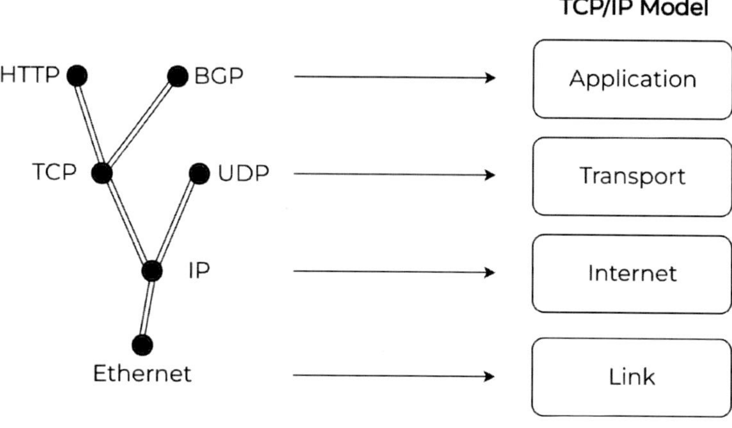

Figure 4.1 – TCP/IP model

In this chapter, we focus on use cases for each of the layers of the TCP/IP model:

- Link
- Internet

- Transport
- Application

Technical requirements

We assume basic familiarity with the command line, Git, and GitHub. You can find the code examples for this chapter in the book's GitHub repository: `https://github.com/PacktPublishing/Network-Automation-with-Go`, under the `ch04` folder.

To run the examples, you'll need to do the following:

1. Install Go 1.17 or later for your operating system. You can follow the instructions in *Chapter 1*, *Introduction*, in the section *Installing Go*, or go to `https://go.dev/doc/install`. Two examples in this chapter, specifically those for the net/netip package, require Go 1.18 or later.
2. Clone the book's GitHub repository with `git clone https://github.com/PacktPublishing/Network-Automation-with-Go.git`.
3. Change the directory to an example folder: `cd Network-Automation-with-Go/ch04/trie`.
4. Execute `go run main.go`.

The link layer

We start with the bottom layer of the TCP/IP model that sends and receives link layer data frames. In this section, we cover the following topics:

- Management of network interfaces
- Basic operations with Ethernet

Network interfaces

As we see more and more network operating systems based on Linux, it makes sense to understand how Go can help us interact with network interfaces in this context.

Linux exposes its networking internals through a kernel interface called Netlink. This interface allows user-space applications such as Go to communicate with the kernel over a standard socket API. Most commonly, TCP/UDP libraries use Netlink sockets to send and receive data, but they can also work with most Linux networking constructs, from interfaces to routes and nftables.

Thankfully, you don't need to learn about or understand the low-level Netlink API, as there are many Go packages that deliver high-level abstractions, making it much easier to work with. Some notable Netlink packages include the following:

- The `syscall` package (*Further reading*) of the Go standard library, which includes several low-level primitives typically used by high-level packages.
- The `vishvananda/netlink` (*Further reading*) third-party Go package is one of the earlier implementations of a high-level Netlink package, widely used by various open source projects such as Docker, Istio, and Kubernetes CNI plugins.
- The ecosystem of plugins based on the `mdlayher/netlink` (*Further reading*) package is a set of relatively recent projects implemented on a common foundation in a more idiomatic and maintainable way.

These Netlink packages have varying levels of feature coverage and the one you choose normally depends on your application requirements. For a demonstration, we show how to toggle the administrative state of an interface, and to do that, we pick one of the rtnetlink packages from the `mdlayher/netlink` ecosystem (*Further reading*).

Let's break down and review this example in three stages. First, we import the Netlink package `rtnetlink/rtnl`, which is one of the loosely related packages developed around the `mdlayher/netlink` package, to establish a connection with a Netlink socket with the `Dial` method and then retrieve the list of all local interfaces with the `Links` method over the connection:

```
func main() {
    conn, err := rtnl.Dial(nil)
    // process error
    defer conn.Close()

    links, err := conn.Links()
    /* ... <continues next > ... */
}
```

This preceding code resembles what we do for all remote connections in Go, which is why Go developers consider this package more idiomatic. Once we have the list of all the interfaces in the variable links, we can iterate over them to find any interface of interest.

Let's say we want to toggle the `lo` interface if it's present in the system. We loop over all the interfaces in the variable links, and we print out the data of the `lo` interface if we find it and store the interface value in a variable we call `loopback`, so we can bring this link down with `LinkDown` and bring it back up with `LinkUp` later:

```
func main() {
    /* ... <continues from before > ... */
    var loopback *net.Interface

    for _, l := range links {
```

```
        if l.Name == "lo" {
            loopback = l
            log.Printf("Name: %s, Flags:%s\n",
                        l.Name, l.Flags)
        }
    }
    /* ... <continues next > ... */
}
```

After running LinkDown and LinkUp, you can verify that the change had the desired effect by retrieving the interface settings from Netlink after each change. We update the loopback variable for a uniform printed statement:

```
func main() {
    /* ... <continues from before > ... */
    conn.LinkDown(loopback)
    loopback, _ = conn.LinkByIndex(loopback.Index)
    log.Printf("Name: %s, Flags:%s\n",
                loopback.Name, loopback.Flags)

    conn.LinkUp(loopback)
    loopback, _ = conn.LinkByIndex(loopback.Index)
    log.Printf("Name: %s, Flags:%s\n",
                loopback.Name, loopback.Flags)
}
```

You can find this example in full in ch04/netlink (*Further reading*) and you must run it with CAP_NET_ADMIN capabilities (*Further reading*) or as root:

```
ch04/netlink $ sudo go run main.go
2021/11/24 20:55:29 Name: lo, Flags:up|loopback
2021/11/24 20:55:29 Name: lo, Flags:loopback
2021/11/24 20:55:29 Name: lo, Flags:up|loopback
```

We've only just scratched the surface of the Netlink API as its abilities extend far beyond the scope of this book. Today, you can use Netlink for everything from IP route management to access lists and from **Quality of Service** (**QoS**) policies to **extended Berkeley Packet Filter** (**eBPF**) program attachments. Hopefully, this section provides enough information to give you an idea of what's involved in Netlink API interactions, as now we have to move on to the next topic and explore how Go deals with the most widely used link layer protocol today: Ethernet.

Ethernet

Working with Ethernet may involve a wide range of activities, from low-level protocol decoding, manipulating, and encoding to interactions with device APIs to collect Ethernet hardware information. Go has a broad spectrum of packages to help you deal with various Ethernet-related tasks:

- One of the most widely used packet processing packages is `google/gopacket` (*Further reading*), which you can use for both packet capturing and protocol decoding. It goes beyond just Ethernet, and we cover it in more detail in *Chapter 10, Network Monitoring*.
- The Netlink API packages we just covered can query link-layer hardware information for Linux-based operating systems.
- Another Ethernet encoding and decoding package `mdlayher/ethernet` (*Further reading*) allows you to convert frames between binary wire format and a static Go type representation.

In the next example, we cover a basic implementation of a `virtual IP` (`VIP`) capability. We loosely based this implementation on the `kube-vip` (*Further reading*) package – a Kubernetes control plane VIP controller. The way it works is a two-step process:

1. It allocates a new **VIP** to one of the local network interfaces.
2. It periodically sends out gratuitous **Address Resolution Protocol** (**ARP**) packets to let everyone in the local broadcast domain know about this VIP.

Let's review this from the first step and see how we assign a VIP to an interface. We'll use the same package to interact with Netlink as we used in the *Network interfaces* section (`rtnetlink/rtnl`), only this time we use the `AddrAdd` method to assign an IP prefix to the interface we specify.

In the program, we pass the name of the interface we want to assign to this VIP address via the CLI using the `flag` package and we store this value in the `intfStr` variable. With this info, we use the `mdlayher/packet` package to send and receive ARP packets over this interface with the `Listen` function:

```
func main() {
    intfStr := flag.String("intf", "", "VIP interface")
    flag.Parse()

    conn, err := rtnl.Dial(nil)
    // process error
    defer conn.Close()

    netIntf, err := net.InterfaceByName(*intfStr)
```

```
    ethSocket, err := packet.Listen(netIntf,
                                    packet.Raw, 0, nil)
    // process error
    defer ethSocket.Close()
    /* ... <continues next > ... */
}
```

To actually assign the VIP address to the interface, we create the `vip` struct type that lets us hold all the information we need to pass to `AddrAdd` to make this happen, as the next output shows:

```
const VIP1 = "198.51.100.1/32"

type vip struct {
    IP      string
    netlink *rtnl.Conn
    intf    *net.Interface
    l2Sock  *raw.Conn
}

func (c *vip) addVIP() error {
    err := c.netlink.AddrAdd(c.intf,
                             rtnl.MustParseAddr(c.IP))
    // process error
    return nil
}

func main() {
    /* ... <continues from before > ... */
    v := &vip{
        IP:      VIP1,
        intf:    netIntf,
        netlink: rtnl,
        l2Sock:  *packet.Conn,
    }

    err = v.addVIP()
     /* ... <continues next > ... */
}
```

Once we have the new VIP assigned, we can start sending out the **Gratuitous ARP** (**GARP**) packets. We do that in a constant `for` loop, which sleeps for 3 seconds and runs again. In this loop, we include an `if` with initialization (`err := v.sendGARP()`) and conditional (`err != nil`) statements. Go executes the initialization statement before evaluating the conditional expression:

```
func main() {
    /* ... <continues from before > ... */
    for {
        select {
        /* ... <omitted for brevity > ... */
        case <-timer.C:
            if err := v.sendGARP(); err != nil {
                log.Printf("fail send GARP %s",
                               err)
                cancel()
            }
        }
    }
}
```

Inside the `sendGARP` method is where we can find most of the Ethernet-related code. Here, we use two packages to help us build the GARP.

We first need to build the GARP payload and populate it with the MAC address of the local interface and the IP address of the VIP. For this, we take advantage of the `mdlayher/arp` (*Further reading*) package:

```
func (c *vip) sendGARP() error {
    /* ... <omitted for brevity > ... */
    arpPayload, err := arp.NewPacket(
        arp.OperationReply,  // op
        c.intf.HardwareAddr, // srcHW
        ip,                  // srcIP
        c.intf.HardwareAddr, // dstHW
        ip,                  // dstIP
    )
    // process error

    arpBinary, err := arpPayload.MarshalBinary()
    /* ... <continues next > ... */
}
```

Then we need to wrap the GARP payload inside an Ethernet frame and set the right Ethernet headers using the `mdlayher/ethernet` (*Further reading*) package:

```
func (c *vip) sendGARP() error {
    /* ... <continues from before > ... */
    ethFrame := &ethernet.Frame{
        Destination: ethernet.Broadcast,
        Source:      c.intf.HardwareAddr,
        EtherType:   ethernet.EtherTypeARP,
        Payload:     arpBinary,
    }

    return c.emitFrame(ethFrame)
}
```

The last step is to send a binary frame and to do that, we use the `mdlayher/packet` (*Further reading*) package that implements the Linux packet socket interface that lets us send and receive packets at the device driver (link-layer) level. We have already opened a raw socket, `ethSocket`, using `Listen` as shown earlier, so now we can write our binary frame into it (`field l2Sock` of the `vip` struct):

```
func (c *vip) emitFrame(frame *ethernet.Frame) error {
    b, err := frame.MarshalBinary()
    // process error

    addr := &packet.Addr{
                HardwareAddr:ethernet.Broadcast}
    if _, err := c.l2Sock.WriteTo(b, addr); err != nil {
        return fmt.Errorf("emitFrame failed: %s", err)
    }

    log.Println("GARP sent")
    return nil
}
```

You can find the full example at `ch04/vip` (*Further reading*). You need to run it with elevated privileges to be able to make changes to network interfaces. The resulting output would look like this:

```
ch04/vip $ sudo go run main.go -intf eth0
2021/11/25 18:47:51 GARP sent
```

```
2021/11/25 18:47:54 GARP sent
^C2021/11/25 18:47:56 Received syscall: interrupt
2021/11/25 18:47:57 Cleanup complete
```

At this point, any host with an overlapping IP subnet on the local network segment should be able to ping the `198.51.100.1` address (if they accept GARPs). To end the program, you can press *Ctrl* + *C* and the program cleans up the VIP from the interface.

It's rare for a network engineer or a developer to interact with Ethernet directly, but it's still worth knowing what it feels like to *talk Ethernet* using Go. In the next section, we move one layer up and cover the internet layer packages and examples.

The internet layer

The internet layer or network layer in the OSI model is in charge of transferring variable-length network packets and routing data from a source to a destination through one or more networks.

The predominant protocol in this layer today is the **Internet Protocol** (**IP**) on either of its two versions: version 4 (IPv4) or version 6 (IPv6). The internet layer also includes diagnostic protocols such as **Internet Control Message Protocol** (**ICMP**), a secure network protocol suite such as **Internet Protocol Security** (**IPsec**), and routing protocols including **Open Shortest Path First** (**OSPF**).

The IP exchanges information via IP datagrams built from a header and a payload, which the link layer then transmits as frames over specific network hardware such as Ethernet. The IP header carries the IP source and destination addresses of a packet used to route it through the internet.

In this section, we review the following:

- How to use the `net` package to parse and perform common tasks with IP addresses
- The new `net/netip` package and what features it brings to the Go standard library
- Examples of real-life Go projects that work with IP addresses

The net package

The `net` package (*Further reading*) from the standard library includes a wide range of tools and resources for network connectivity and, most importantly for this section, defines types and interfaces to work with IP addresses. One of these types is `IP`, represented as a slice of bytes. This type is valid for 4-byte (IPv4) or 16-byte (IPv6) slices:

```
type IP []byte
```

Let's first explore how we can create an `IP` type variable, from the decimal representation of the IPv4 address `192.0.2.1`:

Figure 4.2 – An IPv4 address

One way to turn an IPv4 address into an IP type is by using the `ParseIP` function from the `net` package, which takes a string as an argument and returns an `IP` value:

```
func main() {
	ipv4 := net.ParseIP("192.0.2.1")
	fmt.Println(ipv4)
}
```

IPv6 addresses are a bit harder for our eyes to process, but to Go they are yet another slice of bits just like IPv4:

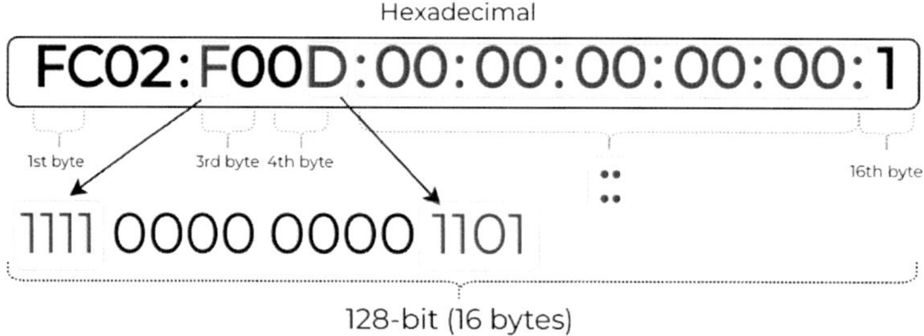

Figure 4.3 – An IPv6 address

The `ParseIP` function can also parse a string representation of an IPv6 to return the variable of the `IP` type:

```
func main() {
	ipv6 := net.ParseIP("FC02:F00D::1")
	fmt.Println(ipv6)
}
```

The `IP` type represents an IP address, so you can use the same IP methods for either IPv4 or IPv6 addresses. Let's say you want to check whether an IP address is within a private address range.

The `IsPrivate` method from the `net` package gives you that answer based on RFC 1918 (Address Allocation for Private Internets) and RFC 4193 (Unique Local IPv6 Unicast Addresses) for both IPv4 and IPv6 automatically:

```
func main() {
    // prints false
    fmt.Println(ipv4.IsPrivate())
    // prints true
    fmt.Println(ipv6.IsPrivate())
}
```

Another interesting type is `IPNet`, which describes an IP prefix or an IP network, so it adds `IPMask` to `IP` to represent its mask:

```
type IPNet struct {
    IP   IP     // network number
    Mask IPMask // network mask
}
```

A mask in the `net` package is also a slice of bytes, which is better explained with the following example using the `CIDRMask` function. Both `ones` and `bits` arguments are integers as the function signature indicates. The first argument, `ones`, is the number of ones in `IPMask` and the remaining bits are all set to zero. The total length of the mask is measured in `bits`:

```
type IPMask []byte

func CIDRMask(ones, bits int) IPMask
```

Let's see an example for IPv4, with a 32-bit mask:

```
func main() {
    // This mask corresponds to a /31 subnet for IPv4.
    // prints [11111111 11111111 11111111 11111110]
    fmt.Printf("%b\n",net.CIDRMask(31, 32))
}
```

IPv6 works similarly but expects a mask length of 128:

```
func main() {
    // This mask corresponds to a /64 subnet for IPv6.
    // prints ffffffffffffffff0000000000000000
```

```
    fmt.Printf("%s\n",net.CIDRMask(64, 128))
}
```

To parse a prefix or network from a string, you can use the `ParseCIDR` function from the `net` package. You get three values – a network address of the `IP` type, an IP prefix of the `IPnet` type, and an error:

```
func main() {
    ipv4Addr, ipv4Net, err := net.ParseCIDR("192.0.2.1/24")
    // process error

    // prints 192.0.2.1
    fmt.Println(ipv4Addr)
    // prints 192.0.2.0/24
    fmt.Println(ipv4Net)
}
```

The next example shows `ParseCIDR` for IPv6 using the same functions as with IPv4:

```
func main() {
    ipv6Addr, ipv6Net, err :=  net.ParseCIDR(
                                "2001:db8:a0b:12f0::1/32")
    // process error

    // prints 2001:db8:a0b:12f0::1
    fmt.Println(ipv6Addr)
    // prints 2001:db8::/32
    fmt.Println(ipv6Net)
}
```

The code for these examples is available at `ch04/net/main.go` (*Further reading*).

This is the standard way of doing basic operations with IP addresses in Go. Yet not long ago there was an effort to add a new IP address type to the standard library, via a package that we review next.

The New netip package

With the goal of improving some things that weren't great about the `net.IP` data structure for IP addresses in Go, a group of Go developers came up with a new IP address type. This was an iterative process that they documented in the blog post *netaddr.IP: a new IP address type for Go* (*Further reading*). This package is now available in Go 1.18 as `net/netip`.

The `net/netip` package defines a new type, `Addr`, that stores both IPv4 and IPv6 addresses as a big-endian 128-bit number. This type also has a special sentinel field `z`, which can have any of these values:

- `nil` means an invalid IP address (for a zero `Addr`).
- `z4` means an IPv4 address.
- `z6noz` means an IPv6 address without a zone.
- Otherwise, it's the IPv6 zone name string.

The data structure in Go looks as follows:

```
type Addr struct {
    addr uint128
    z *intern.Value
}
```

This new `Addr` type has the following major benefits compared to the legacy `net.IP`:

- It takes up less memory.
- It's immutable and, hence, safe to pass around.
- It supports == operations and, hence, you can use it as a map key.

Let's see some examples of how to parse an IP address from a string to get an `Addr` type and use it with some methods available in the package. In the first example, we parse an IPv4 address and check whether it's within the RFC 1112 `224.0.0.0/4` multicast range with the `IsMulticast` method. A second example for IPv6 shows how to parse an IP address from a string with the same function, `ParseAddr`, and checks whether the IPv6 is a Link-Local address or part of the network `FE80::/10` according to the RFC 4291 with the `IsLinkLocalUnicast` method:

```
func main() {
    IPv4, err := netip.ParseAddr("224.0.0.1")
    // process error

    // prints IPv4 address is Multicast
    if IPv4.IsMulticast() {
        fmt.Println("IPv4 address is Multicast")
    }

    IPv6, err := netip.ParseAddr("FE80:F00D::1")
    // process error
```

```
    // prints IPv6 address is Link Local Unicast
    if IPv6.IsLinkLocalUnicast() {
        fmt.Println("IPv6 address is Link Local Unicast")
    }
}
```

Now, if you have an existing program that uses `net.IP`, you can use that type as input for `netip` as well. For both IPv4 and IPv6, it parses the `net.IP` type with the function `AddrFromSlice`. The method `IsX` tells us whether this is an IPv4 or IPv6 address:

```
func main() {
    ipv4 := net.ParseIP("192.0.2.1")
    IPv4s, _ := netip.AddrFromSlice(ipv4)

    fmt.Println(IPv4s.String())
    fmt.Println(IPv4s.Unmap().Is4())
}
```

The code for this example is available at `ch04/parseip` (*Further reading*):

```
ch04/parseip$ go run main.go
::ffff:192.0.2.1
true
```

To represent an IP prefix (CIDR), `net/netip` defines a type called `Prefix` that has an `Addr` and an integer to specify the prefix length (from 0 to 128) in the field `bits`:

```
type Prefix struct {
    ip Addr
    bits int16
}
```

To parse a prefix from a string, you can use the `ParsePrefix` function or `MustParsePrefix`, which calls `ParsePrefix` and panics on error, which means you don't have to check the returned error in your code. Let's look at a program that uses `MustParsePrefix` to generate a prefix, and then checks whether some IP addresses are in the address range of that prefix:

```
func main() {
    addr1 := "192.0.2.18"
    addr2 := "198.51.100.3"
```

```
    network4 := "192.0.2.0/24"
    pf := netip.MustParsePrefix(network4)
    fmt.Printf(
        "Prefix address: %v, length: %v\n",
        pf.Addr(), pf.Bits())

    ip1 := netip.MustParseAddr(addr1)
    if pf.Contains(ip1) {
        fmt.Println(addr1, " is in ", network4)
    }

    ip2 := netip.MustParseAddr(addr2)
    if pf.Contains(ip2) {
        fmt.Println(addr2, " is in ", network4)
    }
}
```

We define the prefix `pf` from the `network4` string `192.0.2.0/24`. Then, we check whether addresses `192.0.2.18` and `198.51.100.3` are in this network by printing a message if they are. This program prints the following:

```
ch04/parseprefix$ go run main.go
Prefix address: 192.0.2.0, length: 24
192.0.2.18  is in  192.0.2.0/24
```

The code for this example is available at `ch04/parseprefix` (*Further reading*).

Working with IP addresses

After parsing IP addresses, you are only one step from several real-world applications you can put into practice. We cover just a few examples here:

- Route lookups
- Geo IP data
- Extra IP address functions

Route lookups

One way to do a route lookup or find the longest prefix match for an IP address is by using a trie data structure (prefix tree). Tries are very efficient in both memory and speed, which is why we use them for IP prefix lookups. To do this in Go, you can use one of the available packages. In this case, we use `cidranger` (*Further reading*).

We start by defining a new path-compressed prefix trie and add a list of parsed IP addresses from the `IPs` variable:

```
func main() {
	ranger := cidranger.NewPCTrieRanger()

	IPs := []string{
		"100.64.0.0/16",
		"127.0.0.0/8",
		"172.16.0.0/16",
		"192.0.2.0/24",
		"192.0.2.0/24",
		"192.0.2.0/25",
		"192.0.2.127/25",
	}

	for _, prefix := range IPs {
		ipv4Addr, ipv4Net, err := net.ParseCIDR(prefix)
		// process error
		ranger.Insert(
				cidranger.NewBasicRangerEntry(*ipv4Net))
	}
	/* ... <continues next > ... */
}
```

Now we can check whether any IP is within the defined list of IP address ranges. Here, we find that `127.0.0.1` is in at least one IP prefix on the list:

```
func main() {
	/* ... <continues from before > ... */
	checkIP := "127.0.0.1"
```

```
    ok, err := ranger.Contains(net.ParseIP(checkIP))
    // process error

    // prints Does the range contain 127.0.0.1?: true
    fmt.Printf("Does the range contain %s?: %v\n",
                checkIP, ok)
    /* ... <continues next > ... */
}
```

One other thing you could do is to request a list of networks that contain an IP address, such as `192.0.2.18` in this case:

```
func main() {
    /* ... <continues from before > ... */
    netIP := "192.0.2.18"

    nets, err := ranger.ContainingNetworks(
                        net.ParseIP(netIP))
    // process error

    fmt.Printf(
    "\nNetworks that contain IP address %s ->\n", netIP)
    for _, e := range nets {
        n := e.Network()
        fmt.Println("\t", n.String())
    }
}
```

This returns `192.0.2.0/24` and `192.0.2.0/25`:

```
ch04/trie$ go run main.go
Networks that contain IP address 192.0.2.18 ->
     192.0.2.0/24
     192.0.2.0/25
```

The code of this example is available at `ch04/trie/main.go` (*Further reading*).

Geo IP data

Another interesting use case is to get the geographical location associated with a public IP address. To make this query, you need access to a database that you can download for free from GeoLite2 Free Geolocation Data (*Further reading*) or you can just use the sample file we included in the book's repo, which has support for a limited number of IP addresses, but enough to run the examples.

We open the database file, and for each IP address in a slice, we query for any available information, which we then print to the terminal:

```
func main() {
    db, err := geoip2.Open("GeoIP2-City-Test.mmdb")
    // process error
    defer db.Close()

    IPs := []string{
        "81.2.69.143",
        /* ... <omitted for brevity > ... */
    }

    fmt.Println("Find information for each prefix:")
    for _, prefix := range IPs {
        ip := net.ParseIP(prefix)
        record, err := db.City(ip)
        // process error

        fmt.Printf("\nAddress: %v\n", prefix)
        fmt.Printf("City name: %v\n",
                        record.City.Names["en"])
        /* ... <omitted for brevity > ... */
    }
}
```

One output example is the following:

```
ch04/geo$ go run main.go
Find information for each prefix:

...
```

```
Address: 81.2.69.143
City name: Norwich
Country name: United Kingdom
ISO country code: GB
Time zone: Europe/London
Coordinates: 52.6259, 1.3032
```

The code for this example is available at `ch04/geo/main.go` (*Further reading*).

Extra IP address functions

If you come from another programming language such as Python, you might be familiar with the `ipaddress` library to manipulate IP addresses and networks. The `iplib` package (*Further reading*) is an effort to bring those features to Go.

In the next example, we see a function to increment an IP address by one (`NextIP`) and another function to increase an IP address by any number (`IncrementIPBy`). We then compute the difference between the original IP address and the result after these two increments with the `DeltaIP` function to find out the number of IP addresses in between.

The last line of the example compares two IP addresses with the `CompareIPs` function. If `a` and `b` are the inputs, it returns `0` if `a == b`, `-1` if `a < b`, and `1` if `a > b`:

```
func main() {
    IP := net.ParseIP("192.0.2.1")
    nextIP := iplib.NextIP(IP)
    incrIP := iplib.IncrementIPBy(nextIP, 19)

    // prints 20
    fmt.Println(iplib.DeltaIP(IP, incrIP))
    // prints -1
    fmt.Println(iplib.CompareIPs(IP, incrIP))
}
```

Because the `iplib` package allows you to compare IP addresses, it means you can use the `sort` package to sort a list of `net.IP` addresses as the next example shows, using the addresses we just created:

```
func main() {
    iplist := []net.IP{incrIP, nextIP, IP}
    // prints [192.0.2.21 192.0.2.2 192.0.2.1]
    fmt.Println(iplist)
```

```
    sort.Sort(iplib.ByIP(iplist))
    // prints [192.0.2.1 192.0.2.2 192.0.2.21]
    fmt.Println(iplist)
}
```

You can also generate an array of IP addresses from a network, starting at any IP address with the `Enumerate` method. In the next example, we take the network `198.51.100.0/24`, count the total available addresses in it with `Count`, to then generate an array of size 3 with `Enumerate`, starting from the first available IP address of the network (index 0):

```
func main() {
    n4 := iplib.NewNet4(net.ParseIP("198.51.100.0"), 24)
    fmt.Println("Total IP addresses: ", n4.Count())

    fmt.Println("First three IPs: ", n4.Enumerate(3, 0))
    fmt.Println("First IP: ", n4.FirstAddress())
    fmt.Println("Last IP: ", n4.LastAddress())
}
```

This program produces the following output:

```
ch04/ipaddr$ go run main.go
...
Total IP addresses:  254
First three IPs:  [198.51.100.1 198.51.100.2 198.51.100.3]
First IP:  198.51.100.1
Last IP:  198.51.100.254
```

The code for this example is available at `ch04/ipaddr/main.go` (*Further reading*).

IP is the fundamental protocol on the internet, which has continued to support its evolution over the last 40 years without major changes, despite the fast pace of technological development in the last few decades. Along with protocols from the transport layer, IP has allowed the decoupling of applications from hardware technologies such as coax cable, fiber optics, and Wi-Fi. Speaking of the transport layer, in the next section, we explore how Go can help you navigate this layer of the TCP/IP model.

The transport layer

The transport layer protocols are the next OSI layer on top of IP and offer a communication channel abstraction. The two most common protocols today are TCP, which offers a connection-oriented communication channel, and UDP, a connectionless protocol.

In Go, the way you interact with both protocols is similar, even though the underlying packet exchange may be completely different. At a high level, there are only a few things that you need to keep in mind when dealing with TCP or UDP:

- Each TCP or UDP application works with a corresponding connection represented by a concrete `TCPConn` or `UDPConn` type, respectively.
- Go has other connection types with overlapping features such as `PacketConn`, which deals with connectionless protocols (UDP and IP); `Conn`, which covers IP, TCP, and UDP; and `UnixConn` for connections to Unix domain sockets. We only focus on `TCPConn` and `UDPConn` in this section.
- Clients use `net.DialTCP` and `net.DialUDP` to open a socket to a remote address.
- Servers use `net.ListenUDP` and `net.ListenTCP` to open a listening socket that accepts connections from different clients.
- Clients and servers can `Read` and `Write` bytes from and to their respective connections.
- When finished, both clients and servers need to close their connections to clean up the underlying file descriptor.

The following figure illustrates the interactions between different types involved in a typical UDP client-server communication:

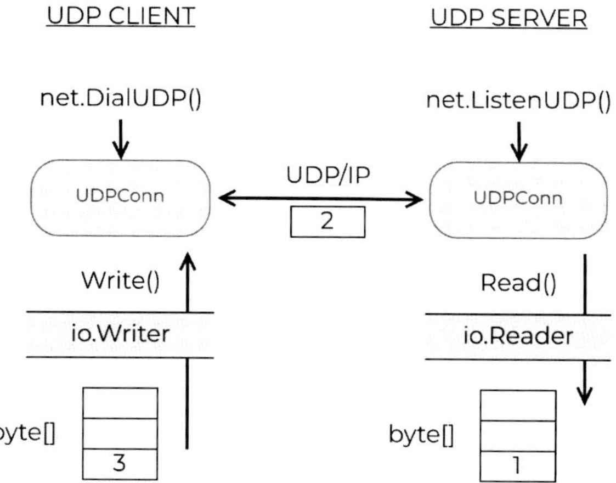

Figure 4.4 – UDP communication in Go

Figure 4.4 shows a UDP client sending one byte at a time, although in reality, the payload can have more bytes. This could be a DNS request or an RTP packet. All network connection types implement `io.Reader` and `io.Writer` interfaces, so reading and writing are similar no matter what protocol you use underneath.

The UDP client creates a UDP connection with `net.DialUDP` and then writes (`Write`) a byte to it, just like when you make a request to the network. On the server side, you read (`Read`) from the connection you would have created earlier with `net.ListenUDP`.

Now, let's move on to something a bit more concrete and see what a real UDP application may look like.

UDP ping application

Ping is one of the most conventional ways of checking remote connectivity and end-to-end latency. Just like the traditional ping, UDP ping uses echo replies to calculate latency and packet loss but encapsulates them in a UDP packet instead of ICMP/NDP. Many monitoring applications use this approach as it allows them to discover and monitor various equal-cost paths in networks with devices that perform 5-tuple hashing. One such application is Cloudprober (*Further reading*), which is the source of inspiration for the next example, as the authors wrote it in Go.

Let's walk through the code of a UDP ping application, focusing on connection establishment and data exchange. You can find the full code in the `ch04/udp-ping` (*Further reading*) folder of the book's repository (*Further reading*). At a high level, our UDP ping application consists of two parts:

1. The server side listens on a UDP port and mirrors back any packets received from its clients.
2. The client that is sending UDP probes to a server receives a stream of mirrored packets coming back to compute the packet loss and end-to-end latency:

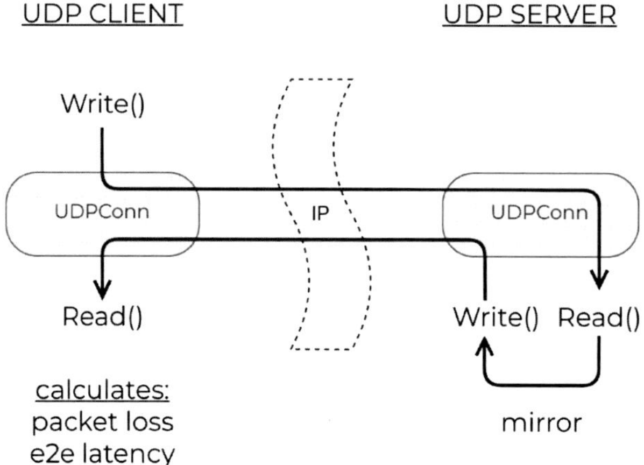

Figure 4.5 – UDP ping application

Let's start the overview of this application with the server side. The program begins by building a `UDPAddr` variable that describes a UDP socket. We then pass this variable to `net.ListenUDP` to create a UDP socket and start listening for incoming packets. The first argument in the `ListenUDP` function is `udp`, which specifies the dual-stack behavior (RFC6724 and RFC6555). You could also use `udp4` or `udp6` to pin the program to either IPv4 or IPv6 respectively:

```
func main() {
    listenAddr      = "0.0.0.0"
    listenPort      = 32767

    listenSoc := &net.UDPAddr{
        IP:   net.ParseIP(listenAddr),
        Port: listenPort,
    }

    udpConn, err := net.ListenUDP("udp", listenSoc)
    // process error
    defer udpConn.Close()
    /* ... <continues next > ... */
}
```

Once we have a listening UDP socket, we can start the main processing loop, which reads an incoming packet into a byte slice with `ReadFromUDP` and writes the entire packet back to the sender with `WriteToUDP`.

Since `ReadFromUDP` is a blocking function, most server implementations add an extra `SetReadDeadline` timeout to make sure the program can be gracefully terminated if needed. In this case, it leads directly to the next loop iteration thanks to the `continue` statement after `ReadFromUDP`:

```
func main() {
    /* ... <continues from before > ... */
    for {
        maxReadBuffer  = 425984
        bytes := make([]byte, maxReadBuffer)

        retryTimeout   = time.Second * 5
        if err := udpConn.SetReadDeadline(
                        time.Now().Add(retryTimeout))
        // process error
```

```
        len, raddr, err := udpConn.ReadFromUDP(bytes)
        if err != nil {
            log.Printf("failed to ReadFromUDP: %s", err)
            continue
        }
        log.Printf("Received a probe from %s:%d",
                        raddr.IP.String(), raddr.Port)

        n, err := udpConn.WriteToUDP(bytes[:len], raddr)
        // process error
    }
}
```

The client-side implementation starts similarly, by building a `UDPAddr` variable and passing it to the `net.DialUDP` function. In the case of TCP, the `net.DialTCP` function would trigger a TCP three-way handshake, but in the case of UDP, the underlying OS opens a network socket without exchanging any packets:

```
func main() {
    rAddr := &net.UDPAddr{
        IP:   net.ParseIP("127.0.0.1"),
        Port: "32767",
    }

    udpConn, err := net.DialUDP("udp", nil, rAddr)
    // process error
    defer udpConn.Close()
    /* ... <continues next > ... */
}
```

At this point, the program branches out in two directions. The logical first step is the packet sending routine, which in this case runs inside the main goroutine of the program. In the background, we also fire off a goroutine that runs the `receive` function, which we discuss a few paragraphs later.

Inside each probe packet we send, we embed a monotonically increasing sequence number and the value of a current timestamp. We serialize the probe packets into a binary slice, `p`, and write them into the UDP connection, `udpConn`, with the `binary.Write` function:

```
func main() {
    /* ... <continues from before > ... */
```

```
    go receive(*udpConn)
    var seq uint8

    for {
        log.Printf("Sending probe %d", seq)
        p := &probe{
            SeqNum: seq,
            SendTS: time.Now().UnixMilli(),
        }

        if err := binary.Write(udpConn,
                        binary.BigEndian, p)
        // process error

        seq++
    }
}
```

Now let's have a closer look at the `receive` function, which we kickstarted just before the sending loop in the last code snippet. Inside this function, we have another loop that performs the following sequence of actions:

1. It receives a mirrored packet and deserializes it into the `p` variable of the `probe` type using the `binary.Read` function.
2. It checks the `SeqNum` sequence number of a received packet to find out whether it's out of order.
3. It calculates the latency by subtracting the current time, `time.Now`, from the time received in the `SendTS` probe.

In Go code, it looks like this:

```
func receive(udpConn net.UDPConn) {
    var nextSeq uint8
    var lost int
    for {
        p := &probe{}

        if err := binary.Read(&udpConn,
                            binary.BigEndian, p)
        // process error
```

```
            if p.SeqNum < nextSeq {
                log.Printf("Out of order packet seq: %d/%d",
                                        p.SeqNum, nextSeq)
                lost -= 1
            } else if p.SeqNum > nextSeq {
                log.Printf("Out of order packet seq: %d/%d",
                                        p.SeqNum, nextSeq)
                lost += int(p.SeqNum - nextSeq)
                nextSeq = p.SeqNum
            }

            latency := time.Now().UnixMilli() - p.SendTS
            log.Printf("E2E latency: %d ms", latency)
            log.Printf("Lost packets: %d", lost)
            nextSeq++
        }
    }
```

We've used `binary.Read` and `binary.Write` in this example to convert between the in-memory data types and binary slices. This is possible thanks to the fixed size of the probe packets. But, if the probes had been of variable size, we could've only used the same functions to pre-parse the fixed-sized part of the header and would've had to read and parse the variable-sized payload manually.

The actual UDP ping application in `ch04/udp-ping` (*Further reading*) has a bit more code to account for further error conditions and graceful program termination. Let's see an example of running the client-side code against a remote UDP ping server, where for each iteration, we can see the total number of lost packets and the latest calculated latency:

```
ch04/udp-ping/client$ sudo go run main.go
2021/12/10 15:10:31 Starting UDP ping client
2021/12/10 15:10:31 Starting UDP ping receive loop
2021/12/10 15:10:32 Sending probe 0
2021/12/10 15:10:32 Received probe 0
2021/12/10 15:10:32 E2E latency: 9 ms
2021/12/10 15:10:32 Lost packets: 0
2021/12/10 15:10:33 Sending probe 1
2021/12/10 15:10:33 Received probe 1
2021/12/10 15:10:33 E2E latency: 8 ms
```

```
2021/12/10 15:10:33 Lost packets: 0
2021/12/10 15:10:34 Sending probe 2
2021/12/10 15:10:34 Received probe 2
2021/12/10 15:10:34 E2E latency: 9 ms
2021/12/10 15:10:34 Lost packets: 0
...
```

The server side does not make any measurements and only logs a client IP address for each received UDP probe:

```
ch04/udp-ping/server$ sudo go run main.go
2021/12/10 15:10:28 Starting the UDP ping server
2021/12/10 15:10:32 Received a probe from 198.51.100.173:59761
2021/12/10 15:10:33 Received a probe from 198.51.100.173:59761
2021/12/10 15:10:34 Received a probe from 198.51.100.173:59761
...
```

You've just seen an example of a binary UDP-based protocol that uses a single message to exchange information and calculate network metrics. Although we think it's important to understand how to work with transport-layer protocols in Go, it's not very common to implement your own application directly on top of TCP or UDP; the only notable exceptions include high-performance messaging protocols such as Kafka, NATS, and AMQP. Most communications these days happen over a higher-level protocol, HTTP. With it, we get wide support for packages and SDKs, a vast ecosystem of communication standards with REST, GRPC, and GraphQL, and standard support from network middleware such as proxies and intrusion detection systems. In the following section, we show how to write a sample HTTP client-server application in Go.

The application layer

In the last section, we explored how to establish a TCP or UDP connection between two nodes to transfer bytes over the network using the Go low-level network primitives we have learned about so far. Now we focus on the top layer of the TCP/IP model and go into the application-level constructs that Go includes in the standard library to implement HTTP clients and servers.

To illustrate this, we go through the steps to build a client-server application that returns the MAC address vendor, IP address owner, or detailed domain information to the requester. On the client side, we need to craft an HTTP request that encapsulates the query to the server address. On the server side, we need to listen for requests and implement the logic to serve them and reply with the information for the argument received.

Working with an HTTP client

On the client side, we first need to put together the URL we send the request to. The URL, for our example, has three components:

- The server address (IP address and port)
- The lookup type to perform (MAC, IP, or domain)
- An argument, which is the value we want to query for

The `net/url` package helps us in this case, to parse the inputs into a URL structure. We hardcode values for the example in the book, but you can input any values you want via flags when you run the code in `ch04/http/client/main.go` (*Further reading*).

We use the `Parse` method from `net/url` to form the first part of the URL: `http://localhost:8080/lookup`. The second part of the example adds the query. We leverage the `Add` method for this, which takes a key-value pair as an argument. The `lookup` variable is the key in this case and the value comes from the `argument` variable. The full URL looks like this: `http://localhost:8080/lookup?domain=tkng.io`.

```
func main() {
	server := "localhost:8080"
	// One of: mac, ip, domain
	lookup := "domain"
	// Examples: 68b5.99fc.d1df, 1.1.1.1, tkng.io
	argument := "tkng.io"
	path := "/lookup"

	addr, err := url.Parse("http://" + server + path)
	// process error

	params := url.Values{}
	params.Add(lookup, argument)
	addr.RawQuery = params.Encode()
	/* ... <continues next > ... */
}
```

To make the actual request to the server, we leverage the `net/http` package. This package has a `Client` type that specifies the mechanism to make an HTTP request. We don't need to stipulate any client details for this example, so we show the type just for reference:

```
type Client struct {
    Transport RoundTripper
    CheckRedirect func(req *Request, via []*Request) error
    Jar CookieJar
    Timeout time.Duration
}
```

If you don't have any preference, you can select a `DefaultClient` that uses a `DefaultTransport`. This client has pre-defined timeouts and proxy settings, which are safe for concurrent use by different goroutines, so we don't need to adjust any of the parameters that the following code snippet from the Go standard library shows, which also depicts the client HTTP transport settings that are available in case you want to fine-tune the behavior of the connection:

```
var DefaultTransport RoundTripper = &Transport{
    Proxy: ProxyFromEnvironment,
    DialContext: (&net.Dialer{
        Timeout:   30 * time.Second,
        KeepAlive: 30 * time.Second,
    }).DialContext,
    ForceAttemptHTTP2:     true,
    MaxIdleConns:          100,
    IdleConnTimeout:       90 * time.Second,
    TLSHandshakeTimeout:   10 * time.Second,
    ExpectContinueTimeout: 1 * time.Second,
}
```

Continuing with the example, `DefaultClient` allows us to use HTTP GET, HEAD, and POST methods. Here, we use HTTP GET with the `Get` method from the `net/http` package to the `addr` address we parsed earlier with `Parse`:

```
func main() {
    /* ... <continues from before > ... */
    res, err := http.DefaultClient.Get(addr.String())
    if err != nil {
        log.Fatal(err)
    }
    defer res.Body.Close()
    io.Copy(os.Stdout, res.Body)
}
```

The last step is to print out the response we get from the server to the terminal. You can use flags from the CLI to submit different queries when running the client application to do these operations:

- A health check:

```
ch04/http/client$ go run main.go -check
OK
```

- A MAC address vendor lookup:

```
ch04/http/client$ go run main.go -lookup mac 68b5.99fc.
d1df
Hewlett Packard
```

- A domain lookup:

```
ch04/http/client$ go run main.go -lookup domain tkng.io
Domain Name: tkng.io
Registry Domain ID: 5cdbf549b56144f5afe00b62ccd8d6e9-
DONUTS
Registrar WHOIS Server: whois.namecheap.com
Registrar URL: https://www.namecheap.com/
Updated Date: 2021-09-24T20:39:04Z
Creation Date: 2021-07-26T19:08:34Z
Registry Expiry Date: 2022-07-26T19:08:34Z
Registrar: NameCheap, Inc.
Registrar IANA ID: 1068
```

- An IP address lookup:

```
ch04/http/client$ go run main.go -lookup ip 1.1.1.1
...
inetnum:        1.1.1.0 - 1.1.1.255
netname:        APNIC-LABS
descr:          APNIC and Cloudflare DNS Resolver project
descr:          Routed globally by AS13335/Cloudflare
descr:          Research prefix for APNIC Labs
country:        AU
```

To get these responses, we need to have a running server first that processes the requests. Let's build it.

Working with an HTTP (server)

To handle the requests and responses, the `net/http` package exposes a `Server` type and a `Handler` interface. `Server` is the data structure for the parameters to run an HTTP server:

```
type Server struct {
	Addr string
	Handler Handler
	TLSConfig *tls.Config
	ReadTimeout time.Duration
	ReadHeaderTimeout time.Duration
	/* ... <omitted for brevity > ... */
}
```

Let's define a `srv` variable of the `Server` type. The zero value for `Server` is a valid configuration, but in this case, we denote `Addr` as `0.0.0.0:8080` to listen on any interface and port `8080` specifically.

The `Server` type has a `ListenAndServe` method to listen on the TCP network address, `Addr`, of the `Server` instance (`srv.Addr` or `0.0.0.0:8080` in the example). It then calls the `Serve` method to accept incoming connections and handle the requests. For each request, it creates a new service goroutine that reads the request and then calls the `Server` instance, `Handler` (`srv.Handler` or `nil` in the example), to reply to them:

```
func main() {
	/* ... <omitted for brevity > ... */
	log.Println("Starting web server at 0.0.0.0:8080")

	srv := http.Server{Addr: "0.0.0.0:8080"}
	// ListenAndServe always returns a non-nil error.
	log.Fatal(srv.ListenAndServe())
}
```

This brings us to the second type in the `net/http` package we mentioned initially, the `Handler` interface. The role of `Handler` is to respond to an HTTP request:

```
type Handler interface {
	ServeHTTP(ResponseWriter, *Request)
}
```

`Handler` responds to HTTP requests via its `ServeHTTP` method, which takes two arguments:

- A `ResponseWriter` interface, which you can use to craft an HTTP header and payload to reply to the request and then return:

```
type ResponseWriter interface {
    Header() Header

    // Write writes the data to the connection
    // as part of an HTTP reply.
    Write([]byte) (int, error)

    // WriteHeader sends an HTTP response header
    // with the provided status code.
    WriteHeader(statusCode int)
}
```

- An HTTP `Request`, which holds the HTTP request received by the server in this case. It could also be a request you want to send from a client:

```
type Request struct {
    // Method specifies the HTTP method
    // (GET, POST, PUT, etc.).
    Method string

    // URL specifies either the URI being requested
    // (for server requests) or the URL to access
    // (for client requests).
    URL *url.URL
    Header Header
    Body io.ReadCloser
    /* ... <omitted for brevity > ... */
}
```

Now, if we look back at our example, we didn't specify our `Handler`, so when we called `ListenAndServe`, our handler was actually null (`nil`). In this scenario, `ListenAndServe` defaults a `DefaultServeMux` to handle the requests that come in. `DefaultServeMux` is an HTTP request multiplexer that the `net/http` package includes. It routes requests to the most appropriate handler based on a list of registered URL patterns.

The next step in the example is to register a handler function for a given pattern. We do this with the `HandleFunc` function, which takes a string pattern and a handler function with the `func(ResponseWriter, *Request)` signature as arguments. Now, when we get an incoming request that has a URL that matches this pattern, the specified handler generates the response.

Going back to the example, in the first code snippet we showed of the main function, we purposely omitted the initial two lines of code, which actually register two URL patterns to match, `/lookup` and `/check`:

```
func main() {
    http.HandleFunc("/lookup", lookup)
    http.HandleFunc("/check", check)
    /* ... <omitted for brevity > ... */
}
```

Normal queries follow the `/lookup` route, but we also included a `/check` option to let us to run a quick health check and verify the server is responding to requests. Each pattern has a corresponding handler function with the `func(ResponseWriter, *Request)` signature as an argument. We conveniently named these functions `lookup` and `check`. *Figure 4.6* shows how `DefaultServeMux` logically determines the `Handler` that handles the user request:

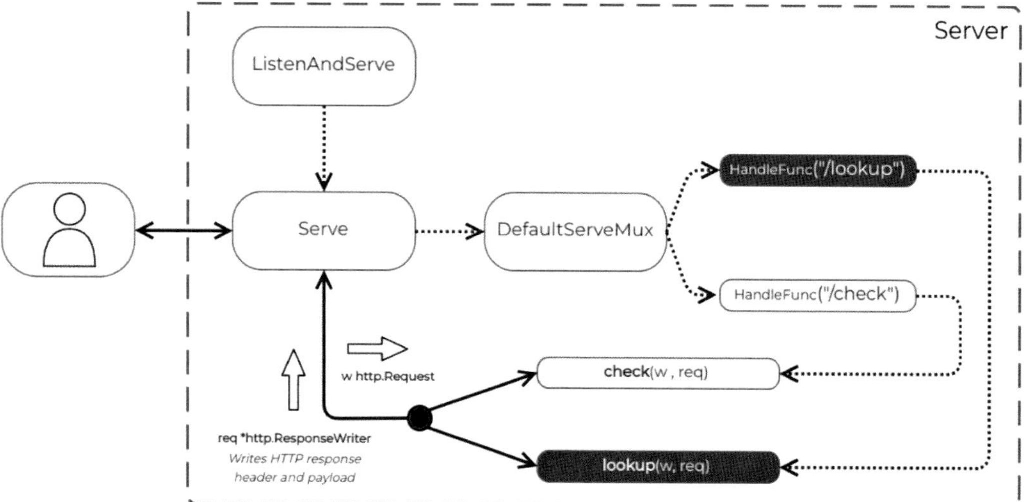

Figure 4.6 – Handling HTTP requests

Now, let's examine the `lookup` handler function. A couple of things stand out:

- We write the response to the request via the first argument, `w`, an `http.ResponseWriter` that satisfies the `io.Writer` interface. This means you can use any mechanism that accepts an `io.Writer` interface to write to it. Here, we use `fmt.Sprintf`.
- We access the user's request via the second argument, `req`. Here, we extract the target URL from the request to print it out in the example with `req.URL.Query`. Also, we get the value of the query to further process the request based on its type, whether this is for a MAC address, IP address, or a domain:

```
func lookup(w http.ResponseWriter, req *http.Request) {
    log.Printf("Incoming %+v", req.URL.Query())
    var response string

    for k, v := range req.URL.Query() {
        switch k {
        case "ip":
            response = getWhois(v)
        case "mac":
            response = getMAC(v)
        case "domain":
            response = getWhois(v)
        default:
            response = fmt.Sprintf(
                        "query %q not recognized", k)
        }
    }
    fmt.Fprintf(w, response)
}
```

When running this on the server side, we need to include all the `.go` files in the folder, not only `main.go`, so you want to run `go run *.go` to get an output like the one in the next snippet:

```
ch04/http/server$ go run *.go
2021/12/13 02:02:39 macDB initialized
2021/12/13 02:02:39 Starting web server at 0.0.0.0:8080
2021/12/13 02:02:56 Incoming map[mac:[68b5.99fc.d1df]]
2021/12/13 02:03:19 Incoming map[domain:[tkng.io]]
2021/12/13 02:03:19 whoisLookup tkng.io@whois.iana.org
```

```
2021/12/13 02:03:19 whoisLookup tkng.io@whois.nic.io
2021/12/13 02:05:09 Incoming map[ip:[1.1.1.1]]
2021/12/13 02:05:09 whoisLookup 1.1.1.1@whois.iana.org
2021/12/13 02:05:09 whoisLookup 1.1.1.1@whois.apnic.net
```

To run this example, you need to open two tabs. You first run `go run *.go` from `ch04/http/server` (*Further reading*) and then from another tab, you can make the client queries from `ch04/http/client` (*Further reading*) with flags as in the outputs in the client part of this section.

Summary

In this chapter, we reviewed the different layers of the TCP/IP model and the applicability of Go to each one. We went from changing the state of network interfaces on Linux systems to working with IP addresses, all the way to building a web application prototype.

Now you are ready to embark on the network automation journey and take all these lessons you've learned so far and apply them to make networks more efficient, reliable, and consistent. This is what we begin to examine in *Chapter 5, Network Automation*.

Further reading

- `syscall` package: `https://pkg.go.dev/syscall`
- `vishvananda/netlink` package: `https://github.com/vishvananda/netlink`
- `mdlayher/netlink` package: `https://github.com/mdlayher/netlink`
- `mdlayher/netlink` ecosystem: `https://github.com/mdlayher/netlink#ecosystem`
- `ch04/netlink`: `https://github.com/PacktPublishing/Network-Automation-with-Go/tree/main/ch04/netlink`
- `CAP_NET_ADMIN` capabilities: `https://man7.org/linux/man-pages/man7/capabilities.7.html`
- `google/gopacket` package: `https://github.com/google/gopacket`
- `mdlayher/ethernet` package: `https://github.com/mdlayher/ethernet`
- `kube-vip` package: `https://github.com/kube-vip/kube-vip/tree/main/pkg/vip`
- `mdlayher/arp` package: `https://github.com/mdlayher/arp`
- `mdlayher/packet` package: `https://github.com/mdlayher/packet`

- `ch04/vip`: `https://github.com/PacktPublishing/Network-Automation-with-Go/tree/main/ch04/vip`
- `net` package: `https://pkg.go.dev/net`
- `ch04/net/main.go`: `https://github.com/PacktPublishing/Network-Automation-with-Go/blob/main/ch04/net/main.go`
- *netaddr.IP: a new IP address type for Go*: `https://tailscale.com/blog/netaddr-new-ip-type-for-go/`
- `ch04/parseip`: `https://github.com/PacktPublishing/Network-Automation-with-Go/tree/main/ch04/parseip`
- `ch04/parseprefix`: `https://github.com/PacktPublishing/Network-Automation-with-Go/tree/main/ch04/parseprefix`
- `cidranger`: `https://github.com/yl2chen/cidranger`
- `ch04/trie/main.go`: `https://github.com/PacktPublishing/Network-Automation-with-Go/blob/main/ch04/trie/main.go`
- GeoLite2 Free Geolocation Data: `https://dev.maxmind.com/geoip/geolite2-free-geolocation-data`
- `ch04/geo/main.go`: `https://github.com/PacktPublishing/Network-Automation-with-Go/blob/main/ch04/geo/main.go`
- `iplib` package: `https://github.com/c-robinson/iplib`
- `ch04/ipaddr/main.go`: `https://github.com/PacktPublishing/Network-Automation-with-Go/blob/main/ch04/ipaddr/main.go`
- cloudprober: `https://github.com/cloudprober/cloudprober`
- `ch04/udp-ping`: `https://github.com/PacktPublishing/Network-Automation-with-Go/tree/main/ch04/udp-ping`
- The book's GitHub repository: `https://github.com/PacktPublishing/Network-Automation-with-Go`
- `ch04/http/client/main.go`: `https://github.com/PacktPublishing/Network-Automation-with-Go/blob/main/ch04/http/client/main.go`
- `ch04/http/server`: `https://github.com/PacktPublishing/Network-Automation-with-Go/blob/main/ch04/http/server`
- `ch04/http/client`: `https://github.com/PacktPublishing/Network-Automation-with-Go/blob/main/ch04/http/client`

Part 2: Common Tools and Frameworks

This part describes the existing challenges and objectives of network automation. You will learn how organizations are approaching this major undertaking and where we are headed.

This part of the book comprises the following chapters:

- *Chapter 5, Network Automation*
- *Chapter 6, Configuration Management*
- *Chapter 7, Automation Frameworks*

5
Network Automation

Up until this point, we've covered some Go fundamentals required to perform common network-related activities. Now, it's time to focus on the principal topic of this book — network automation. Before we review the solutions, tools, and code libraries, let's take a step back and look at network automation as a discipline. In this chapter, we aim to find an answer to the following questions:

- What is network automation and why is it often considered a dedicated skill that's distinct from, say, network engineering?
- What is its impact on network operations and its benefits for the business?
- What are some common automation use cases you can tackle individually?
- How can you string these individual use cases together into a bigger network automation system and why would anyone want that?

This chapter is light on code but heavy on words and may contain arguments that not everyone may agree on. We, as authors of this book, are trying to express our opinions as objectively as possible, but our views are ultimately based on subjective experiences that we've had in our careers. Still, we have tried our best to steer away from the most controversial topics such as automation reducing the need for human operators and, where possible, provided evidence to support our arguments.

In this chapter we will cover the following topics:

- What is network automation?
- Automating network operation tasks
- Systems approach

Technical requirements

You can find the code examples for this chapter in this book's GitHub repository (specified in the *Further reading* section), under the `ch05` folder.

What is network automation?

As a relatively new discipline, it's not uncommon to see a broad spectrum of network automation definitions that vary in scope and goals. Network automation isn't about one use case or technology in particular, but rather what can be of help in your environment and benefit your business.

Some engineers would argue that routing protocols already automate networks and the CLI is the intent-based API, transforming individual network commands into a dynamic network state. We don't try to argue with this point of view, as there are some grains of truth in these statements, but it's certainly not the most popular definition in the industry.

Instead, let's define network automation as a set of processes to automate common manual workflows performed by a network operator, such as provisioning services, performing software upgrades, or telemetry processing. This includes tasks that network engineers would otherwise traditionally have to click their way through, combined with running a set of CLI commands.

More complex network automation solutions may involve reacting to operational events by adjusting network configuration, applying traffic engineering policies, or even enforcing some design constraints. One common trait that unites all these activities is the ability to describe the desired behavior in a concrete sequence of steps that lead to the expected outcome. This may rule out some iterative activities such as network troubleshooting or creative activities such as network design, although they are making considerable progress in these areas with static configuration analysis (Batfish: *Further reading*) and mathematical network modeling (Forward: *Further reading*), for example, so we could eventually borrow concepts from the software world such as **test-driven development** (**TDD**) to automate the development and testing (whole-network **quality assurance** (**QA**) and regression) of configuration templates of a network design.

Why network automation exists

Probably a more interesting question to answer is why network automation exists as a discipline unlike, say, systems administration, which has evolved into site reliability engineering and now encompasses not only plain infrastructure provisioning but also observability, automation, and even systems software development.

The way we run and operate networks has changed very little in the last few decades. Network management still mainly focuses on executing CLI commands and working with unstructured data, despite the wide acceptance that CLI-driven operations are error-prone and not scalable. Often, this leads to a lack of standardization that leaves network engineers with manual processes taking up most of their workday and making networks difficult to scale, support, and secure.

Network automation has emerged as a response to this to improve efficiency and reduce the overhead of mundane tasks. The goal is to produce more reliable and repeatable processes, which increases productivity. This also helps make networks more consistent and simpler to operate, while at the same time reducing the likelihood of an outage, thus minimizing downtime.

Despite this, not all network engineers have embarked on the journey of network automation. Some reasons we think this could be the case are as follows:

- Lack of standard and vendor-agnostic APIs for network management that return structured data. Network vendors typically offer proprietary configuration syntax or CLIs designed primarily for human interaction.
- Automation requires a completely new skill set and, since network engineers generally don't come from a computer science background, programming remains a big skill gap.
- Learning automation requires time and not every employer is happy to dedicate part of their employees' time to something with no immediate benefit.
- Automation speed can also propagate a failure rapidly, which may not help build trust in automation early on. It takes time to create systems that are reliable, secure, and offer enough visibility.
- Given the large number of network automation tools, libraries, and frameworks with overlapping scopes, choosing the right one for a particular task can be challenging and introduces the risk of over-investing in something that may end up being a wrong choice.
- Shifting from *it's always been done this way* is hard. Sometimes, we follow the path of least resistance and, thus, are reluctant to change.

Introducing network automation into your environment brings a different set of gains and perils, depending on your point of view. So, let's try to unpack what it means to both engineers operating the network and the upper management operating the business for whom a network can be a cost or a profit center.

Bottom-up view

Some network operation activities that lend themselves well to automation include configuration changes, running audits or compliance checks, software and device life cycle management, and more. Several organizations have playbooks or require change management forms, documenting every operational step of these processes. Many companies already use a form of automation when a senior engineer prepares a change that a junior engineer later executes.

These activities usually have a set of very well-defined inputs, such as an inventory of devices, a list of commands to execute, a set of well-defined outputs, and maybe a filled-out spreadsheet or a new software version running on a device. These attributes make these activities suitable candidates for automation.

One of the commonly cited benefits of automation is its ability to scale – the relative cost of making a change to one device is the same as making a change to thousands of devices or making a hundred changes to hundreds of devices. Although scale and speed are important, they may not be the most valuable outcomes of process automation.

For some networking teams with relatively small-scale networks or low change rates, network automation may bring other benefits, such as the following:

- **Consistency**: Since computers perform these changes, you can expect them to yield the same result every time. Also, you can enforce the same configurations, templates, or policies across elements.
- **Reliability**: Instructions are code, which computers interprets unambiguously. You can also add automatic checks to validate inputs or results.
- **Visibility**: All future and past changes in the network can be viewed by all members of the team, to embrace peer review and ease troubleshooting.
- **Ubiquity**: The same tools are used across different teams, which simplifies interactions and improves knowledge sharing.

When introducing network automation to your peers, it's important to emphasize that this is not a single product or a solution, but rather a journey – a vector in a new direction with no fixed destination.

Keep in mind that not all manual processes may be completely automatable, and it may take years to develop new practices and update existing procedures. This is why it's also very important to get your organization's management on board.

Top-down view

Network engineers can understand the preceding technical points and can judge for themselves whether a network automation project is worth their time and effort to deploy.

By contrast, the same arguments may not be enough to convince management if you don't look at the bigger picture (the business). This could be one of the primary reasons a network automation initiative may fail. If the business benefits are not clear, then management may decide it's not worth the investment of time. But the reverse is also true – a network automation initiative is more likely to succeed when it has support within the organization's management structure.

Here is a list of business values that you can use as a starting point in discussions with management. Depending on the company, a network can be a cost center or a profit center, so adjust or re-prioritize them to fit your circumstances:

- **Cost management**: Generate cost savings through resource optimization. You reduce the costs of running the network by troubleshooting fewer human errors, not having to manually compile audit reports, or having to work on overtime changes.
- **Speed of delivery**: Increase the speed to configure and validate changes in the network, allowing you to deliver customer services faster or even on-demand.
- **Risk management**: Enforce security policies consistently with every operation to reduce risk. Reduce the number of incidents that impact services and hence your revenue.

- **Business capabilities**: Depending on how your organization defines value, network automation can help discover opportunities. Increased visibility could help improve capacity planning or spot unused capacity or hot spots. New services or business capabilities can be an outcome of streamlined cross-team interactions due to the well-defined interfaces, inputs, and outputs of an automated system.

Despite the rise of awareness about the benefits of network automation, some people are still hesitant to embrace it as an internal organizational practice, so getting support from them may require extra effort. Each situation is unique and, thus, may require a slightly distinct set of arguments. In the end, network automation is becoming an important part of network engineering and its relevance in the industry continues to increase.

Now that we've defined what network automation is and why we need it, it's time to dig deeper and start looking at concrete use cases and areas where you can apply it in the traditional network engineering discipline.

Automating network operation tasks

This section introduces some common network operation tasks and use cases where you can introduce automation without causing too much friction with the existing tools and processes. We aim to take a series of manual steps normally performed by a human operator and explore how you can convert them into code so that a computer can execute them for you, all while keeping the original inputs and outputs unchanged. We will divide this section into three categories:

- Configuration management
- Network state analysis
- Network audits and reporting

Let's get started.

Configuration management

This is the most popular area of the network engineering discipline that spans beyond network operations and often includes design and architecture stages. Most people see this as the lowest-hanging fruit to test, or where to start using, network automation. Let's look at some common use cases that fall under this category.

Config generation

Before we can make any changes to a network device, we need to craft the desired configuration for that target device. Traditionally, we would do this manually in a text editor, which involves a lot of copy/paste and search/replace actions.

You can use the following Go packages to automate this process and generate a network device configuration based on a set of inputs:

- `text/template`: A package from the standard library that uses a special Go templating language to generate an unstructured text document based on the input program variables. We will use this package in the *Interacting with network devices via SSH* section in *Chapter 6, Configuration Management.*
- `flosch/pongo2`: A Django-syntax-like templating language for those that are more familiar with Jinja2 (the `gonja` fork).
- `encoding`: This package includes encoders and decoders for YAML and JSON to parse and generate documents you can use with structured network APIs (for example, YANG or OpenAPI). We will use this package in the *Getting config inputs from other systems via HTTP* section in *Chapter 6, Configuration Management.*
- `regexp`: Another standard library package that implements efficient regular expression pattern matching and string manipulation. We will use this package in the example at the end of this chapter.

Once you sort out the configuration details, you can send this config to the target device, which brings us to the next set of use cases.

Configuration changes, backups, and restore

Working with device configuration may involve backing up and replacing the entire device configuration or making scoped changes to provision new services or update existing configuration snippets. Making these changes often involves logging into each device individually and executing a set of vendor-specific commands in a sequence.

The following Go packages can help with the transport abstractions that are common across different networking vendors to streamline the steps to make changes to, back up, or restore your network configurations:

- `crypto/ssh`: A standard library package that implements base SSH connectivity. We will use this package in the *Interacting with network devices via SSH* section in *Chapter 6, Configuration Management.*
- `scrapli/scrapligo`: A third-party package that builds on top of crypto/SSH and offers various convenient helper functions to work with different CLI prompts and commands from major networking vendors. You can also use this package as a NETCONF client. We will use this package in the *Automating routine SSH tasks* section in *Chapter 6, Configuration Management.*

- `net/http`: A standard library package that you can use to talk to HTTP-based APIs, such as RESTCONF or OpenAPI. We will use this package in the *Getting config inputs from other systems via HTTP* section in *Chapter 6, Configuration Management*.

The preceding list is by no means exclusive and several more third-party packages are available, including some that are specifically designed to work with **RESTCONF** (*Further reading*) or **NETCONF** (*Further reading*), but they all vary in their levels of activity or openness to outside contributions.

It always helps to look around, especially when choosing an external package, to make sure it fits your needs and has a healthy community of contributors.

Configuration diffs and compliance checks

After you have applied the desired configuration, you may need to run periodic compliance checks to make sure certain invariants remain unchanged or to detect any configuration drift. These use cases rely on string searching, pattern matching, and computing differences. You can leverage the following Go packages for this purpose:

- `strings`: A package from the standard library that can offer basic string comparison and pattern matching with the `Compare` and `Contains` functions. We will use this package in the example at the end of this chapter.
- `sergi/go-diff`: A third-party package that can compare, match, or patch plain text (a Go port of the `google/diff-match-patch` package).
- `homeport/dyff`: Another third-party package and a command-line tool you can use to compare structured documents, such as JSON or YAML.

While keeping your device configuration in check is crucial, you can't derive everything that happens in the network from them. That's why we need to complement our analysis with the operational data we gather from the network.

Network state analysis

The operational state that results from an applied configuration is often hard to predict. You can spend a significant amount of time fine-tuning monitoring and collecting information from the network. But these use cases are often a good first step into network automation because of their low-risk profile, so they present a very attractive opportunity to start using Go.

Collecting operational state

Depending on the target **network operating system** (**NOS**), collecting operational data from a network device can be a quick API call – for example, an HTTP GET with a URL parameter of `?rev=operational` indicates that the returned data should come from the operational data store.

In contrast, for a human-first NOS, this may require extra steps to parse the CLI output you get from it. You can do this in Go in a few different ways:

- `regexp`: Using regular expressions is the most battle-tested and well-known way of parsing unstructured text into variables. Keep in mind that writing robust regular expressions and troubleshooting them can be a challenge. We will use this package in the example at the end of this chapter.
- `sirikothe/gotextfsm`: This package offers a higher-level abstraction built on top of the `regexp` package, designed to parse semi-formatted text, meaning text with visual structure, such as tables, but represented as a single string. We will use this package indirectly in the *Checking routing information* section in *Chapter 6, Configuration Management*.
- `scrapli/scrapligo`: This package embeds the `textfsm` package and allows you to parse the responses you get from networking devices using the `TextFsmParse(template string)` function. We will use this package in the *Checking routing information* section in *Chapter 6, Configuration Management*.

You can get the operational state of the network and parse it into in-memory data structures before and after a maintenance window, for example, to compare them and vet the success of the work performed during this time. This is what we'll discuss next.

State snapshots and validation

Validating the operational state, to make sure that the values we receive are what we expect to see, is something network engineers do when they configure network devices, run troubleshooting sessions, provision services, perform software upgrades, and carry out other daily activities as part of their job assignments.

As we automate the collection of this data and since we can often pre-calculate the intended state, the next step is to check whether the state is as expected and then make sure that this state persists over time. For example, BGP neighbors should be in an *established* state and all connected interfaces should be *up*. As we collect new data from the network, we record it in a structured format to compare it with the intended state and to trigger another action if we find a difference.

Comparing arbitrary data normally requires writing some custom code to traverse these data structures and look at the values that matter. But there are a few packages that can simplify this task:

- `reflect.DeepEqual`: This package is part of the Go standard library and can use runtime reflection to compare values that are of the same type.
- `mitchellh/hashstructure`: A third-party package that can calculate a unique hash from arbitrary Go values that you can use to quickly answer the question if the operational state matches the one you expect. We will use this package in the example at the end of this chapter.

- `r3labs/diff`: Another third-party package that supports several standard Go types and relies on runtime reflection to produce a detailed log of all the differences between two Go structs or values.

We can't classify all operational states as *intended*. Some values are more dynamic and their change is not always actionable. An example of this is MAC and IP address tables – their values fluctuate over time and long-term churn is normal.

Keeping track of the dynamic state of the network can be helpful during routine maintenance, such as in software upgrades, where you make snapshots of the network state and can quickly compare the pre - and post-change values to spot any inconsistencies. Programmatically, this is just like the generic state validation use case. You use the same set of tools and libraries but save these snapshots as a structured document on a disk or inside a database over time.

Network audits and reporting

The scope of network audits can vary greatly, from trying to identify obsolete hardware or end-of-life software to measuring the quality of the service or the rate of control plane updates. Normally, the goal is to collect and process state information from a large set of devices and produce some human-readable output.

We discussed state collection and validation tasks in the preceding section, and you can scale this process to target hundreds or thousands of network devices with goroutines, which we covered in *Chapter 3, Getting Started with Go*. The missing part that we haven't discussed yet is report generation. Here, Go also offers several resources that you can use to generate human-readable outputs:

- `text/tabwriter`: This is a package from the standard library you should consider if you want to send information to standard output. You can use this package to print tabbed data. Other feature-rich options exist outside of the standard library, one of which is the `jedib0t/go-pretty/v6` package, which can you can use to colorize text or print tables, lists, and progress bars.
- `unidoc/unioffice`: This package or `qax-os/excelize` are good options if you want to produce a spreadsheet. You can also use `unidoc/unioffice` to work with Word, Excel, or PowerPoint documents.
- `html/template` and `text/template`: These are the two most common templating libraries. Hugo, the popular static site generator, uses both the `html` and `text` template packages, for example.
- `go:embed`: This is a Go directive that you could use to allow templates to be embedded inside a compiled Go binary to simplify code distribution.

The use cases we've introduced in this section are all relatively independent. Once you automate them, they can become so-called automation islands, completely isolated from one another at first, but once their number grows, they may merge into more complex multi-stage workflows or even complete closed-loop systems. This is what we'll explore in the next section.

Systems approach

As you start automating different tasks with an incremental approach, you may envision a path where you chain a subset of these automated tasks together to orchestrate a workflow.

You can also look at this from a different angle. You initially break down your existing manual processes into smaller chunks of work that you can automate independently, so you don't need to wait until you get the full end-to-end process automated to start taking advantage of automation, while at the same time you are mindful of the bigger picture.

In this context, you take the first steps to interconnect different building blocks, which become part of a larger system that delivers a business outcome with eventually no human intervention that originally may have involved several teams. That's what we call a systems approach.

One common example is when you mix the processes of configuring network services and collecting operational data from the network, which is what we'll discuss next.

Closed-loop automation

One of the first things every network engineer does after configuring anything on a network device is to check the status of that service, protocol, or resource configured via a CLI command. If an automated system performs this configuration, the network engineer still needs to log into a network device or group of network devices to execute commands, or maybe go to a web portal to check the logs or graphs that show the statistics for the network devices. This time-consuming, repetitive process that is error-prone for humans becomes a natural fit for automation as well.

Now, you not only push the configuration or instructions down to the network but also ingest real-time operational data from the network, which you can process to determine whether it matches the intended state of the network.

If we abstract away the network device details, a closed-loop application would consume **network intelligence** on one interface, and push intent down to the network. We can loosely define these as follows:

- **Intent**: This would be the declarative definition of the operational state or measurable outcome you expect in the context of the network (topology, inventory, protocol, and so on) without requiring you to specify an exact procedure to get to it (those are implementation details).
- **Network intelligence**: This would be telemetry from the network that is actionable after some level of processing to make it useful. Keep in mind that events, metrics, stats, or alarms do not necessarily translate into actionable intelligence. Network operators get so many alarms that it's

hard to know what's real and what's noise. Hence, network intelligence results from correlating this data, running analytics, or any other process that helps tie this to the desired intent.

The following is a high-level diagram of a closed-loop application:

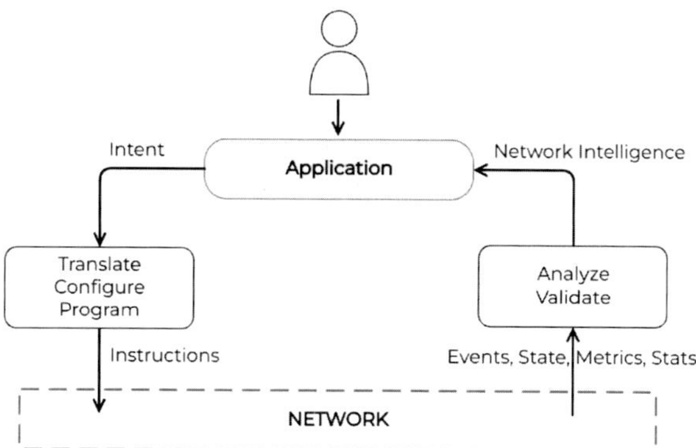

Figure 5.1 – Closed-loop automation – 10,000 foot view

The intent translates into configuration syntax or programmatic instructions, which are specific to the network device. We can adjust these instructions based on the feedback we get from the network, enabling us to close the loop and automate the life cycle of network services.

You can think of a closed-loop system as a continuous loop that learns from the networks and adapts to them. This could replace pre - and post-snapshot checks as you would compare the network at arbitrary times and for arbitrary deltas continuously. But what we see in networks today is somewhat closer to systems that react to the network feedback only during the time window in which they provision a service. This is what we will replicate in the following example.

Demo application

For the demo application, we could either build a distributed system where all the different components communicate and coordinate via messages over the network, or run everything on just one node in a single application. Because the goal is to illustrate the notion of closed-loop automation and not to show how distributed systems work, we will keep the application simple and run all the components as functions of a monolith application, as shown in the following diagram:

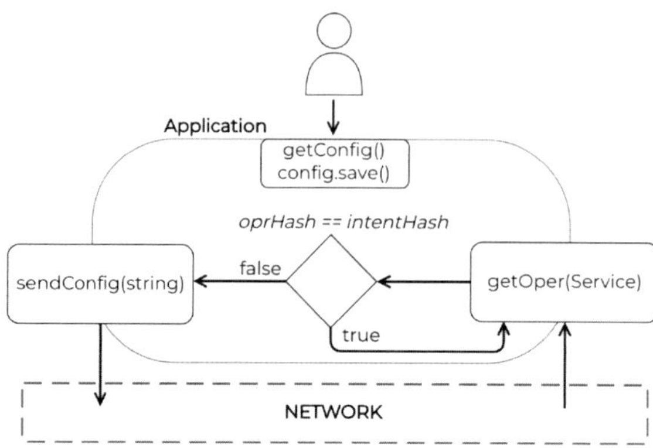

Figure 5.2 – Closed-loop automation sample application

The application starts by reading the input data from the user. It reads the target device information for this example from a file, `input.yml`, as shown in the following code snippet. We hard code the parameters of the service to configure a variable (`intent`) in the code. The service we want to configure in this case is **gRPC**, listening on IPv4 port `57777` with `TLS` enabled:

```
# input.yml
router:
- hostname: sandbox-iosxr-1.cisco.com
  platform: cisco_iosxr
  strictkey: false
  username: admin
  password: C1sco12345
```

We encapsulate the service information in a `Service` definition that acts as a higher layer of abstraction than what a network device configuration represents, which translates into the intent for this example. We also compute a hash of this value so that we can compare it later with the operational information we receive from the network:

```
func main() {
    /* ... <omitted for brevity > ... */
    intent := Service{
        Name:     "grpc",
        Port:     "57777",
        AF:       "ipv4",
        Insecure: false,
        CLI:      "show grpc status",
```

```
    }
    intentHash, err := hashstructure.Hash(intent,
        hashstructure.FormatV2, nil)
    /* ... <omitted for brevity > ... */
}
```

Before the application configures the service, we have the chance to perform a series of pre-maintenance tasks, such as running a network audit to report whether the service is present already, so you may not need to configure it. Another good idea is to make a backup of the network device's configuration in case we need to roll back the changes.

In this example, we must make a configuration backup of the target device with the `getConfig` method and then save it in a folder with the `save` method:

```
func main() {
    /* ... <omitted for brevity > ... */
    config, err := iosxr.getConfig()
    // process error

    err = config.save()
    /* ... <omitted for brevity > ... */
}
```

With the pre-work done, the application enters a continuous enforcement loop that runs, in this example, every 30 seconds. Inside the loop, the application collects the operational state of the service with the `getOper` method. This method sends a CLI command to the target device to gather the operational details of the service we need:

```
func (r Router) getOper(s Service) (o DeviceInfo, err error) {
    rs, err := r.Conn.SendCommand(s.CLI)
    // process error
    o = DeviceInfo{
        Device:    r.Hostname,
        Output:    rs.Result,
        Timestamp: time.Now(),
    }
    return o, nil
}
```

Once we receive the response, we parse the information with regular expressions while using the `regexp` package to generate a new `Service` value with it that captures whether the service has `TLS` enabled, for example, as well as the rest of the `Service` attributes. Then, we calculate a new hash for this `Service` type instance, which we compare with the original hash we have to validate whether the operational state of the service matches the intent:

```
if oprHash == intentHash {
    continue
}
```

If these values match, we can proceed to the next iteration (`continue`). Otherwise, we need to configure the router to bring the service to the desired state. Then, the loop starts over again. We get the service configuration in the target device's syntax by using a template with the `genConfig` method and the `text/template` package, which we then send to the target device with the `sendConfig` function:

```
func (r Router) sendConfig(conf string) error {
    c, err := cfg.NewCfgDriver(r.Conn, r.Platform)
    // process error
    err = c.Prepare()
    // process error
    _, err = c.LoadConfig(conf, false)
    // process error
    _, err = c.CommitConfig()
    // process error
    return nil
}
```

If you want to see this example in action, you can run the code from the `ch05/closed-loop` folder. While it's running, open an SSH session to the target Cisco DevNet device in a separate terminal window with `sshpass -p "C1sco12345" ssh admin@sandbox-iosxr-1.cisco.com` and execute the following to disable `TLS`:

```
conf
grpc no-tls
commit
```

In the program's output, you will see that it eventually catches this discrepancy, so it proceeds to remediate it by re-configuring TLS. The code for this example is available at `ch05/closed-loop/main.go` (*Further reading*):

```
ch05/closed-loop$ go run main.go
Entering to continuous loop ====>
 Loop at 15:31:22
  Operational state from device:
   service: grpc
   addr-family: ipv4
   port: 57777
   TLS: true

 Loop at 15:31:52
  Operational state from device:
   service: grpc
   addr-family: ipv4
   port: 57777
   TLS: false

Configuring device ====>

 Loop at 15:32:22
  Operational state from device:
   service: grpc
   addr-family: ipv4
   port: 57777
   TLS: true

...
```

The intelligence in this scenario only considers a boolean outcome, without a qualitative assessment of the network situation. You can also explore how to get a more involved assessment of the data you retrieve from the network to make a decision tree that goes beyond just a simple fix network yes or no.

Likewise, with intent, we only cover a direct predetermined relationship between the intent and the configuration you require to enable it. Real deployments likely have more moving parts and decisions on which parts you need.

Summary

In this chapter, we discussed what network automation is, its impact on network operations, and its benefits for the business. We talked about different use cases, from configuration management and network state analysis to running network audits and reporting, to finally look at how to put different pieces together to create a closed-loop system that can help you enforce the desired intent of the network.

In the next chapter, we'll examine configuration management in detail, one of the more recurrent network automation use cases, and navigate through the options that Go presents to us to automate it.

Further reading

For more information about the topics that were covered in this chapter, take a look at the following resources:

- This book's GitHub repository: `https://github.com/PacktPublishing/Network-Automation-with-Go`
- Batfish: `https://www.batfish.org/`
- Forward: `https://forwardnetworks.com/forward-enterprise/`
- RESTCONF: `https://github.com/freeconf/restconf`
- NETCONF: `https://github.com/Juniper/go-netconf`
- `ch05/closed-loop/main.go`: `https://github.com/PacktPublishing/Network-Automation-with-Go/blob/main/ch05/closed-loop/main.go#L1`

6
Configuration Management

Configuration management is a process that helps us enforce the desired configuration state on an IT system. It's a way to make sure a network device, in our context, performs as expected as we roll out new settings. As this becomes a mundane task we perform repeatedly, it's no surprise network configuration management is the most common network automation use case according to the NetDevOps 2020 Survey (*Further reading*).

In the previous chapter, we discussed common configuration management tasks, along with some helpful tools and libraries that can help you write programs to automate those tasks in Go. In this chapter, we will focus on a few concrete examples, taking a closer look at how Go can help us connect and interact with network devices from different networking vendors using standard protocols. We will cover four areas in this chapter:

- Before we introduce any new examples, we will define a three-node multi-vendor virtual network lab to test the code examples in this chapter and later chapters of this book.
- Next, we will explore how we can use Go and SSH to interact with network devices.
- Then, we will repeat the exercise following the same program structure as with SSH but using HTTP to contrast these different options.
- Finally, we will extract and parse the resulting operational state to verify that our configuration changes have been successful.

Note that we have deliberately avoided talking about YANG-based APIs here as we will cover them extensively in the last few chapters of this book.

In this chapter, we will cover the following topics:

- Environment setup
- Interacting with network devices via SSH
- Interacting with network devices via HTTP
- State validation

Technical requirements

You can find the code examples for this chapter in the book's GitHub repository: `https://github.com/PacktPublishing/Network-Automation-with-Go`, under the `ch06` folder.

> **Important Note**
>
> We recommend that you execute the Go programs in this chapter in a virtual lab environment. Refer to the *Appendix* for prerequisites and instructions on how to build it.

Environment setup

One of the easiest and safest ways to learn and experiment with network automation is to build a lab environment. Thanks to the progress we've had in the last decade, today, we have access to virtualized and containerized network devices from different networking vendors and plenty of tools that can help us build a virtual topology from them.

In this book, we will use one of those tools: **Containerlab**. This tool, which is written in Go, allows you to build arbitrary network topologies from container images. The fact that you can create and run topologies based on a plain YAML file in a matter of seconds makes it a strong choice to run quick tests. Please refer to the *Appendix* for installation instructions and recommendations for host operating systems.

Creating the topology

Throughout the rest of this book, we will work with a base network topology consisting of three containerized network devices running different **network operating systems** (**NOSes**):

- `srl`: Running Nokia's **Service Router Linux** (**SR Linux**)
- `cvx`: Running NVIDIA's Cumulus Linux
- `ceos`: Running Arista's EOS

The following diagram depicts the device interconnections. They all come up with their default (blank) configuration:

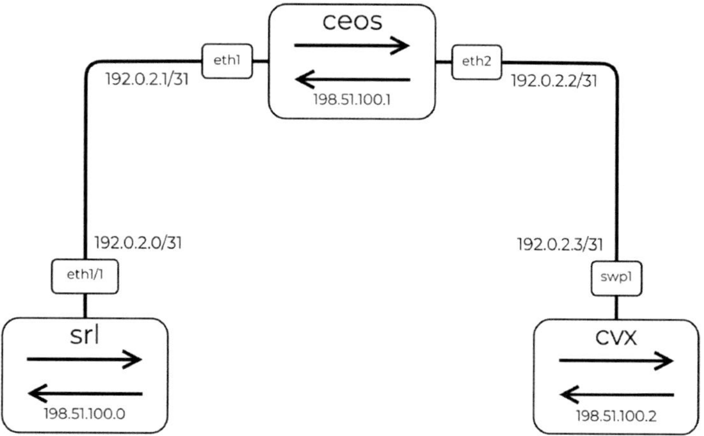

Figure 6.1 – Test topology

We can describe this topology with the following YAML file, which is a representation that **Containerlab** can interpret and translate into a running topology:

```
name: netgo

topology:
  nodes:
    srl:
      kind: srl
      image: ghcr.io/nokia/srlinux:21.6.4
    ceos:
      kind: ceos
      image: ceos:4.26.4M
    cvx:
      kind: cvx
      image: networkop/cx:5.0.0
      runtime: docker

  links:
    - endpoints: ["srl:e1-1", "ceos:eth1"]
    - endpoints: ["cvx:swp1", "ceos:eth2"]
```

You can find this YAML file, like the rest of the code examples, in this book's GitHub repository, specifically in the `topo-base` directory. If you go through the *Appendix* to learn more about Containerlab or you have it running already, you can bring up the entire lab with the following command:

```
topo-base$ sudo containerlab deploy -t topo.yml --reconfigure
```

Once the lab is up, you can access each device by its hostname using the credentials shown in the following table:

Device	Username	Password
clab-netgo-srl	admin	admin
clab-netgo-ceos	admin	admin
clab-netgo-cvx	cumulus	cumulus

Table 6.1 – Containerlab access credentials

For example, to access NVIDIA's device via SSH, you would execute `ssh cumulus@clab-netgo-cvx`:

```
⇨  ssh cumulus@clab-netgo-cvx
cumulus@clab-netgo-cvx's password: cumulus
Linux cvx 5.14.10-300.fc35.x86_64 #1 SMP Thu Oct 7 20:48:44 UTC 
2021 x86_64

Welcome to NVIDIA Cumulus (R) Linux (R)

cumulus@cvx:mgmt:~$ exit
```

If you want to learn more about Containerlab or run this lab setup in the cloud, check out the instructions in the *Appendix* of this book.

Interacting with network devices via SSH

Secure Shell (**SSH**) is the predominant protocol that network engineers use to securely access and configure network devices via a **command-line interface** (**CLI**) that transports unstructured data to display to end users. This interface simulates a computer terminal, so we've used it traditionally for human interactions.

One of the first steps network engineers take when they embark on the journey of automating mundane tasks is to create scripts that run a set of CLI commands for them in sequence to achieve an outcome. Otherwise, they would run the commands themselves interactively via an SSH pseudo-terminal.

While this gives us speed, this is not the only benefit of network automation. As we cover different technologies through the rest of this book, other benefits, such as reliability, repeatability, and consistency, to name a few, become a common theme. For now, we will start by crafting an SSH connection to a network device in Go and send configuration commands line by line, to then take advantage of a higher-level package in Go that abstracts away the connection details of the different networking vendors, making the development experience simpler for network engineers.

Describing the network device configurations

The first task we want to do with Go is to configure each of the devices of the three-node topology we defined in the preceding section. As a learning exercise, we will create three different Go programs to configure each device independently so that you can contrast the different approaches. While each program is unique, they all follow the same design structure. One program uses SSH to connect and configure a device, another one uses Scrapligo, and the last one uses HTTP, as we'll cover in the next section.

To make the code examples meaningful, but at the same time not overly complicated, we have limited the device configurations to apply to the following sections:

- A unique IPv4 address on each of the transit links
- A **Border Gateway Protocol** (**BGP**) peering established between those IPs
- A unique loopback address that is also redistributed into BGP

The goal of these settings is to establish reachability between all three loopback interfaces.

In real-life automation systems, developers strive to find a common data model you can use to represent device configurations for any vendor. The two main examples of this are IETF and OpenConfig YANG models. We will do the same in this case by defining a standard schema for the input data we will use for all three network devices but using Go directly to define the data structures instead of the YANG modeling language. This schema has just enough information to meet the goal of establishing end-to-end reachability:

```
type Model struct {
    Uplinks  []Link `yaml:"uplinks"`
    Peers    []Peer `yaml:"peers"`
    ASN      int    `yaml:"asn"`
    Loopback Addr   `yaml:"loopback"`
}

type Link struct {
    Name   string `yaml:"name"`
```

```
    Prefix string `yaml:"prefix"`
}

type Peer struct {
    IP  string `yaml:"ip"`
    ASN int    `yaml:"asn"`
}

type Addr struct {
    IP string `yaml:"ip"`
}
```

In each of the programs, we supply the parameters to the data model to generate the device's configuration via the `input.yml` file, which is available in the program's folder. For the first example, this file looks as follows:

```
# input.yml
asn: 65000

loopback:
  ip: "198.51.100.0"

uplinks:
  - name: "ethernet-1/1"
    prefix: "192.0.2.0/31"

peers:
  - ip: "192.0.2.1"
    asn: 65001
```

After we open this file for reading, we deserialize this information into an instance of a `Model` type – which represents the data model – with the `Decode` method. The following output represents these steps:

```
func main() {
    src, err := os.Open("input.yml")
    // process error
    defer src.Close()
```

```
    d := yaml.NewDecoder(src)

    var input Model
    err = d.Decode(&input)
    // process error
}
```

Then, we pass the input variable (of the `Model` type) to a config generator function (`devConfig`), which transforms this information into syntax that the target device can understand. The result of this transformation is a vendor-specific configuration serialized into bytes that you can transfer to the remote device.

A transport library establishes the connection to the remote device using default credentials, which you can overwrite via command-line flags. The session we have created has an `io.Writer` element that we can use to send the configuration to the remote device:

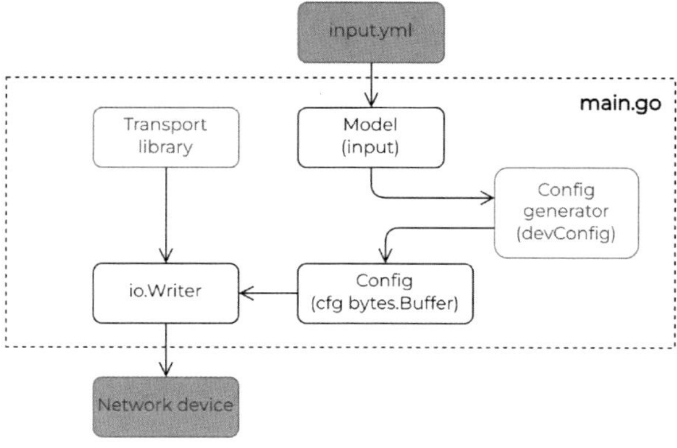

Figure 6.2 – Program structure

Now that we're familiar with the structure of the program, let's explore different implementations of it to learn more about the Go packages that are available to communicate with network devices, starting with SSH and Scrapligo.

Using Go's SSH package to access network devices

The first device from the topology that we are configuring is the containerized Nokia **SR Linux**. Although this NOS supports a variety of interfaces, including structured APIs such as gNMI and NETCONF, in this case, we are configuring it interactively via SSH, using the same commands that a human operator would use. We will execute these commands as a multi-line string, which we can craft using Go's `text/template` template package.

Go's SSH package, `golang.org/x/crypto/ssh`, belongs to a set of packages that are still part of the Go project but developed outside the main Go tree under looser compatibility requirements. Although this is not the only SSH Go client, other packages tend to reuse parts of this package, so they become higher-level abstractions.

As described in the general program design, we use the `Model` data structure to hold the device configuration inputs and merge them with the `srlTemplate` template to produce a valid device configuration as a buffer of bytes:

```
const srlTemplate = `
enter candidate
{{- range $uplink := .Uplinks }}
set / interface {{ $uplink.Name }} subinterface 0 ipv4 address
{{ $uplink.Prefix }}
set / network-instance default interface {{ $uplink.Name }}.0
{{- end }}
...
`
```

The `srlTemplate` constant has a template that starts by looping (using the `range` keyword) over the uplinks of a `Model` instance. For each `Link`, it takes the `Name` and `Prefix` properties of it to create a couple of CLI commands we can place in a buffer. In the following code, we are running the `Execute` method to pass the inputs via the `in` variable and put the binary representation of interactive CLI commands on `b`, which we later expect to send to the remote device (`cfg`):

```
func devConfig(in Model)(b bytes.Buffer, err error){
    t, err := template.New("config").Parse(srlTemplate)
    // process error

    err = t.Execute(&b, in)
    // process error
    return b, nil
}

func main() {
    /* ... <omitted for brevity > ... */
    var input Model
    err = d.Decode(&input)
    // process error
```

```
    cfg, err := devConfig(input)
    /* ... <continues next > ... */
}
```

We have hardcoded the authentication credentials to the correct values to fit the lab, but you can override them if necessary. We use these arguments to establish initial connectivity with the `srl` network device:

```
func main() {
    /* ... <continues from before > ... */
    settings := &ssh.ClientConfig{
        User: *username,
        Auth: []ssh.AuthMethod{
            ssh.Password(*password),
        },
        HostKeyCallback: ssh.InsecureIgnoreHostKey(),
    }
    conn, err := ssh.Dial(
        "tcp",
        fmt.Sprintf("%s:%d", *hostname, sshPort),
        settings,
    )
    // process error
    defer conn.Close()
    /* ... <continues next > ... */
}
```

If the authentication credentials are correct and there are no connectivity problems, the `ssh.Dial` function returns a connection handler (`conn`), representing a single SSH connection. This connection acts as a single transport for potentially various channels. One such channel is a pseudo-terminal session used for interactive communication with the remote device, but it may also include extra channels that you can use for port forwarding.

The following code snippet spawns a new terminal session and sets the expected terminal parameters, such as terminal height, width, and **TeleTYpe** (**TTY**) speed. The `ssh.Session` type provides functions to retrieve standard input and standard output pipes that connect to the remote terminal:

```
func main() {
    /* ... <continues from before > ... */
    session, err := conn.NewSession()
```

```
    // process error
    defer session.Close()

    modes := ssh.TerminalModes{
        ssh.ECHO:          1,
        ssh.TTY_OP_ISPEED: 115200,
        ssh.TTY_OP_OSPEED: 115200,
    }

    if err := session.RequestPty("xterm", 40, 80, modes);
err != nil {
        log.Fatal("request for pseudo terminal failed: ", err)
    }

    stdin, err := session.StdinPipe()
    // process error

    stdout, err := session.StdoutPipe()
    // process error

    session.Shell()
    /* ... <continues next > ... */
}
```

In conformance with the rest of the Go packages, standard input and standard output pipes implement the `io.Writer` and `io.Reader` interfaces, respectively. This means you can use them to write data in to and read output from the remote network device. We will go back to the `cfg` buffer with the CLI config and use the `WriteTo` method to send this config over to the target node:

```
func main() {
    /* ... <continues from before > ... */
    log.Print("connected. configuring...")
    cfg.WriteTo(stdin)
}
```

This is the expected output of this program:

```
ch06/ssh$ go run main.go
go: downloading golang.org/x/crypto v0.0.0-20220112180741-
```

```
5e0467b6c7ce
go: downloading gopkg.in/yaml.v2 v2.4.0
2022/02/07 21:11:44 connected. configuring...
2022/02/07 21:11:44 disconnected. dumping output...

enter candidate
set / interface ethernet-1/1 subinterface 0 ipv4 address
192.0.2.0/31
set / network-instance default interface ethernet-1/1.0
...
set / network-instance default protocols bgp ipv4-unicast
admin-state enable
commit now
quit
Using configuration file(s): []
Welcome to the srlinux CLI.
Type 'help' (and press <ENTER>) if you need any help using
this.
--{ running }--[  ]--
A:srl#
--{ running }--[  ]--
A:srl# enter candidate
--{ candidate shared default }--[  ]--
A:srl# set / interface ethernet-1/1 subinterface 0 ipv4 address
192.0.2.0/31
--{ * candidate shared default }--[  ]--
.......
--{ * candidate shared default }--[  ]--
A:srl# commit now
All changes have been committed. Leaving candidate mode.
--{ + running }--[  ]--
A:srl# quit
```

You can find the complete example in the `ch06/ssh` folder (*Further reading*).

Automating routine SSH tasks

Common network elements, such as routers and switches, display data for people rather than computers via the CLI. We rely on screen scraping to let our programs consume this human-readable data. One popular screen-scraping Python library, whose name comes from *scrape cli*, is Scrapli.

Scrapli has a version in Go, which we will explore in the following example, called Scrapligo. The goal of this package is to offer the next layer of abstraction on top of SSH and hide away some transport complexities while providing several convenient functions and supporting the CLI flavors of different networking vendors.

To show `scrapligo` in action, we will configure another network device in the topology: Arista's cEOS (`ceos`). Just like we did with `srl`, we will use a list of CLI commands to push the desired network state so that the initial steps of parsing and instantiating a string from a template are the same. What changes is the template, which uses Arista EOS's syntax:

```
const ceosTemplate = `
...
!
router bgp {{ .ASN }}
  router-id {{ .Loopback.IP }}
{{- range $peer := .Peers }}
  neighbor {{ $peer.IP }} remote-as {{ $peer.ASN }}
{{- end }}
  redistribute connected
!
`
```

The difference starts when we get to the SSH connection setup. We create a device driver (`GetNetworkDriver`) to connect to the remote device with the device hostname and authentication credentials. The platform definition comes from the `platform` package of `scrapligo`. From then on, it only takes a single method call on this driver to open an SSH connection to the remote device:

```
func main() {
    /* ... <omitted for brevity > ... */
    conn, err := platform.NewPlatform(
        *nos,
        *hostname,
        options.WithAuthNoStrictKey(),
        options.WithAuthUsername(*username),
        options.WithAuthPassword(*password),
```

```
    )
    // process error

    driver, err := conn.GetNetworkDriver()
    // process error

    err = driver.Open()
    // process error
    defer driver.Close()
    /* ... <continues next > ... */
}
```

One of the extra features that `scrapli` offers is the `cscrapligocfg` package, which defines a high-level API to work with a remote network device's configuration. This API understands different CLI flavors, it can sanitize a configuration before sending it to the device, and it can generate configuration diffs for us. But, most importantly, this package allows for a single function call to load the entire device configuration as a string, taking care of things such as privilege escalation and configuration merging or replacement. We will do this here with the `LoadConfig` method:

```
func main() {
    /* ... <continues from before > ... */
    conf, err := cfg.NewCfg(driver, *nos)
    // process error

    // sanitize config by removing keywords like "!" and "end"
    err = conf.Prepare()
    // process error

    response, err = conf.LoadConfig(config.String(), false)
    // process error
}
```

These are all the steps you need to configure the device in this case. After you run the program with `go run`, you can `ssh` to the device to check that the configuration is now there:

```
ch06/scrapli$ go run main.go
2022/02/14 17:06:16 Generated config:
!
configure
```

```
!
ip routing
!
interface Ethernet1
  no switchport
  ip address 192.0.2.1/31
!
...
```

Normally, to get a response coming back from a device, we need to read the response buffer carefully until we see a command-line prompt, as it normally ends with an **end-of-file** (**EOF**). Although we don't show it here, `scrapligo` can do this for us by reading the received buffer and converting the response into a string.

Another popular Go SSH package that provides a high-level API to execute commands at scale is `yahoo/vssh`. We won't cover it here, but you can find an example in the `ch06/vssh` directory of this book's repository (*Further reading*) to configure the network devices of the topology.

Interacting with network devices via HTTP

Over the last decade, networking vendors have begun to include **application programming interfaces** (**APIs**) to manage their devices as a supplement to the CLI. It's not uncommon to find network devices with a robust RESTful API that gives you read and write access to it.

A RESTful API is a stateless client-server communication architecture that runs over HTTP. The request and responses generally transport structured data (JSON, XML, and so on), but they might as well carry plain text. This makes the RESTful API a better-suited interface for machine-to-machine interactions.

Using Go's HTTP package to access network devices

The remaining device to configure is NVIDIA's Cumulus Linux (`cvx`). We will use its OpenAPI-based RESTful API to configure it. We will encode the configuration in a JSON message and send it over an HTTP connection with Go's `net/http` package.

As in the SSH examples, we normally load the input data and transform it into the shape the target device expects with the `devConfig` function, but in this case, it's a JSON payload. Because of this, we no longer need templates to build the network device configuration, as we can now use data structures in Go to encode and decode data from JSON or any other encoding format.

The data structures represent the configuration data model of the target device. Ideally, this data model would match the one we defined previously, so we don't need to define anything else. But that's not what we see in the field, where all the network vendors have proprietary data models. The good news is that both IETF and OpenConfig offer vendor-agnostic models; we'll explore these later in *Chapter 8, Network APIs*. For now, these are some of the data structures we will use for this device's configuration:

```
type router struct {
    Bgp
}

type bgp struct {
    ASN      int
    RouterID string
    AF       map[string]addressFamily
    Enabled  string
    Neighbor map[string]neighbor
}

type neighbor struct {
    RemoteAS int
    Type     string
}
```

Inside the main function, we parse the program flags and use them to store the HTTP connection settings inside a data structure with all the details required to build an HTTP request, including any non-default transport settings for an HTTP client. We do this entirely for convenience purposes as we want to pass these details to different functions:

```
type cvx struct {
    url   string
    token string
    httpC http.Client
}

func main() {
    /* ... <omitted for brevity > ... */
    device := cvx{
        url:   fmt.Sprintf("https://%s:%d", *hostname,
defaultNVUEPort),
        token: base64.StdEncoding.EncodeToString([]byte(fmt.
Sprintf("%s:%s", *username, *password))),
```

```
        httpC: http.Client{
            Transport: &http.Transport{
                TLSClientConfig: &tls.
Config{InsecureSkipVerify: true},
            },
        },
    }
    /* ... <continues next > ... */
}
```

Now, we can send the configuration over and make it a candidate config on the target device. We can later apply this configuration on the device by referencing the revision ID we associate our desired configuration with. Let's look at the steps to do this that showcase different attributes to consider when working with HTTP.

First, we will create a new revision ID, which we include as a query parameter (`?rev=<revisionID>`) in the URL to connect to the device API. Now, the `addr` is variable the target device URL that contains `device hostname` and `revisionID`:

```
func main() {
    /* ... <continues from before > ... */
    // create a new candidate configuration revision
    revisionID, err := createRevision(device)
    // process error

    addr, err := url.Parse(device.url + "/nvue_v1/")
    // process error
    params := url.Values{}
    params.Add("rev", revisionID)
    addr.RawQuery = params.Encode()
    /* ... <continues next > ... */
}
```

With the URL linked to the revision ID, we put together the PATCH request for the configuration change. This points to `addr` and `cfg`, which is the JSON device configuration that the `devConfig` function returns. We also add an HTTP `Authorization` header with the encoded username and password and signal that the payload is a JSON message:

```
func main() {
    /* ... <continues from before > ... */
```

```
    req, err := http.NewRequest("PATCH", addr.String(), &cfg)
    // process error
    req.Header.Add("Content-Type", "application/json")
    req.Header.Add("Authorization", "Basic "+device.token)
    /* ... <continues next > ... */
}
```

Once we have the HTTP request built, we can pass it to the device HTTP client's method, `Do`, which serializes everything into a binary format, sets up a TCP session, and sends the HTTP request over it.

Finally, to apply the candidate configuration changes, we must make another PATCH request inside the `applyRevision` function:

```
func main() {
    /* ... <continues from before > ... */
    res, err := device.httpC.Do(req)
    // process error
    defer res.Body.Close()

    // Apply candidate revision
    if err := applyRevision(device, revisionID); err != nil {
        log.Fatal(err)
    }
}
```

You can find the code for this example in the `ch06/http` directory of this book's GitHub repository (*Further reading*). This is what you should see when you run this program:

```
ch06/http$ go run main.go
2022/02/14 16:42:26 generated config {
 "interface": {
  "lo": {
   "ip": {
    "address": {
     "198.51.100.2/32": {}
...
 "router": {
  "bgp": {
   "autonomous-system": 65002,
```

```
    "router-id": "198.51.100.2"
   }
  },
  "vrf": {
   "default": {
    "router": {
     "bgp": {
...
      "enable": "on",
      "neighbor": {
       "192.0.2.2": {
        "remote-as": 65001,
        "type": "numbered"
       },
       "203.0.113.4": {
        "remote-as": 65005,
        "type": "numbered"
       }
...
}
2022/02/14 16:42:27 Created revisionID: changeset/
cumulus/2022-02-14_16.42.26_K4FJ
{
  "state": "apply",
  "transition": {
    "issue": {},
    "progress": ""
  }
}
```

Just like with SSH, we rarely use `net/http` directly in our programs to interact with a REST API and normally use a higher-level package instead.

Getting config inputs from other systems via HTTP

Until this point, the data to generate a particular device configuration has come from a static file that is present in the program's folder. These values are network device vendor-agnostic.

In real-world network automation systems, these values can come from other systems. For example, an **IP address management** (**IPAM**) tool can allocate IP addresses dynamically via a REST API call for a particular device, which you can use to build its configuration. The collection of systems that supply these parameters becomes what some refer to as the *source of truth*. Nautobot is an infrastructure resource modeling application that falls into this category.

This also highlights the fact that to automate networks, we not only need to interact with network devices but also integrate with other systems such as Nautobot. This is why we are dedicating this example to exploring how to Go use to interact with a free public instance of Nautobot available for anyone at `https://demo.nautobot.com/`.

The Go client package for Nautobot is automatically generated from its OpenAPI specification, which means its structure might be familiar to you if you have already worked with other OpenAPI-derived packages, which is an advantage of machine-generated code.

In the following example, we are using the auto-generated Nautobot Go package to define a Nautobot API client pointing to `https://demo.nautobot.com/` with an API token:

```
func main() {
    token, err := NewSecurityProviderNautobotToken("...")
    // process error

    c, err := nb.NewClientWithResponses(
        "https://demo.nautobot.com/api/",
        nb.WithRequestEditorFn(token.Intercept),
    )
    /* ... <continues next > ... */
}
```

The `c` client allows us to interact with the remote Nautobot instance. In this example, we want to add one of the lab topology nodes (`ceos`) to the **data center infrastructure management** (**DCIM**) resource collection of the Nautobot instance. The device details are in the `device.json` file:

```
{
    "name": "ams01-ceos-02",
    "device_type": {
        "slug": "ceos"
    },
    "device_role": {
        "slug": "router"
    },
```

```
        "site": {
            "slug": "ams01"
        }
    }
```

Before we can add the device to Nautobot, we must make sure the device type, device role, and site we are referencing in the `device.json` file exist by name already in Nautobot. The `createResources` function takes care of this. Then, we get the IDs of these resources (device type, device role, and site) with the `getDeviceIDs` function, to associate the new device with its type, role, and site:

```
func main() {
    /* ... <continues from before > ... */
    err = createResources(c)
    // process error

    dev, err := os.Open("device.json")
    // process error
    defer dev.Close()

    d := json.NewDecoder(dev)

    var device nb.Device
    err = d.Decode(&device)
    // process error

    found, devWithIDs, err := getDeviceIDs(c, device)
    /* ... <continues next > ... */
}
```

If the device is not already in Nautobot, we can create it with the auto-generated `DcimDevicesCreateWithResponse` function:

```
func main() {
    /* ... <continues from before > ... */
    created, err := c.DcimDevicesCreateWithResponse(
        context.TODO(),
        nb.DcimDevicesCreateJSONRequestBody(*devWithIDs))
```

```
    check(err)
}
```

After running the program with `go run nautobot` from the `ch06/nautobot` folder, you should see the following in the Nautobot graphical interface at `https://demo.nautobot.com/`:

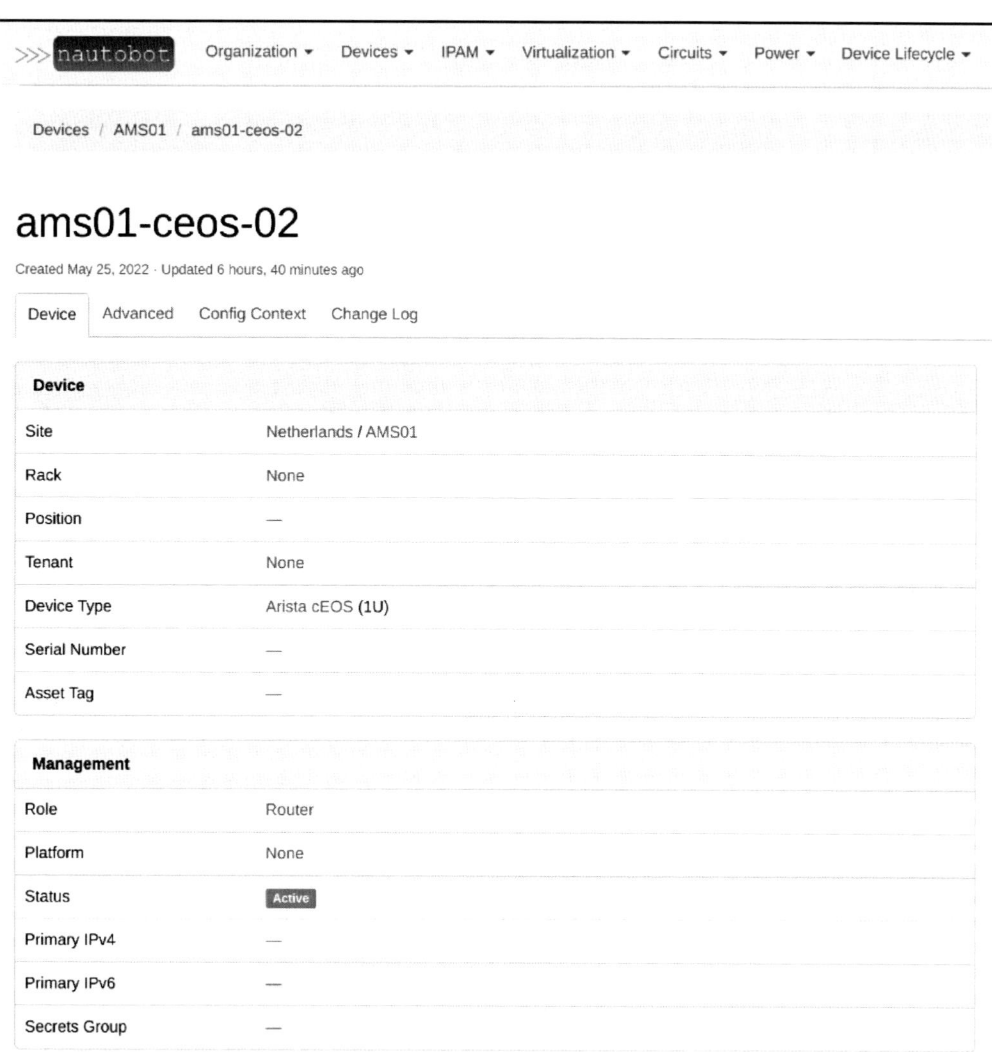

Figure 6.3 – Nautobot screenshot

The data that we pass to these Dcim functions ends up in HTTP requests, just like the ones we built manually earlier in this chapter. Here, we don't deal with URL queries, HTTP paths, or JSON payloads directly as the package abstracts away all that from us. This allows the developers to focus more on business value and less on implementation details. It makes the API easier to consume.

The focus of this chapter so far has been more on pushing configurations down to network devices and less on reading the state of the network after this operation. While configuration management's primary focus is on producing and deploying configurations in the correct format, state validation can play a key role in verifying your configuration changes have been successful. In the next section, we will learn how to retrieve and parse operational data from a remote device.

State validation

The way network devices model and store their state internally is often different from their configuration data model. Traditional CLI-first network devices display the state in a tabular format to the end user, making it easier for network operators to interpret and reason about it. In API-enabled network operating systems, they can present the state in a structured format, making the data friendlier for automation, but we still need to prepare the right data model for deserialization.

In this section, we will look at three different methods you could use to read the state from a network device through a code example that gathers operational data from the devices we just configured with `crypto/ssh`, `net/http`, and `scrapligo` in the preceding sections of this chapter. For each network device, we will use one of these resources to get the data in the format we need:

- **RESTful API calls**: To retrieve and parse data from an HTTP interface
- **Regular expressions**: To parse plain text received via SSH
- **TextFSM templates**: To simplify parsing tabular data

Checking routing information

At this point, you should have a three-node topology running. Each network device has a loopback address we redistribute into BGP. Arista cEOS's loopback address is `198.51.100.1/32`, for example. The goal of the next program is to verify the setup. We retrieve the routing table information from every device to check whether all three IPv4 loopback addresses are present. This way, we can verify our configuration intent – established end-to-end reachability between all devices.

The program has two building blocks:

- `GetRoutes`: A method that connects to the network device, gets the information we need, and puts it in a common format
- `checkRoutes`: A function that reads the routes from `GetRoutes` and compares them to the list of loopback addresses we expect to see (`expectedRoutes`)

One caveat is that the API type a network device supports to access its operational data remotely may vary, from the transport protocol to the format of the textual representation of the data. In our example, this translates into different implementation details of `GetRoutes` per networking vendor. Here, we take it a bit to the extreme for educational purposes and make the implementation per vendor completely different from one another to showcase REST APIs, regular expressions, and TextFSM independently:

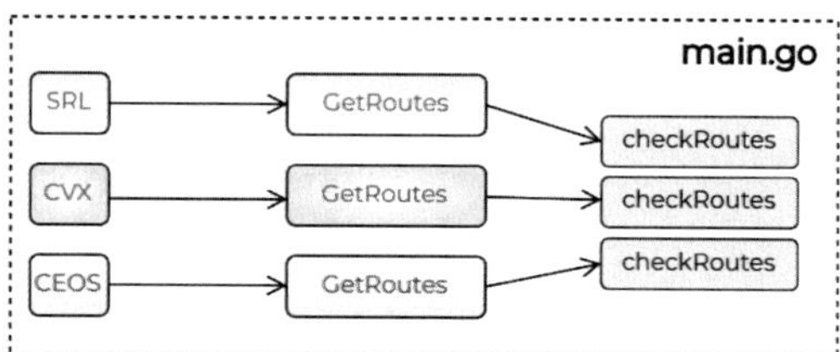

Figure 6.4 – Checking routing information

Each network device has its own data structure. For example, we create SRL for SR Linux. The `SRL`, `CVX`, and `CEOS` types implement the `Router` interface, as each one has a `GetRoutes` method that contains the implementation details for that specific vendor.

In the main program, a user only needs to initialize the devices with the authentication details, so it creates a variable of the type we created for that device. Then, it can run the route collection tasks concurrently by firing off a goroutine for each device that runs the device type's `GetRoutes` method. The `Router` interface successfully hides away the implementation details of a particular vendor from the user, as the call is always the same `router.GetRoutes`:

```
type Router interface {
    GetRoutes(wg *sync.WaitGroup)
}

func main() {
     cvx := CVX{
     Hostname: "clab-netgo-cvx",
      Authentication: Authentication{
      Username: "cumulus",
     Password: "cumulus",
     },
    }
    srl := SRL{
     Hostname: "clab-netgo-srl",
     Authentication: Authentication{
      Username: "admin",
      Password: "admin",
```

```
        },
    }
    ceos := CEOS{
        Hostname: "clab-netgo-ceos",
        Authentication: Authentication{
            Username: "admin",
            Password: "admin",
        },
    }

    log.Printf("Checking reachability...")

    devices := []Router{cvx, srl, ceos}

    var wg sync.WaitGroup
    for _, router := range devices {
        wg.Add(1)
        go router.GetRoutes(&wg)
    }
    wg.Wait()
}
```

Because all `GetRoutes` instances run in the background in their own goroutine, we added a `wg` wait group to make sure we don't finish the main goroutine until we have collected and verified all the devices. Before the end of each `GetRoutes` method, we call the `expectedRoutes` function to process the routes we get from that device.

We verify the parsed state (routes) by checking that each `expectedRoutes`, which contains a unique set of loopback addresses, is present in each device's routing table. For every IPv4 prefix received, we check whether it's present in `expectedRoutes` and change a boolean flag to signal this. If, by the end of this, we have prefixes in `expectedRoutes` with a Boolean value of `false`, it means they were not present in the device's routing table, and we create a log message:

```
func checkRoutes(device string, in []string, wg *sync.
WaitGroup) {
    defer wg.Done()
    log.Printf("Checking %s routes", device)

    expectedRoutes := map[string]bool{
```

```
        "198.51.100.0/32": false,
        "198.51.100.1/32": false,
        "198.51.100.2/32": false,
    }

    for _, route := range in {
        if _, ok := expectedRoutes[route]; ok {
            log.Print("Route ", route,
                        " found on ", device)
            expectedRoutes[route] = true
        }
    }

    for route, found := range expectedRoutes {
        if !found {
            log.Print("! Route ", route,
                        " NOT found on ", device)
        }
    }
}
```

Following this, we examine each of the `GetRoutes` method implementations. As with the rest of the examples, you can find the complete program in the `ch06/state` folder of this book's GitHub repository (*Further reading*).

Parsing command outputs with regular expressions

We use regular expressions to parse and extract information from unstructured data. The Go standard library includes the `regexp` package, which understands the RE2 syntax. This is a regular expression library designed with safety as one of its primary goals. One of the main consequences of that decision is the lack of back-references and look-around operations, which are unsafe and can lead to denial of service exploits.

In this case, the `GetRoutes` method uses `scrapligo` to connect and sends a `show` command to extract the routing table information from an SRL device type in this case. One way to parse this information is to iterate over the output line by line while matching expected patterns with regular expressions, close to what we did for the `ch05/closed-loop` example (*Further reading*):

```
func (r SRL) GetRoutes(wg *sync.WaitGroup) {
    lookupCmd := "show network-instance default route-table
```

```
ipv4-unicast summary"

    conn, err := platform.NewPlatform(
        "nokia_srl",
        r.Hostname,
        options.WithAuthNoStrictKey(),
        options.WithAuthUsername(r.Username),
        options.WithAuthPassword(r.Password),
        options.WithTermWidth(176),
    )
    // process error

    driver, err := conn.GetNetworkDriver()
    // process error
    err = driver.Open()
    // process error
    defer driver.Close()

    resp, err := driver.SendCommand(lookupCmd)
    // process error

    ipv4Prefix := regexp.
            MustCompile(`(\d{1,3}\.){3}\d{1,3}\/\d{1,2}`)

    out := []string{}
    for _, match := range ipv4Prefix.FindAll(
    resp.RawResult, -1) {
        out = append(out, string(match))
    }
    go checkRoutes(r.Hostname, out, wg)
}
```

To make things a bit simpler, we assume that anything that matches the IPv4 address pattern in the entire output is a prefix installed in the routing table. This way, instead of reading and parsing a tabular data structure, we tell our program to find all text occurrences that match the IPv4 route pattern and put them on a string slice (`out`) that we pass to the `checkRoutes` function for further processing.

Parsing semi-formatted command outputs with templates

Parsing various output formats with regular expressions can be tedious and error-prone. This is why Google created `TextFSM`, initially as a Python library, to implement a template-based parsing of semi-formatted text. They designed it specifically to parse information from network devices and it has a wide range of community-developed templates maintained in **ntc-templates** (*Further reading*).

We will use one of these community templates to parse the `ip` route command's output in the implementation of `GetRoutes` for Arista cEOS. Scrapligo embeds a Go port of TextFSM and can conveniently parse the response using the `TextFsmParse` function:

```
func (r CEOS) GetRoutes(wg *sync.WaitGroup) {
    template := "https://raw.githubusercontent.com/
networktocode/ntc-templates/master/ntc_templates/templates/
arista_eos_show_ip_route.textfsm"

    lookupCmd := "sh ip route"

    conn, err := core.NewEOSDriver(
        r.Hostname,
        base.WithAuthStrictKey(false),
        base.WithAuthUsername(r.Username),
        base.WithAuthPassword(r.Password),
    )
    // process error

    err = conn.Open()
    // process error
    defer conn.Close()

    resp, err := conn.SendCommand(lookupCmd)
    // process error

    parsed, err := resp.TextFsmParse(template)
    // process error

    out := []string{}
    for _, match := range parsed {
```

```
        out = append(out, fmt.Sprintf(
                "%s/%s", match["NETWORK"], match["MASK"]))
    }
    go checkRoutes(r.Hostname, out, wg)
}
```

The `parsed` variable that stores the parsed data is a slice that contains `map[string]interface{}` values, where keys correspond to the TextFSM values defined in a template. Thus, just by looking at the `show ip route` template, we can extract the network and mask (prefix length) information and append it to a string slice (`out`) that we pass to the `checkRoutes` function for further processing.

Getting JSON-formatted data with REST API requests

Thus far in this chapter, we've seen two different ways of interacting with a REST API – one using the `net/http` package and another using an auto-generated high-level package (`nautobot`). But you also have other options, such as `go-resty`, which builds on top of `net/http` to offer an improved user experience when interacting with REST API endpoints.

In the following implementation of `GetRoutes`, we are taking advantage of `go-resty` to build the required HTTP headers for authentication, extend the URL with query parameters, and unmarshal a response into a user-defined data structure (`routes`):

```
Code Block 1:
func (r CVX) GetRoutes(wg *sync.WaitGroup) {
    client := resty.NewWithClient(&http.Client{
        Transport: &http.Transport{
            TLSClientConfig: &tls.
Config{InsecureSkipVerify: true},
        },
    })
    client.SetBaseURL("https://" + r.Hostname + ":8765" )
    client.SetBasicAuth(r.Username, r.Password)

    var routes map[string]interface{}
    _, err := client.R().
        SetResult(&routes).
        SetQueryParams(map[string]string{
            "rev": "operational",
        }).
        Get("/nvue_v1/vrf/default/router/rib/ipv4/route")
```

```
        // process error

        out := []string{}
        for route := range routes {
                out = append(out, route)
        }
        go checkRoutes(r.Hostname, out, wg)
}
```

We have created a REST API client to request the routing table information (`...rib/ipv4/route`) from the target device (type CVX). We decoded the JSON payload response with the routing table prefixes as keys into the `routes` variable of the `map[string]interface{}` type. Next, we looped through `routes` to append all keys to a string slice (`out`) we can pass to the `checkRoutes` function.

Validating end-to-end reachability

You can run this program to check whether all three routers in the topology can reach one another from the `ch06/state` folder (*Further reading*). Make sure all the devices have the configs from the examples that used `crypto/ssh`, `net/http`, and `scrapligo` to configure them earlier in this chapter. The expected output should look as follows:

```
ch06/state$ go run main.go
2022/03/10 17:06:30 Checking reachability...
2022/03/10 17:06:30 Collecting CEOS routes
2022/03/10 17:06:30 Collecting CVX routes
2022/03/10 17:06:30 Collecting SRL routes
2022/03/10 17:06:30 Checking clab-netgo-cvx routes
2022/03/10 17:06:30 Route 198.51.100.0/32 found on clab-netgo-
cvx
2022/03/10 17:06:30 Route 198.51.100.1/32 found on clab-netgo-
cvx
2022/03/10 17:06:30 Route 198.51.100.2/32 found on clab-netgo-
cvx
2022/03/10 17:06:31 Checking clab-netgo-ceos routes
2022/03/10 17:06:31 Route 198.51.100.0/32 found on clab-netgo-
ceos
2022/03/10 17:06:31 Route 198.51.100.1/32 found on clab-netgo-
ceos
```

```
2022/03/10 17:06:31 Route 198.51.100.2/32 found on clab-netgo-
ceos
2022/03/10 17:06:34 Checking clab-netgo-srl routes
2022/03/10 17:06:34 Route 198.51.100.0/32 found on clab-netgo-
srl
2022/03/10 17:06:34 Route 198.51.100.1/32 found on clab-netgo-
srl
2022/03/10 17:06:34 Route 198.51.100.2/32 found on clab-netgo-
srl
```

If any of the routes were not present on any of the devices, we would've seen messages such as these:

```
2022/03/10 15:59:55 ! Route 198.51.100.0/32 NOT found on clab-
netgo-cvx
2022/03/10 15:59:55 ! Route 198.51.100.1/32 NOT found on clab-
netgo-cvx
```

Summary

Configuration generation, deployment, reporting, and compliance remain the most popular network automation operations. This is where the immediate benefits of introducing automation are greatest and most visible, making it the first logical step into the world of automation and DevOps. Configuration management is one of those repetitive tasks network engineers spend most of their time on, so it's a natural fit for automation. But sending a new configuration to a device is just part of a broader process that should consider failure handling, from syntax errors in the configuration to how to recover properly if the connection to a remote device drops. In this context, you can abstract some repetitive tasks with reusable code that offers generic functionality to reduce the time and effort to automate your use cases. This is what automation frameworks offer, which we will discuss in the next chapter.

Further reading

To learn more about the topics that were covered in this chapter, take a look at the following resources:

- NetDevOps 2020 Survey: `https://dgarros.github.io/netdevops-survey/reports/2020`
- `topo` directory: `https://github.com/PacktPublishing/Network-Automation-with-Go/blob/main/topo-base/topo.yml`
- `ch06/ssh` folder: `https://github.com/PacktPublishing/Network-Automation-with-Go/tree/main/ch06/ssh`

- `ch06/vssh` directory: `https://github.com/PacktPublishing/Network-Automation-with-Go/tree/main/ch06/vssh`
- `ch06/http` directory: `https://github.com/PacktPublishing/Network-Automation-with-Go/tree/main/ch06/http`
- demo.nautobot.com: `https://demo.nautobot.com/`
- `ch06/state` directory: `https://github.com/PacktPublishing/Network-Automation-with-Go/tree/main/ch06/ssh`
- `ch05/closed-loop` example: `https://github.com/PacktPublishing/Network-Automation-with-Go/blob/main/ch05/closed-loop/main.go#L138`
- ntc-templates: `https://github.com/networktocode/ntc-templates`

7

Automation Frameworks

Most engineers start their automation journey by writing small ad hoc scripts. Over time, as these scripts grow in size and number, we need to think about the operating model for the solutions we create and how strong the foundations we are building upon are. Ultimately, we have to coordinate automation practices across different teams to generate business outcomes at scale.

To reduce the time and effort spent automating their use cases, some organizations try to standardize their tools and reuse generic components in their solutions, which often leads them to automation frameworks.

Automation frameworks allow different teams to come together under the same umbrella, break silos that may lead to inefficiencies, embrace common practices and code reusability, and enforce policies across domains to make the developed solutions more secure.

When choosing what best fits your environment and use cases, make sure you evaluate different automation frameworks. In this chapter, we will review some of them and focus specifically on how they can integrate with Go. In particular, we will look at the following:

- How Go programs can become Ansible modules
- The development of a custom Terraform provider
- An overview of the rest of the well-known Go-based frameworks

We close this chapter by looking at the current trends in the industry and how the new generation of automation frameworks may develop in the future.

Technical requirements

You can find the code examples for this chapter in the book's GitHub repository (see the *Further reading* section), in the `ch07` folder.

> **Important Note**
>
> We recommend you execute the Go programs in this chapter in a virtual lab environment. Refer to the appendix for the prerequisites and instructions on how to build it.

Ansible

Ansible is an open source project, framework, and automation platform. Its descriptive automation language has captured the attention of many network engineers who see it as an introduction with minimal friction into the world of network automation and something that can help them become productive relatively quickly.

Ansible has an agentless push-based architecture. It connects to the hosts it manages via SSH and runs a series of tasks. These tasks are small programs that we call Ansible modules, which are the units of code that Ansible abstracts away from the user. A user only has to give the input arguments and can rely on Ansible modules to do all the heavy work for them. Although the level of abstraction may vary, Ansible modules allow users to focus more on the desired state of their infrastructure and less on the individual commands required to achieve that state.

Overview of Ansible components

Playbooks are at the core of Ansible. These text-based declarative YAML files define a set of automation tasks that you can group in different plays. Each task runs a module that comes from either the Ansible code base or a third-party content collection:

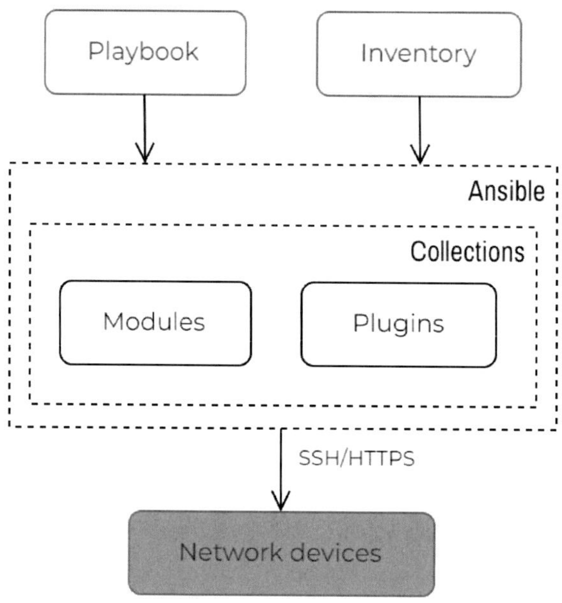

Figure 7.1 – Ansible high-level diagram

We use an Ansible inventory to describe the hosts or network devices we want to manage with Ansible. *Figure 7.1* provides a high-level overview of these elements.

Inventory

An inventory is a list of managed hosts you can define statically in a text file or pull dynamically from an external system. You can manage hosts individually or collectively using groups. The following code snippet shows an Ansible inventory file:

```
[eos]
clab-netgo-ceos

[eos:vars]
ansible_user=admin
ansible_password=admin
ansible_connection=ansible.netcommon.network_cli
```

You can also use inventory to define group- and host-level variables that become available to Ansible playbooks.

Playbooks, plays, and tasks

Ansible playbooks are files that you write using a YAML-based **Domain-Specific Language** (**DSL**). A playbook can have one or more plays on it. Each Ansible play targets a host or a group of hosts from an inventory to perform a series of tasks in a specific order. The following code output shows an example of a playbook with a single play and two tasks:

```
- name: First Play - Configure Routers
  hosts: routers
  gather_facts: true

  tasks:
    - name: Run Nokia Go module on local system with Go
      go_srl:
        host: "{{ inventory_hostname }}"
        user: "{{ ansible_user }}"
        password: "{{ ansible_password }}"
        input: "{{ hostvars[inventory_hostname] | string |
b64encode }}"
      delegate_to: localhost
      when: ('srl' in group_names)

    - name: Run NVIDIA compiled Go module on remote system
```

```
without Go
        go_cvx:
          host: localhost
          user: "{{ ansible_user }}"
          password: "{{ ansible_password }}"
          input: "{{ hostvars[inventory_hostname] | string |
b64encode }}"
        when: ('cvx' in group_names)
```

The last example is a snippet from a larger playbook (see *Further reading*) included in the `ch07/ansible` folder of this book's GitHub repository. That playbook has four tasks spread across two different plays. We use that playbook to review different concepts throughout this section.

Modules

Each task executes an Ansible module. Although implementations may vary, the goal of an Ansible module is to be idempotent, so no matter how many times you run it against the same set of hosts, you always get the same outcome.

Ansible ships with several modules written mostly in Python, but it doesn't stop you from using another programming language, which is what we explore in this section.

Working with Ansible modules

The code of an Ansible module can execute either on a remote node, for hosts such as Linux servers, or locally, on the node running the playbook. The latter is what we typically do when the managed node is an API service or a network device because they both lack an execution environment with dependencies such as Linux shell and Python. Luckily, modern network operating systems meet those requirements, which give us both options of running the code locally or remotely.

If you look at the preceding playbook snippet, you can see how we implemented these two options. The first task invokes the `go_srl` module that gets delegated to the localhost. This means it runs from the machine running Ansible and targets a remote host provided in the host argument. The second task executes the `go_cvx` module, which is not delegated and thus runs on a remote node, targeting its API calls at the localhost.

The rest of the playbook uses a combination of local and remote execution environments, as denoted by the gear symbols in the following diagram:

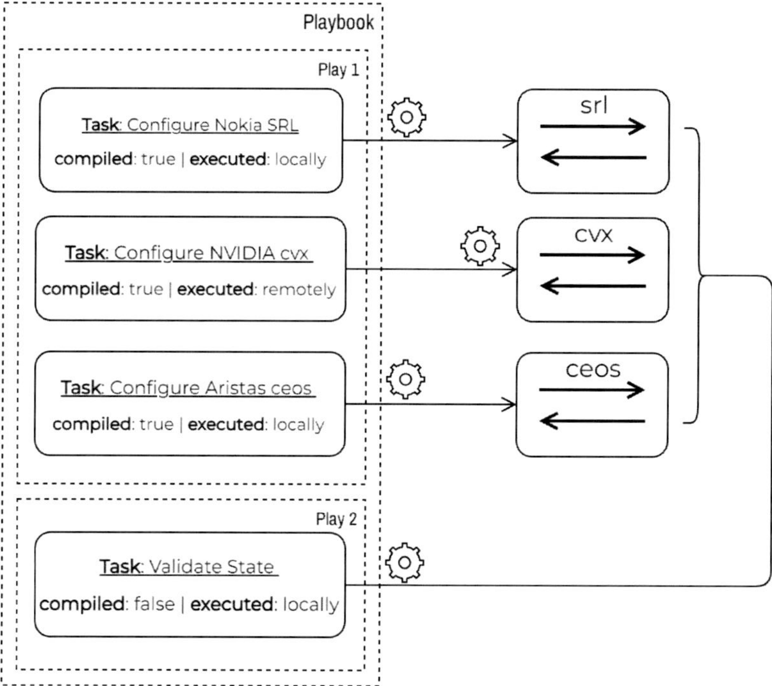

Figure 7.2 – Playbook example

The Ansible playbook first runs an Ansible play to configure each node of the topology with these high-level objectives:

- Configure the SR Linux node (`srl`) using a compiled Go code we execute locally on the machine running Ansible
- Configure the NVIDIA Cumulus node (`cvx`) using a compiled Go code we execute on the remote node
- Configure the Arista EOS node (`ceos`) using a compiled Go code we execute locally on the machine running Ansible

The choice of local or remote execution environments in the preceding playbook is random and only serves to show the two different approaches. Since all our lab devices are Linux-based, we can change this behavior without reworking the Ansible modules we use.

The second play has a single task that verifies the configured state on all three devices using a non-compiled code we execute using the `go run` command. We use this last task to show an alternative approach to concurrency that uses Go native primitives instead of Ansible forks to execute tasks on several nodes at the same time. We discuss this later in this section.

Developing an Ansible module

While Ansible developers write most Ansible modules in Python, there are different reasons to write a module in another programming language:

- Your company might use another programming language already.
- Maybe you know or feel more comfortable writing in a different language.
- The code is already available and there is no business justification to rewrite it in another programming language.
- You want to take advantage of a feature that is not available in Python.

Ansible's role is not to rip and replace everything that you have, especially if it's working for you already. To illustrate this, we will take a set of Go programs from other chapters and turn them into Ansible modules we can execute in a playbook to configure our lab topology.

Ansible module interface

You can extend Ansible by adding custom modules. Their implementation code should go into the `library` folder. When Ansible runs into a task with a module that is not installed in the system, it looks for a file with the module's name in the `library` folder and tries to run it as a module, going through the following sequence of steps:

1. It saves all module arguments in a temporary file, for example, `/tmp/foo`.
2. It executes that module as a child process, passing it the filename as the first and only argument, for example, `./library/my_module /tmp/foo`.
3. It waits for the process to complete and expects to receive a structured response in its standard output.

While Ansible always expects a response in a JSON format, the input file format Ansible passes to the module depends on whether the module is a script or a binary. All binary modules get their input arguments as a JSON file, while script modules receive their input arguments as Bash files or just a list of key-value pairs.

From Go's code perspective, to make this input behavior uniform, we normalize the input format to JSON before running any non-compiled Go programs. We do this using a wrapper Bash script that transforms the Bash input into JSON before calling the `go run` command, as you can see in the `ch07/ansible/library/go_state` file of this book's GitHub repository (see *Further reading*).

Adapting your Go code to interact with Ansible

Ultimately, a custom Ansible module can do anything as long as it understands how to parse the input arguments and knows how to return the expected output. We would need to change the Go programs from other chapters to make them an Ansible module. But the amount of changes necessary is minimal. Let's examine this.

First, for this example, we need to create a struct to parse the module arguments we receive in the input JSON file. These arguments include login credentials and the input data model:

```
// ModuleArgs are the module inputs
type ModuleArgs struct {
  Host     string
  User     string
  Password string
  Input    string
}

func main() {
  if len(os.Args) != 2 {
    // generate error
  }

  argsFile := os.Args[1]
  text, err := os.ReadFile(argsFile)
  // check error

  var moduleArgs ModuleArgs
  err = json.Unmarshal(text, &moduleArgs)
  // check error
  /* ... <continues next > ... */
```

The input data model we use for Ansible remains the same as the one that we used in other chapters. This data is in the `ch07/ansible/host_vars` directory for this example. With Ansible, this data model becomes just a subset of all variables defined for each host. We pass it, along with the rest of the host variables, as a base64-encoded string. Inside our module, we decode the input string and decode it into the same `Model` struct we used before:

```
import (
  "encoding/base64"
  "gopkg.in/yaml.v2"
)
```

```
type Model struct {
  Uplinks  []Link `yaml:"uplinks"`
  Peers    []Peer `yaml:"peers"`
  ASN      int    `yaml:"asn"`
  Loopback Addr   `yaml:"loopback"`
}

func main() {
  /* ... <continues from before > ... */
  src, err :=
      base64.StdEncoding.DecodeString(moduleArgs.Input)
  // check error
  reader := bytes.NewReader(src)
  d := yaml.NewDecoder(reader)
  var input Model
  d.Decode(&input)
  /* ... <continues next > ... */
```

At this point, we've parsed enough information for our Go program to configure a network device. This part of the Go code does not require any modifications. The only thing you need to be mindful of is that instead of logging to the console, you now need to send any log messages as a response to Ansible.

When all the work is complete, we need to prepare and print the response object for Ansible. The following code snippet shows the *happy path* when all changes have gone through:

```
// Response is the values returned from the module
type Response struct {
  Msg     string `json:"msg"`
  Busy    bool   `json:"busy"`
  Changed bool   `json:"changed"`
  Failed  bool   `json:"failed"`
}

func main() {
  /* ... <continues from before > ... */
  var r Response
  r.Msg = "Device Configured Successfully"
  r.Changed = true
```

```
    r.Failed = false

    response, err = json.Marshal(r)
    // check error
    fmt.Println(string(response))
    os.Exit(0)
}
```

Using a similar pattern to what we just described, we have created a custom module for each one of the three lab devices and one module to verify the state of the lab topology as we did in *Chapter 6, Configuration Management*. You can find these modules in the `ch07/ansible/{srl|cvx|ceos|state}` directories of this book's GitHub repository (see *Further reading*).

Before we move on to the execution, we want to show one way we can make use of Go's built-in features to speed up and optimize concurrent task execution in Ansible.

Taking advantage of Go's concurrency

Ansible's default behavior is to run each task on all hosts before moving on to the next one (linear strategy). Of course, it doesn't just run one task on one host at a time; instead, it uses several independent processes attempting to run simultaneously on as many hosts as the number of forks you define in the Ansible configuration. Whether these processes run in parallel depends on the hardware resources available to them.

A less expensive approach from a resource utilization perspective is to leverage Go concurrency. This is what we do in the `go_state` Ansible module, where we target a single node from the inventory, the implicit localhost, and leave the concurrent communication with the remote nodes to Go.

For the following module, we reuse the code example from the *State validation* section of *Chapter 6, Configuration Management* that has the access details embedded in the code already, but you could also pass these access details as arguments to the module to achieve the same result:

```
- name: Run Validate module on Systems with Go installed
  go_state:
    host: "{{ inventory_hostname }}"
```

The trade - off of this approach is that we gain speed and get more efficient use of resources, but we lose the inventory management side of Ansible. Be mindful of this when trying to decide whether this is the right fit for your use case.

Running the playbook

You can find the complete example involving four Go Ansible modules in the `ch07/ansible` directory. To run it, first make sure the lab topology is running from the root folder of the repository with `make lab-up`, then run the playbook with the `ansible-playbook` command:

```
ch07/ansible$ ansible-playbook playbook.yml
# output omitted for brevity.
PLAY RECAP ***************************************************
***************************************************************
**************************************
clab-netgo-ceos           : ok=5    changed=0    unreachable=0
failed=0    skipped=4    rescued=0    ignored=0
clab-netgo-cvx            : ok=2    changed=1    unreachable=0
failed=0    skipped=7    rescued=0    ignored=0
clab-netgo-srl            : ok=2    changed=1    unreachable=0
failed=0    skipped=7    rescued=0    ignored=0
localhost                 : ok=1    changed=0    unreachable=0
failed=0    skipped=0    rescued=0    ignored=0
```

Now that we've covered how Go programs can integrate with Ansible, we will move on to another popular automation framework: Terraform.

Terraform

Terraform is an open source software solution for declarative infrastructure management. It allows you to express and manage the desired state of your infrastructure with code. It has gained initial popularity as a framework to automate public cloud infrastructure but now supports a variety of on-premises and public cloud resources, platforms, services—almost anything that has an API.

One of the key distinctions of Terraform is the way it manages state. Once it creates a remote resource initially, it saves the resulting state in a file and relies on that state to be there for its next runs. As you update and develop your infrastructure code, the state file enables Terraform to manage the entire life cycle of a remote resource, calculating the precise sequence of API calls to transition between states. This ability to manage state and the declarative configuration language and the agentless, API-first architecture allowed Terraform to become deeply entrenched in the cloud infrastructure space and become a critical part of DevOps and Infrastructure-as-Code toolchains.

If we look at the Terraform registry (see *Further reading*), we can see over a hundred providers in the networking category ranging from SDN appliances and firewalls to various cloud services. This number is on a rising trend, as more people adopt a declarative approach to manage their infrastructure as code. This is why we believe it's important for network automation engineers to know Terraform and be able to extend its capabilities using Go.

Overview of Terraform components

The entire Terraform ecosystem is a collection of Go packages. They distribute the main CLI tool, often referred to as *Terraform Core*, as a statically compiled binary. This binary implements the command-line interface and can parse and evaluate instructions written in **Hashicorp Configuration Language (HCL)**. On every invocation, it builds a resource graph and generates an execution plan to reach the desired state described in the configuration file. The main binary only includes a few plugins but can discover and download the required dependencies.

Terraform plugins are also distributed as standalone binaries. Terraform Core starts and terminates the required plugins as child processes and interacts with them using an internal gRPC-based protocol. Terraform defines two types of plugins:

- **Providers**: Interact with a remote infrastructure provider and implement the required changes
- **Provisioners**: Implement a set of imperative actions, declared as a set of terminal commands, to bootstrap a resource that a provider created before

The following diagram demonstrates what we have described and shows how different Terraform components communicate internally and externally:

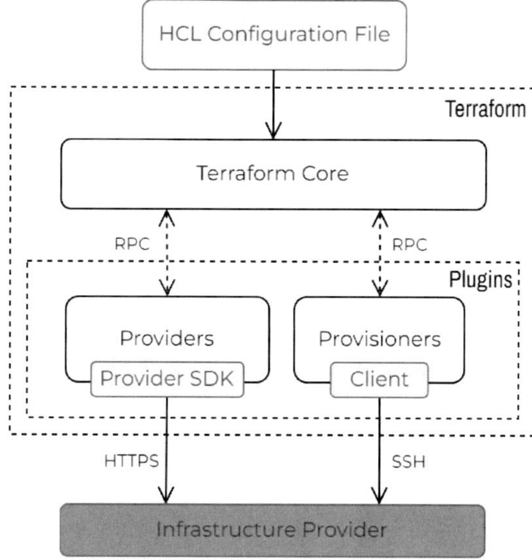

Figure 7.3 – Terraform high-level diagram

The vast majority of Terraform plugins are providers as they implement the declarative resource actuation and communicate with an upstream API. A provider defines two types of objects that you can use to interact with a remote API:

- **Resources**: Represent the actual managed infrastructure objects, such as virtual machines, firewall policies, and DNS records
- **Data Sources**: Offer a way to query information that is not managed by Terraform, such as a list of supported cloud regions, VM images, or **Identity and Access Management** (**IAM**) roles

It's up to the Terraform provider maintainers to decide what resources and data sources to implement, so the coverage may vary, especially between official and community-supported providers.

Working with Terraform

A typical Terraform workflow involves several stages that need to happen in sequence. We first need to define a provider that determines what infrastructure we would manage, and then describe the state of our infrastructure using a combination of resources and data sources. We will walk through these stages by following a configuration file, `ch07/terraform/main.tf`, we've created in this book's GitHub repository (see *Further reading*).

Defining a provider

Providers define connection details for the upstream API. They can point at the public AWS API URL or an address of a private vCenter instance. In the next example, we show how to manage the demo instance of Nautobot running at `https://demo.nautobot.com/`.

Terraform expects to find a list of required providers, along with their definition, in one file in the current working directory. For the sake of simplicity, we include those details at the top of the `main.tf` file and define credentials in the same file. In production environments, these details may live in a separate file, and you should source credentials externally, for example, from environment variables:

```
terraform {
  required_providers {
    nautobot = {
      version = "0.2.4"
      source  = "nleiva/nautobot"
    }
  }
}

provider "nautobot" {
  url = "https://demo.nautobot.com/api/"
```

```
  token = "aaaaaaaaaaaaaaaaaaaaaaaaaaaaaaaaaaaaaaaa"
}
```

With this information defined, we can initialize Terraform. The following command instructs Terraform to perform plugin discovery and download any dependencies into a local `./terraform` directory:

```
ch07/terraform$ terraform init -upgrade

Initializing the backend...

Initializing provider plugins...
- Finding nleiva/nautobot versions matching "0.2.4"...
- Installing nleiva/nautobot v0.2.4...
- Installed nleiva/nautobot v0.2.4 (self-signed, key ID
A33D26E300F155FF)
```

At the end of this step, Terraform creates a lock file, `.terraform.lock.hcl`, to record the provider selections it just made. Include this file in your version control repository so that Terraform can guarantee to make the same selections by default when you run `terraform init` on a different machine.

Creating a resource

To create a resource, we define it in a configuration block with zero or more arguments that assign values to resource fields. The following resource creates a new `Manufacturer` object in Nautobot with the specified name and description:

```
resource "nautobot_manufacturer" "new" {
  description = "Created with Terraform"
  name        = "New Vendor"
}
```

Now we can run `terraform plan` to check whether the current configuration matches the existing state. If they don't match, Terraform creates an execution plan with the proposed changes to make the remote objects match the current configuration. We could skip the `terraform plan` command and move straight to `terraform apply`, which generates the plan and also executes it in a single step:

```
ch07/terraform$ terraform apply --auto-approve

Terraform used the selected providers to generate the following
execution plan. Resource actions
are indicated with the following symbols:
```

```
  + create

Terraform will perform the following actions:

  # nautobot_manufacturer.new will be created
  + resource "nautobot_manufacturer" "new" {
      + created             = (known after apply)
      + description         = "Created with Terraform"
      + devicetype_count    = (known after apply)
      + display             = (known after apply)
      + id                  = (known after apply)
      + inventoryitem_count = (known after apply)
      + last_updated        = (known after apply)
      + name                = "New Vendor"
      + platform_count      = (known after apply)
      + slug                = (known after apply)
      + url                 = (known after apply)
    }

Plan: 1 to add, 0 to change, 0 to destroy.
```

You can see the result of running this plan in Nautobot's web UI at `https://demo.nautobot.com/dcim/manufacturers/new-vendor/`, or you can check the resulting state using the following command:

```
ch07/terraform$ terraform state show 'nautobot_manufacturer.
new'
# nautobot_manufacturer.new:
resource "nautobot_manufacturer" "new" {
    created             = "2022-05-04"
    description         = "Created with Terraform"
    devicetype_count    = 0
    display             = "New Vendor"
    id                  = "09219670-3e28-..."
    inventoryitem_count = 0
    last_updated        = "2022-05-04T18:29:06.241771Z"
    name                = "New Vendor"
    platform_count      = 0
```

```
    slug                    = "new-vendor"
    url                     = "https://demo.nautobot.com/api/dcim/
manufacturers/09219670-3e28-.../"
}
```

At the time of writing, there was no Terraform provider available for Nautobot, so the last example used a custom provider we created specifically for this book. Creating a new provider can enable many new use cases and it involves writing Go code, so this is what we cover next.

Developing a Terraform provider

Eventually, you may come across a provider with limited or missing capabilities, or a provider may not even exist for a platform that is part of your infrastructure. This is when knowing how to build a provider can make a difference, to either extend or fix a provider or build a brand new one. The only prerequisite to get started is the availability of a Go SDK for the target platform. For example, Nautobot has a Go client package that gets automatically generated from its OpenAPI model, which we used already in the *Getting config inputs from other systems via HTTP* section of *Chapter 6, Configuration Management*, so we have all we need to develop its Terraform provider.

The recommended way to create a new Terraform provider is to start with the terraform-provider-scaffolding project (see *Further reading*). This repository provides enough boilerplate to allow you to focus on the internal logic while it provides function stubs and implements **Remote Procedure Call** (**RPC**) integration. We used this template to create the Nautobot provider, so you can compare our final result with the template to see what changes we made.

As a by-product of developing a Terraform provider using the scaffolding project, you can register your Git repository in the Terraform registry and get the benefit of automatically rendered provider documentation (see *Further reading*).

Defining a provider

The provider's internal code (`internal/provider/provider.go` (see *Further reading*)) starts with a schema definition for the provider itself as well as its managed resources and data sources. Inside the provider's schema, we define two input arguments—`url` and `token`. You can extend each schema struct with more constraints, default values, and validation functions:

```
func New(version string) func() *schema.Provider {
  return func() *schema.Provider {
    p := &schema.Provider{
      Schema: map[string]*schema.Schema{
        "url": {
          Type:          schema.TypeString,
```

```
            Required:      true,
            DefaultFunc:
            schema.EnvDefaultFunc("NAUTOBOT_URL", nil),
            ValidateFunc: validation.IsURLWithHTTPorHTTPS,
            Description:  "Nautobot API URL",
          },
          "token": {
            Type:          schema.TypeString,
            Required:      true,
            Sensitive:     true,
            DefaultFunc:
              schema.EnvDefaultFunc("NAUTOBOT_TOKEN", nil),
            Description: "Admin API token",
          },
        },
        DataSourcesMap: map[string]*schema.Resource{
          "nautobot_manufacturers":
              dataSourceManufacturers(),
        },
        ResourcesMap: map[string]*schema.Resource{
          "nautobot_manufacturer": resourceManufacturer(),
        },
      }
      p.ConfigureContextFunc = configure(version, p)

      return p
    }
  }
```

With login information defined, the provider can initialize an API client for the target platform. This happens inside a local function where `url` and `token` get passed to the Nautobot's Go SDK, which creates a fully authenticated HTTP client. We save this client in a special `apiClient` struct, which gets passed as an argument to all provider resources, as we show later on:

```
import nb "github.com/nautobot/go-nautobot"

type apiClient struct {
```

```
    Client *nb.ClientWithResponses
    Server string
}

func configure(
    version string,
    p *schema.Provider,
) func(context.Context, *schema.ResourceData) (interface{},
diag.Diagnostics) {
    return func(ctx context.Context, d *schema.ResourceData)
(interface{}, diag.Diagnostics) {
        serverURL := d.Get("url").(string)
        _, hasToken := d.GetOk("token")
        /* ... <omitted for brevity > ... */

        token, _ :=
            NewSecurityProviderNautobotToken(
                d.Get("token").(string))

        c, err := nb.NewClientWithResponses(
                    serverURL,
                    nb.WithRequestEditorFn(token.Intercept),
                )
        // process error

        return &apiClient{
            Client: c,
            Server: serverURL,
        }, diags
    }
}
```

Now that we have prepared a remote API client, we can start writing code for our managed resources.

Defining resources

Just like how we defined a schema for our provider, we now need to define a schema for each managed resource and data source. For educational purposes, we only implement a single resource type,

`Manufacturer`, and a corresponding data source you can use to retrieve the list of all existing manufacturers in Nautobot.

When we define a schema, our goal is to match the upstream API as closely as possible. This should reduce the number of required data transformations and make the implementation work much easier. Let's look at Nautobot's Go SDK code:

```
type Manufacturer struct {
  Created       *openapi_types.Date
    `json:"created,omitempty"`
  CustomFields  *Manufacturer_CustomFields
    `json:"custom_fields,omitempty"`
  Description   *string `json:"description,omitempty"`
  /* ... <omitted for brevity > ... */
  Url           *string `json:"url,omitempty"`
}

type Manufacturer_CustomFields struct {
  AdditionalProperties map[string]interface{} `json:"-"`
}
```

The schema that we define for the `Manufacturer` resource in `resource_manufacturer.go` closely follows the fields and types defined in the preceding output:

```
func resourceManufacturer() *schema.Resource {
  return &schema.Resource{
    Description: "This object manages a manufacturer",

    CreateContext: resourceManufacturerCreate,
    ReadContext:   resourceManufacturerRead,
    UpdateContext: resourceManufacturerUpdate,
    DeleteContext: resourceManufacturerDelete,

    Schema: map[string]*schema.Schema{
      "created": {
        Description: "Manufacturer's creation date.",
        Type:        schema.TypeString,
        Computed:    true,
      },
```

```
        "description": {
          Description: "Manufacturer's description.",
          Type:        schema.TypeString,
          Optional:    true,
        },
        "custom_fields": {
          Description: "Manufacturer custom fields.",
          Type:        schema.TypeMap,
          Optional:    true,
        },
        /* ... <omitted for brevity > ... */
        "url": {
          Description: "Manufacturer's URL.",
          Type:        schema.TypeString,
          Optional:    true,
          Computed:    true,
        },
      },
    }
  }
```

Once we have defined all schemas with their constraints, types, and descriptions, we can start implementing resource operations. The scaffolding project provides stubs for each one of the CRUD functions, so we only need to fill them out with code.

The create operation

We first look at the `resourceManufacturerCreate` function, which gets invoked when Terraform determines that it must create a new object. This function has two very important arguments:

- `meta`: Stores the API client we created earlier
- `d`: Stores all resource arguments defined in the HCL configuration file

We extract the user-defined configuration from `d` and use it to build a new `nb.Manufacturer` object from the Nautobot's SDK. We can then use the API client to send that object to Nautobot and save the returned object ID:

```
func resourceManufacturerCreate(ctx context.Context, d *schema.
ResourceData, meta interface{}) diag.Diagnostics {
    c := meta.(*apiClient).Client
```

```
        var m nb.Manufacturer

        name, ok := d.GetOk("name")
        n := name.(string)
        if ok {
            m.Name = n
        }
        /* ... <omitted for brevity > ... */

        rsp, err := c.DcimManufacturersCreateWithResponse(
            ctx,
            nb.DcimManufacturersCreateJSONRequestBody(m))
        // process error

        // process returned HTTP response

        d.SetId(id.String())
        return resourceManufacturerRead(ctx, d, meta)
}
```

Typically, we don't define all optional fields when we create a new object. A remote provider assigns the unique ID and initializes default values as it creates a new object. Some platforms return the newly created object back, but there is no guarantee of that. Hence, it's a common pattern in Terraform provider implementations to call a read function at the end of the create function to synchronize and update a local state.

The read operation

The read function updates the local state to reflect the latest state of an upstream resource. We've seen in the preceding example how the create function calls the read at the end of its execution to update the state of a newly created object.

But the most important use of read is to detect configuration drift. When you do `terraform plan` or `terraform apply`, read is the first thing that Terraform executes and its goal is to retrieve the current upstream state and compare it with the state file. This allows Terraform to understand whether users have manually changed a remote object, so it needs to reconcile its state, or whether it's up to date and no updates are necessary.

Read has the same signature as the rest of the CRUD functions, which means it gets the latest version of a managed resource as `*schema.ResourceData` and an API client stored in `meta`. The first thing we need to do in this function is fetch the upstream object:

```
import "github.com/deepmap/oapi-codegen/pkg/types"

func resourceManufacturerRead(ctx context.Context, d *schema.
ResourceData, meta interface{}) diag.Diagnostics {
    c := meta.(*apiClient).Client
    id := d.Get("id").(string)
    rsp, err := c.DcimManufacturersListWithResponse(
        ctx,
        &nb.DcimManufacturersListParams{
            IdIe: &[]types.UUID{types.UUID(id)},
        })
  /* ... <continues next > ... */
}
```

We use the data we get back to update the local Terraform state:

```
func resourceManufacturerRead(ctx context.Context, d *schema.
ResourceData, meta interface{}) diag.Diagnostics {
    /* ... <continues from before > ... */

    d.Set("name", item["name"].(string))
    d.Set("created", item["created"].(string))
    d.Set("description", item["description"].(string))
    d.Set("display", item["display"].(string))
    /* ... <omitted for brevity > ... */

    return diags
}
```

At this stage, our local state should be in sync with the upstream and Terraform can decide whether any changes are necessary as a result.

Remaining implementations

In this chapter, we only cover a subset of the Nautobot provider code. The remaining sections we need to implement include the following:

- The resource **update** and **delete** functions
- **Data source** implementation

For the sake of brevity, we don't include this code in the book, but the full implementation for the `Manufacturer` resource and data source is available in our demo Nautobot provider repository (see *Further reading*).

Networking providers

Writing a provider and keeping it up to date is a major undertaking. At the beginning of this section, we mentioned that Terraform has several providers in the networking category of the Terraform registry (see *Further reading*). We invite you to explore them and always check whether there's an existing provider before implementing your own.

Terraform's guarantees of declarative configuration and state management are very appealing to network engineers trying to adopt DevOps and GitOps practices. As the interest grows, so does the number of new network-related providers, with the following notable recent additions:

- **JUNOS Terraform Automation Framework** (see *Further reading*): Allows you to create a custom JunOS Terraform provider from YANG files
- **Terraform Provider for Cisco IOS XE** (see *Further reading*): Manages the configuration of Cisco Catalyst IOS XE devices including switches, routers, and wireless LAN controllers
- **terraform-provider-junos** (see *Further reading*): An unofficial Terraform provider for Junos OS devices with the NETCONF protocol
- **terraform-provider-ciscoasa** (see *Further reading*): DevNet provider to configure Cisco ASA firewall rules

This completes the overview of Terraform and its network-related use cases. We hope that its adoption continues to increase and the number of networking providers grows. In the next section, we wrap up with a brief overview of a few other automation frameworks.

Other automation frameworks

Our industry has many more automation frameworks and solutions that we would have liked to cover in this chapter. The best we can do is just scratch the surface, leaving much of the exploration up to you. At the same time, we don't want to leave you thinking there's nothing out there besides Ansible and Terraform. This section gives you an overview of other automation frameworks and solutions that you can use or adapt to use within a networking context.

Gornir

Nornir (see *Further reading*) is a popular network automation framework for Python that offers a pure programming experience by ditching DSL in favor of the Python API. It has a pluggable architecture where you can replace or extend almost any element of the framework, from inventory to device connections. It also has a flexible way to parallelize groups of tasks without having to deal with Python's concurrency primitives directly.

Gornir (see *Further reading*) is a Nornir implementation in Go. Keeping with the same principles, it offers things such as inventory management, concurrent execution of tasks, and pluggable connection drivers. Gornir ships with a minimal set of drivers, but its core provides Go interfaces to improve upon and extend this feature. If you're coming to Go from Python and are familiar with Nornir, Gornir may offer a very smooth transition through a familiar API and workflows.

Consul-Terraform-Sync

In the preceding section, we examined how you can use Terraform to manage resources declaratively on a remote target, using Nautobot as an example. Hashicorp, the same company behind Terraform, has developed another automation solution that builds on top of it. It's called Consul-Terraform-Sync (see *Further reading*) and it enables automatic infrastructure management by combining Terraform with Consul and linking them together with a synchronization agent.

Consul is a distributed key/value store used for service discovery, load balancing, and access control. It works by setting up a cluster of nodes that use the Raft consensus protocol to have a consistent view of their internal state. Server nodes communicate with their clients and broadcast relevant updates to make sure clients have an up-to-date version of the relevant part of the internal state. All this happens behind the scenes, with minimal configuration, which makes Consul a very popular choice for service discovery and data storage.

The main idea of the Consul-Terraform-Sync solution is to use Consul as a backend for Terraform configuration and state. The synchronization agent connects to Consul, waits for updates, and automatically triggers Terraform reconciliation as it detects any changes.

Consul-Terraform-Sync allows you to automate Terraform deployments for any of these providers and ensures that your state always matches your intent thanks to the automated reconciliation process.

mgmt

`mgmt` (see *Further reading*) is another infrastructure automation and management framework written completely in Go. It has its own DSL and synchronizes its state using a baked-in etcd cluster. It uses a few interesting ideas, such as a declarative and functional DSL, resource graphs, and dynamic state transitions triggered by closed-loop feedback. Just like Gornir, `mgmt` ships with a set of plugins that users can extend, but none of these plugins is specifically for network devices since the main use case for mgmt is Linux server management.

Looking into the future

In this chapter, we have covered popular network automation frameworks in use today. All these frameworks are at a different stage of development—some have already reached their peak while others are still crossing the chasm (see *Further reading*). But it's important to remember that automation frameworks are not a solved problem with well-established projects and well-understood workflows. This field is constantly developing, and new automation approaches are emerging on the horizon.

These alternative approaches do not resemble what we had seen before. One big trend that we're seeing lately is the departure from an imperative automation paradigm, where a human operator manually triggers actions and tasks. We briefly discussed this trend in *Chapter 5, Network Automation*, and we want to revisit it here to show how the *closed-loop* automation approach changes the landscape of infrastructure management systems. Most modern automation frameworks develop into systems that exhibit some or all the following characteristics:

- Focus on the complete life cycle management of a system as opposed to individual stages, such as bootstrapping, provisioning, or decommissioning.
- Exclusive use of declarative state definition and automatic reconciliation, or self-healing implemented internally.
- Separation of state definitions from the platform managing this state through practices such as GitOps.
- Offer a cloud-native self-service experience via APIs, reducing the friction in consuming of these services both manually and programmatically.

We're currently at a point when these systems and their building blocks are becoming a reality, with some notable examples including Crossplane, Nokia Edge Network Controller, and Anthos Config Sync. They build these systems as Kubernetes controllers, leveraging the Operator model, allowing them to expose their APIs in a standard way, so other systems can talk to them with the same set of tools. We still don't know whether these systems could become mainstream and displace the incumbent frameworks, since they increase the level of complexity and they introduce a steep learning curve. Regardless of that, it's an area to explore, like other potential new trends that might develop, since infrastructure management is far from being a solved problem.

Summary

Whether to choose Ansible, Terraform, or a programming language to solve a particular use case depends on many variables. But don't fall into the trap of looking at this as a binary decision. Most times, different technologies complement each other to offer solutions, as we showed in this chapter. In the next chapter, we will explore newer and more advanced techniques to interact with networking devices and Go.

Further reading

- This book's GitHub repository: `https://github.com/PacktPublishing/Network-Automation-with-Go`
- Playbook: `https://github.com/PacktPublishing/Network-Automation-with-Go/blob/main/ch07/ansible/playbook.yml`
- Terraform registry: `https://registry.terraform.io/browse/providers?category=networking`
- terraform-provider-scaffolding project: `https://github.com/hashicorp/terraform-provider-scaffolding`
- Provider documentation: `https://registry.terraform.io/providers/nleiva/nautobot/latest/docs?pollNotifications=true`
- Provider's internal code: `https://github.com/nleiva/terraform-provider-nautobot/blob/main/internal/provider/provider.go`
- `resource_manufacturer.go`: `https://github.com/nleiva/terraform-provider-nautobot/blob/main/internal/provider/resource_manufacturer.go`
- Nautobot provider repository: `https://github.com/nleiva/terraform-provider-nautobot`
- JUNOS Terraform Automation Framework: `https://github.com/Juniper/junos-terraform`
- Terraform Provider for Cisco IOS XE: `https://github.com/CiscoDevNet/terraform-provider-iosxe`
- terraform-provider-junos: `https://github.com/jeremmfr/terraform-provider-junos`
- terraform-provider-ciscoasa: `https://github.com/CiscoDevNet/terraform-provider-ciscoasa`
- Nornir: `https://github.com/nornir-automation/nornir/`
- Gornir: `https://github.com/nornir-automation/gornir`

- Consul-Terraform-Sync: `https://learn.hashicorp.com/tutorials/consul/consul-terraform-sync-intro?in=consul/network-infrastructure-automation`
- mgmt: `https://github.com/purpleidea/mgmt`
- `https://en.wikipedia.org/wiki/Diffusion_of_innovations`

Part 3: Interacting with APIs

As the way that networks are built, deployed, and operated has evolved, new protocols and interfaces have emerged to facilitate machine-to-machine communication as an enabler of network automation. In these chapters, we will navigate through some of these new capabilities and how to take advantage of them with Go.

This part of the book comprises the following chapters:

8
Network APIs

As the ways we build, deploy, and operate networks evolve, new protocols and interfaces are emerging to ease machine-to-machine communication—a primary enabler of network automation. In this and the following chapters, we'll navigate through some of these new capabilities and explore how to take advantage of them in the context of the Go programming language.

The network **Command-Line Interface** (**CLI**) is what we, network engineers, have used for decades to operate and manage network devices. As we move toward a more programmatic approach to managing networks, simply relying on faster CLI command execution might not be enough to deploy network automation solutions at scale.

Solutions that don't have a strong foundation are brittle and unstable. Hence, when possible, we prefer to build network automation projects based on structured data and machine-friendly **Application Programming Interfaces** (**APIs**). The target use case for these interfaces isn't direct human interaction, so you can rely on Go to translate between remote API calls and a local, user-facing interface.

When we talk about APIs, we generally refer to different things that make up the API developer experience, which you need to consider when evaluating an API:

- A set of **Remote Procedure Calls** (**RPCs**) defining the rules of interaction between a client and a server—at the very least, this would include a standard set of create, get, update, and delete operations.
- The structure and data type exchanged—product vendors can define this using data model specification languages such as YANG or OpenAPI.
- The underlying protocol that wraps the modeled data, which you can serialize into one of the standard formats, such as XML or JSON, and transports it between a client and a server—this could be SSH or, more often these days, HTTP.

In the networking world, we have another dimension in the API landscape that determines the origin of a model specification document. While every networking vendor is free to write their own data models, there are two sources of vendor-agnostic models—IETF and OpenConfig—that strive to offer a vendor-neutral way of configuring and monitoring network devices. Because of this variability in the API ecosystem, it's impossible to cover all protocols and standards, so in this chapter, we'll only cover a subset of network APIs, selected based on availability, practicality, and usefulness:

- We'll start by looking at OpenAPI as one of the most prevalent API specification standards in a wider infrastructure landscape.
- We'll then move on to JSON-RPC, which uses vendor-specific YANG models.
- After that, we'll show an example of an RFC-standard HTTP-based protocol called RESTCONF.
- Finally, we'll look at how you can leverage **Protocol Buffers** (**protobuf**) and gRPC to interact with network devices and stream telemetry.

In this chapter, we'll focus only on these network APIs, as the others are outside of the scope. The most notable absentee is the **Network Configuration Protocol** (**NETCONF**)—one of the oldest network APIs, defined originally by IETF in 2006. We're skipping NETCONF mainly because of the lack of support for XML in some Go packages we use throughout this chapter. Although NETCONF is in use today and offers relevant capabilities, such as different configuration datastores, configuration validation, and network-wide configuration transactions, in the future, it may get displaced by technologies running over HTTP and TLS, such as RESTCONF, gNMI, and various proprietary network APIs.

Technical requirements

You can find the code examples for this chapter in the book's GitHub repository (refer to the *Further reading* section), under the `ch08` folder.

> **Important Note**
>
> We recommend you execute the Go programs in this chapter in a virtual lab environment. Refer to the appendix for prerequisites and instructions on how to build it.

API data modeling

Before we look at any code, let's review what data modeling is, what its key components are, and their relationships. While we focus on the configuration management side of model-driven APIs for this explanation, similar rules and assumptions apply to workflows involving state data retrieval and verification.

The main goal of a configuration management workflow is to transform some input into a serialized data payload whose structure adheres to a data model. This input is usually some user-facing data, which has its own structure and may contain only a small subset of the total number of configuration values. But this input has a one-to-one relationship with the resulting configuration, meaning that rerunning the same workflow should result in the same set of RPCs with the same payloads and the same configuration state on a network device.

At the center of it all is a data model—a text document that describes the hierarchical structure and types of values of a (configuration) data payload. This document becomes a contract with all potential clients—as long as they send their data in the right format, a server should be able to understand it and parse it. This contract works both ways so that when a client requests some information from a server, it can expect to receive it in a predetermined format.

The following diagram shows the main components of a model-driven configuration management workflow and their relationships:

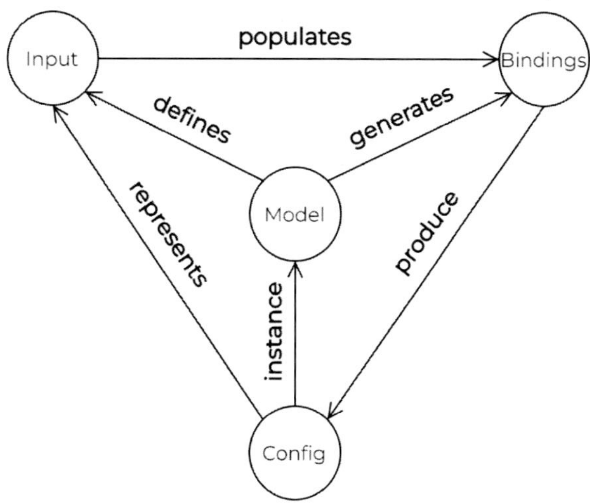

Figure 8.1 – Data modeling concepts

Thus far, we've discussed a model, its input, and the resulting configuration. The only thing we haven't mentioned until now is the *bindings*. We use this term to refer to a broad set of tools and libraries that can help us generate the final configuration data payload programmatically, that is, without resorting to a set of text templates or building these data payloads manually, both of which we consider an anti-pattern in any network automation workflow. We produce these bindings based on the data model and they represent a programmatic view of the model. They may also include several helper functions to serialize and deserialize data structures into one of the expected output formats, for example, JSON or protobuf. We'll spend most of this chapter discussing and interacting with bindings as they become the main interface for a data model inside of the programming language.

Now that we've covered some theory, it's time to put it into practice. In the following section, we'll examine OpenAPI models and one way you can instantiate and validate them.

OpenAPI

Within a greater infrastructure landscape, HTTP and JSON are two commonly used standards for machine-to-machine communication. Most web-based services, including public and private clouds, use a combination of these technologies to expose their externally facing APIs.

The OpenAPI Specification allows us to define and consume RESTful APIs. It lets us describe the enabled HTTP paths, responses, and JSON schemas for the corresponding payloads. It serves as a contract between an API provider and its clients to allow for a more stable and reliable API consumer experience and enables API evolution through versioning.

We don't widely use OpenAPI in networking, arguably for historical reasons. YANG and its ecosystem of protocols predate OpenAPI and the rate of change in network operating systems is not as fast as you might expect. But we often find OpenAPI support in network appliances—SDN controllers, monitoring and provisioning systems or **Domain Name System** (**DNS**), **Dynamic Host Configuration Protocol** (**DHCP**), and **IP Address Management** (**IPAM**) products. This makes working with OpenAPI a valuable skill to have for any network automation engineer.

In *Chapters 6* and *7*, we went through an example of how to interact with Nautobot's external OpenAPI-based interface. We used a Go package produced by an open source code generation framework based on Nautobot's OpenAPI specification. One thing to be mindful of with automatic code generation tools is that they rely on a certain version of the OpenAPI Specification. If the version of your API specification is different (there are nine different OpenAPI versions today; refer to the *Further reading* section), the tool may not generate the Go code. Hence, we want to explore an alternative approach.

In this section, we'll configure NVIDIA's Cumulus Linux device (`cvx`), which has an OpenAPI-based HTTP API, using **Configure Unify Execute** (**CUE**; refer to the *Further reading* section)—an open source **Domain-Specific Language** (**DSL**) designed to define, generate, and validate structured data.

CUE's primary user-facing interface is CLI, but it also has first-class Go API support, so we'll focus on how to interact with it entirely within Go code while providing the corresponding shell commands where appropriate.

The following figure shows a high-level overview of the Go program we'll discuss next:

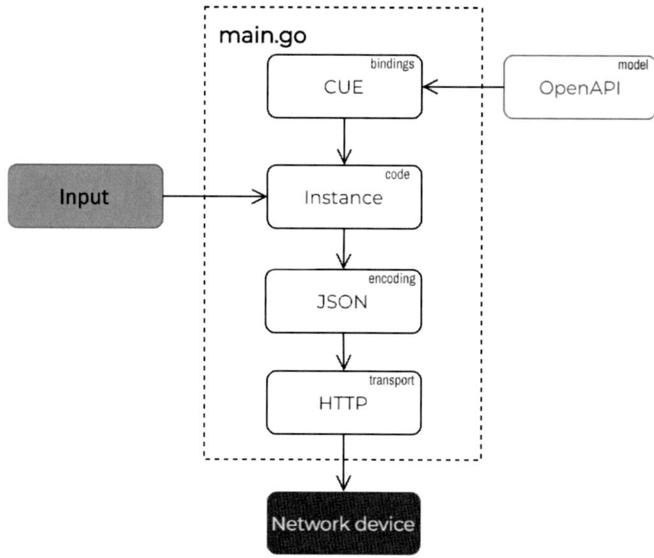

Figure 8.2 – Working with OpenAPI data models

Data modeling

Starting from the top of the diagram, the first thing we need to do is produce the CUE code we can use to generate the data structures to configure a network device.

Although CUE can import existing structured data and generate CUE code, it may take a few iterations to get to a point where the code organization is optimal. It turned out to be faster to write this code from scratch for the example we present here. The result is in the `ch08/cue/template.cue` file (refer to the *Further reading* section).

> **Important Note**
> We won't cover CUE syntax or any of its core concepts and principles in this book but will instead focus on its Go API. For more details about the language, please refer to CUE's official documentation, linked in the *Further reading* section.

CUE resembles JSON with heavy influences from Go. It allows you to define data structures and map values between different data structures via references. Data generation in CUE thus becomes an exercise of data transformation with strict value typing and schema validation. Here's a snippet from the `template.cue` file mentioned earlier, which defines three top-level objects for interfaces, routing, and VRF configuration:

```
package cvx

import "network.automation:input"

interface: _interfaces
router: bgp: {
    _global_bgp
}
vrf: _vrf

_global_bgp: {
    "autonomous-system": input.asn
    enable:              "on"
    "router-id":         input.loopback.ip
}

_interfaces: {
    lo: {
        ip: address: "\(input.LoopbackIP)": {}
        type: "loopback"
    }
    for intf in input.uplinks {
        "\(intf.name)": {
            type: "swp"
            ip: address: "\(intf.prefix)": {}
        }
    }
}
/* ... omitted for brevity ... */
```

> **Important Note**
>
> You can refer to CUE's *References and Visibility* tutorial (linked in the *Further reading* section) for explanations about emitted values, references, and the use of underscores.

This file has references to an external CUE package called input, which provides the required input data for the data model in the preceding output. This separation of data templates and their inputs allows you to distribute these files separately and potentially have them come from different sources. CUE provides a guarantee that the result is always the same, no matter the order you follow to assemble those files.

Data input

Now, let's see how we define and provide inputs to the preceding data model. We use the same data structure we used in *Chapters 6*, *Configuration Management*, and *Chapter 7*, *Automation Frameworks*, in a YAML file (`input.yaml`), which for the `cvx` lab device looks as follows:

```
# input.yaml
asn: 65002
loopback:
  ip: "198.51.100.2"
uplinks:
  - name: "swp1"
    prefix: "192.0.2.3/31"
peers:
  - ip: "192.0.2.2"
    asn: 65001
```

Using CUE, we can validate that this input data is correct by building a corresponding object and introducing constraints, for example, a valid ASN range or IPv4 prefix format. CUE allows you to define extra values directly inside the schema definition, either by hardcoding defaults (`input.VRFs`) or referencing other values from the same context (`input.LoopbackIP`):

```
package input

import (
    "net"
)

asn: <=65535 & >=64512
loopback: ip: net.IPv4 & string
uplinks: [...{
    name:   string
    prefix: net.IPCIDR & string
```

```
}]
peers: [...{
    ip:  net.IPv4 & string
    asn: <=65535 & >=64512
}]
LoopbackIP: "\(loopback.ip)/32"
VRFs: [{name: "default"}]
```

In the main function of the example program, we use the `importInput` helper function to read the input YAML file and generate a corresponding CUE file:

```
import "cuelang.org/go/cue/load"

func main() {
    err := importInput()
    /* ... <continues next > ... */
}
```

The program saves the resulting file as `input.cue` in the local directory. The implementation details of this function are not too important as you can perform the same action from the command line with `cue import input.yaml -p input`.

At this stage, we can validate that our input conforms to the schema and constraints shown earlier. For example, if we had set the `asn` value in `input.yaml` to something outside of the expected range, CUE would've caught and reported this error:

```
ch08/cue$ cue eval network.automation:input -c
asn: invalid value 10 (out of bound >=64512):
    ./schema.cue:7:16
    ./input.cue:3:6
```

Device configuration

Now we have all the pieces in place to configure our network device. We produce the final configuration instance by compiling the template defined in the `cvx` package into a concrete CUE value. We do this in three steps.

First, we load all CUE files from the local directory, specifying the name of the package containing the template (`cvx`):

```
func main() {
    /* ... <continues from before > ... */
    bis := load.Instances([]string{"."}, &load.Config{
        Package: "cvx",
    })
    /* ... <continues next > ... */
}
```

Second, we compile all loaded files into a CUE value, which resolves all imports and combines the input with the template:

```
func main() {
    /* ... <continues from before > ... */
    ctx := cuecontext.New()
    i := ctx.BuildInstance(instances[0])
    if i.Err() != nil {
        msg := errors.Details(i.Err(), nil)
        fmt.Printf("Compile Error:\n%s\n", msg)
    }
    /* ... <continues next > ... */
}
```

Finally, we validate that we can resolve all references and that the input provides all the required fields:

```
func main() {
    /* ... <continues from before > ... */
    if err := i.Validate(
        cue.Final(),
        cue.Concrete(true),
    ); err != nil {
        msg := errors.Details(err, nil)
        fmt.Printf("Validate Error:\n%s\n", msg)
    }
    /* ... <continues next > ... */
}
```

Once we know the CUE value is concrete, we can safely marshal it into JSON and send it directly to the `cvx` device. The body of the `sendBytes` function implements the three-stage commit process we discussed in *Chapter 6, Configuration Management*:

```
func main() {
    /* ... <continues from before > ... */
    data, err := e.MarshalJSON()
    // check error

    if err := sendBytes(data); err != nil {
        log.Fatal(err)
    }

    log.Printf("Successfully configured the device")
}
```

You can find the full program in the `ch08/cue` directory (refer to the *Further reading* section) of this book's GitHub repository (refer to the *Further reading* section). The same directory includes the complete version of the CUE files with a data template and input schema and the input YAML file. Successful execution of this program should produce an output like this:

```
ch08/cue$ go run main.go
main.go:140: Created revisionID: changeset/
cumulus/2022-05-25_20.56.51_KF9A
{
  "state": "apply",
  "transition": {
    "issue": {},
    "progress": ""
  }
}
main.go:69: Successfully configured the device
```

Keep in mind that although we focus on CUE's Go API in this chapter, you can do the same set of actions using the CUE CLI (executable binary). This even includes the three-stage commit to submit and apply the `cvx` configuration. Using the built-in CUE scripting language, you can define any sequence of tasks, such as making HTTP calls or checking and parsing responses. You can save these actions or tasks in a special *tool* file and they automatically become available in the `cue` binary. You can read more about this in the `ch08/cue` readme document and find example source code in the `ch08/cue/cue_tool.cue` file (refer to the *Further reading* section).

CUE has many use cases outside of what we've just described and different open source projects such as **Istio** and **dagger.io** (refer to the *Further reading* section) have adopted it and use it in their products. We encourage you to explore other CUE use cases beyond what's covered in this book, as well as similar configuration languages such as **Jsonnet** and **Dhall** (refer to the *Further reading* section).

We've covered a few different ways of interacting with an OpenAPI provider. For the rest of this chapter, we'll focus on YANG-based APIs. The first one we'll introduce is a JSON-RPC interface implementation from Nokia.

JSON-RPC

JSON-RPC is a lightweight protocol you can use to exchange structured data between a client and a server. It can work over different transport protocols, but we'll focus only on HTTP. Although JSON-RPC is a standard, it only defines the top-level RPC layer, while payloads and operations remain specific to each implementation.

In this section, we'll show how to use Nokia-specific YANG models to configure the srl device from our lab topology, as SR Linux supports sending and receiving YANG payloads over JSON-RPC (refer to the *Further reading* section).

We'll try to avoid building YANG data payloads manually or relying on traditional text templating methods. The sheer size of some YANG models, as well as model deviations and augmentations, make it impossible to build the payloads manually. To do this at scale, we need to rely on a programmatic approach to build configuration instances and retrieve state data. This is where we use openconfig/ygot (YANG Go Tools) (refer to the *Further reading* section)—a set of tools and APIs for automatic code generation from a collection of YANG models.

At a high level, the structure of the example program is analogous to the one in the *OpenAPI* section. *Figure 8.3* shows the building blocks of the program we'll review in this section:

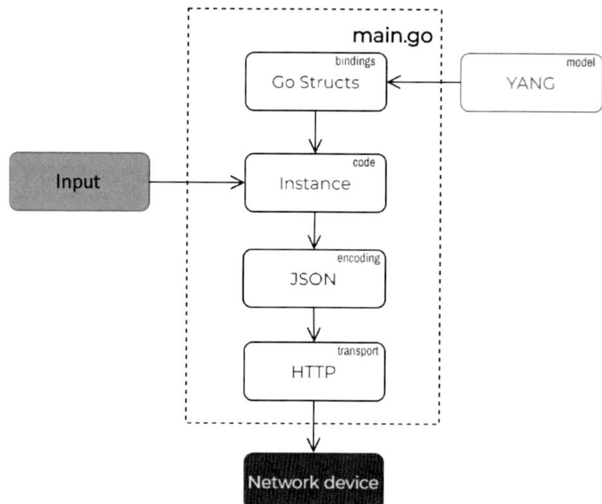

Figure 8.3 – Working with YANG data models

We'll start by combining the auto-generated Go bindings with the input data and building a configuration instance to provision the `srl` device.

Code generation

Starting from the top of the preceding diagram, the first step is to generate the corresponding Go code from a set of Nokia's YANG models (refer to the *Further reading* section). We'll only use a subset of Nokia's YANG models to generate the bindings to configure what we need, namely L3 interfaces, BGP, and route redistribution. This way, we keep the size of the generated Go package small and constrained to our specific use case.

Sadly, there is no universal rule for how to pinpoint the list of models you need apart from reading and understanding YANG models or reverse-engineering them from an existing configuration. Thankfully, Nokia has developed a YANG browser (refer to the *Further reading* section) that includes a pattern-matching search that highlights the relevant XPaths and can help you find the right set of YANG models.

Once we've identified which models we need, we can use the ygot generator tool to build a Go package based on them. We won't describe all the flags of this tool, as ygot's official documentation (refer to the *Further reading* section) covers them. Still, we want to highlight the most important options we'll use:

- `generate_fakeroot`: This encapsulates all generated Go data structures in a top-level *fake* root data structure called `Device` to join all modules in a common hierarchy. Because there isn't a YANG model that defines a universal root top-level container for all devices, network devices just add the YANG modules they support at the root (`/`). `ygot` represents the root via this *fake* root container.

- `path`: This flag helps `ygot` find and resolve any YANG data model imports.

The complete command to auto-generate the `srl` package and place it in the `./pkg/srl/` directory we used is this:

```
ch08/json-rpc$ go run \
  github.com/openconfig/ygot/generator \
    -path=yang \
    -generate_fakeroot -fakeroot_name=device \
    -output_file=pkg/srl/srl.go \
    -package_name=srl \
    yang/srl_nokia/models/network-instance/srl_nokia-bgp.yang \
    yang/srl_nokia/models/routing-policy/srl_nokia-routing-
policy.yang \
    yang/srl_nokia/models/network-instance/srl_nokia-ip-route-
tables.yang
```

Since the preceding command has several flags, it may be desirable to remember their exact set to make the build reproducible in the future. One alternative is to include it in a code build utility, such as make. Another, more Go-native option is to include it in the source code using the `//go:generate` directive, as you can see in the `ch08/json-rpc/main.go` file (refer to the *Further reading* section). Thus, you can generate the same `srl` repeatedly using this command:

```
ch08/json-rpc$ go generate ./...
```

Building configuration

Now that we've built a YANG-based Go package, we can create a programmatic instance of our desired configuration state and populate it. We do all this within Go, with the full flexibility of a general-purpose programming language at our disposal.

For example, we can design the configuration program as a set of methods, with the input model being the receiver argument. After we read and decode the input data, we create an empty *fake* root device we extend iteratively until we build the complete YANG instance with all the relevant values we want to configure.

The benefit of using a root device is that we don't need to worry about individual paths. We can send our payload to `/`, assuming that the resulting YANG tree hierarchy starts from the root:

```
import (
  api "json-rpc/pkg/srl"
)
```

```
// Input Data Model
type Model struct {
  Uplinks  []Link `yaml:"uplinks"`
  Peers    []Peer `yaml:"peers"`
  ASN      int    `yaml:"asn"`
  Loopback Addr   `yaml:"loopback"`
}

func main() {
  /* ... <omitted for brevity > ... */
  var input Model
  d.Decode(&input)

  device := &api.Device{}

  input.buildDefaultPolicy(device)
  input.buildL3Interfaces(device)
  input.buildNetworkInstance(device)
  /* ... <continues next (main) > ... */
}
```

The preceding code calls three methods on input. Let's zoom in on `buildNetworkInstance`, responsible for L3 routing configuration. This method is where we define a *network instance*, which is a commonly used abstraction for **VPN Routing and Forwarding** (VRF) instances and **Virtual Switch Instances** (VSIs). We create a new network instance from the top-level root device to ensure we attach it to the top of the YANG tree:

```
func (m *Model) buildNetworkInstance(dev *api.Device) error {
  ni, err := dev.NewNetworkInstance(defaultNetInst)
  /* ... <continues next (buildNetworkInstance) > ... */
}
```

In the next code snippet, we move all uplinks and a loopback interface into the newly created network instance by defining each subinterface as a child of the default network instance:

```
func (m *Model) buildNetworkInstance(dev *api.Device) error {
  // ... <continues from before (buildNetworkInstance) >
  links := m.Uplinks
```

```
    links = append(
      links,
      Link{
        Name:   srlLoopback,
        Prefix: fmt.Sprintf("%s/32", m.Loopback.IP),
      },
    )
    for _, link := range links {
      linkName := fmt.Sprintf("%s.%d", link.Name,
                                  defaultSubIdx)
      ni.NewInterface(linkName)
    }
    /* ... <continues next (buildNetworkInstance) > ... */
  }
```

Next, we define the global BGP settings by manually populating the BGP struct and attaching it to the `Protocols.Bgp` field of the `default` network instance:

```
  func (m *Model) buildNetworkInstance(dev *api.Device) error {
    // ... <continues from before (buildNetworkInstance) >
    ni.Protocols =
    &api.SrlNokiaNetworkInstance_NetworkInstance_Protocols{
      Bgp:
      &api.
      SrlNokiaNetworkInstance_NetworkInstance_Protocols_Bgp{
        AutonomousSystem: ygot.Uint32(uint32(m.ASN)),
        RouterId:         ygot.String(m.Loopback.IP),
        Ipv4Unicast:
        &api.
  SrlNokiaNetworkInstance_NetworkInstance_Protocols_Bgp_
  Ipv4Unicast{
          AdminState: api.SrlNokiaBgp_AdminState_enable,
        },
      },
    }
    /* ... <continues next (buildNetworkInstance) > ... */
  }
```

The final part of the configuration is BGP neighbors. We iterate over a list of peers defined in the input data model and add a new entry under the BGP struct we set up earlier:

```
func (m *Model) buildNetworkInstance(dev *api.Device) error {
  // ... <continues from before (buildNetworkInstance) >
  ni.Protocols.Bgp.NewGroup(defaultBGPGroup)
  for _, peer := range m.Peers {
    n, err := ni.Protocols.Bgp.NewNeighbor(peer.IP)
    // check error
    n.PeerAs = ygot.Uint32(uint32(peer.ASN))
    n.PeerGroup = ygot.String(defaultBGPGroup)
  }
  /* ... <continues next (buildNetworkInstance) > ... */
}
```

When we finish populating the Go structs, we make sure that all provided values are correct and match the YANG constraints. We can do this with a single call to the `Validate` method on the parent container:

```
func (m *Model) buildNetworkInstance(dev *api.Device) error {
    /* ... <continues from before (buildNetworkInstance) > ...
*/
    if err := ni.Validate(); err != nil {
        return err
    }
    return nil
}
```

Device configuration

Once we have populated a YANG model instance with all the input values, the next step is to send it to the target device. We do this in a few steps:

1. We use a `ygot` helper function to produce a map from the current YANG instance. This map is ready to be serialized into JSON according to the rules defined in RFC7951.
2. We use the standard `encoding/json` library to build a single JSON-RPC request that updates the entire YANG tree with our configuration changes.

3. Using the standard `net/http` package, we send this request to the `srl` device:

```
func main() {
    /* ... <continues from before (main) > ... */
    v, err := ygot.ConstructIETFJSON(device, nil)
    // check error

    value, err := json.Marshal(RpcRequest{
        Version: "2.0",
        ID:      0,
        Method:  "set",
        Params: Params{
            Commands: []*Command{
                {
                    Action: "update",
                    Path:   "/",
                    Value:  v,
                },
            },
        },
    })
    // check error

    req, err := http.NewRequest(
        "POST",
        hostname,
        bytes.NewBuffer(value),
    )
    resp, err := client.Do(req)
     // check error
    defer resp.Body.Close()

    if resp.StatusCode != http.StatusOK {
        log.Printf("Status: %s", resp.Status)
    }
```

You can find the complete program that configures the srl device in the `ch08/json-rpc` directory (refer to the *Further reading* section) of this book's GitHub repository. To run it, `cd` into this folder and run the following command:

```
ch08/json-rpc$ go run main.go
2022/04/26 13:09:03 Successfully configured the device
```

This program only verifies that we executed the RPC successfully; it doesn't yet check to confirm that it had the desired effect, which we will discuss later in this chapter. As with most HTTP-based protocols, a single RPC is a single transaction, so you can assume the target device applied the changes, as long as you receive a successful response. It's worth mentioning that some JSON-RPC implementations have more session control functions that allow multistage commits, rollbacks, and other features.

In the following section, we'll take a similar approach of configuring a network device based on its YANG models but introduce a couple of twists to show OpenConfig models and the RESTCONF API.

RESTCONF

The IETF designed RESTCONF as an HTTP-based alternative to NETCONF that offers **Create, Read, Update, and Delete** (**CRUD**) operations on a conceptual datastore containing YANG-modeled data. It may lack some NETCONF features, such as different datastores, exclusive configuration locking, and batch and rollback operations, but the exact set of supported and unsupported features depends on the implementation and network device capabilities. That said, because it uses HTTP methods and supports JSON encoding, RESTCONF reduces the barrier of entry for external systems to integrate and inter-operate with a network device.

RESTCONF supports a standard set of CRUD operations through HTTP methods: POST, PUT, PATCH, GET, and DELETE. RESTCONF builds HTTP messages with the YANG XPath translated into a REST-like URI and it transports the payload in the message body. Although RESTCONF supports both XML and JSON encoding, we will only focus on the latter, with the rules of the encoding defined in RFC7951. We'll use Arista's EOS as a test device, which has its RESTCONF API enabled when launching the lab topology.

The structure of the program we'll create in this section is the same as for the JSON-RPC example illustrated in *Figure 8.3*.

Code generation

The code generation process is almost the same as the one we followed in the *JSON-RPC* section. We use openconfig/ygot (refer to the *Further reading* section) to generate a Go package from a set of YANG models that EOS supports. But there are a few notable differences that are worth mentioning before moving forward:

- Instead of vendor-specific YANG models, we use vendor-neutral OpenConfig models, which Arista EOS supports.
- When generating Go code with openconfig/ygot (refer to the *Further reading* section), you might run into situations when more than one model is defined in the same namespace. In those cases, you can use the `-exclude_modules` flag to ignore a certain YANG model without having to remove its source file from the configured search path.
- We enable OpenConfig path compression to optimize the generated Go code by removing the YANG containers containing `list` nodes. Refer to the `ygen` library design documentation for more details (*Further reading*).
- We also show an alternative approach where we don't generate a *fake* root device. As a result, we can't apply all the changes in a single RPC. Instead, we have to make more than one HTTP call, each with its own unique URI path.

Before we can generate the Go code, we need to identify the supported set of Arista YANG models (refer to the *Further reading* section) and copy them into the `yang` directory. We use the following command to generate the `eos` Go package from that list of models:

```
ch08/restconf$ go run github.com/openconfig/ygot/generator \
  -path=yang \
  -output_file=pkg/eos/eos.go \
  -compress_paths=true \
  -exclude_modules=ietf-interfaces \
  -package_name=eos \
  yang/openconfig/public/release/models/bgp/openconfig-bgp.yang
\
  yang/openconfig/public/release/models/interfaces/openconfig-
if-ip.yang \
  yang/openconfig/public/release/models/network-instance/
openconfig-network-instance.yang \
  yang/release/openconfig/models/interfaces/arista-intf-
augments-min.yang
```

For the same reasons we described in the *JSON-RPC* section, we can also embed this command into the Go source code to generate the same Go package using the following command instead:

```
ch08/restconf$ go generate ./...
```

Building configuration

In this example, we won't apply all changes in a single HTTP call so that we can show you how to update a specific part of a YANG tree without affecting other, unrelated parts. In the preceding section, we worked around that by using an `Update` operation, which merges the configuration we send with the existing configuration on the device.

But in certain cases, we want to avoid the *merge* behavior and ensure that only the configuration we send is present on the device (declarative management). For that, we could've imported all existing configurations and identified the parts that we want to keep or replace before sending a new configuration version to the target device. Instead, we create a configuration for the specific parts of a YANG tree via a series of RPCs.

To simplify RESTCONF API calls, we create a special `restconfRequest` type that holds a URI path and a corresponding payload to send to the device. The `main` function starts with parsing the inputs for the data model and preparing a variable to store a set of RESTCONF RPCs:

```
type restconfRequest struct {
    path    string
    payload []byte
}

func main() {
    /* ... <omitted for brevity > ... */
    var input Model
    err = d.Decode(&input)
    // check error

    var cmds []*restconfRequest
    /* ... <continues next > ... */
}
```

As in the JSON-RPC example, we build the desired configuration instance in a series of method calls. This time, each method returns one `restConfRequest` that has enough details to build an HTTP request:

```
func main() {
    /* ... <continues from before > ... */
    l3Intfs, err := input.buildL3Interfaces()
    // check error
    cmds = append(cmds, l3Intfs...)
```

```
    bgp, err := input.buildBGPConfig()
    // check error
    cmds = append(cmds, bgp)

    redistr, err := input.enableRedistribution()
    // check error
    cmds = append(cmds, redistr)
    /* ... <continues next > ... */
}
```

Let's examine one of these methods that creates a YANG configuration from our inputs. The `enableRedistribution` method generates a configuration to enable redistribution between a directly connected table and the BGP **Routing Information Base** (**RIB**). OpenConfig defines a special `TableConnection` struct that uses a pair of YANG enums to identify the redistribution source and destination:

```
const defaultNetInst = "default"

func (m *Model) enableRedistribution() (*restconfRequest,
error) {
    netInst := &api.NetworkInstance{
        Name: ygot.String(defaultNetInst),
    }

    _, err := netInst.NewTableConnection(
        api.OpenconfigPolicyTypes_INSTALL_PROTOCOL_TYPE_
DIRECTLY_CONNECTED,
        api.OpenconfigPolicyTypes_INSTALL_PROTOCOL_TYPE_BGP,
        api.OpenconfigTypes_ADDRESS_FAMILY_IPV4,
    )

    /* ... <omitted for brevity > ... */
    value, err := ygot.Marshal7951(netInst)
    // check error

    return &restconfRequest{
        path: fmt.Sprintf(
```

```
            "/network-instances/network-instance=%s",
            defaultNetInst,
        ),
        payload: value,
    }, nil
}
```

The rest of the code in *Figure 8.3* shows the building blocks of the program we review in this section.

Device configuration

Once we've prepared all the required RESTCONF RPCs, we can send them to the device. We iterate over each `restconfRequest` and pass it to a helper function, catching any returned errors.

The `restconfPost` helper function has just enough code to build an HTTP request using the `net/http` package and send it to the `ceos` device:

```
const restconfPath = "/restconf/data"

func restconfPost(cmd *restconfRequest) error {
  baseURL, err := url.Parse(
    fmt.Sprintf(
      "https://%s:%d%s",
      ceosHostname,
      defaultRestconfPort,
      restconfPath,
    ),
  )
  // return error if not nil
  baseURL.Path = path.Join(restconfPath, cmd.path)
  req, err := http.NewRequest(
    "POST",
    baseURL.String(),
    bytes.NewBuffer(cmd.payload),
  )
  // return error if not nil
  req.Header.Add("Content-Type", "application/json")
  req.Header.Add(
    "Authorization",
```

```
        "Basic "+base64.StdEncoding.EncodeToString(
          []byte(
            fmt.Sprintf("%s:%s", ceosUsername, ceosPassword),
          ),
        ),
      )

    client := &http.Client{Transport: &http.Transport{
          TLSClientConfig:
            &tls.Config{
              InsecureSkipVerify: true
            },
        }
    }
    resp, err := client.Do(req)
    /* ... <omitted for brevity > ... */
}
```

You can find the complete program in the `ch08/restconf` directory (refer to the *Further reading* section) of this book's GitHub repository. Running it from a host running the lab topology should produce a similar output to this:

```
ch08/restconf$ go run main.go
2022/04/28 20:49:16 Successfully configured the device
```

At this point, we should have all three nodes of our lab topology fully configured. Still, we haven't confirmed that what we've done has had the desired effect. In the next section, we'll go through a process of state validation and show how you can do it using network APIs.

State validation

In the last three sections of this chapter, we pushed device configs without verifying that the configuration changes had the desired effect. This is because we need all devices configured before we can validate the resulting converged operational state. Now, with all the code examples from the *OpenAPI*, *JSON-RPC*, and *RESTCONF* sections executed against the lab topology, we can verify whether we achieved our configuration intent—establish end-to-end reachability between loopback IP addresses of all three devices.

In this section, we'll use the same protocols and modeling language we used earlier in this chapter to validate that each lab device can see the loopback IP address of the other two lab devices in its

Forwarding Information Base (**FIB**) table. You can find the complete code for this section in the `ch08/state` directory (refer to the *Further reading* section) of this book's GitHub repository. Next, we'll examine a single example of how you can do this with Arista's cEOS (`ceos`) lab device.

Operational state modeling

One thing we need to be mindful of when talking about the operational state of a network element is the difference between the applied and the derived state, as described by the YANG operational state IETF draft (refer to the *Further reading* section). The former refers to the currently active device configuration and should reflect what an operator has already applied. The latter is a set of read-only values that result from the device's internal operations, such as CPU or memory utilization, and interaction with external elements, such as packet counters or BGP neighbor state. Although we aren't explicitly mentioning it when we're talking about an operational state, assume we're referring to the derived state unless we state otherwise.

Historically, there've been different ways to model the device's operational state in YANG:

- You could either enclose everything in a top-level container or read from a separate `state` datastore, completely distinct from the `config` container/datastore we use for configuration management.
- Another way is to create a separate `state` container for every YANG sub-tree alongside the `config` container. This is what the YANG operational state IETF draft (refer to the *Further reading* section) describes.

Depending on which approach you use, you may need to adjust how you construct your RPC request. For example, the `srl` device needs an explicit reference to the `state` datastore. What we show in the next code example is the alternative approach, where you retrieve a part of the YANG sub-tree and extract the relevant state information from it.

It's worth noting that OpenAPI is less strict about the structure and composition of its models and the state may come from a different part of a tree or require a specific query parameter to reference the operational datastore, depending on the implementation.

Operational state processing

Configuration management workflows typically involve the processing of some input data to generate a device-specific configuration. This is a common workflow that we often use to show the capabilities of an API. But there is an equally important workflow that involves operators retrieving state data from a network device, which they process and verify. In that case, the information flows in the opposite direction—from a network device to a client application.

At the beginning of this chapter, we discussed the configuration management workflow, so now we want to give a high-level overview of the state retrieval workflow:

1. We start by querying a remote API endpoint, represented by a set of URL and HTTP query parameters.
2. We receive an HTTP response, which has a binary payload attached to it.
3. We unmarshal this payload into a Go struct that follows the device's data model.
4. Inside this struct, we look at the relevant parts of the state we can extract and evaluate.

The following code snippet from the `ch08/state` program (refer to the *Further reading* section) is a concrete example of this workflow. The program structure follows the same pattern we described in the *State validation* section of *Chapter 6, Configuration Management*. Hence, in this chapter, we'll only zoom in on the most relevant part—the `GetRoutes` function, which connects to the `ceos` device and retrieves the content of its routing table.

It starts by building an HTTP request with the device-specific login information:

```
func (r CEOS) GetRoutes(wg *sync.WaitGroup) {
  client := resty.NewWithClient(&http.Client{
    Transport: &http.Transport{
      TLSClientConfig: &tls.Config{
        InsecureSkipVerify: true},
    },
  })
  client.SetBaseURL("https://" + r.Hostname + ":6020")
  client.SetBasicAuth(r.Username, r.Password)

  resp, err := client.R().
    SetHeader("Accept", "application/yang-data+json").
    Get(fmt.Sprintf("/restconf/data/network-instances/network-
instance=%s/afts", "default"))
  /* ... <continues next > ... */
}
```

The **Abstract Forwarding Table** (**AFT**) in the code example is an OpenConfig representation of the FIB (routing) table and the GET API call retrieves a JSON representation of the default **Virtual Routing and Forwarding** (**VRF**) routing table.

Next, we create an instance of the Go struct corresponding to the part of the YANG tree we queried and pass it to the `Unmarshal` function for deserialization. The resulting Go struct now has one `Ipv4Entry` value for each entry in the default FIB and we store that list of prefixes in the `out` slice:

```
import eosAPI "restconf/pkg/eos"

func (r CEOS) GetRoutes(wg *sync.WaitGroup) {
  /* ... <continues from before > ... */

  response := &eosAPI.NetworkInstance_Afts{}
  err := eosAPI.Unmarshal(resp.Body(), response)
  // process error

  out := []string{}
  for key := range response.Ipv4Entry {
    out = append(out, key)
  }
  /* ... <omitted for brevity > ... */

  go checkRoutes(r.Hostname, out, expectedRoutes, wg)
}
```

In this example, we import the `eos` package (`restconf/pkg/eos`) we auto-generated in the *RESTCONF* section of this chapter, which lives outside the root directory of this program. To do this, we add the `replace restconf => ../restconf/` instruction to this program's `go.mod` file (`ch08/state/go.mod`; refer to the *Further reading* section).

For the remaining lab devices, we follow a similar state retrieval workflow. The only difference is in the YANG paths and the model-based Go structs we use for deserialization. You can find the full program code in the `ch08/state` directory (refer to the *Further reading* section) of this book's GitHub repository.

In this chapter, we have covered network APIs based on HTTP version 1.1 that use common encoding formats, such as JSON. Although HTTP is still very popular and this is unlikely to change soon, it has its own limitations that may manifest themselves in large-scale deployments. HTTP 1.1 is a text-based protocol, which means it's not efficient on the wire and its client-server origins make it difficult to adapt it for bi-directional streaming. The next version of this protocol, HTTP/2, overcomes these shortcomings. HTTP/2 is the transport protocol of the gRPC framework, which is what we'll examine in the next section.

gRPC

Network automation opens a door that until recently seemed closed or at least prevented network engineers from reusing technologies that have had success in other areas, such as microservices or cloud infrastructure.

One of the most recent advances in network device management is the introduction of gRPC. We can use this high-performance RPC framework for a wide range of network operations, from configuration management to state streaming and software management. But performance is not the only thing that is appealing about gRPC. Just like with YANG and OpenAPI apps, gRPC auto-generates client and server stubs in different programming languages, which enables us to create an ecosystem of tools around the API.

In this section, we'll go over the following topics to help you understand the gRPC API better:

- Protobuf
- gRPC transport
- Defining gRPC services
- Configuring network devices with gRPC
- Streaming telemetry from a network device with gRPC

Protobuf

gRPC uses protobuf as its **Interface Definition Language** (**IDL**) to allow you to share structured data between remote software components that may be written in different programming languages.

When working with protobuf, one of the first steps is to model the information you're serializing by creating a protobuf file. This file has a list of *messages* defining the structure and type of data to exchange.

If we take the input data model we have been using throughout this book as an example and encode it in a `.proto` file, it would look something like this:

```
message Router {
  repeated Uplink uplinks = 1;
  repeated Peer peers = 2;
  int32 asn = 3;
  Addr loopback = 4;
}

message Uplink {
    string name = 1;
```

```
    string prefix = 2;
}

message Peer {
    string ip = 1;
    int32 asn = 2;
}

message Addr {
  string ip = 1;
}
```

Each field has an explicit type and a unique sequence number that identifies it within the enclosing message.

The next step in the workflow, just like with OpenAPI or YANG, is to generate bindings for Go (or any other programming language). For this, we use the protobuf compiler, protoc, which generates the source code with data structures and methods to access and validate different fields:

```
ch08/protobuf$ protoc --go_out=. model.proto
```

The preceding command saves the bindings in a single file, `pb/model.pb.go`. You can view the contents of this file to see what structs and functions you can use. For example, we automatically get this `Router` struct, which is what we had to define manually before:

```
type Router struct {
  Uplinks  []*Uplink
  Peers    []*Peer
  Asn      int32
  Loopback *Addr
}
```

Protobuf encodes a series of key-value pairs in a binary format similar to how routing protocols encode **Type-Length-Values (TLVs)**. But instead of sending the key name and a declared type for each field, it just sends the field number as the key with its value appended to the end of the byte stream.

As with TLVs, Protobuf needs to know the length of each value to encode and decode a message successfully. For this, Protobuf encodes a wire type in the 8-bit key field along with the field number that comes from the `.proto` file. The following table shows the wire types available:

Type	Meaning	Used For
0	Varint	int32, int64, uint32, uint64, sint32, sint64, bool, enum
1	64-bit	fixed64, sfixed64, double
2	Length-delimited	string, bytes, embedded messages, packed repeated fields
5	32-bit	fixed32, sfixed32, float

Table 8.1 – Protobuf wire types

This generates a dense message (small output) that a CPU can process faster compared to a JSON- or XML-encoded message. The downside is the message you generate is not human-readable in its native format and it's only meaningful if you have the message definition (proto file) to find out the name and type for each field.

Protobuf on the wire

One of the easiest ways to see how protobuf looks in a binary format is to save it into a file. In our book's GitHub repository, we have an example in the `ch08/protobuf/write` directory (refer to the *Further reading* section) that reads a sample `input.yaml` file and populates the data structure generated from the `.proto` file we discussed earlier. We then serialize and save the result into a file we name `router.data`. You can use the following command to execute this example:

```
ch08/protobuf/write$ go run protobuf
```

You can see the content of the generated protobuf message by viewing the file with `hexdump -C router.data`. If we group some bytes for convenience and refer to the proto definition file, we can make sense of the data, as shown in the following figure:

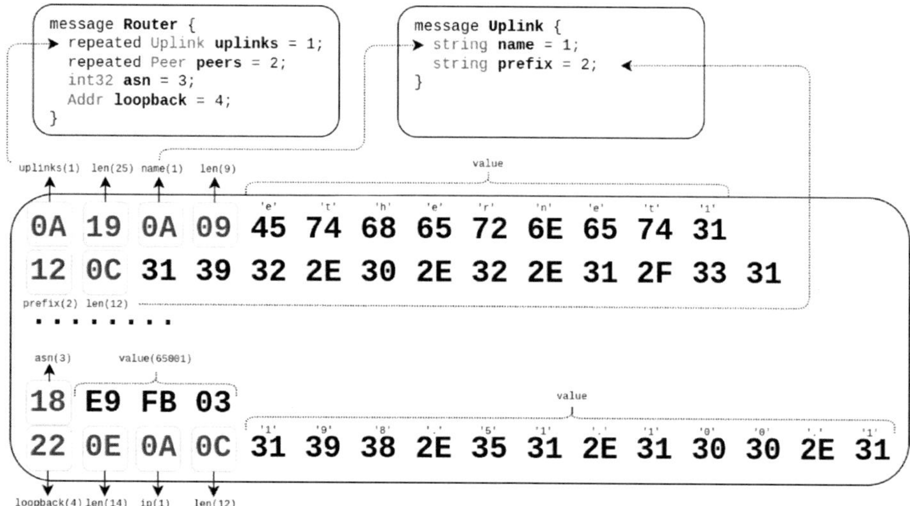

Figure 8.4 – Protobuf-encoded message

To give you an idea of how efficient the protobuf encoding is, we've included a couple of JSON files encoding the same data. The `router.json` file is a compact (space-free) JSON encoding. The second version, called `router_ident.json`, has the same JSON payload indented with extra spaces, which can happen if you generate JSON from a text template or use *pretty print* functions before sending the data over the network:

```
ch08/protobuf$ ls -ls router* | awk '{print $6, $10}'
108 router.data
454 router_indent.json
220 router.json
```

The difference between JSON and protobuf is quite stark and can become very important when transferring and encoding/decoding large datasets.

Now that we know some basics about gRPC data encoding, we can move on to the protocol used to transfer these messages.

gRPC transport

Besides efficient binary encoding and enabling simpler framing to serialize your data—compared to newline-delimited plain text—the gRPC framework also attempts to exchange those messages as efficiently as possible over the network.

While you can only process one request/response message at a time with HTTP/1.1, gRPC makes use of HTTP/2 to multiplex parallel requests over the same TCP connection. Another benefit of HTTP/2 is that it supports header compression. *Table 8.2* shows the various transport methods used by different APIs:

API	Transport	RPC/Methods
NETCONF	SSH	get-config, edit-config, commit, lock
RESTCONF	HTTP	GET, POST, DELETE, PUT
gRPC	HTTP/2	Unary, server streaming, client streaming, bidirectional streaming

Table 8.2 – API comparative table

Compared to the older network APIs, gRPC not only allows you to make unary or single requests, but it also supports full-duplex streaming. Both the client and server can stream data simultaneously, so you no longer need to work around the limitations of the traditional client-server mode of interaction.

Defining gRPC services

gRPC uses Protobuf to define statically typed services and messages in a file that we can use to generate the code for client and server applications to consume. gRPC abstracts the underlying transport and serialization details, allowing developers to focus on the business logic of their applications instead.

A gRPC service is a collection of RPCs that accept and return protobuf messages. In the following output, you can see a snippet from Cisco IOS XR's proto file called `ems_grpc.proto` (refer to the *Further reading* section). This file defines a gRPC service called `gRPCConfigOper` with several RPCs to perform a standard set of configuration management operations:

```
syntax = "proto3";

service gRPCConfigOper {

  rpc GetConfig(ConfigGetArgs) returns(stream ConfigGetReply)
{};

  rpc MergeConfig(ConfigArgs) returns(ConfigReply) {};

  rpc DeleteConfig(ConfigArgs) returns(ConfigReply) {};

  rpc ReplaceConfig(ConfigArgs) returns(ConfigReply) {};

  /* ... <omitted for brevity > ... */

  rpc CreateSubs(CreateSubsArgs) returns(stream
CreateSubsReply) {};
}
```

As well as the configuration management operations, this Cisco IOS XR protobuf definition includes a streaming telemetry subscription (`CreateSubs`) RPC. The message format for the request and response is also part of the `ems_grpc.proto` file (refer to the *Further reading* section). For example, to invoke the telemetry subscription RPC, the client has to send a `ConfigArgs` message and the server (router) should reply with a stream of `CreateSubsReply` messages.

Unlike with NETCONF, where **Request for Comments** (**RFC**) documents predefine all RPCs, networking vendors didn't initially push for a standard set of gRPC services. This flexibility comes with a cost, as any other vendor could define a similar service, but with different names and message types. Here, you can see a snippet from Juniper's telemetry protobuf file called `telemetry.proto` (refer to the *Further reading* section):

```
syntax = "proto3";

service OpenConfigTelemetry {
  rpc telemetrySubscribe(SubscriptionRequest) returns (stream
```

```
OpenConfigData) {}

  /* ... <omitted for brevity > ... */

  rpc getTelemetryOperationalState(GetOperationalStateRequest)
returns(GetOperationalStateReply) {}

  rpc getDataEncodings(DataEncodingRequest) returns
(DataEncodingReply) {}
}
```

This is something that the OpenConfig community is addressing with the definition of vendor-agnostic services, such as gNMI (`gnmi.proto`; refer to the *Further reading* section), which we will explore in the next chapter:

```
service gNMI {
  rpc Capabilities(CapabilityRequest) returns
(CapabilityResponse);

  rpc Get(GetRequest) returns (GetResponse);

  rpc Set(SetRequest) returns (SetResponse);

  rpc Subscribe(stream SubscribeRequest) returns (stream
SubscribeResponse);
}
```

Now, let's see how you can use these RPCs with Go.

Configuring network devices with gRPC

In our example program, we configure an IOS XR device with the `ReplaceConfig` RPC, defined in a service called `gRPCConfigOper`. You can find all the source code for this program in the `ch08/grpc` directory of this book's GitHub repository (refer to the *Further reading* section). You can use the following command to execute this program against a test device in Cisco's DevNet sandbox:

```
ch08/grpc$ go run grpc
```

Following the same configuration management workflow we've used throughout this chapter, we'll start by generating the code for the following gRPC service:

```
service gRPCConfigOper {
  rpc ReplaceConfig(ConfigArgs) returns(ConfigReply) {};
}

message ConfigArgs {
  int64 ReqId = 1;
  string yangjson = 2;
  bool   Confirmed = 3;
  uint32  ConfirmTimeout = 4;
}
```

One thing to remember when working with gRPC-based network APIs is that they might not define the full data tree natively as protobuf schemas. In the preceding example, one field defines a string called `yangjson` that expects a YANG-based JSON payload, not exploring any further what might be inside that "string." Carrying a YANG-based JSON payload is what we also did in the JSON-RPC and RESTCONF examples. In a sense, gRPC serves as a thin RPC wrapper in this example, not too different from JSON-RPC. We are still doing the configuration management work with YANG-based data structures.

Since we're now using both gRPC and YANG schemas, we have to use `protoc` together with `ygot` to generate their respective bindings. We run the `protoc` command to generate the code from the proto definition in `ch08/grpc/proto` (refer to the *Further reading* section) and `ygot` to generate code from a set of OpenConfig YANG models. You can find the exact set of commands in the `ch08/grpc/generate_code` file (refer to the *Further reading* section).

Before we can connect to the target device, we need to gather all the information we need to run the program, so we reuse the data structures from *Chapter 6, Configuration Management*, to store this data:

```
type Authentication struct {
  Username string
  Password string
}

type IOSXR struct {
  Hostname string
  Authentication
}
```

```
type xrgrpc struct {
  IOSXR
  conn *grpc.ClientConn
  ctx  context.Context
}
```

We start the `main` function of the program by populating the access credentials and processing the device configuration inputs, just like in other examples in the book:

```
func main() {
  iosxr := xrgrpc{
    IOSXR: IOSXR{
      Hostname: "sandbox-iosxr-1.cisco.com",
      Authentication: Authentication{
        Username: "admin",
        Password: "C1sco12345",
      },
    },
  }

  src, err := os.Open("input.yml")
  // process error
  defer src.Close()

  d := yaml.NewDecoder(src)
  var input Model
  err = d.Decode(&input)
  /* ... <continues next > ... */
}
```

Next, we use the `ygot` Go bindings from the `grpc/pkg/oc` package to prepare the `yangjson` payload. We build the BGP configuration in the `buildNetworkInstance` method in the same way we showed in the *JSON-RPC* section of this chapter. Once the `oc.Device` struct is fully populated, we serialize it into a JSON string:

```
func main() {
  /* ... <continues from before > ... */
```

```
    device := &oc.Device{}

    input.buildNetworkInstance(device)

    payload, err := ygot.EmitJSON(device,
    &ygot.EmitJSONConfig{
      Format: ygot.RFC7951,
      Indent: "  ",
      RFC7951Config: &ygot.RFC7951JSONConfig{
        AppendModuleName: true,
      },
    })
    /* ... <continues next > ... */
}
```

To simplify the interactions with the target device, we created a thin wrapper around the gRPC API. We define a handful of method receivers for the `xrgrpc` type that implement things such as initial connection establishment and deleting or replacing RPCs. This is how we connect and replace the target device's configuration:

```
func main() {
  /* ... <continues from before > ... */
  iosxr.Connect()
  defer router.conn.Close()

  iosxr.ReplaceConfig(payload)
  /* ... <continues next > ... */
}
```

Looking closer at the `ReplaceConfig` method, we can see exactly how to invoke the required RPC. We dynamically generate a random ID and populate the `ConfigArg` message with the YANG-based JSON payload that we generated with `ygot` a couple of steps before. The inner `ReplaceConfig` method is the one that the `protoc` command automatically generated for us:

```
func (x *xrgrpc) ReplaceConfig(json string) error {
  // Random int64 for id
  id := rand.Int63()

  // 'g' is the gRPC stub.
```

```
    g := xr.NewGRPCConfigOperClient(x.conn)

    // We send 'a' to the router via the stub.
    a := xr.ConfigArgs{ReqId: id, Yangjson: json}

    // 'r' is the result that comes back from the target.
    r, err := g.ReplaceConfig(x.ctx, &a)
    // process error
    return nil
}
```

The configuration payload we send in this case is a string blob, but we can also encode the content fields with protobuf if the target devices support this. This is what we'll examine next with a streaming telemetry example.

Streaming telemetry from a network device with gRPC

gRPC streaming capabilities allow network devices to send data over a persistent TCP connection either continuously (stream) or on demand (poll). We'll continue with the same program we started earlier and reuse the same connection we set up to configure a network device to subscribe to a telemetry stream.

Even though we initiated a connection to the Cisco IOS XR device, the data now flows in the opposite direction. This means we need to be able to decode the information we receive and there are two different ways of doing this.

Once we've configured the device, we request it to stream the operational state of all BGP neighbors. In the first scenario, we'll cover the case where you have the BGP neighbor proto definition to decode the messages you get. Then, we'll examine a less efficient option where a proto definition is unnecessary.

Decoding YANG-defined data with Protobuf

We use the `CreateSubs` RPC to subscribe to a telemetry stream. We need to submit the subscription ID we want to stream and choose an encoding option between `gpb` for protobuf or `gpbkv` for an option we'll explore at the end of this chapter. The following output shows the proto definition of this RPC and its message types:

```
service gRPCConfigOper {
  rpc CreateSubs(CreateSubsArgs) returns(stream
CreateSubsReply) {};
}
```

```
message CreateSubsArgs {
  int64 ReqId = 1;
  int64 encode = 2;
  string subidstr = 3;
  QOSMarking qos = 4;
  repeated string Subscriptions = 5;
}

message CreateSubsReply {
  int64 ResReqId = 1;
  bytes data = 2;
  string errors = 3;
}
```

Similar to the configuration part of the program, we create a helper function to submit the request to the router. The main difference is that now the reply is a data stream. We store the result of `CreateSubs` in a variable we call `st`.

For data streams, gRPC gives us the `Recv` method, which blocks until it receives a message. To continue processing in the main thread, we run an anonymous function in a separate goroutine that calls the auto-generated `GetData` method. This method returns the `data` field of each message we get and we send it over a channel (`b`) back to the main goroutine:

```
func (x *xrgrpc) GetSubscription(sub, enc string) (chan []byte,
chan error, error) {
  /* ... <omitted for brevity > ... */

  // 'c' is the gRPC stub.
  c := xr.NewGRPCConfigOperClient(x.conn)

  // 'b' is the bytes channel where telemetry is sent.
  b := make(chan []byte)

  a := xr.CreateSubsArgs{
        ReqId: id, Encode: encoding, Subidstr: sub}

  // 'r' is the result that comes back from the target.
  st, err := c.CreateSubs(x.ctx, &a)
  // process error
```

```
    go func() {
      r, err := st.Recv()
      /* ... <omitted for brevity > ... */
      for {
        select {
        /* ... <omitted for brevity > ... */
        case b <- r.GetData():
        /* ... <omitted for brevity > ... */
        }
      }
    }()
    return b, e, err
  }
```

The `data` field, and hence the data we receive in channel `b`, consist of arrays of bytes that we need to decode. We know this is a streaming telemetry message, so we use its proto-generated code to decode its fields. *Figure 8.5* shows an example of how we can get to BGP state information by following the proto file definitions:

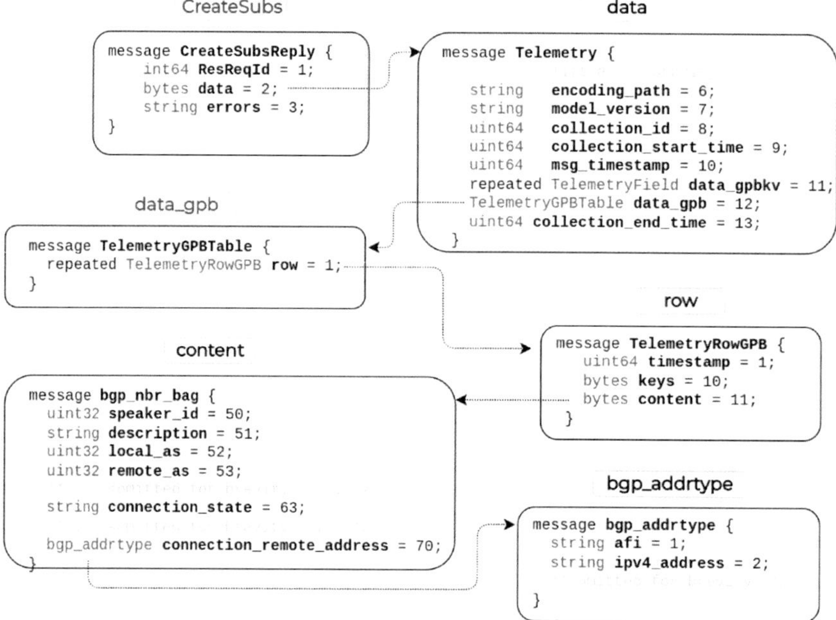

Figure 8.5 – Protobuf telemetry message (protobuf)

Back in the main goroutine, we listen out for what the `GetSubscription` channel returns and iterate over each message we get. We unmarshal the data received into a `Telemetry` message. At this point, we have access to the general telemetry data, so we can use the auto-generated functions to access some of its fields, such as the timestamp and the encoding path:

```
func main() {
  /* ... <omitted for brevity > ... */
  ch, errCh, err := router.GetSubscription("BGP", "gpb")
  // process error

  for msg := range ch {
    message := new(telemetry.Telemetry)
    proto.Unmarshal(msg, message)

    t := time.UnixMilli(int64(message.GetMsgTimestamp()))
    fmt.Printf(
      "Time: %v\nPath: %v\n\n",
      t.Format(time.ANSIC),
      message.GetEncodingPath(),
    )

    /* ... <continues next > ... */
  }
}
```

Following that, we extract the content of the `data_bgp` field to access the BGP data encoded with protobuf. Cisco IOS XR lists the items in rows, so for each one, we unmarshal the content into the auto-generated `BgpNbrBag` data structure, from where we can access all operational information of a BGP neighbor. This way, we get the connection state and the IPv4 address of the BGP peer, which we print to the screen:

```
func main() {
  for msg := range ch {
    /* ... <continues from before > ... */
    for _, row := range message.GetDataGpb().GetRow() {
      content := row.GetContent()
      nbr := new(bgp.BgpNbrBag)
      err = proto.Unmarshal(content, nbr)
```

```
        if err != nil {
          fmt.Printf("could decode Content: %v\n", err)
          return
        }
        state := nbr.GetConnectionState()
        addr := nbr.GetConnectionRemoteAddress().Ipv4Address

        fmt.Println("  Neighbor: ", addr)
        fmt.Println("  Connection state: ", state)
      }
    }
  }
```

If you don't have access to the BGP message definition (proto file), gRPC can still represent the fields with protobuf, but it has to add the name and value type for each one, so the receiving end can parse them. This is what we'll examine next.

Protobuf self-describing messages

While self-describing messages in a way defeat the purpose of protobuf by sending unnecessary data, we've included an example here to contrast how you could parse a message in this scenario:

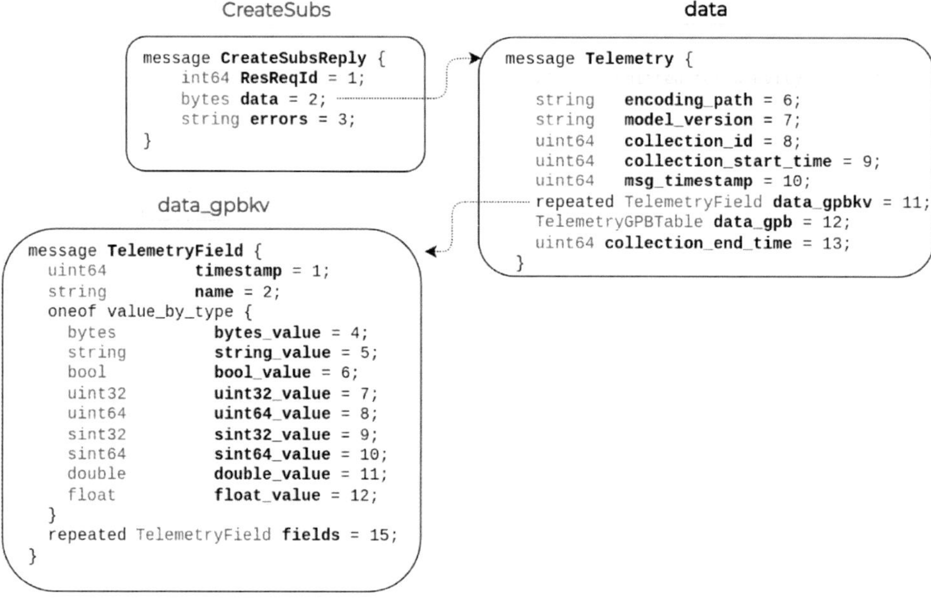

Figure 8.6 – Protobuf self-describing telemetry message (JSON)

The telemetry header is the same, but when you choose `gpbkv` as the encoding format, Cisco IOS XR sends the data in the `data_bgpkv` field instead:

```
func main() {

  for msg := range ch {
    message := new(telemetry.Telemetry)
    err := proto.Unmarshal(msg, message)
    /* ... <omitted for brevity > ... */

    b, err := json.Marshal(message.GetDataGpbkv())
    check(err)
    j := string(b)

    // https://go.dev/play/p/uyWenG-1Keu
    data := gjson.Get(
      j,
      "0.fields.0.fields.#(name==neighbor-address).ValueByType.
StringValue",
    )
    fmt.Println("  Neighbor: ", data)

    data = gjson.Get(
      j,
      "0.fields.1.fields.#(name==connection-state).ValueByType.
StringValue",
    )
    fmt.Println("  Connection state: ", data)
  }
}
```

At this point, what you have is a big JSON file you can navigate using a Go package of your preference. Here, we've used `gjson`. To test this program, you can rerun the same program we described earlier with an extra flag to enable the self-describing key-value messages:

```
ch08/grpc$ go run grpc -kvmode=true
```

While this method might seem less involved, not only do you compromise the performance benefits but also, by not knowing the Go data structures beforehand, it opens up room for bugs and typos, it prevents you from taking advantage of the auto-completion features of most IDEs, and it makes your code less explicit. All of that has a negative impact on code development and troubleshooting.

Summary

In this chapter, we explored different ways to use APIs and RPCs to interact with network devices. One common theme we saw throughout this chapter was having a model for any data we exchange. Although the network community has embraced YANG as the standard language to model network configuration and operational state data, the implementation differences across networking vendors still impede its wide adoption.

In the next chapter, we'll look at how OpenConfig tries to increase the adoption of declarative configuration and model-driven management and operations by defining a set of vendor-neutral models and protocols.

Further reading

- The book's GitHub repository: `https://github.com/PacktPublishing/Network-Automation-with-Go`
- OpenAPI versions: `https://swagger.io/specification/#appendix-a-revision-history`
- CUE: `https://cuelang.org/`
- `ch08/cue/template.cue`: `https://github.com/PacktPublishing/Network-Automation-with-Go/blob/main/ch08/cue/template.cue`
- CUE's *References and Visibility* tutorial: `https://cuelang.org/docs/tutorials/tour/references/`
- The `ch08/cue` directory: `https://github.com/PacktPublishing/Network-Automation-with-Go/blob/main/ch08/cue`
- `ch08/cue/cue_tool.cue`: `https://github.com/PacktPublishing/Network-Automation-with-Go/blob/main/ch08/cue/cue_tool.cue`
- Istio: `https://istio.io/`
- dagger.io: `https://dagger.io/`
- Jsonnet: `https://github.com/google/go-jsonnet`
- Dhall: `https://github.com/philandstuff/dhall-golang`
- JSON-RPC: `https://documentation.nokia.com/srlinux/SR_Linux_HTML_R21-11/SysMgmt_Guide/json-interface.html`
- openconfig/ygot: `https://github.com/openconfig/ygot`

- Nokia's YANG models: https://github.com/nokia/srlinux-yang-models
- The YANG browser: https://yang.srlinux.dev/v21.6.4/
- ygot's official documentation: https://github.com/openconfig/ygot#introduction
- The ch08/json-rpc/main.go file: https://github.com/PacktPublishing/Network-Automation-with-Go/blob/main/ch08/json-rpc/main.go
- The ch08/json-rpc directory: https://github.com/PacktPublishing/Network-Automation-with-Go/blob/main/ch08/json-rpc
- The yget library design documentation: https://github.com/openconfig/ygot/blob/master/docs/design.md#openconfig-path-compression
- Arista YANG models: https://github.com/aristanetworks/yang
- The ch08/restconf directory: https://github.com/PacktPublishing/Network-Automation-with-Go/tree/main/ch08/restconf
- The ch08/state directory: https://github.com/PacktPublishing/Network-Automation-with-Go/tree/main/ch08/state
- IETF draft: https://datatracker.ietf.org/doc/html/draft-openconfig-netmod-opstate-01
- The ch08/state program: https://github.com/PacktPublishing/Network-Automation-with-Go/tree/main/ch08/state
- ch08/state/go.mod: https://github.com/PacktPublishing/Network-Automation-with-Go/blob/main/ch08/state/go.mod
- The ch08/protobuf/write directory: https://github.com/PacktPublishing/Network-Automation-with-Go/tree/main/ch08/protobuf/write
- ems_grpc.proto: https://github.com/nleiva/xrgrpc/blob/master/proto/ems/ems_grpc.proto
- telemetry.proto: https://github.com/Juniper/jtimon/blob/master/telemetry/telemetry.proto
- gnmi.proto: https://github.com/openconfig/gnmi/blob/master/proto/gnmi/gnmi.proto
- ch08/grpc/proto: https://github.com/PacktPublishing/Network-Automation-with-Go/tree/main/ch08/grpc/proto
- ch08/grpc/generate_code: https://github.com/PacktPublishing/Network-Automation-with-Go/blob/main/ch08/grpc/generate_code

9
OpenConfig

OpenConfig is a group of network operators (see the *Further reading* section) with the common goal of streamlining the way we manage and operate networks. They welcome anyone operating a production network as a member and, more recently, have started to accept contributions from vendors when more than one of them implements the same feature (that they want to include in a YANG model).

Their initial focus was to create a set of vendor-neutral YANG data models based on common operational use cases and requirements from the field. This later expanded to include vendor-neutral **Remote Procedure Calls** (**RPCs**) for configuring, streaming telemetry, performing operational commands, and manipulating forwarding entries (see *Further reading*) on network devices. In this chapter, we will focus primarily on the OpenConfig RPCs, as we already covered YANG data models in *Chapter 8, Network APIs*.

One thing that sets OpenConfig apart from other similar initiatives is that they not only work publicly on the specifications but also write open source code that implements these specifications, helping you to interact with OpenConfig-compliant devices. They write most of these projects in Go, including but not limited to ygot, gNxI Tools, the gNMI collector, the gNMI CLI utility, the gNMI test framework, gRPC tunnels, and IS-IS LSDB parsing (see *Further reading*). We encourage you to explore those projects, especially the ones we do not cover in this book, as they target a wide range of network-related applications.

At the time of writing, OpenConfig includes four gRPC services:

- **gRPC Network Management Interface** (**gNMI**): For streaming telemetry and configuration management
- **gRPC Network Operations Interface** (**gNOI**): For executing operational commands on network devices
- **gRPC Routing Information Base Interface** (**gRIBI**): To let an external client inject routing entries on a network element
- **gRPC Network Security Interface** (**gNSI**): Infrastructure services for securing access to a compliant network device

In the following sections, we will examine the following common operational tasks:

- Device provisioning, with the gNMI `Set` RPC, to label correctly the primary and backup interfaces between two nodes in the lab topology
- Streaming telemetry, with the `Subscribe` RPC, where a Go program reacts to a gNMI telemetry stream to make changes to the network
- Network operations, with a `traceroute` example with the gNOI `Traceroute` RPC, to check that all the forwarding paths in the network are working as expected

Technical requirements

You can find the code examples for this chapter in the book's GitHub repository (see *Further reading*), in the `ch09` folder.

> **Important Note**
>
> We recommend you execute the Go programs in this chapter in a virtual lab environment. Refer to the appendix for prerequisites and instructions on how to build the fully configured network topology.

The first example we discuss in the following section explores gNMI to configure network devices with Go.

Device provisioning

In *Chapter 6, Configuration Management*, we discussed applying the desired configuration state on a network device. Network engineers routinely have to log in to network devices to provision new services, bring up new connections, or remove outdated configurations. We covered the different transport options available to configure network devices such as SSH or HTTP in the same chapter, and in *Chapter 8, Network APIs*, we added gRPC as another option.

We briefly touched on modeling network device configurations with a data modeling language such as YANG, so we could move from configuring networks with semi-structured vendor-specific CLI syntax to a model where we exchange structured data with the network to change its configuration state.

OpenConfig defines a gRPC service specifically for configuration management called gNMI. It aims to provide a common gRPC protobuf definition that any vendor can implement, alongside their existing proprietary gRPC services.

The protobuf definition for gNMI is as follows:

```
service gNMI {
    rpc Capabilities(CapabilityRequest) returns
```

```
(CapabilityResponse);
   rpc Get(GetRequest) returns (GetResponse);
   rpc Set(SetRequest) returns (SetResponse);
   rpc Subscribe(stream SubscribeRequest) returns (stream
SubscribeResponse);
}
```

gNMI particularly offers configuration management capabilities via the `Set` RPC that you can use to make changes on a target node. The gNMI specification (see *Further reading*) has extensive documentation on all available gNMI RPCs. In this section, we will focus on `Set`.

Set RPC

The `Set` RPC lets you change the state of a target network device. You do this by sending a `SetRequest` message that encodes all changes you want to make.

You can update, replace, or delete values in the data tree of the target device in a single transaction, using dedicated fields of the `SetRequest` message. This means that unless the target can apply every specified change, it must roll all of them back and return to its previous state. The following protobuf definition shows the options you have in a `SetRequest` message:

```
message SetRequest {
   Path prefix = 1;
   repeated Path delete = 2;
   repeated Update replace = 3;
   repeated Update update = 4;
   repeated gnmi_ext.Extension extension = 5;
}
```

The field called `Path` in `SetRequest` encodes a YANG data tree path. It's worth noting that gNMI is not limited to using OpenConfig YANG models; it works equally well with vendor-defined YANG models. gNMI describes the data tree path as a series of `PathElem` (path elements). Each one of these is a data tree node that has a name, and it may have one or more attributes (keys) associated with it:

```
message Path {
  string origin = 2;
  repeated PathElem elem = 3;
  string target = 4;
}

message PathElem {
```

```
  string name = 1;
  map<string, string> key = 2;
}
```

For instance, the `/interfaces/interface[name=Ethernet2]/config/description` path lets you set the description on the `Ethernet2` interface on a target device. The only data node in this case that has an attribute is `interface`, which needs a `name`. To configure an IPv4 address on the native VLAN in that same interface, you can use a path that looks like this: `/interfaces/interface[name=Ethernet2]/subinterfaces/subinterface[index=0]/ipv4/addresses/address[ip=192.0.2.2]`. In this case, you need to add the `subinterface` index, as the interface could have IP addresses on different sub-interfaces.

Once you have identified the data path, you need to build the content that has the new values you want to set on the target device, which is a data instance of a YANG schema. You only need this for `replace` and `update`. For `delete`, the path is enough to tell the target device what to remove from the configuration.

An `Update` message that you would use to send the values for either `replace` or `update` has a `Path` and `TypedValue` pair. The latter lets you encode the content in different formats:

```
message Update {
  Path path = 1;
  TypedValue val = 3;
  uint32 duplicates = 4;
}

message TypedValue {
  oneof value {
    string string_val = 1;
    int64 int_val = 2;
    uint64 uint_val = 3;
    bool bool_val = 4;
    bytes bytes_val = 5;
    double double_val = 14;
    ScalarArray leaflist_val = 8;
    google.protobuf.Any any_val = 9;
    bytes json_val = 10;
    bytes json_ietf_val = 11;
    string ascii_val = 12;
    bytes proto_bytes = 13;
```

```
    }
}
```

A value could be a string for an interface description, such as `PRIMARY: TO -> CVX:swp1` or a JSON value to describe the IPv4 address of an interface such as `{"config":{"ip":"192.0.2.2","prefix-length":31}}`.

Using gNMI to configure network interfaces

The virtual lab topology for this chapter, which you can bring up by running `make lab-full` from the root of this book's GitHub repository, has two connections between `ceos` and `cvx`. They have IPv4 addresses configured already, but they don't have a description that lets you identify the roles of these interfaces, whether they are the primary or the backup link:

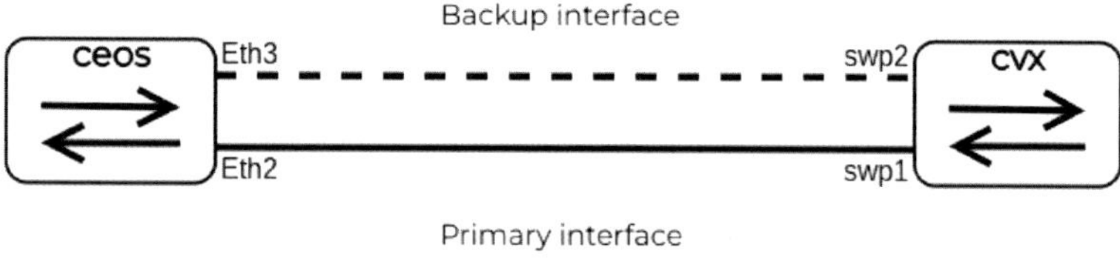

Figure 9.1 – A dual link between ceos and cvx

In the next example, we add a description to those interfaces on the `ceos` side via gNMI. To do this, we use the gNMIc package (`karimra/gnmic/api`). We chose gNMIc over the official gNMI package (`openconfig/gnmi`) because it's more developer-friendly and higher-level. It lets us conveniently encode the gNMI paths as strings, instead of Go data structures, as the gNMIc docs (see *Further reading*) describe. You can find the code for this example in the `ch09/gnmi` directory of this book's GitHub repository (see *Further reading*).

The gNMIc package has a `NewTarget` function that creates a new gNMI target device. In the following example, we wrap this function in the `createTarget` method:

```
func (r Router) createTarget() (*target.Target, error) {
	return api.NewTarget(
		api.Name("gnmi"),
		api.Address(r.Hostname+":"+r.Port),
		api.Username(r.Username),
		api.Password(r.Password),
		api.Insecure(r.Insecure),
	)
}
```

The first step in the code is to read the connection details from a YAML file (`input.yml`) to create this target device:

```
# input.yml
- hostname: clab-netgo-ceos
  port: 6030
  insecure: true
  username: admin
  password: admin
```

We store all target devices in the `Routers` data structure. In our case, we only have one device (`clab-netgo-ceos`) but the connection details are a list, so we could've added more devices if we wanted to. Now, with the target data, we use the `CreateGNMIClient` method to set up the underlying gRPC connection to the target device (`clab-netgo-ceos:6030`):

```
func main() {
  /* ... <omitted for brevity > ... */
  for _, router := range inv.Routers {
    tg, err := router.createTarget()
    // process error

    ctx, cancel := context.WithCancel(
    context.Background())
    defer cancel()

    err = tg.CreateGNMIClient(ctx)
    // process error
    defer tg.Close()
  /* ... <continues next > ... */
}
```

With the connection established, we now can send the `Set` requests. Another YAML file (`api-ceos.yml`) has a list of parameters for each request: `prefix`, `encoding`, `path`, and `value`. You can add `prefix` when you want to reduce the length of a path. In our Go program, we save this list of parameters in the `info` slice:

```
# api-ceos.yml
- prefix: "/interfaces/interface[name=Ethernet2]"
  encoding: "json_ietf"
```

```
  path: '/subinterfaces/subinterface[index=0]/ipv4/addresses/
address[ip=192.0.2.2]'
  value: '{"config":{"ip":"192.0.2.2","prefix-length":31}}'

- prefix: ""
  encoding: "json_ietf"
  path: '/interfaces/interface[name=Ethernet2]/config/
description'
  value: 'PRIMARY: TO -> CVX:swp1''
## ... <omitted for brevity > ... ##
```

The last step is to iterate over the `info` slice, build a `Set` request with the `NewSetRequest` function, and send it to the target device using the `Set` method:

```
func main() {
  /* ... <continues from before > ... */
    for _, data := range info {
      setReq, err := api.NewSetRequest(
              api.Update(
                    api.Path(data.Prefix+data.Path),
                    api.Value(data.Value, data.Encoding)),
      )
      // process error

      configResp, err := tg.Set(ctx, setReq)
      // process error

      fmt.Println(prototext.Format(configResp))
    }
  }
}
```

Here, `NewSetRequest` has only one `Update` message, but you could include several messages in a single request.

You get the following output when running this example:

```
ch09/gnmi$ go run main.go
response: {
```

```
path: {
  elem: {
    name: "interfaces"
  }
  elem: {
    name: "interface"
    key: {
      key: "name"
      value: "Ethernet2"
    }
  }
  elem: {
    name: "subinterfaces"
  }
  elem: {
    name: "subinterface"
    key: {
      key: "index"
      value: "0"
    }
  }
  elem: {
    name: "ipv4"
  }
  elem: {
    name: "addresses"
  }
  elem: {
    name: "address"
    key: {
      key: "ip"
      value: "192.0.2.2"
    }
  }
}
op: UPDATE
```

```
}
timestamp: 1660148355191641746

response: {
  path: {
    elem: {
      name: "interfaces"
    }
    elem: {
      name: "interface"
      key: {
        key: "name"
        value: "Ethernet2"
      }
    }
    elem: {
      name: "config"
    }
    elem: {
      name: "description"
    }
  }
  op: UPDATE
}
timestamp: 1660148355192866023
## ... <omitted for brevity > ... ##
```

What you see on the terminal screen are the `SetResponse` messages, containing the `path`, `response`, and `timestamp` values of the operation:

```
message SetResponse {
  Path prefix = 1;
  repeated UpdateResult response = 2;
  int64 timestamp = 4;
  repeated gnmi_ext.Extension extension = 5;
}
```

If you connect to the ceos device now, you will see the following in its running configuration:

```
interface Ethernet2
   description PRIMARY: TO -> CVX:swp1
   no switchport
   ip address 192.0.2.2/31
!
interface Ethernet3
   description BACKUP: TO -> CVX:swp2
   no switchport
   ip address 192.0.2.4/31
!
```

Configuring network devices is one of those repetitive tasks that most network engineers spend a good amount of time on, so automating this process has the potential to have a good return on investment.

The years of work of the OpenConfig working group, which released the official gNMI package (`openconfig/gnmi`), set the path for the emergence of other open source packages and libraries such as gNMIc (`karimra/gnmic`) and pyGNMI (`akarneliuk/pygnmi`), creating a community around these vendor-neutral gRPC services to drive consistent automation practices in our networks.

In the following section, we will cover another OpenConfig gRPC service that enhances your network visibility capabilities.

Streaming telemetry

Traditionally, network engineers have relied on the **Simple Network Management Protocol** (**SNMP**) to gather state information from network devices. Devices encode this information in a binary format using the **Abstract Syntax Notation One** (**ASN.1**) and send it to a receiver, typically a collector or a **Network Management System** (**NMS**). The latter would use one of the **Management Information Bases** (**MIBs**) to decode the received information and store it locally for further processing.

This has been the way we've done network monitoring for decades, but this approach has room for improvement:

- The limited number of vendor-neutral data models means that even the basic things require unique MIBs that you may need to update every time you do a major network OS upgrade.
- MIBs use a notation defined by a subset of ASN.1, which isn't the best way to structure values. It has no concept of lists or key-value pairs. Instead, you must implement these with indexed values and extra lookup tables.

- SNMP uses UDP as its transport protocol to avoid putting an extra burden on the collector. This means that you could miss some events completely, leaving blind spots in the stream of telemetry data.
- Since SNMP primarily relies on polling, we can only see aggregated values and may miss important state transitions.
- SNMP does not generally timestamp when a value changes. Collectors can only infer timing based on the time of collection.

gNMI offers a new approach to network monitoring via a dedicated `Subscribe` RPC. At the very least, it offers the same capabilities as SNMP but takes it further, making the protocol more feature-rich and versatile:

- One of the greatest improvements is telemetry streaming. Now, you can continuously receive any value of the operational YANG tree from a network device, which gives you better visibility into all state transitions along with their timestamps.
- You have a choice to receive telemetry data only when there is a change as opposed to a periodic transmission.
- Thanks to the underlying gRPC transport, gNMI supports both dial-in and dial-out connection methods and delivers messages using a reliable HTTP/2 protocol.
- OpenConfig defines vendor-neutral YANG models to describe the operational state of a network device, which enables clients to parse and process the received data from different vendors in a standard pipeline.

> **Important Note**
>
> Even with streaming telemetry, you are not necessarily getting an update for every counter increment. Network devices have local processes that periodically poll internal data stores to get the latest metrics or stats, such as interface packet counters, which they feed to their gNMI process. Hence, how real-time the data you receive is depends not only on how often you get streaming messages but also on the internal polling cadence. Still, you will probably see the most relevant system events, such as BGP state transitions, which you would otherwise miss with SNMP.

These features are just a subset of the gNMI capabilities. The gNMI specification (see *Further reading*) can serve as a good reference for all gNMI protocol features. Next, we examine the gNMI protobuf message for the telemetry service to help you understand how it works.

Subscribe RPC

gNMI defines a single RPC to subscribe to a telemetry stream. Network devices receive one or more `SubscribeRequest` messages and respond with a stream of `SubscribeResponse` messages:

```
service gNMI {
    rpc Subscribe(stream SubscribeRequest) returns (stream
SubscribeResponse);
}
```

gNMI clients have different options to control their telemetry subscriptions. The following figure shows the composition of the `SubscribeRequest` message, highlighting some of these options:

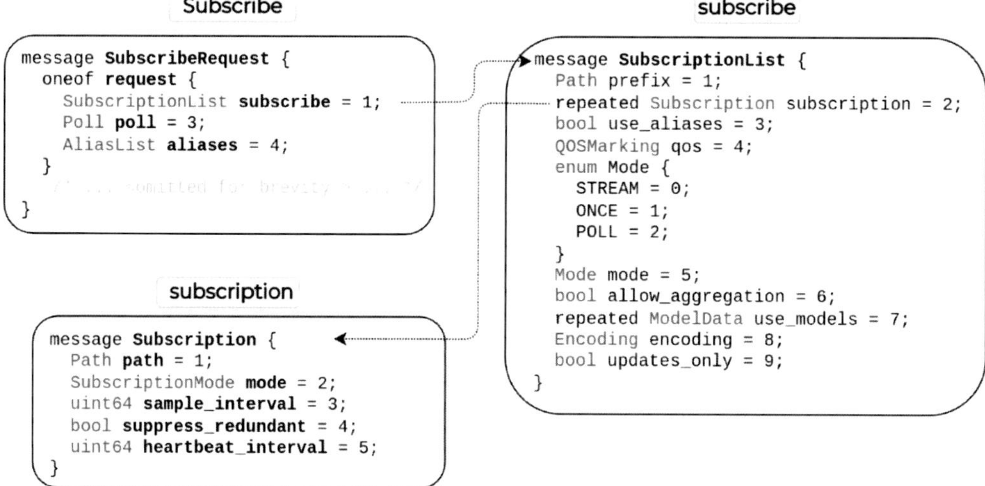

Figure 9.2 – gNMI subscribe protobuf messages

The most basic way to control the telemetry subscription is by specifying `Path` and `SubscriptionMode`:

- **Path**: References the part of the YANG tree you want to monitor. You can subscribe to anything, from the entire device state to just a single leaf value. It follows the gNMI path convention (see *Further reading*).
- **SubscriptionMode**: Determines whether to send the telemetry on-change or periodically:

```
enum SubscriptionMode {
    TARGET_DEFINED = 0;
    ON_CHANGE      = 1;
    SAMPLE         = 2;
}
```

In return, a network device sends you a stream of response messages with the following information:

- **TypedValue**: The most critical field, containing the actual telemetry value
- **Path**: The full gNMI path of the value, which identifies the unique YANG leaf node
- **timestamp**: To help you arrange and process received data in the right order or find out when a value last changed for those that do not change frequently:

```
message Notification {
      int64 timestamp = 1;
      Path prefix = 2;
      string alias = 3;
      repeated Update update = 4;
      repeated Path delete = 5;
      bool atomic = 6;
}

message Update {
      Path path = 1;
      TypedValue val = 3;
      uint32 duplicates = 4;
}
```

We are just scratching the surface of the `Subscribe` RPC. You can check the `gnmi.proto` file to see the complete set of protobuf messages and read the telemetry section of the gNMI specification (see *Further reading*) to get a better idea of the capabilities and features offered by the protocol. Here are some features you can learn about that we don't cover in this book:

- gNMI lets you poll or take an instant one-off (`ONCE`) snapshot of telemetry values.
- Some network devices can send several `Update` messages bundled in a single `SubscribeResponse`. This comes at the expense of reduced timestamp accuracy, since there's only a single timestamp for all transported values.
- If you are not interested in seeing every single value, you can let a network device aggregate those values.
- For values that different YANG models define, you can specify the definition you prefer to use.

Important Note

As with OpenConfig YANG models, the exact set of implemented features varies from vendor to vendor.

Streaming telemetry processing pipelines with gNMI

To receive or collect the data from a gNMI-compliant network device, you could use the Go gNMI client implementation from the official gNMI repository (see *Further reading*). Another alternative is gNMIc (see *Further reading*), which builds on top of the official gNMI client and provides more capabilities, such as data transformation and wide support of northbound interfaces.

gNMIc can serve as a link between a network device and a **Time-Series Database** (**TSDB**) or a message queue, as it can transform the received telemetry data into a format popular open source projects, such as Prometheus, InfluxDB, NATS, and Kafka, can understand. You can run gNMIc as a command-line tool to interact with network devices or as a daemon, subscribing to telemetry data and publishing it into a message queue or a database.

Event-manager sample program

Let's examine one example of a telemetry processing pipeline via an implementation of a primitive event-manager application. The goal of this program is to react to an increased packet rate by temporarily enabling a backup interface to redistribute incoming traffic. The following diagram depicts the high-level architecture of the telemetry processing pipeline and includes the following main components:

- A gNMIC process running as a daemon, collecting and processing network telemetry data
- A TSDB (Prometheus) storing the collected telemetry data
- AlertManager (see *Further reading*) processing alerts received from Prometheus and triggering external events
- A Go program that implements the event-manager business logic:

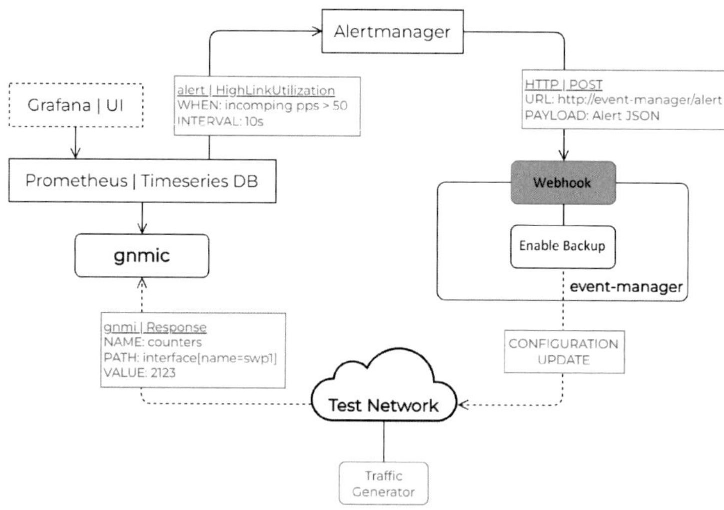

Figure 9.3 – The event-manager application

You can spin up these components with `make gnmic-start` from the root of this book's GitHub repository (see *Further reading*). This command starts the gNMIc daemon and brings up Prometheus, Grafana, and AlertManager using `docker-compose`. These applications now run alongside our test lab topology and interact with it over standard network interfaces:

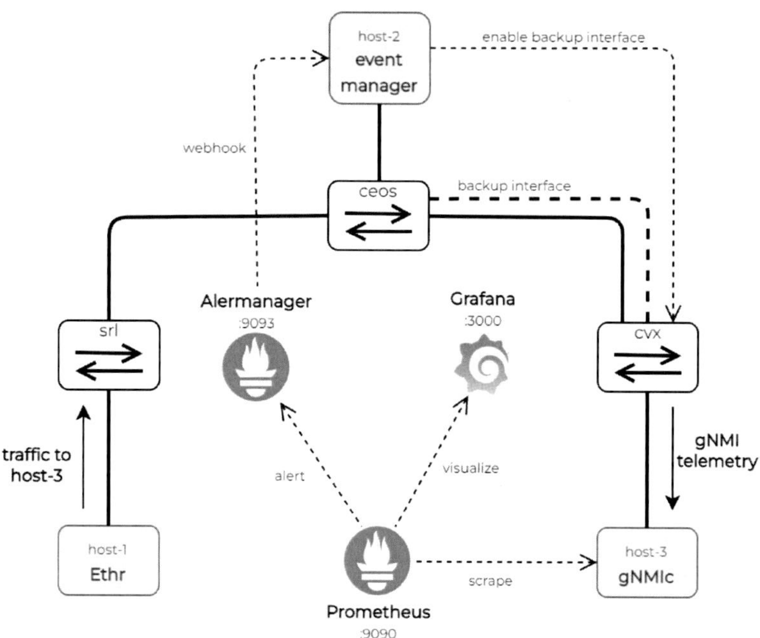

Figure 9.4 – The event-manager topology

We configured these applications using a series of files located in the `topo-full/workdir/` (see *Further reading*) directory of this book's GitHub repository (see *Further reading*). These files get mounted into their respective containers, as we define in the configuration files of either Containerlab (`topo.yml` – see *Further reading*) or Docker Compose (`docker-compose.yml` – see *Further reading*). Here's a brief description of the role these applications play in our setup:

- The gNMIc daemon process runs in `Host-3` of the test topology. It subscribes to telemetry data from the `cvx` device and exposes it as Prometheus-style metrics. We manage these settings in the `gnmic.yaml` file that looks like this:

```
targets:
 "clab-netgo-cvx:9339":
    username: cumulus
    password: cumulus
```

```
subscriptions:
  counters:
    target: netq
    paths:
      - /interfaces
    updates-only: true

outputs:
  prom-output:
    type: prometheus
    listen: ":9313"
```

- You can find the Prometheus configuration values in the `prometheus.yml` file. We configure it to scrape the gNMIc endpoint every 2 seconds and store the collected data in its TSDB:

```
scrape_configs:
  - job_name: 'event-trigger'
    scrape_interval: 2s
    static_configs:
      - targets: ['clab-netgo-host-3:9313']
```

- The same configuration file includes a reference to the alert definition file, called `alert.rules`, and the connection details of the AlertManager:

```
rule_files:
  - 'alert.rules'

alerting:
  alertmanagers:
  - scheme: http
    static_configs:
    - targets:
      - "alertmanager:9093"
```

- Inside of the `alert.rules` file, we define a single alert we call `HighLinkUtilization`. Every 10 seconds, Prometheus checks whether the incoming packet rate has exceeded a predefined threshold of 50 packets per 30-second interval, in which case it fires an alert and sends it to the AlertManager:

```
groups:
- name: thebook
  interval: 10s
  rules:
  - alert: HighLinkUtilization
    expr: rate(interfaces_interface_state_counters_in_
pkts[30s]) > 50
    for: 0m
    labels:
      severity: warning
    annotations:
      summary: Transit link {{ $labels.interface_name }}
is under high load
      description: "Transit link {{ $labels.interface_
name }} is under high load LABELS = {{ $labels }}"
      value: '{{ $value }}'
```

- AlertManager has its own configuration file, called `alertmanager.yml`, that controls how to aggregate and route incoming alerts from Prometheus. In our case, we have a single alert type, so we only need one route. We decrease the default aggregation timers to enable faster reaction time and specify the webhook URL where to send these alerts:

```
route:
  receiver: 'event-manager'
  group_wait: 5s
  group_interval: 10s

receivers:
  - name: 'event-manager'
    webhook_configs:
    - url: http://clab-netgo-host-2:10000/alert
```

- event-manager parses the alert and toggles a backup interface to re-balance the traffic coming into the `cvx` device. Its behavior is fairly static, so we don't need a configuration file for it.

The event-manager program implements a standard web server that listens to incoming requests and dispatches them to a handler function. Here, we decode the received Prometheus alert and invoke the `toggleBackup` function based on its status:

```
func alertHandler(w http.ResponseWriter, req *http.Request) {
  log.Println("Incoming alert")
  var alerts Alerts
  err := json.NewDecoder(req.Body).Decode(&alerts)
  // process error

  for _, alert := range alerts.Alerts {
    if alert.Status == "firing" {
      if err := toggleBackup(alert.Labels.InterfaceName,
"permit"); err != nil {
        w.WriteHeader(http.StatusInternalServerError)
        return
      }
      continue
    }

    if err := toggleBackup(alert.Labels.InterfaceName, "deny");
err != nil {
      w.WriteHeader(http.StatusInternalServerError)
      return
    }
  }
  w.WriteHeader(http.StatusOK)
}
```

We have two *uplinks* between the `cvx` and `ceos` devices, and we only use one of them by default. The backup uplink does BGP ASN prepending and only receives traffic when we announce more specific or disaggregated prefixes. The `toggleBackup` function does this by toggling a permit/deny statement on an IP prefix list (on `cvx`), thereby enabling or disabling the BGP disaggregation behavior:

```
var (
  backupRules = map[string][]int{
    "swp1": {10, 20},
  }
)
```

```
func toggleBackup(intf string, action string) error {
  log.Printf("%s needs to %s backup prefixes",
            intf, action)
  ruleIDs, ok := backupRules[intf]
  // process error

  var pl PrefixList
  pl.Rules = make(map[string]Rule)
  for _, ruleID := range ruleIDs {
    pl.Rules[strconv.Itoa(ruleID)] = Rule{
      Action: action,
    }
  }


  var payload nvue
  payload.Router.Policy.PrefixLists = map[string]PrefixList{
    plName: pl,
  }

  b, err := json.Marshal(payload)
  // process error

  return sendBytes(b)
}
```

The final `sendBytes` function applies the constructed configuration using the three-stage commit process we discussed in *Chapter 6, Configuration Management*.

Visualizing the data

You can connect to the local instance of Grafana running at `:3000` using `admin` as the username/password to test the complete telemetry-driven pipeline in action. This Grafana instance comes up pre-integrated with Prometheus as its data source, and it includes a pre-built `event-manager` dashboard that plots the incoming packet rate for both `cvx` links to `ceos`.

Run `make traffic-start` from the root of this book's GitHub repository (see *Further reading*) to generate traffic in the lab topology. All traffic should initially flow over the primary connection between `cvx` and `ceos` (`swp1`).

Next, we want to start the event-manager application so that we can load-balance traffic across both connections. To do this, run the event-manager Go application inside the `host-2` container. This translates to the command that we execute in the following snippet:

```
$ sudo ip netns exec clab-netgo-host-2 /usr/local/go/bin/go run ch09/event-manager/main.go
AlertManager event-triggered webhook
2022/08/01 21:51:13 Starting web server at 0.0.0.0:10000
```

Open a new terminal window or tab and run `make traffic-start` again, but increase the traffic generation period from the default `60s` using the `DURATION` variable. For example, the following command would generate traffic for 2 minutes:

```
$ DURATION=2m make traffic-start
```

This can help you see the longer-term effect of traffic re-balancing. Logs should show that the traffic rate has triggered an alert and the application implemented corrective actions:

```
$ sudo ip netns exec clab-netgo-host-2 /usr/local/go/bin/go run ch09/event-manager/main.go
AlertManager event-triggered webhook
2022/08/01 21:51:13 Starting web server at 0.0.0.0:10000
ch09/event-manager/main.go
2022/08/01 21:53:10 Incoming alert
2022/08/01 21:53:10 swp1 needs to permit backup prefixes
2022/08/01 21:53:10 Created revisionID: changeset/cumulus/2022-08-01_21.53.10_ASPO
{
  "state": "apply",
  "transition": {
    "issue": {},
    "progress": ""
  }
}
2022/08/01 21:54:00 Incoming alert
2022/08/01 21:54:00 swp1 needs to deny backup prefixes
2022/08/01 21:54:00 Created revisionID: changeset/
```

```
cumulus/2022-08-01_21.54.00_ASP2
{
  "state": "apply",
  "transition": {
    "issue": {},
    "progress": ""
  }
}
2022/08/01 21:54:00 swp2 needs to permit backup prefixes
2022/08/01 21:54:00 Could not find a backup prefix for swp2
2022/08/01 21:54:20 Incoming alert
2022/08/01 21:54:20 swp2 needs to deny backup prefixes
2022/08/01 21:54:20 Could not find a backup prefix for swp2
2022/08/01 21:54:30 Incoming alert
2022/08/01 21:54:30 swp1 needs to permit backup prefixes
2022/08/01 21:54:30 Created revisionID: changeset/
cumulus/2022-08-01_21.54.30_ASP4
{
  "state": "apply",
  "transition": {
    "issue": {},
    "progress": ""
  }
}
2022/08/01 21:55:20 Incoming alert
2022/08/01 21:55:20 swp1 needs to deny backup prefixes
2022/08/01 21:55:20 Created revisionID: changeset/
cumulus/2022-08-01_21.55.20_ASP6
{
  "state": "apply",
  "transition": {
    "issue": {},
    "progress": ""
  }
}
```

All three of the tests we performed should get you a similar-looking graph:

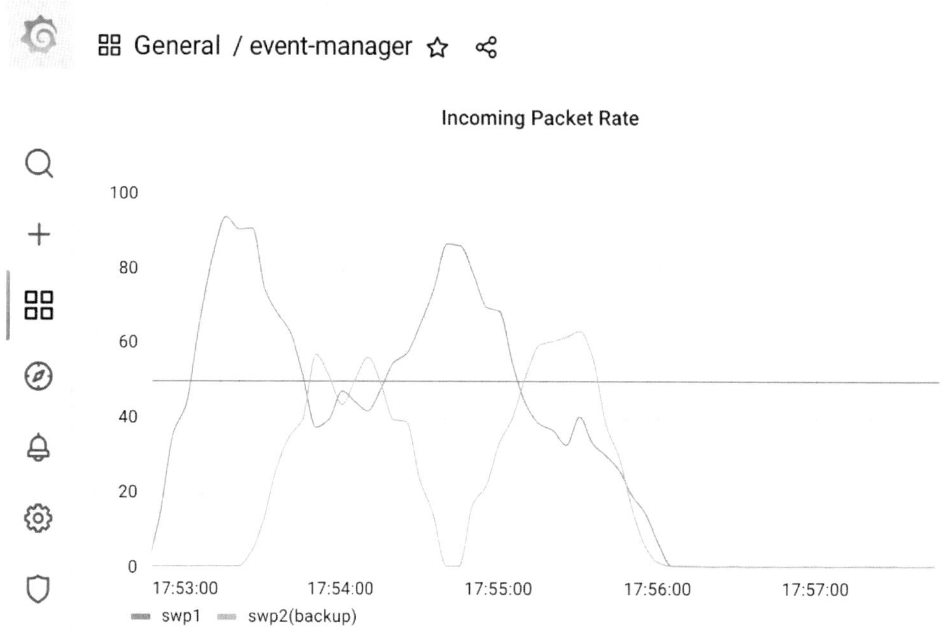

Figure 9.5 – Event-manager visualization

Streaming telemetry is a powerful capability that you can adapt to a wide variety of business use cases. However, most of these use cases are specific to the operating network environment, so it's hard to come up with a set of *killer applications* that would apply to every network. Hence, it's important to know how to implement the required business logic in code, which is what we have tried to show you in this chapter.

In the following section, we cover another OpenConfig gRPC service you can use to automate operational tasks.

Network operations

In the preceding sections, we explored how the OpenConfig management interface approaches two common network automation use cases: configuration management and operational state collection. These two tasks alone can get you a long way in your network automation journey, but there is a set of common operational tasks that don't fall into either of these categories.

To automate all aspects of network operations, we need to perform tasks such as network device reloads, software life cycle management, and counter and adjacency resets. You normally execute these activities as part of interactive CLI workflows, with prompts and warnings that assume a human operator is involved in the process. This makes the automation of these tasks a major undertaking, as we have to resort to screen-scraping, which increases the already high risk of these tasks.

To address these challenges, OpenConfig proposed a new gRPC API, designed to abstract away the interactive commands and surface these network operations capabilities in a standard, vendor-neutral way.

gNOI

gNOI defines a list of gRPC services that address a wide range of network operations use cases. Each service represents one operational process with a set of actions, and the following table includes a few examples to give you an idea of the challenges gNOI attempts to solve:

Service	Description	RPC examples
OS	NOS package management	Install, Activate, and Verify
File	File operations	Get, Transfer, Put, and Remove
L2	L2 protocols operations	ClearNeighborDiscovery and ClearLLDPInterface
Cert	Certificate management	Rotate, Install, GenerateCSR, and RevokeCertificates
System	System operations	Ping, Traceroute, Reboot, and Time

Table 9.1 – gNOI use case examples

Some RPCs are a one-shot with immediate response, some stream responses synchronously until complete or canceled, and some work asynchronously.

The gNOI GitHub repository (see *Further reading*) protobuf files have the most recent list of actions for each service. At the time of writing, this is the top-level definition of the `system.proto` file (see *Further reading*):

```
service System {
     rpc Ping(PingRequest) returns (stream PingResponse) {}
     rpc Traceroute(TracerouteRequest) returns (stream
TracerouteResponse) {}
     rpc Time(TimeRequest) returns (TimeResponse) {}
     rpc SetPackage(stream SetPackageRequest) returns
(SetPackageResponse) {}
     rpc SwitchControlProcessor(SwitchControlProcessorRequest)
       returns (SwitchControlProcessorResponse) {}
     rpc Reboot(RebootRequest) returns (RebootResponse) {}
     rpc RebootStatus(RebootStatusRequest) returns
(RebootStatusResponse) {}
     rpc CancelReboot(CancelRebootRequest) returns
(CancelRebootResponse) {}
```

```
    rpc KillProcess(KillProcessRequest) returns
(KillProcessResponse) {}
}
```

We don't cover all gNOI RPCs in this book. Instead, we focus on just one and include an example program built around it.

Traceroute RPC

Most, if not all, network engineers are familiar with the `traceroute` command. This is a common way to explore the forwarding path between a pair of network endpoints. When you run `traceroute` from a network device's interactive shell, the terminal prints the result on your screen. With gNOI, `traceroute` is an action we request via an RPC with a `TracerouteRequest` message in the payload, and the result is a stream (one or many) of `TracerouteResponse` messages:

```
service System {
    rpc Traceroute(TracerouteRequest) returns (stream
TracerouteResponse) {}
```

As with the `traceroute` command-line arguments and flags, the request message lets you specify options such as source address, the maximum number of hops, and whether to perform reverse DNS lookups:

```
message TracerouteRequest {
    string source = 1;        // Source addr to ping from.
    String destination = 2; // Destination addr to ping.
    Uint32 initial_ttl = 3; // Initial TTL. (default=1)
    int32 max_ttl = 4;        // Maximum number of hops.
    Int64 wait = 5;           // Response wait-time (ns).
    Bool do_not_fragment = 6;
    bool do_not_resolve = 7;
    /* ... <omitted for brevity > ... */
}
```

Each response message includes the results of a single measurement cycle, including the hop count, the round-trip time, and the responding address extracted from a probe reply:

```
message TracerouteResponse {
    /* ... <omitted for brevity > ... */
    int32 hop = 5;           // Hop number. required.
    string address = 6;      // Address of responding hop.
```

```
        string name = 7;        // Name of responding hop.
        int64 rtt = 8;          // Round trip time in nanoseconds.
        /* ... <omitted for brevity > ... */
}
```

Now, let's see an example of how to use the gNOI interface with Go.

Path verifier application

In the streaming telemetry section of this chapter, we explored the implementation of an event-manager application that enables or disables a backup link as the traffic through the primary interface crosses a pre-defined threshold. We used Grafana to plot the traffic rate for both interfaces to confirm that the application works as intended.

In real-world automation use cases involving complex workflows, relying on visual clues is not always the right approach. Ideally, we need a programmatic way to verify that the backup link is actually working. We use the gNOI `Traceroute` RPC to check this in the next code example. The goal is to explore diverse network paths and confirm that we are forwarding some traffic flows over the backup interface. You can find the code example for this section in the `ch09/gnoi-trace` directory of this book's GitHub repository (see *Further reading*).

We start by setting up a gRPC session to the `ceos` virtual network device and creating a new API client for the gNOI `System` service:

```
var target = "clab-netgo-ceos:6030"

import (
        "google.golang.org/grpc"
        "github.com/openconfig/gnoi/system"
)

func main() {
        conn, err := grpc.Dial(target, grpc.WithInsecure())
        // process error
        defer conn.Close()

        sysSvc := system.NewSystemClient(conn)
        ctx, cancel := context.WithCancel(context.Background())
        defer cancel()
```

```
    /* ... <continues next > ... */
}
```

Next, we create a `sync.WaitGroup` to coordinate all goroutines running traceroutes to different destinations. These goroutines send the collected results back to the `main` goroutine over the `traceCh` channel. For each traceroute destination encoded as `string`, the traceroute result includes a list of responded IP addresses per network hop.

To make it easier to compare lists of IP addresses in the following steps, we store them as a set using the `deckarep/golang-set` (`mapset`) third-party package, because Go doesn't implement sets natively in the standard library. We encode the hop count implicitly as the index of the `[]mapset.Set` array:

```
var destinations = []string{
            "203.0.113.251",
            "203.0.113.252",
            "203.0.113.253",
}

func main() {
    /* ... <continues from before > ... */
    var wg sync.WaitGroup
    wg.Add(len(destinations))

    traceCh := make(chan map[string][]mapset.Set,
                    len(destinations))
  /* ... <continues next > ... */
}
```

Each goroutine runs a single traceroute, and we only specify the source and destination fields of the `TracerouteRequest` message, leaving the rest options as default. As we receive responses, we store the results in the `route` slice. When the traceroute stops, which is when the error type is `io.EOF`, we send the accumulated response over the `traceCh` channel and call `wg.Done`:

```
var source = "203.0.113.3"

func main() {
  /* ... <continues from before > ... */
  for _, dest := range destinations {
    go func(d string) {
```

```
    defer wg.Done()
    retryMax := 3
    retryCount := 0

  START:
    response, err := sysSvc.Traceroute(ctx,
                      &system.TracerouteRequest{
                              Destination: d,
                              Source: source,
    })
    // process error


    var route []mapset.Set
    for {
      resp, err := response.Recv()
      if errors.Is(err, io.EOF) {
      // end of stream, traceroute completed
        break
      }
      // process error

      // timed out, restarting the traceroute
      if int(resp.Hop) > len(route)+1 {
        if retryCount > retryMax-1 {
          goto FINISH
        }
        retryCount += 1
        goto START
      }

      // first response
      if len(route) < int(resp.Hop) {
        route = append(route, mapset.NewSet())
      }
```

```
            // subsequent responses
              route[resp.Hop-1].Add(resp.Address)
            }

        FINISH:
          traceCh <- map[string][]mapset.Set{
                       d: route,
                   }
        }(dest)
    }
    wg.Wait()
    close(traceCh)
    /* ... <continues next > ... */
}
```

Since network devices have default control plane security settings that may restrict them from processing every incoming **ICMP** packet they receive, you might see gaps in your traceroute results. To overcome this, we use Go's labels and `goto` statements in the code to retry a traceroute in case we don't get any information for any one hop. `START` and `FINISH` are the two labels we used to implement this retry logic, with the latter serving as a fall-through case when we don't get a result after several attempts.

Once we have completed all traceroute requests, we can process and analyze the results. To simplify the code logic, we first transform the data to store a map between a hop count and a set of IP addresses per traceroute destination:

```
func main() {
  /* ... <continues from before > ... */
  routes := make(map[int]map[string]mapset.Set)

  for trace := range traceCh {
    for dest, paths := range trace {
      for hop, path := range paths {
        if _, ok := routes[hop]; !ok {
          routes[hop] = make(map[string]mapset.Set)
        }
        routes[hop][dest] = path
      }
    }
  }
```

```
    /* ... <continues next > ... */
}
```

Finally, we can traverse over each hop and check whether there is a discrepancy between a set of responding IP addresses for different traceroute destinations, which would mean that the packets went over different paths. If we detect this, we print it on the screen:

```
func main() {
    /* ... <continues from before > ... */
    for hop, route := range routes {
        if hop == len(routes)-1 {
            continue
        }
        found := make(map[string]string)
        for myDest, myPaths := range route {
            for otherDest, otherPaths := range route {
                if myDest == otherDest {
                    continue
                }
                diff := myPaths.Difference(otherPaths)
                if diff.Cardinality() == 0 {
                    continue
                }

                v, ok := found[myDest]
                if ok && v == otherDest {
                    continue
                }

                log.Printf("Found different paths at hop %d", hop)
                log.Printf("Destination %s: %+v", myDest, myPaths)
                log.Printf(
                        "Destination %s: %+v",
                                otherDest,
                                otherPaths,
                                )
```

```
        found[otherDest] = myDest
      }
    }
  }
  log.Println("Check complete")
}
```

You can run this program from the `ch09/gnoi-trace` folder. Make sure `lab-full` is up and running first. You should see output like the following:

```
ch09/gnoi-trace$ go run main.go
2022/06/26 16:51:10 Checking if routes have different paths
2022/06/26 16:51:16 Missed at least one hop in 203.0.113.251
2022/06/26 16:51:16 retrying 203.0.113.251
2022/06/26 16:51:17 Check complete
```

Generate traffic with `make traffic-start` and run this program again. In another tab, run simultaneously the event-manager application from the `clab-netgo-host-2` host to activate the backup link:

```
$ DURATION=2m make traffic-start
docker exec -d clab-netgo-cvx systemctl restart hsflowd
docker exec -d clab-netgo-host-3 ./ethr -s
docker exec -d clab-netgo-host-1 ./ethr -c 203.0.113.253 -b
900K -d 2m -p udp -l 1KB
docker exec -d clab-netgo-host-1 ./ethr -c 203.0.113.252 -b
600K -d 2m -p udp -l 1KB
docker exec -d clab-netgo-host-1 ./ethr -c 203.0.113.251 -b
400K -d 2m -p udp -l 1KB


$ sudo ip netns exec clab-netgo-host-2 /usr/local/go/bin/go run
ch09/event-manager/main.go
AlertManager event-triggered webhook
2022/09/14 21:02:57 Starting web server at 0.0.0.0:10000
2022/09/14 21:02:58 Incoming alert
2022/09/14 21:02:58 swp1 needs to permit backup prefixes
2022/09/14 21:02:58 Created revisionID: changeset/
cumulus/2022-09-14_21.02.58_S4SQ
{
```

```
  "state": "apply",
  "transition": {
    "issue": {},
    "progress": ""
  }
}
2022/09/14 21:03:40 Incoming alert
2022/09/14 21:03:40 swp1 needs to deny backup prefixes
2022/09/14 21:03:40 Created revisionID: changeset/
cumulus/2022-09-14_21.03.40_S4SS
{
  "state": "apply",
  "transition": {
    "issue": {},
    "progress": ""
  }
}
2022/09/14 21:03:40 swp2 needs to permit backup prefixes
2022/09/14 21:03:40 Could not find a backup prefix for swp2
2022/09/14 21:04:10 Incoming alert
2022/09/14 21:04:10 swp1 needs to permit backup prefixes
2022/09/14 21:04:10 Created revisionID: changeset/
cumulus/2022-09-14_21.04.10_S4SV
{
  "state": "apply",
  "transition": {
    "issue": {},
    "progress": ""
  }
}
2022/09/14 21:04:10 swp2 needs to deny backup prefixes
2022/09/14 21:04:10 Could not find a backup prefix for swp2
```

The output of the program would look like this:

```
ch09/gnoi-trace$ go run main.go
2022/09/14 21:03:29 Checking if routes have different paths
2022/09/14 21:03:34 Missed at least one hop in 203.0.113.253
2022/09/14 21:03:34 retrying 203.0.113.253
2022/09/14 21:03:34 Found different paths at hop 0
2022/09/14 21:03:34 Destination 203.0.113.252: Set{192.0.2.5}
2022/09/14 21:03:34 Destination 203.0.113.253: Set{192.0.2.3}
2022/09/14 21:03:34 Found different paths at hop 0
2022/09/14 21:03:34 Destination 203.0.113.251: Set{192.0.2.5}
2022/09/14 21:03:34 Destination 203.0.113.253: Set{192.0.2.3}
2022/09/14 21:03:34 Found different paths at hop 0
2022/09/14 21:03:34 Destination 203.0.113.253: Set{192.0.2.3}
2022/09/14 21:03:34 Destination 203.0.113.252: Set{192.0.2.5}
2022/09/14 21:03:34 Check complete
```

The last output shows that the path that `203.0.113.252/32` and `203.0.113.251/32` follow is different from the path that `203.0.113.253/32` follows (primary link). This is because the event-manager disaggregated `.252` and `.251` from the main `203.0.113.250/30` prefix. Now, we know that the backup link is working as expected, as it is carrying traffic for these two IP addresses.

Historically, networking vendors were not incentivized to create vendor-neutral APIs and data models, as it doesn't allow them to differentiate themselves from the competition. And while standards bodies such as the Internet Engineering Task Force (IETF) produce standards for the networking industry, they can't always influence what vendors actually implement. Also, some vendors might still perceive technological lock-ins as an effective way to keep their existing customer base.

By contrast, the OpenConfig community of network operators has more leverage to influence networking vendors to adopt vendor-independent data models and APIs. OpenConfig adoption is still relatively low, in both model and feature coverage, but, as long as the OC participants continue to push for more, the coverage will increase, which, in turn, will drive the adoption in the wider networking community.

Even today, OpenConfig provides a vendor-neutral way of doing a lot of common networking tasks, including configuration management, monitoring, and operations. In this chapter, we've shown the two most popular interfaces, gNMI and gNOI, ignoring the less common gRIBI, which is outside of the scope of this book. We hope this chapter provides enough examples of tools and workflows that you can use with Go to consume and interact with OpenConfig-compliant devices.

Summary

In this chapter, by introducing streaming telemetry, we have started exploring the world of network monitoring, a critical task for a business. The ability to observe network-wide state and collect and process data plane information are all important in determining the health of your network. In the next chapter, we will examine a few concrete examples of network monitoring tasks and use cases and learn how Go can help us automate them.

Further reading

- Network operators: `https://www.openconfig.net/about/participants/`
- Manipulating forwarding entries: `https://github.com/openconfig/gribi/blob/master/doc/motivation.md#grpc-service-for-rib-injection`
- gNMI collector: `https://github.com/openconfig/gnmi/tree/master/cmd/gnmi_collector`
- gNMI CLI utility: `https://github.com/openconfig/gnmi/tree/master/cmd/gnmi_cli`
- gNMI Test framework: `https://github.com/openconfig/gnmitest`
- gRPC tunnel: `https://github.com/openconfig/grpctunnel`
- IS-IS LSDB parsing: `https://github.com/openconfig/lsdbparse`
- Ygot: `https://github.com/openconfig/ygot`
- gNxI Tools: `https://github.com/google/gnxi`
- Book's GitHub repository: `https://github.com/PacktPublishing/Network-Automation-with-Go`
- gNMI specification: `https://github.com/openconfig/reference/blob/master/rpc/gnmi/gnmi-specification.md`
- gNMIc docs: `https://gnmic.kmrd.dev/user_guide/golang_package/intro/#set-request`
- gNMI path convention: `https://github.com/openconfig/reference/blob/master/rpc/gnmi/gnmi-path-conventions.md`
- gNMI repository: `https://github.com/openconfig/gnmi`
- gNMIc: `https://gnmic.kmrd.dev/`
- AlertManager: `https://prometheus.io/docs/alerting/latest/alertmanager/`
- `full/workdir/`: `https://github.com/PacktPublishing/Network-Automation-with-Go/tree/main/topo-full/workdir`

- `topo.yml`: `https://github.com/PacktPublishing/Network-Automation-with-Go/blob/main/topo-full/topo.yml`
- `docker-compose.yml`: `https://github.com/PacktPublishing/Network-Automation-with-Go/blob/main/ch09/docker-compose.yml`
- gNOI GitHub repository: `https://github.com/openconfig/gnoi`
- `system.proto` file: `https://github.com/openconfig/gnoi/blob/master/system/system.proto`

10
Network Monitoring

Despite the popularity of configuration management, we actually spend more time monitoring networks than configuring them. As networks become more and more complex, with new layers of encapsulation and IP address translations, our ability to understand whether a network functions correctly to let us meet customer **service-level agreements** (**SLAs**) is becoming increasingly difficult.

Engineers working in the cloud infrastructure space have come up with the term *observability*, referring to the ability to reason about the internal state of a system by observing its external outputs. Translated into networking terms, this may include passive monitoring through logs and state telemetry collection or active monitoring using distributed probing, data processing, and visualization.

The ultimate goal of all this is to reduce the **mean time to repair** (**MTTR**), adhere to customer SLAs, and shift to proactive problem resolution. Go is a very popular language of choice for these kinds of tasks, and in this chapter we will examine a few of the tools, packages, and platforms that can help you with network monitoring. Here are the highlights of this chapter:

- We will explore traffic monitoring by looking at how to capture and parse network packets with Go.
- Next, we will look at how to process and aggregate data plane telemetry to get meaningful insights into the current network behavior.
- We show how you can use active probing to measure network performance, and how to produce, collect, and visualize performance metrics.

We will deliberately avoid talking about YANG-based telemetry, as we covered this already in *Chapter 8, Network APIs*, and *Chapter 9, OpenConfig*.

Another area that we haven't touched on so far and that we want to discuss briefly in this chapter is the developer experience. As we write more code, maintaining existing software becomes an important part of our day-to-day operations. We introduce one tool per section of this chapter, acknowledging that we are just scratching the surface and that this topic could be the subject of an entire book. In the end, we don't strive to give a comprehensive overview of all tools there are out there but just want to give you an idea of what developing Go code in production may feel like.

Technical requirements

You can find the code examples for this chapter in the book's GitHub repository (see the *Further reading* section), under the `ch10` folder.

> **Important Note**
>
> We recommend you execute the Go programs in this chapter in a virtual lab environment. Refer to the *Appendix* for prerequisites and instructions on how to build the fully configured network topology.

The first example we will discuss in the following section explores packet capturing and parsing capabilities in Go.

Data plane telemetry processing

Network activities such as capacity planning, billing, or **distributed denial-of-service** (**DDoS**) attack monitoring require insights into the traffic flowing through a network. One way we can offer such visibility is by deploying a packet sampling technology. The premise is that at a high-enough rate, it's possible to capture only a randomly sampled subset of packets to build a good understanding of the overall network traffic patterns.

While it's the hardware that samples the packets, it's the software that aggregates them into flows and exports them. NetFlow, sFlow, and **IP Flow Information Export** (**IPFIX**) are the three main protocols we use for this, and they define the structure of the payload and what metadata to include with each sampled packet.

One of the first steps in any telemetry processing pipeline is information ingestion. In our context, this means receiving and parsing data plane telemetry packets to extract and process flow records. In this section, we will look at how you can capture and process packets with the help of the `google/gopacket` package (see *Further reading*).

Packet capturing

In *Chapter 4, Networking (TCP/IP) with Go*, we discussed how to build a UDP ping application using the `net` package from Go's standard library. And while we should probably take a similar approach when building an sFlow collector, we will do something different for the next example.

Instead of building a data plane telemetry collector, we designed our application to tap into an existing flow of telemetry packets, assuming the network devices in the topology are sending them to an existing collector somewhere in the network. This allows you to avoid changing the existing telemetry service configuration while still being able to capture and process telemetry traffic. You can use a program like this when you want a transparent tool that can run directly on a network device, on demand, and for a short period of time.

In the test lab topology, the `cvx` node runs an agent that exports sampled metrics using the sFlow protocol. The sFlow traffic flows toward `host-2`, where it gets intercepted by the example application using a tap:

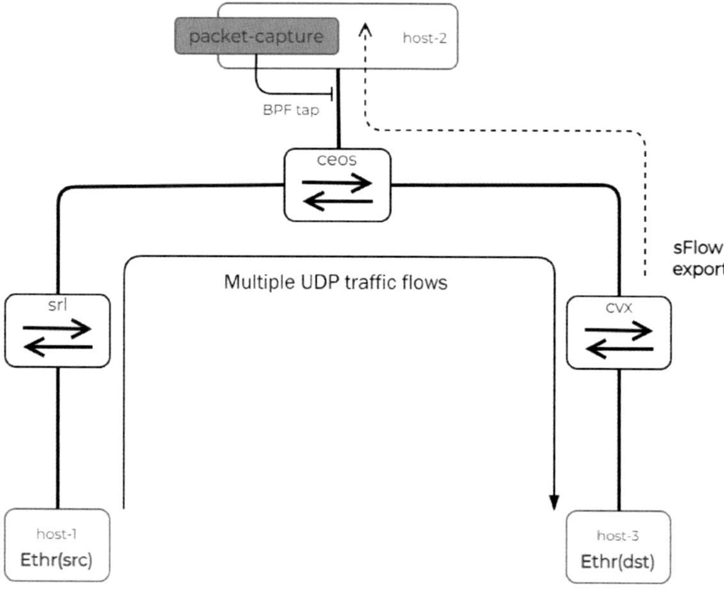

Figure 10.1 – sFlow application

To show you the packet-capturing capabilities of the `google/gopacket` package, we intercept all sFlow packets using `pcapgo` – a native Go implementation of the traffic-capturing API in Linux. Although it's less feature-rich than its counterpart `pcap` and `pfring` packages, the benefit of `pcapgo` is that it doesn't rely on any external C libraries and can work natively on any Linux distribution.

In the first part of the `packet-capture` program, which you can find in the `ch10/packet-capture` folder of this book's GitHub repository, we set up a new `af_packet` socket handler with the `pcapgo.NewEthernetHandle` function, passing it the name of the interface to monitor:

```
import (
	"github.com/google/gopacket/pcapgo"
)

var (
	intf = flag.String("intf", "eth0", "interface")
)

func main() {
```

```
    handle, err := pcapgo.NewEthernetHandle(*intf)
    /* ... <continues next > ... */
}
```

At this point, `handle` gives us access to all packets on the `eth0` interface.

Packet filtering

While we could just capture all packets through the interface, for the sake of experimenting, we will include an example of how to filter the traffic we capture with a **Berkeley Packet Filter** (**BPF**) program in Go.

First, we generate a compiled packet-matching code in a human-readable format, using the `-d` option of the `tcpdump` command to filter IP and UDP packets:

```
$ sudo tcpdump -p -ni eth0 -d "ip and udp"
(000) ldh      [12]
(001) jeq      #0x800          jt 2    jf 5
(002) ldb      [23]
(003) jeq      #0x11           jt 4    jf 5
(004) ret      #262144
(005) ret      #0
```

Then, we convert each of the preceding instructions into a corresponding `bpf.Instruction` from the `golang.org/x/net/bpf` package. We assemble these instructions into a set of `[]bpf.RawInstruction` that are ready to load into a BPF virtual machine:

```
import (
  "golang.org/x/net/bpf"
)

func main() {
/* ... <continues from before > ... */

  rawInstructions, err := bpf.Assemble([]bpf.Instruction{
    // Load "EtherType" field from the ethernet header.
    bpf.LoadAbsolute{Off: 12, Size: 2},
    // Skip to last instruction if EtherType isn't IPv4.
    bpf.JumpIf{Cond: bpf.JumpNotEqual, Val: 0x800,
                SkipTrue: 3},
```

```
      // Load "Protocol" field from the IPv4 header.
      bpf.LoadAbsolute{Off: 23, Size: 1},
      // Skip to the last instruction if Protocol is not UDP.
      bpf.JumpIf{Cond: bpf.JumpNotEqual, Val: 0x11,
                  SkipTrue: 1},
      // "send up to 4k of the packet to userspace."
      bpf.RetConstant{Val: 4096},
      // Verdict is "ignore packet and return to the stack."
      bpf.RetConstant{Val: 0},
    })


    handle.SetBPF(rawInstructions)
    /* ... <continues next > ... */
}
```

We can attach the result to the `EthernetHandle` function we created earlier, to act as a packet filter and reduce the number of packets received by the application.

In summary, we copy all packets that match the `0x800` EtherType and the `0x11` IP protocol to the user space process, where our Go program runs, while all the other packets, including the ones we match, continue through the network stack. This makes this program completely transparent to any existing traffic flows, and you can use it without having to change the configuration of the sFlow agent.

Packet processing

All packets that the kernel sends to the user space become available in the Go application through the `PacketSource` type, which we build by combining the `EthernetHandle` function we created with an Ethernet packet decoder:

```
func main() {
  /* ... <continues from before > ... */
     packetSource := gopacket.NewPacketSource(
           handle,
           layers.LayerTypeEthernet,
     )
     /* ... <continues next > ... */
}
```

This `PacketSource` structure sends each received and decoded packet over a Go channel, which means we can use a `for` loop to iterate over them one by one. Inside this loop, we use `gopacket` to match packet layers and extract information about L2, L3, and L4 networking headers, including protocol-specific details such as the sFlow payload:

```
func main() {
  /* ... <continues from before > ... */
  for packet := range packetSource.Packets() {
    sflowLayer := packet.Layer(layers.LayerTypeSFlow)
    if sflowLayer != nil {
      sflow, ok := sflowLayer.(*layers.SFlowDatagram)
      if !ok {
        continue
      }

      for _, sample := range sflow.FlowSamples {
        for _, record := range sample.GetRecords() {
          p, ok := record.(layers.SFlowRawPacketFlowRecord)
          if !ok {
            log.Println("failed to decode sflow record")
            continue
          }

          srcIP, dstIP := p.Header.
            NetworkLayer().
            NetworkFlow().
            Endpoints()
          sPort, dPort := p.Header.
            TransportLayer().
            TransportFlow().
            Endpoints()
          log.Printf("flow record: %s:%s <-> %s:%s\n",
            srcIP,
            sPort,
            dstIP,
            dPort,
          )
```

```
                }
            }
        }
    }
}
```

The benefit of using `gopacket` specifically for sFlow decoding is that it can parse and create another `gopacket.Packet` based on the sampled packet's headers.

Generating traffic

To test this Go application, we need to generate some traffic in the lab topology, so the `cvx` device can generate sFlow records about it. Here, we use `microsoft/ethr` – a Go-based traffic generator that offers a user experience and features comparable to `iperf`. It can generate and receive a fixed volume of network traffic and measure bandwidth, latency, loss, and jitter. In our case, we only need it to generate a few low-volume traffic flows over the lab network to trigger the data plane flow sampling.

The `packet-capture` application taps into the existing sFlow traffic, parses and extracts flow records, and prints that information on the screen. To test the program, run `make capture-start` from the root of this book's GitHub repository (see *Further reading*):

```
$ make capture-start
docker exec -d clab-netgo-cvx systemctl restart hsflowd
docker exec -d clab-netgo-host-3 ./ethr -s
docker exec -d clab-netgo-host-1 ./ethr -c 203.0.113.253 -b
900K -d 60s -p udp -l 1KB
docker exec -d clab-netgo-host-1 ./ethr -c 203.0.113.252 -b
600K -d 60s -p udp -l 1KB
docker exec -d clab-netgo-host-1 ./ethr -c 203.0.113.251 -b
400K -d 60s -p udp -l 1KB
cd ch10/packet-capture; go build -o packet-capture main.go
docker exec -it clab-netgo-host-2 /workdir/packet-capture/
packet-capture
2022/02/28 21:50:25  flow record: 203.0.113.0:60087 <->
203.0.113.252:8888
2022/02/28 21:50:25  flow record: 203.0.113.0:60087 <->
203.0.113.252:8888
2022/02/28 21:50:27  flow record: 203.0.113.0:40986 <->
203.0.113.252:8888
```

```
2022/02/28 21:50:29 flow record: 203.0.113.0:60087 <->
203.0.113.252:8888
2022/02/28 21:50:29 flow record: 203.0.113.0:49138 <->
203.0.113.251:8888
2022/02/28 21:50:30 flow record: 203.0.113.0:60087 <->
203.0.113.252:8888
2022/02/28 21:50:30 flow record: 203.0.113.0:49138 <->
203.0.113.251:8888
```

As promised, before we move on to the next section, let's review the first *developer experience* tool of the chapter.

Debugging Go programs

Reading and reasoning about an existing code base is a laborious task, and it gets even harder as programs mature and evolve. This is why, when learning a new language, it's very important to have at least a basic understanding of the debugging process. Debugging allows us to halt the execution of a program at a pre-defined place and step through the code line by line while examining in-memory variables and data structures.

In the following example, we use Delve to debug the `packet-capture` program we just ran. Before you can start, you need to generate some traffic through the lab topology with `make traffic-start`:

```
$ make traffic-start
docker exec -d clab-netgo-cvx systemctl restart hsflowd
docker exec -d clab-netgo-host-3 ./ethr -s
docker exec -d clab-netgo-host-1 ./ethr -c 203.0.113.253 -b
900K -d 60s -p udp -l 1KB
docker exec -d clab-netgo-host-1 ./ethr -c 203.0.113.252 -b
600K -d 60s -p udp -l 1KB
docker exec -d clab-netgo-host-1 ./ethr -c 203.0.113.251 -b
400K -d 60s -p udp -l 1KB
```

The Delve binary file is already pre-installed in the `host` lab containers, so you can connect to the `host-2` container with the `docker exec -it` command and start the Delve shell with the `dlv debug` command:

```
$ docker exec -it clab-netgo-host-2 bash
root@host-2:/# cd workdir/ch10/packet-capture/
root@host-2:/workdir/packet-capture# dlv debug main.go
```

Once in the `dlv` interactive shell, you can use different built-in commands to control the execution of the program (you can use `help` to view the full list of commands). Set a breakpoint at line 49 of `main.go` and run the program until the point where we receive the first packet:

```
(dlv) break main.go:49
Breakpoint 1 set at 0x5942ce for main.main() ./main.go:49
(dlv) continue
> main.main() ./main.go:49 (hits goroutine(1):1 total:1) (PC: 0x5942ce)
    44:     packetSource := gopacket.NewPacketSource(
    45:       handle,
    46:       layers.LayerTypeEthernet,
    47:     )
    48:     for packet := range packetSource.Packets() {
=>  49:       if l4 := packet.TransportLayer(); l4 == nil {
    50:         continue
    51:       }
    52:
    53:       sflowLayer := packet.Layer(layers.LayerTypeSFlow)
    54:       if sflowLayer != nil {
```

When execution stops at a breakpoint, you can examine the local variables using the `locals` command:

```
(dlv) locals
err = error nil
handle = ("*github.com/google/gopacket/pcapgo.EthernetHandle")
(0xc000162200)
rawInstructions = []golang.org/x/net/bpf.RawInstruction len: 6,
cap: 6, [...]
packetSource = ("*github.com/google/gopacket.PacketSource")
(0xc00009aab0)
packet = github.com/google/gopacket.Packet(*github.com/google/
gopacket.eagerPacket) 0xc0000c3c08
```

You can print the variable contents on a screen, as in the following example for the `packet` variable:

```
(dlv) print packet
github.com/google/gopacket.Packet(*github.com/google/gopacket.
eagerPacket) *{
  packet: github.com/google/gopacket.packet {
```

```
    data: []uint8 len: 758, cap: 758, [170,193,171,140,219,204,
170,193,171,198,150,242,8,0,69,0,2,232,40,71,64,0,63,17,18,182,
192,0,2,5,203,0,113,2,132,19,24,199,2,212,147,6,0,0,0,5,0,0,0,1
,203,0,113,129,0,1,134,160,0,0,0,39,0,2,...+694 more],
    /* ... < omitted > ... */
    last: github.com/google/gopacket.Layer(*github.com/google/
gopacket.DecodeFailure) ...,
    metadata: (*"github.com/google/gopacket.PacketMetadata")
(0xc0000c6200),
    decodeOptions: (*"github.com/google/gopacket.
DecodeOptions")(0xc0000c6250),
    link: github.com/google/gopacket.LinkLayer(*github.com/
google/gopacket/layers.Ethernet) ...,
    network: github.com/google/gopacket.NetworkLayer(*github.
com/google/gopacket/layers.IPv4) ...,
    transport: github.com/google/gopacket.
TransportLayer(*github.com/google/gopacket/layers.UDP) ...,
    application: github.com/google/gopacket.ApplicationLayer
nil,
    failure: github.com/google/gopacket.ErrorLayer(*github.com/
google/gopacket.DecodeFailure) ...,},}
```

The text-based navigation and verbosity of the output may be intimidating for beginners, but luckily, we have alternative visualization options.

Debugging from an IDE

If debugging in a console is not your preferred option, most of the popular **Integrated Development Environments** (**IDEs**) come with some form of support for Go debugging. For example, Delve integrates with **Visual Studio Code** (**VSCode**) and you can also configure it for remote debugging.

Although you can set up VSCode for remote debugging in different ways, in this example, we run Delve manually inside a container in the `headless` mode while specifying the port at which to listen for incoming connections:

```
$ docker exec -it clab-netgo-host-2 bash
root@host-2:/# cd workdir/ch10/packet-capture/
root@host-2:/workdir/ch10/packet-capture#  dlv debug main.go
--listen=:2345 --headless --api-version=2
API server listening at: [::]:2345
```

Now, we need to tell VSCode how to connect to the remote Delve process. You can do this by including a JSON config file in the `.vscode` folder next to the `main.go` file. Here's an example file you can find in `ch10/packet-capture/.vscode/launch.json` in this book's GitHub repository:

```
{
      "version": "0.2.0",
      "configurations": [
          {
              "name": "Connect to server",
              "type": "go",
              "request": "attach",
              "mode": "remote",
              "remotePath": "/workdir/ch10/packet-capture",
              "port": 2345,
              "host": "ec2-3-224-127-79.compute-1.amazonaws.com",

          },
      ]
}
```

You need to replace the `host` value with the one where the lab is running and then start an instance of VSCode from the root of the Go program (`code ch10/packet-capture`):

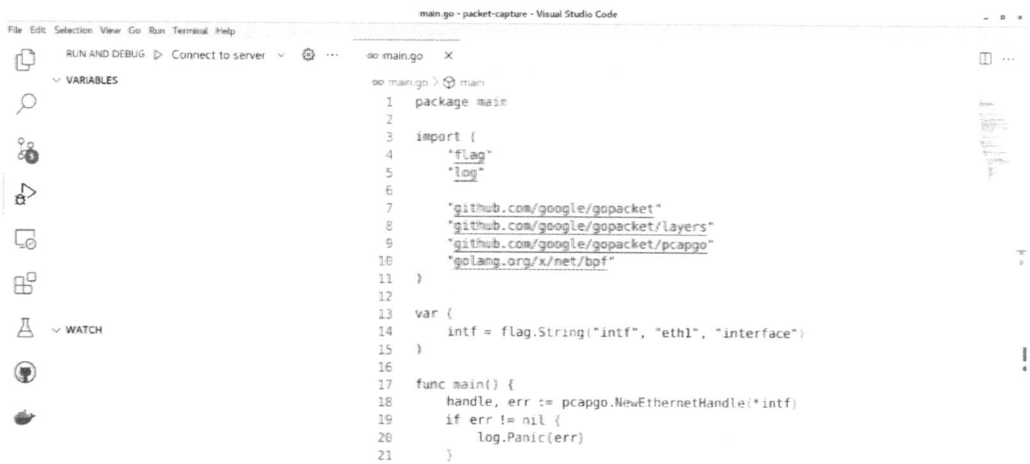

Figure 10.2 – VSCode development environment

In VSCode, now you can go to the debug icon in the left menu to get to **RUN AND DEBUG**, where you should see the **Connect to server** option that reads the preceding JSON config file. Click on the green arrow to connect to the remote debugging process.

At this point, you can navigate through the code and examine local variables inside the VSCode **user interface** (**UI**), while the debugging process is running inside a container:

Figure 10.3 – VSCode debugging

In the next section, we will look at how to add value to the data plane telemetry we collect and process by aggregating it to generate a report of the highest bandwidth consumers.

Data plane telemetry aggregation

After collecting and parsing data plane telemetry, we need to think about what to do with it next. Looking at raw data is not always helpful because of the sheer number of flows and lack of any meaningful context. Hence, the next logical step in a telemetry processing pipeline is data enrichment and aggregation.

Telemetry enrichment refers to the process of adding extra metadata to each flow based on some external source of information. For example, these external sources can provide a correlation between a public IP and its country of origin or BGP ASN, or between a private IP and its aggregate subnets or device identity.

Another technique that can help us interpret and reason about the telemetry we collect is aggregation. We can combine different flow records either based on the IP prefix boundary or flow metadata, such as a BGP ASN, to help network operators draw meaningful insights and create high-level views of the data.

You could build the entire telemetry processing pipeline out of open source components with ready-to-use examples (see *Further reading*) available on the internet, but sooner or later, you might need to write some code to meet your specific business requirements. In the following section, we will work on a scenario where we need to aggregate data plane telemetry to better understand the traffic patterns in our network.

Top talkers

In the absence of long-term telemetry storage, getting a just-in-time snapshot of the highest bandwidth consumers can be quite helpful. We refer to this application as *top talkers*, and it works by displaying a list of network flows that are sorted based on their relative interface bandwidth utilization.

Let's walk through an example Go application that implements this feature.

Exploring telemetry data

In our `top-talkers` application, we collect sFlow records with `netsampler/goflow2`, a package designed specifically to collect, enrich, and save sFlow, IPFIX, or NetFlow telemetry. This package ingests raw protocol data and produces normalized (protocol-independent) flow records. By default, you can save these normalized records in a file or send them to a Kafka queue. In our case, we store them in memory for further processing.

To store the flow records in memory, we save the most relevant fields of each flow record we receive in a user-defined data structure we call `MyFlow`:

```
type MyFlow struct {
	Key        string
	SrcAddr    string `json:"SrcAddr,omitempty"`
	DstAddr    string `json:"DstAddr,omitempty"`
	SrcPort    int    `json:"SrcPort,omitempty"`
	DstPort    int    `json:"DstPort,omitempty"`
	Count      int    // times we've seen this flow sample
}
```

Additionally, we create a flow key as a concatenation of the ports and IP addresses of the source and destination to uniquely identify each flow:

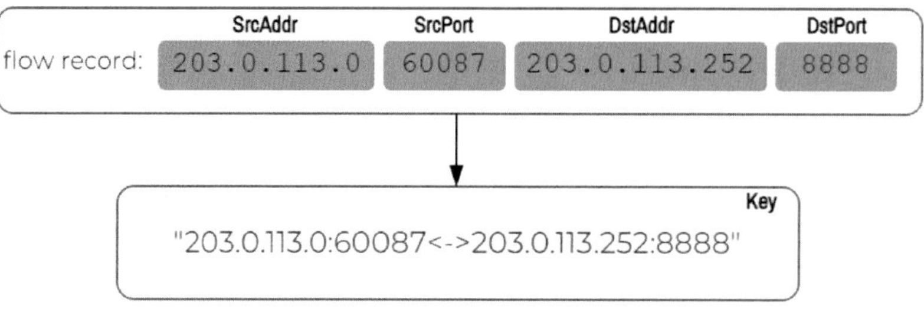

Figure 10.4 – A flow key

To help us calculate the final result, we create another data structure we call `topTalker`, which has two fields:

- `flowMap`: A map to store a collection of `MyFlow`-type flows. We use the key we created to index them.
- `Heap`: A helper data structure that keeps track of the most frequently seen flows:

```
type Heap []*MyFlow

type topTalker struct {
	flowMap map[string]*MyFlow
	heap    Heap
}
```

Since we use a high-level sFlow package (`goflow2`), we don't need to worry about setting up a UDP listener or receiving and decoding packets, but we need to tell `goflow2` the format to report flow records (`json`) and point to a custom transport driver (`tt`) that determines what to do with the data after the sFlow package normalizes the received flow records:

```
import (
  "github.com/netsampler/goflow2/format"
  "github.com/netsampler/goflow2/utils"
)

func main() {
	tt := topTalker{
		flowMap: make(map[string]*MyPacket),
```

```
        heap:    make(Heap, 0),
    }

    formatter, err := format.FindFormat(ctx, "json")
    // process error

    sSFlow := &utils.StateSFlow{
        Format:    formatter,
        Logger:    log.StandardLogger(),
        Transport: &tt,
    }

    go sSFlow.FlowRoutine(1, hostname, 6343, false)
}
```

The `Transport` field in the `utils.StateSFlow` type of the preceding code snippet accepts any type that implements `TransportInterface`. This interface expects a single method (`Send()`) where all the enrichment and aggregation may take place:

```
type StateSFlow struct {
    Format    format.FormatInterface
    Transport transport.TransportInterface
    Logger    Logger
    /* ... < other fields > ... */
}

type TransportInterface interface {
    Send(key, data []byte) error
}
```

The `Send` method accepts two arguments, one representing the source IP of an sFlow datagram and the second one containing the actual flow record.

Telemetry processing

In our implementation of the `Send` method (to satisfy the `TransportInterface` interface), we first parse the input binary data and deserialize it into a `MyFlow` data structure:

```
func (c *topTalker) Send(key, data []byte) error {
    var myFlow MyFlow
```

```
        json.Unmarshal(data, &myFlow)
        /* ... <continues next > ... */
}
```

Bearing in mind that sFlow can capture packets going in either direction, we need to ensure that both flows count toward the same in-memory flow record. This means creating a special flow key that satisfies the following two conditions:

- It must be the same for both ingress and egress packets of the same flow.
- It must be unique for all bidirectional flows.

We do this by sorting the source and destination IPs when constructing the bidirectional flow key, as the next code snippet shows:

```
var flowMapKey = `%s:%d<->%s:%d`

func (c *topTalker) Send(key, data []byte) error {
  /* ... <continues from before > ... */
  ips := []string{myFlow.SrcAddr, myFlow.DstAddr}
  sort.Strings(ips)
  var mapKey string
  if ips[0] != myFlow.SrcAddr {
    mapKey = fmt.Sprintf(
      flowMapKey,
      myFlow.SrcAddr,
      myFlow.SrcPort,
      myFlow.DstAddr,
      myFlow.DstPort,
    )
  } else {
    mapKey = fmt.Sprintf(
      flowMapKey,
      myFlow.DstAddr,
      myFlow.DstPort,
      myFlow.SrcAddr,
      myFlow.SrcPort,
    )
  }
```

```
    /* ... <continues next > ... */
}
```

With a unique key that represents both directions of a flow, we can save it in the map (`flowMap`) to store in memory. For each received flow record, the `Send` method performs the following checks:

- If this is the first time we've seen this flow, then we save it on the map and set the count number to `1`.
- Otherwise, we update the flow by incrementing its count by one:

```
func (c *topTalker) Send(key, data []byte) error {
    /* ... <continues from before > ... */
        myFlow.Key = mapKey
        foundFlow, ok := c.flowMap[mapKey]
        if !ok {
                myFlow.Count = 1
                c.flowMap[mapKey] = &myFlow
                heap.Push(&c.heap, &myFlow)
                return nil
        }

        c.heap.update(foundFlow)

        return nil
}
```

Now, to display the top talkers in order, we need to sort the flow records we have saved. Here, we use the `container/heap` package from the Go standard library. It implements a sorting algorithm, offering O(log n) (logarithmic) upper-bound guarantees, which means it can do additions and deletions of data very efficiently.

To use this package, you only need to teach it how to compare your items. As you add, remove, or update elements, it will sort them automatically. In our example, we want to sort flow records saved as the `MyFlow` data type. We define `Heap` as a list of pointers to `MyFlow` records. The `Less()` method instructs the `container/heap` package to compare two `MyFlow` elements, based on the `Count` field that stores the number of times we have *seen* a flow record:

```
type Heap []*MyFlow
```

```
func (h Heap) Less(i, j int) bool {
     return h[i].Count > h[j].Count
}
```

With this, we now have an in-memory flow record store with elements sorted according to their `Count`. We can now iterate over the `Heap` slice and print its elements on the screen. As in the earlier example with `gopacket`, we use `ethr` to generate three UDP flows with different throughputs to get a consistently sorted output. You can trigger the flows in the topology with `make top-talkers-start`:

```
Network-Automation-with-Go $ make top-talkers-start
docker exec -d clab-netgo-cvx systemctl restart hsflowd
docker exec -d clab-netgo-host-3 ./ethr -s
docker exec -d clab-netgo-host-1 ./ethr -c 203.0.113.253 -b
900K -d 60s -p udp -l 1KB
docker exec -d clab-netgo-host-1 ./ethr -c 203.0.113.252 -b
600K -d 60s -p udp -l 1KB
docker exec -d clab-netgo-host-1 ./ethr -c 203.0.113.251 -b
400K -d 60s -p udp -l 1KB
```

Then, run the Top-talkers Go application with `go run main.go` from within the `host-2` container (`clab-netgo-host-2`) to get a real-time Top-talkers table:

```
$ cd ch10/top-talkers; sudo ip netns exec clab-netgo-host-2 /
usr/local/go/bin/go run main.go; cd ../../
Top Talkers
+---+-------------------+--------------------+------
| # | FROM              | TO                 | PROTO
+---+-------------------+--------------------+------
| 1 | 203.0.113.253:8888 | 203.0.113.0:48494 | UDP |
| 2 | 203.0.113.252:8888 | 203.0.113.0:42912 | UDP |
| 3 | 203.0.113.251:8888 | 203.0.113.0:42882 | UDP |
+---+-------------------+--------------------+------
```

Note that due to low traffic volume, random packet sampling, and limited test duration, your results may be slightly different but should converge to a similar distribution after several test iterations.

Testing Go programs

Code testing is an integral part of any production software development process. Good test coverage improves application reliability and increases tolerance to bugs introduced at later stages of software development. Go has native support for testing with its `testing` package from the standard library and built-in command-line tool, `go test`. With test coverage built into the Go tool, it's uncommon to see third-party packages used for testing Go code.

Table-driven testing is one of the most popular testing methodologies in Go. The idea is to describe test cases as a slice of custom data structures, with each one providing both inputs and expected results for each test case. Writing test cases as a table makes it easier to create new scenarios, consider corner cases, and interpret existing code behaviors.

We can test part of the code of the `top-talkers` example we just reviewed by building a set of table tests for the heap implementation we used to sort the flow records.

Let's create a test file, `main_test.go`, with a single test function in it:

```
package main

import (
	"container/heap"
	"testing"
)

func TestHeap(t *testing.T) {
  // code tests
}
```

Both the `_test.go` filename suffix and the `Test<Name>` function prefix are naming conventions that allow Go to detect testing code and exclude it during binary compilation.

We design each test case to have all the relevant information, including the following:

- A name to use in error messages
- A set of unique flows described by their starting counters and resulting positions:

```
type testFlow struct {
	startCount   int
	timesSeen    int
	wantPosition int
	wantCount    int
}

type testCase struct {
	name  string
```

```
        flows map[string]testFlow
    }
```

Given the preceding definitions, we create a test suite for a different combination of input and output values to cover as many non-repeating scenarios as possible:

```
var testCases = []testCase{
 {
   name: "single packet",
   flows: map[string]testFlow{
     "1-1": {
       startCount:   1,
       timesSeen:    0,
       wantPosition: 0,
       wantCount:    1,
     },
   },
 },{
   name: "last packet wins",
   flows: map[string]testFlow{
     "2-1": {
       startCount:   1,
       timesSeen:    1,
       wantPosition: 1,
       wantCount:    2,
     },
     "2-2": {
       startCount:   2,
       timesSeen:    1,
       wantPosition: 0,
       wantCount:    3,
     },
   },
 },
```

We tie all this together in the body of the TestHeap function, where we iterate over all test cases. For each test case, we set up its preconditions, push all flows on the heap, and update their count timeSeen number of times:

```
func TestHeap(t *testing.T) {
	for _, test := range testCases {
		h := make(Heap, 0)
		// pushing flow on the heap
		for key, f := range test.flows {
			flow := &MyFlow{
				Count: f.startCount,
				Key:   key,
			}
			heap.Push(&h, flow)

			// updating packet counts
			for j := 0; j < f.timesSeen; j++ {
				h.update(flow)
			}
		}
	/* ... <continues next > ... */
}
```

Once we have updated all flows, we remove them off the heap, one by one, based on the highest count, and check whether the resulting position and count match what we had described in the test case. In case of a mismatch, we generate an error message using the *testing.T type injected by the testing package:

```
func TestHeap(t *testing.T) {
  /* ... < continues from before > ... */
  for i := 0; h.Len() > 0; i++ {
		f := heap.Pop(&h).(*MyFlow)

		tf := test.flows[f.Key]
		if tf.wantPosition != i {
				t.Errorf(
				  "%s: unexpected position for
packet key %s: got %d, want %d", test.name, f.Key, i,
tf.wantPosition)
```

```
                }

                if tf.wantCount != f.Count {
                        t.Errorf(
                                "%s: unexpected count for
packet key %s: got %d, want %d", test.name, f.Key, f.Count,
tf.wantCount)
                }
        }
}
```

Thus far, we've only discussed data plane telemetry, which is crucial, but not the only element of network monitoring. In the following section, we will explore network control plane telemetry by building a complete end-to-end telemetry processing pipeline.

Measuring control plane performance

Most network engineers are familiar with tools such as `ping`, `traceroute`, and `iperf` to verify network data plane connectivity, reachability, and throughput. At the same time, control plane performance often remains a black box, and we can only assume how long it takes for our network to re-converge. In this section, we aim to address this problem by building a control plane telemetry solution.

Modern control plane protocols, such as BGP, distribute large volumes of information from IP routes to MAC addresses and flow definitions. As the size of our networks grows, so does the churn rate of the control plane state, with users, VMs, and applications constantly moving between different locations and network segments. Hence, it's critical to have visibility of how well our control plane performs to troubleshoot network issues and take any preemptive actions.

The next code example covers the telemetry processing pipeline we built to monitor the control plane performance of the lab network. At the heart of it, there is a special `bgp-ping` application that allows us to measure the round-trip time of a BGP update. In this solution, we take advantage of the features of the following Go packages and applications:

- `jwhited/corebgp`: A pluggable implementation of a BGP finite state machine that allows you to run arbitrary actions for different BGP states.
- `osrg/gobgp`: One of the most popular BGP implementations in Go; we use it to encode and decode BGP messages.
- `cloudprober/cloudprober`: A flexible distributed probing and monitoring framework.
- `Prometheus` and `Grafana`: A popular monitoring and visualization software stack.

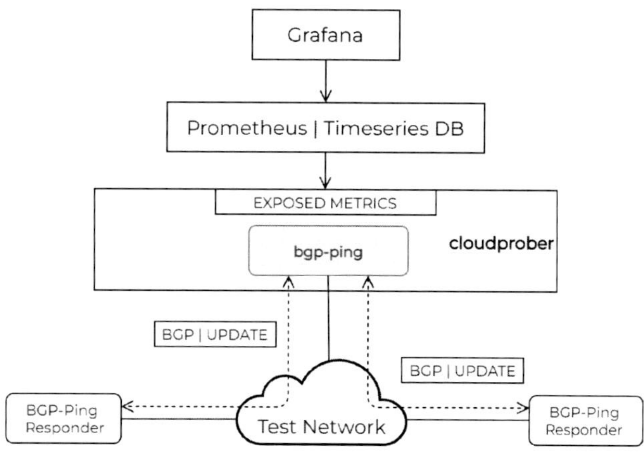

Figure 10.5 – Telemetry pipeline architecture

To bring up this entire setup, you can run `make bgp-ping-start` from the root of this book's GitHub repository (see *Further reading*):

```
Network-Automation-with-Go $ make bgp-ping-start
cd ch10/bgp-ping; go build -o bgp-ping main.go
docker exec -d clab-netgo-host-3 /workdir/bgp-ping/bgp-ping -id host-3 -nlri 100.64.0.2 -laddr 203.0.113.254 -raddr 203.0.113.129 -las 65005 -ras 65002 -p
docker exec -d clab-netgo-host-1 /workdir/bgp-ping/bgp-ping -id host-1 -nlri 100.64.0.0 -laddr 203.0.113.0 -raddr 203.0.113.1 -las 65003 -ras 65000 -p
docker exec -d clab-netgo-host-2 /cloudprober -config_file /workdir/workdir/cloudprober.cfg
cd ch10/bgp-ping; docker-compose up -d; cd ../../
Creating prometheus ... done
Creating grafana    ... done
http://localhost:3000
```

The final line of the preceding output shows the URL that you can use to access the deployed instance of Grafana, using `admin` as both `username` and `password`:

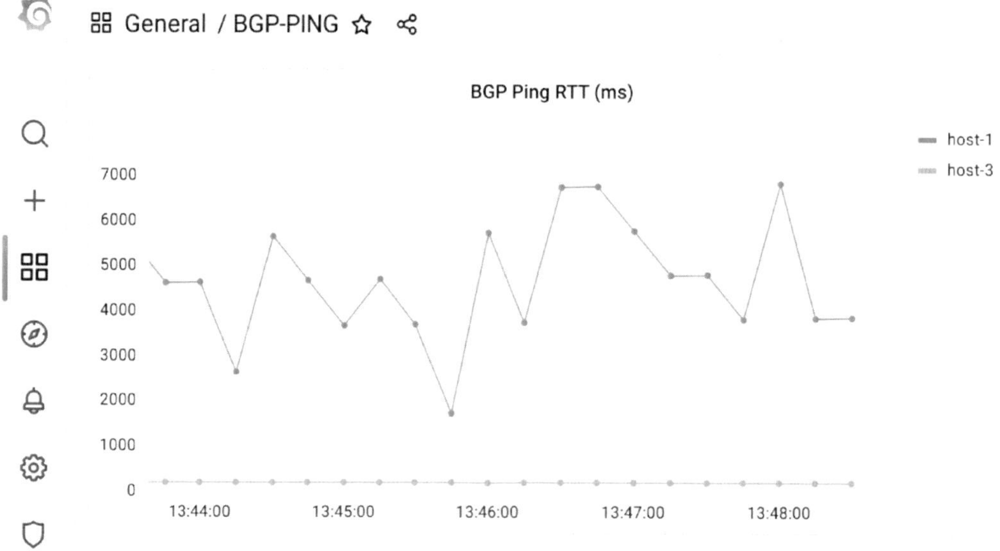

Figure 10.6 – BGP ping dashboard

This instance has a pre-created dashboard called `BGP-Ping` that plots the graph of BGP round-trip times in milliseconds.

It's important to note that there's a lot more to routing protocol convergence and performance than the update propagation time. Other important factors may include update churn due to transient events or **Forwarding Information Base** (**FIB**) programming time. We focus on a single-dimension metric in this example, but in reality, you may want to consider other performance metrics as well.

Measuring BGP Update propagation time

As the standard `ping`, the `bgp-ping` application works by sending and receiving probe messages. A sender embeds a probe in a BGP Update message and sends it to its BGP neighbor. We encode the probe as a custom BGP optional transitive attribute, which allows it to propagate transparently throughout the network until it reaches one of the `bgp-ping` responders.

A `bgp-ping` responder recognizes this custom transitive attribute and reflects it back to the sender. This gives the sender a measure of BGP Update propagation delay within the network, which is then reported to an external metric consumer or printed on a screen.

Since the `bgp-ping` application needs to inter-operate with real BGP stacks, at the very least it has to implement the initial exchange of `Open` messages to negotiate the BGP session capabilities, followed by the periodic exchange of `Keepalive` messages. We also need to do the following:

1. Send BGP Update messages triggered by different events.
2. Encode and decode custom BGP attributes.

Let's see how we can implement these requirements using open source Go packages and applications.

Event-driven BGP state machine

We use CoreBGP (`jwhited/corebgp`) to establish a BGP session with a peer and keep it alive until it's shut down. This gets us the `Open` and `Keepalive` messages we just discussed.

Inspired by the popular DNS server CoreDNS, CoreBGP is a minimalistic BGP server that you can extend through event-driven plugins.

In practice, you extend the initial capabilities by building a custom implementation of the `Plugin` interface. This interface defines different methods that can implement user-defined behavior at certain points of the BGP **finite state machine** (**FSM**):

```
type Plugin interface {
     GetCapabilities(...) []Capability
     OnOpenMessage(...) *Notification
     OnEstablished(...) handleUpdate
     OnClose(...)
}
```

For the `bpg-ping` application, we only need to send and receive BGP Update messages, so we focus on implementing the following two methods:

- `OnEstablished`: To send BGP Update messages.
- `handleUpdate`: We use this to process received updates, identify ping requests, and send a response message.

The following diagram shows the main functional blocks of this application:

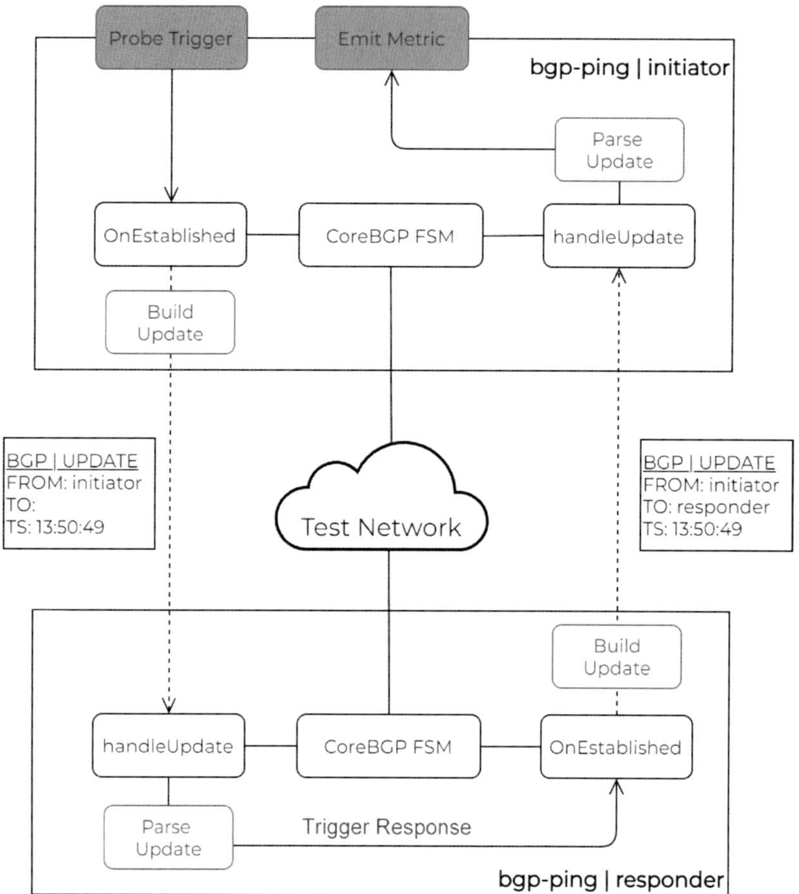

Figure 10.7 – BGP Ping Design

Let's start the code overview by examining the BGP Update handling logic (`handleUpdate`). Since our goal is to parse and process BGP ping probes, we can make sure we discard any other BGP updates early in the code. For every BGP Update message we receive, we check whether any of the BGP attributes have the custom `bgpPingType` transitive attribute we created to signal the probe or ping. We silently ignore BGP updates that don't have this attribute with a `continue` statement:

```
import bgp "github.com/osrg/gobgp/v3/pkg/packet/bgp"

const (
      bgpPingType = 42
```

```
)

func (p *plugin) handleUpdate(
     peer corebgp.PeerConfig,
     update []byte,
) *corebgp.Notification {

     msg, err := bgp.ParseBGPBody(
           &bgp.BGPHeader{Type: bgp.BGP_MSG_UPDATE},
           update,
     )
     // process error

     for _, attr := range msg.Body.
                    (*bgp.BGPUpdate).PathAttributes {
           if attr.GetType() != bgpPingType {
                      continue
           }
     /* ... <continues next > ... */
}
```

Once we have determined that it's a BGP ping message, we deal with two possible scenarios:

- If it's a **ping response**, we calculate the round-trip time using the timestamp extracted from the `bgpPingType` path attribute.
- If it's a **ping request**, we trigger a ping response by sending parsed data over a channel to the `OnEstablished` function:

```
func (p *plugin) handleUpdate(
  peer corebgp.PeerConfig,
  update []byte,
) *corebgp.Notification {
    /* ... < continues from before > ... */
    source, dest, ts, err := parseType42(attr)
    // process error
    sourceHost := string(bytes.Trim(source, "\x00"))
    destHost := string(bytes.Trim(dest, "\x00"))
```

```
    /* ... <omitted for brevity > ... */

    // if src is us, may be a response. id = router-id
    if sourceHost == *id {
      rtt := time.Since(ts).Nanoseconds()
      metric := fmt.Sprintf(
        "bgp_ping_rtt_ms{device=%s} %f\n",
        destHost,
        float64(rtt)/1e6,
      )

    p.store = append(p.store, metric)
                 return nil
    }

    p.pingCh <- ping{source: source, ts: ts.Unix()}
    return nil
}
```

The event-driven logic to send BGP updates lives in the `OnEstablished()` method that has a three-way select statement to listen for triggers over Go channels, representing three different states of the `bgp-ping` application:

- Responding to a received ping request, triggered by a request coming from the `handleUpdate` function
- Firing a new ping request, triggered by an external signal
- Sending a scheduled withdraw message at the end of the probing cycle:

```
func (p *plugin) OnEstablished(
  peer corebgp.PeerConfig,
  writer corebgp.UpdateMessageWriter,
) corebgp.UpdateMessageHandler {
  log.Println("peer established, starting main loop")
  go func() {
    for {
      select {
      case pingReq := <-p.pingCh:
```

```
            // Build the ping response payload
            bytes, err := p.buildUpdate(
                          type42PathAttr,
                          peer.LocalAddress,
                          peer.LocalAS,
            )
            // process error
            writer.WriteUpdate(bytes)
            /* ... < schedule a withdraw > ... */

        case <-p.probeCh:
            // Build the ping request payload
            bytes, err := p.buildUpdate(
                          type42PathAttr,
                          peer.LocalAddress,
                          peer.LocalAS,
            )
            // process error
            writer.WriteUpdate(bytes)
            /* ... < schedule a withdraw > ... */

        case <-withdraw.C:
            bytes, err := p.buildWithdraw()
            // process error
            writer.WriteUpdate(bytes)
        }
      }
    }()
    return p.handleUpdate
}
```

One caveat of CoreBGP is that it doesn't include its own BGP message parser or builder. It sends any raw bytes that may confuse or even crash a standard BGP stack, so always use it with caution.

Now, we need a way to parse and craft a BGP message, and here is where we can use another Go library called GoBGP.

Encoding and decoding BGP messages

GoBGP is a full-blown BGP stack and supports most of the BGP address families and features. However, since we already use CoreBGP for BGP state management, we limit the use of GoBGP to message encoding and decoding.

For example, whenever we need to build a BGP withdraw update message, we call a helper function (`buildWithdraw`) that uses GoBGP to build the message. GoBGP allows us to include only the relevant information, such as a list of **Network Layer Reachability Information** (**NLRI**), while it takes care of populating the rest of the fields, such as type, length, and building a syntactically correct BGP message:

```
func (p *plugin) buildWithdraw() ([]byte, error) {
	myNLRI := bgp.NewIPAddrPrefix(32, p.probe.String())
	withdrawnRoutes := []*bgp.IPAddrPrefix{myNLRI}
	msg := bgp.NewBGPUpdateMessage(
		withdrawnRoutes,
		[]bgp.PathAttributeInterface{},
		nil,
	)
	return msg.Body.Serialize()
}
```

Here's another example of how to use GoBGP to parse a message received by CoreBGP. We take a slice of bytes and use the `ParseBGPBody` function to deserialize it into GoBGP's `BGPMessage` type:

```
func (p *plugin) handleUpdate(
	peer corebgp.PeerConfig,
	update []byte,
) *corebgp.Notification {
	msg, err := bgp.ParseBGPBody(
		&bgp.BGPHeader{Type: bgp.BGP_MSG_UPDATE},
		update,
	)
	// process error

	if err := bgp.ValidateBGPMessage(msg); err != nil {
		log.Fatal("validate BGP message ", err)
	}
```

You can now further parse this BGP message to extract various path attributes and NLRIs, as we've seen in the earlier overview of the `handleUpdate` function.

Collecting and exposing metrics

The `bgp-ping` application can run as a standalone process and print the results on a screen. We also want to be able to integrate our application into more general-purpose system monitoring solutions. To do that, it needs to expose its measurement results in a standard format that an external monitoring system can understand.

You can implement this capability natively by adding a web server and publishing your metrics for external consumers, or you can use an existing tool that collects and exposes metrics on behalf of your application. One tool that does this is Cloudprober, which enables automated and distributed probing and monitoring, and offers native Go integration with several external probes.

We integrate the `bgp-ping` application with the Cloudprober via its `serverutils` package, which allows you to exchange probe requests and replies over the **standard input (stdin)** and **standard output (stdout)**. When we start `bgp-ping` with a `-c` flag, it expects all probe triggers to come from Cloudprober and sends its results back in a `ProbeReply` message:

```
func main() {
  /* ... < continues from before > ... */
  probeCh := make(chan struct{})
  resultsCh := make(chan string)

  peerPlugin := &plugin{
            probeCh: probeCh,
          resultsCh: resultsCh,
  }

  if *cloudprober {
    go func() {
      serverutils.Serve(func(
        request *epb.ProbeRequest,
        reply *epb.ProbeReply,
      ) {
        probeCh <- struct{}{}
        reply.Payload = proto.String(<-resultsCh)
        if err != nil {
          reply.ErrorMessage = proto.String(err.Error())
```

```
            }
          })
        }()
      }
    }
```

The Cloudprober application itself runs as a pre-compiled binary and requires minimal configuration to tell it about the `bgp-ping` application and its runtime options:

```
probe {
  name: "bgp_ping"
  type: EXTERNAL
  targets { dummy_targets {} }
  timeout_msec: 11000
  interval_msec: 10000
  external_probe {
    mode: SERVER
    command: "/workdir/bgp-ping/bgp-ping -id host-2 -nlri
100.64.0.1 -laddr 203.0.113.2 -raddr 203.0.113.3 -las 65004
-ras 65001 -c true"
  }
}
```

All measurement results are automatically published by Cloudprober in a format that most popular cloud monitoring systems can understand.

Storing and visualizing metrics

The final stage in this control plane telemetry processing pipeline is metrics storage and visualization. Go is a very popular choice for these systems, with examples including Telegraf, InfluxDB, Prometheus, and Grafana.

The current telemetry processing example includes Prometheus and Grafana with their respective configuration files and pre-built dashboards. The following configuration snippet points Prometheus at the local Cloudprober instance and tells it to scrape all available metrics every 10 seconds:

```
scrape_configs:
  - job_name: 'bgp-ping'
    scrape_interval: 10s
```

```
    static_configs:
      - targets: ['clab-netgo-host-2:9313']
```

Although we discuss little of it here, building meaningful dashboards and alerts is as important as doing the measurements. Distributed systems observability is a big topic that is extensively covered in existing books and online resources. For now, we will stop at the point where we see a visual representation of the data in a Grafana dashboard but don't want to imply that a continuous linear graph of absolute values is enough. Most likely, to make any reasonable assumptions, you'd want to present your data as an aggregated distribution and monitor its outlying values over time, as this would give a better sign of increasing system stress and may serve as a trigger for any further actions.

Developing distributed applications

Building a distributed application, such as `bgp-ping`, can be a major undertaking. Unit testing and debugging can help spot and fix a lot of bugs, but these processes can be time-consuming. In certain cases, when an application has different components, developing your code iteratively may require some manual orchestration. Steps such as building binary files and container images, starting the software process, enabling logging, and triggering events are now something you need to synchronize and repeat for all the components that include your application.

The final developer experience tool that we will cover in this chapter was specifically designed to address the preceding issues. Tilt helps developers automate manual steps, and it has native integration with container and orchestration platforms, such as Kubernetes or Docker Compose. You let it know which files to monitor, and it will automatically rebuild your binaries, swap out container images, and restart existing processes, all while showing you the output logs of all applications on a single screen.

It works by reading a special `Tiltfile` containing a set of instructions on what to build and how to do it. Here's a snippet from a Tiltfile that automatically launches a `bgp-ping` process inside one of the host containers and restarts it every time it detects a change to `main.go`:

```
local_resource('host-1',
  serve_cmd='ip netns exec clab-netgo-host-1 go run main.go -id
host-1 -nlri 100.64.0.0 -laddr 203.0.113.0 -raddr 203.0.113.1
-las 65003 -ras 65000 -p',
  deps=['./main.go'])
```

The full `Tiltfile` has two more resources for the other two hosts in our lab network. You can bring up all three parts of the application with `sudo tilt up`:

```
Network-Automation-with-Go $ cd ch10/bgp-ping
Network-Automation-with-Go/ch10/bgp-ping $ sudo tilt up
Tilt started on http://localhost:10350/
```

Tilt has both a console (text) and a web UI that you can use to view the logs of all resources:

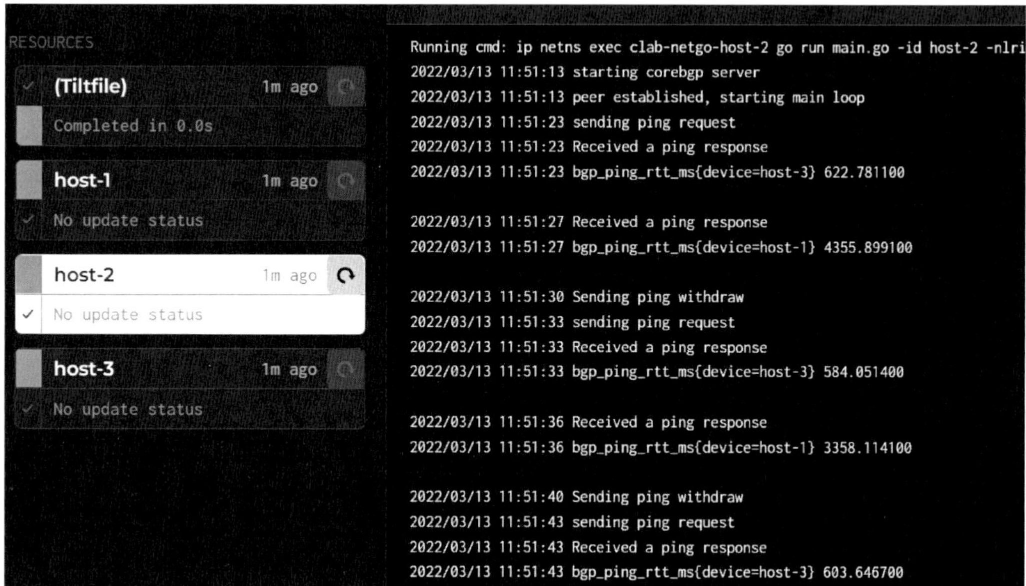

Figure 10.8 – Tilt

Any change to the source code of the `bgp-ping` application would trigger a restart of all affected resources. By automating a lot of manual steps and aggregating the logs, this tool can simplify the development process of any distributed application.

Summary

This concludes the chapter about network monitoring. We have only touched upon a few selected subjects and admit that the topic of this chapter is too vast to cover in this book. However, we hope we have provided enough resources, pointers, and ideas for you to continue the exploration of network monitoring, as it's one of the most vibrant and actively growing areas of the network engineering discipline.

Further reading

- Book's GitHub repository: `https://github.com/PacktPublishing/Network-Automation-with-Go`
- `google/gopacket` package: `https://github.com/google/gopacket`
- gdb documentation: `https://go.dev/doc/gdb`
- `vscode-go`: `https://code.visualstudio.com/docs/languages/go`

- `ch10/packet-capture/.vscode/launch.json`: `https://github.com/PacktPublishing/Network-Automation-with-Go/blob/main/ch10/packet-capture/.vscode/launch.json`
- Open source components with ready-to-use examples: `https://github.com/netsampler/goflow2/tree/main/compose/kcg`
- CoreBGP documentation: `https://pkg.go.dev/github.com/jwhited/corebgp#section-readme`

11
Expert Insights

As we're getting closer to the end of the book, we want to do something special. Instead of a more traditional final chapter that reiterates the main points and tries to look into the future, we have done something different and, hopefully, more entertaining for you.

We reached out to several people who have real-world hands-on experience with network automation and/or are using Go for network-related tasks and activities so that they could share their perspectives with us.

We hope that their thoughts, lessons learned, ideas, and opinions will provide you with guidance and more food for thought about the role and importance of automation in the networking industry and reinforce the point that Go is not an esoteric, niche language, but one that is used extensively today for a wide range of network-related use cases.

Without further ado, we present to you the *Expert Insights* chapter.

David Barroso

David is a Principal Engineer working in the intersection between infrastructure and software engineering. Among other things, he is responsible for creating open source projects such as NAPALM, Nornir, and Gornir.

Traditionally, the networking space has been very stable. Most innovations came through standard bodies that took years to be ratified. In addition, vendors promoted certifications with clear and structured learning guides and courses. This meant that network engineers had a clear path to start their careers and become certified experts without having to worry too much about being sidetracked and even without having to bother to figure out what came next for them; someone else had already decided that.

However, the year is 2022 and our everyday vocabulary has gone from acronyms such as MPLS-over-GRE-over-IPSec to others such as IaC, CI, PR, and DevSecOps. Our vendor-driven, slow-changing, cozy life is no more and now we need to keep up with the latest industry buzzwords and the breaking changes in the latest update of our framework/library of choice (luckily, we don't need to keep up with JavaScript frameworks, for now). But do not despair—take the red pill and be ready to choose your own path.

My advice to keep up with this ever-changing crazy world is as follows: rely less on vendor-driven certifications unless they are a hard requirement for your job. Instead, grab books such as the one you are reading now. Get familiar with the ideas and concepts without worrying too much about the tiny details. Instead of setting up impossible lab scenarios, collaborate with open source projects and learn from the community, the tooling used to develop and maintain the project, the processes, the frameworks, the ideas, and so on. Finally, do not get overwhelmed. People will come up with new buzzwords, libraries, projects, and so on all the time, but if you focus on the ideas, you quickly notice that things are not as earth-shattering as they claim to be and the industry doesn't move as fast as advertised.

Stuart Clark

Stuart is a Senior Developer Advocate Of Community AWS, author for Cisco Press, and a Cisco-Certified DevNet Expert #20220005.

It would be fair to say I would not be where I am now/today without network automation. I was not the first person on the "automate everything" bus, though. I fully admit I was late to the game, or so I felt back in 2014. Since starting in networking in 2008, a number of people have said how they could automate many of their daily tasks, but yet, my ego said my CLI was still better. What held me back? Mostly fear, failure, and not knowing where to begin. It wasn't until the summer of 2014 that I rolled up my sleeves and said, *I am going to master this now*. Being a network genius, I could easily do this! Nope. This humbled me and I found I could not brute-force learn to code the same way I learned network engineering. For me, a more logical approach was required. This started as just an hour a day in the morning when my brain was fresh and my day of customer network issues and network projects kicked off. I often found I would be stuck in areas for days, too. I could complete labs or copy the examples, but understanding concepts I would often struggle with, so I started making mini projects based on my current day tasks. This often was the same script, but I kept adding and building on this day after day, adding better error handling or validation. Having someone with more experience look over your work and get feedback is great too. After a while, your code has evolved into a work tool that your whole team now uses, and that kick-started many other exciting new workflows. It takes time, but it comes a year or 2 years later.

When anyone asks me about careers, learning new things, or applying for a new role, I always ask: *Where do you want to be in 2 years' time and 5 years' time?* Your skills always need to be sharpened and to do that, you need to hone your skills and learn new things. It is not today we are preparing for, it is our future, and each step of the way requires discipline and consistency. That is where all the magic in you happens. I do not believe we are born with a skill. Sure, we might learn something faster than others. I believe we can be whoever we want to be, and if you have the passion and desire and are willing to put in the work, you can achieve anything.

Good luck in all you do.

Claudia de Luna

After graduating from Stanford University, Claudia started working for NASA JPL initially in software development and then moving into enterprise networking. In 2006, she left JPL and worked in several verticals, including biotech and financial. In 2015, while working for one of the largest Cisco VARs, she began automating network workflows. Today, she works for a boutique consulting firm, Enterprise Infrastructure Acceleration, Inc., helping Fortune 100 companies deploy network and security programs at speed.

Network automation truths... so far...

1 – Automation will not replace network engineers

Make no mistake, the discipline of network engineering is not going anywhere. How we interact with devices is amid revolution to be sure, but the knowledge of how a TCP three-way handshake takes place or how a routing protocol works is, and will continue to be, essential. In fact, the depth of this knowledge will likely increase as scripting networking workflows will require an in-depth understanding. I never truly understood Cisco's **Application Centric Infrastructure** (**ACI**) until I scripted a complete data center ACI fabric build-out.

2 – The power of text and revision control

This does not get said often enough (or ever), but text is all-powerful. It is the lowest common denominator as well as the input to rich typesetting output with which to convey a written language (programming or otherwise). While putting together a richly formatted book or a computer script, you can take the simple text and snapshot its evolution over time. In this way, you know the exact nature of every change. This is revision control. Originally developed to track code changes, today, as with network automation, you can put configurations, configuration templates, state, diagrams, documents, and almost anything under revision control. Before you leap into scripting, take a little bit of time to learn a revision control system such as Git and GitHub.

While we are on the topic of text, get a real text editor! Notepad and TextEdit are only handy if you have no other option (and learn `vi`—see *9 – Linux and regular expressions*). Invest the time to get familiar with more advanced text editors such as Sublime or Atom.

3 – Just start

Approaching something new and unfamiliar can be daunting. Just start. If you are new to programming, search for resources on basic programming concepts or programming fundamentals. This is an important step if you are *NOT* familiar with the concepts of variables, scopes, operators, control structures, and namespaces.

Once you have a footing in these concepts, write down a particular problem you want to solve, pick a language, and **dive right in**. For me, it was generating configurations. In fact, for every new programming language I learn, that is the first problem I solve. I'm just working with text and not actual devices, so I can't get into too much trouble. If there is a small problem at work that you are comfortable tackling, start there. Define the problem clearly, detail the desired outcome, and just start. Jot down the specific steps and tackle each one individually.

Let's say you want to generate configuration commands for configuring the same VLAN on 10 devices and, just to keep it simple, output the necessary commands you need to run on each device to the screen. Your first script could be as simple as taking a list of devices and printing out to the screen the following configuration:

```
!Switch01 vlan 10
name Vlan10_on_Switch01
```

Once you have that, you will want to save the output to a text file. After that, you will want a file for each switch. After that, you will start to customize each switch. You get the idea. Every enhancement will teach you something new. Every new feature will expand your experience.

4 – Embrace the landscape

Doubly daunting is the fact that you are trying to learn something new, but there is so much to learn! See *3 – Just start*. The experience you get from learning something and then abandoning it for something better is invaluable. Being able to articulate why you prefer one solution over another or why you are recommending a particular approach will immediately set you apart and will instantly generate credibility. This makes you a true engineer.

I believe there is as much value in trying something and abandoning it as there is in trying something and adopting it. This process makes you credible. It moves you from someone who says, *You should use X. Why? Uh.. because ...* to the person who says, *For what you are trying to do, you should use X because X has these features or is easier to support in your environment or ....* Cultivate the ability to articulate why you are recommending something, along with why you are not recommending something.

That experience, that *credibleness*, has served me well as a female in a largely male-dominated industry. I've shown up for a job or a meeting with males and had the client speak only to my male counterparts. That credibility and these fact-based recommendations always win the day. They may start out talking only to my male teammates, but they end up speaking with me. That will always hold true and not just for gender.

5 – Share and package

It's tempting to code for yourself but think about the impact you can have if you empower your team. To that end, as you write your scripts, think about how you would write them if you had to share them. Think about teaching a teammate who has zero programming or even CLI experience to execute one of your scripts. This will get you thinking about how to package your script. There are many options, including turning your script into a Windows executable if that is your *audience*, or front-ending your script by a GUI or web page if your team leverages different operating systems.

6 – No limits

In network automation, it's very easy to focus solely on automation for infrastructure. Don't do that! Think about an environment where your final documentation was automatically generated by the configurations. Have to do lots of change control tickets that are often similar? Think about an environment where your change control information was generated by a script. And the closeout is also generated by a script. Want to add a diagram to your documentation? Think about a world where your diagram was autogenerated from your new topology. Have to interface with another team and share information with them? How appreciative would they be if you shared just the information that they needed in a consistent format rather than making them slog through an email thread or an exasperating Excel spreadsheet?

7 – Understand data structures

How you put your data together has far-reaching implications. Get comfortable with complex data structures. By data structures, I mean lists and dictionaries and every combination thereof. Ask yourself: will my code be clearer if I iterate over a list of dictionaries or if I pick data from a set of keys? Get comfortable extracting the data you need when these data structures are highly nested. For more on this topic, see my post *Decomposing Data Structures* (in the *Further reading* section).

8 – Learn about and use APIs

Many modern network devices now offer APIs. These APIs will generally return the answers to queries in structured data (See *7 – Understand data structures*). If you don't have to log in to a switch, pull a configuration, or show a command in semi-formatted text and then parse that text, don't! Use an API. In addition to APIs offered by infrastructure appliances and network devices, there is a wealth of data available, often with open and free APIs.

Need to look up the vendor OUI of a MAC address? There is a public and free API for that. Need to look up the physical location of an IP address? There is a public and free API for that. Enrich your data, reports, and information with APIs.

9 – Linux and regular expressions

I can't stress this enough. A background in Unix is invaluable. Many infrastructure devices start out with a Unix or Linux base. Having this background will further distinguish you from the run-of-the-mill network engineer. Part of having some Linux knowledge should include knowledge of regular expressions. Because network automation invariably requires some parsing, having a familiarity with regular expressions will help you do your own parsing and will help you work with other parsing modules. The more sophisticated text editors understand regular expressions to facilitate your searches.

10 – Wander and explore

Finally, set aside time to explore. I try to set aside at least two Sunday mornings a month where I take something I heard about or read about or saw and start exploring, or I take a problem and research solutions. No destination in mind, I just see where it takes me. Half the time, I start with one thing and wind up basically on another planet. I'm going to take an Udemy course on MongoDB and I wind up trying to create the best regular expression I can for matching an IP address. *I'm not hung up on this completion thing* (at least on Sundays).

Alexis de Talhouët

Alexis de Talhouët is an avid network automation expert always trying to lessen network complexity by getting involved in open source communities; he was mainly involved with OpenDaylight (ODL) and Open Network Automation Platform (ONAP), both hosted by The Linux Foundation, where he held Technical Steering Committee membership.

I initially started my career as a Java developer, with a massive passion for networking. At first, it felt very weird to build systems automating networks without really understanding them. But throughout the years, I learned to be sufficiently proficient in networking to properly build automation platforms around it. Such knowledge can be acquired either by building labs, following workshops, or, for the luckiest ones, spending some time in a network operation center.

Something that struck me the most, and is still true, is how much the path to network automation can be different if you come from a software developer versus a network engineering background. Both have their own acronyms, processes, standards, and so on, and yet, with the rise of cloud-native, Infra as Code, Network as Code, GitOps, and so on, we saw both worlds adopting similar concepts, methodologies, and tooling to do the initial provisioning and operate the entire life cycle of what was automated. So, at a high level, the *how* to perform the automation became fairly common, whereas the *what* still remains fairly domain-specific. When embarking on such a journey, we should really take advantage of this ecosystem to accelerate our automation strategies.

In my opinion, the basis of network automation is the configuration to apply a (golden) template of that configuration with well-defined (typed) parameters, and the protocol used to apply that configuration. Another very important element required for service assurance is the notion of telemetry, to retrieve the running state and get updates on state changes and state.

With my developer hat on, what matters most is the API/contract exposed by the network equipment/ network function; these are commonly represented by the device YANG models. The main issue is, given the network is non-homogeneous, each vendor has its own models, and exposes more or less its functionalities. Even though there is a lot of effort being put into standardizing the configuration and monitoring of network equipment (OpenConfig, OpenROADM, and IETF), this is certainly not fully adopted, and thus still requires a lot of *cookie-cutter* handling.

Network automation strategies must account for this and accordingly design their platform to accept any type of network automation techniques. Of course, the more the said platform attempts to abstract that non-homogeneous environment, the more maintenance there is, as the shim layer that will convert from the device's native API to that higher-level business API will have to keep up with the pace of device upgrade and device model change.

This put forward the following design decision: should you strive to have one abstraction layer for your entire network and maintain a shim layer that talks southbound to devices?

If yes, you'd better be armed with a team of developers to build and maintain that abstraction.

If not, I suggest solving the issue by letting the network engineers build that golden template for each network service and have a platform to load, version, and interact with them. And that interaction might be a shell script, a Python snippet, a Go program, an Ansible playbook, and so on: whatever might work for that specific team, as long as the said platform exposes a REST API with the ability to execute it. That way, network teams are empowered to automate by exposing the API and can stop worrying about the platform. The onus of keeping these golden templates and scriptlets becomes theirs.

Another important aspect is having an orchestration engine enabling the definition of a workflow consuming these domain-specific APIs. With maturity and governance, enforcing pre-check and post-check tasks should become a must-have in these workflows. Also, always consider how to roll back if the post-check isn't successful. Applying and rolling back configuration can be tricky when doing network-wide transactions; consider building helper functions to increase reusability.

These orchestration engines can either be distributed or centralized, but often there will be an end-to-end service orchestration that will consume these exposed domain-specific workflows.

Finally, one of the key components to keep in mind is the inventory of the network elements/functions. As soon as a workflow does something, it is important to have and keep the inventory up to date so that service assurance workflows can properly act upon the active and available state of the network.

Given most of the network automation is currently done either through NETCONF or gNxI southbound protocols, YANG has become the de facto model standard to define and express device configuration, and the tooling around YANG is mature enough to rely on XML/JSON for the golden templates. Rendering these templates is also something easily doable, regardless of the technology used, even if enforcing YANG-defined types. Considering all of this, when starting a network automation journey, I wouldn't advocate for a specific programming/scripting language, but rather let each team manage that for themselves. But I would definitely advocate for standardizing as much as possible the southbound protocol and interaction. As the journey matures, and you feel that, as an organization, you have a better handle on a specific technology, then you can build more helpers and start putting forward some company-wide practice for automation.

As the network automation domain evolves, infrastructure provisioning is also evolving. With the rise of Kubernetes, the latest trend is to extend the Kubernetes API to provide **Custom Resource Definition (CRD)** abstracting hardware and software configuration, and supporting their entire lifecycle through the use of an Operator. An Operator exposes the CRD as a K8S native API and contains the logic for managing the end-to-end lifecycle of a CRD instance. This is shifting the responsibility of operation to the Operator provider and is fostering intent-driven automation. As network equipment vendors adopt this concept, network automation will become even closer to application lifecycle management. And with this trend, one of the main programming languages being put forward is Go.

One project to look at is Nephio, the latest Linux Foundation networking initiative aiming at providing network controllers using Kubernetes API extensions.

Happy coding!

John Doak

John Doak is a Principal Software Engineer Manager at Microsoft, an ex-Google Network Systems Engineer (SRE), and an ex-LucasArts/Lucasfilm Network Engineer.

I cut my teeth in networking at LucasArts after I asked the Director of IT what my next career step was. He made me a network engineer on the spot and said to go buy a Cisco book and configure a router for a new T1 we just got. There is nothing quite like staring at a box in a closet, hoping that the Cisco book you have placed on top of your head will give you knowledge via osmosis. I spent the next several years there automating my way out of doing work (portals that reset network MAC security parameters, moved ports to new VLANs, auto-balanced inbound BGP traffic using route maps, and so on).

I moved from there to Google, where I spent the bulk of my time automating the vendor backbone known as **Backend Backbone** (**B2**). I wrote the first autonomous services that programmed the various routers. Then, I built the first workflow orchestration system for the network with some very talented software engineers (Sridhar Srinivasan, Benjamin Helsley, and Wencheng Lu), and then I went on to build the next version (because you never get it right the first time). The biggest change between the first and second was moving from Python to Go. We were able to decrease our bugs, increase the number of workflows by 10x, and made it possible to refactor the code without breaking everything. I spent the next few years migrating all of NetOps onto Go from Python and building automations that configured the network on a daily basis (BGP mesh deployments, LSP metrics, SRLG configuration deployments, edge router turn-ups, BGP-LU updates, ISIS metrics, LSP optimizations, and so on). One of the keys for making that scalable was another service I wrote that allows sending an RPC that could configure any vendor router we supported for a change (such as configuring a BGP peer).

Now, I work at Microsoft where I no longer am working in networking, but write Go SDKs and manage a software group that deploys software to validate data, supply gating controls, audit data sources, and so on. This includes running Kubernetes clusters, deploying software, and building tools to run these systems.

Finally, I'm the author of the book *Go For DevOps*.

If I could give one piece of advice for network automation: use a centralized workflow orchestration system. The benefits of a centralized workflow system to allow visibility into what is happening in your network, allow emergency controls, and provide policy enforcement have been proven time and time again.

So, what do I mean by centralized workflow enforcement? You want an RPC service that exists and has a set of actions that the service can do. Your tools submit an RPC describing the set of actions and monitor the running of that from the server.

This means all executions are running out of the same place. You can then build emergency tools to stop problem network executions in case there are issues (or simply pause them). You can enforce concurrency limits on how many network devices can be touched within a time period. You can provide network health checks that have to run before an automation can run.

Centralization is key to controlling the automation on your network. When you're in a small group, it is easy to know what is going on. When your group grows much beyond five people, this starts to become impossible.

Two of the largest outages I witnessed at Google were due to engineers running scripts on their desktops that mutated the network while they were working outside their time zone. Backtracking to who/what was causing the issue required scanning TACACS logs to find the culprits. And if the scripts had been making ongoing changes, no one could have stopped it without tracking down someone in security to disable their credentials. That precious time might mean that your entire network is down.

If you'd like to look at a basic workflow system that could be used for network actions, see my *Designing for Chaos* chapter in the *Go For DevOps* book.

The packets must flow!

Roman Dodin

Roman is a Network Automation Engineer with a product management hat signed by Nokia. Besides his professional affiliation, he is a renowned open source leader, maintainer, and contributor in the network automation landscape. You might recognize him as the current maintainer of the Containerlab project, which you will come across while working on the practical exercises provided within this book.

I assume you are already into Go, and you want to see how Go can apply to the network automation problem space, or you're curious to know *why Go for network automation*. Allow me to share why I once switched to Go, what were the main drivers for that move, and why I think it is a perfect time for network engineers to start looking at Go.

Before delving into Go, I used Python for all things network automation; no big surprises here. For the past couple of decades, the *usual* network automation workflow revolved around crafting/templating CLI commands, sending them over SSH/Telnet to the network element's CLI process, parsing the replies, and processing them. Back then, you were lucky to have any kind of vendor-provided REST

API. Hence, most automation projects were using screen scraping libraries with all the pains of dealing with unstructured data in an ad hoc way.

Meanwhile, in the IT realm, the proliferation of containerization, micro-segmentation, and Infra-as-Code paradigms was coupled with the Go language mounting solid ground. The simplicity of the language syntax, coupled with a rich standard library, compiled nature, first-class concurrency, and decent performance, made Go win lots of developers' hearts. In no time, we witnessed a new ecosystem—**Cloud Native Computing Foundation** (**CNCF**)—emerge with a new set of requirements on how applications get deployed, run, and interface with one another. Consequently, the community revisited the networking layer to comply with the new way of running applications in an API-first, cloud-native setting.

With time, the waves made in the sea of IT reached the networking island. Nowadays, any decent network OS carries on top a set of management APIs with structured and modeled data for anyone to consume. The modern automation workflow assumes leveraging those APIs solely in a concurrent, performant, and cloud-native way. And you guessed it right: being able to write concurrent, performant, easily deployable applications leveraging the sheer set of cloud-native tools and libraries is what Go offers to network automation engineers out of the box.

Even with the inertia levels we have in networking, the ecosystem of network-focused projects is growing fast. As you will see for yourself, getting through the chapters of this book, typical network-related libraries have been created for Go already.

Another critical player in the network automation/management field is the OpenConfig consortium. Spearheaded by Google with the participation of network operators, OpenConfig conceived many network automation projects that gravitate toward Go—`goyang`, `ygot`, `kne`, `ondatra`, and `featureprofiles`. Those who want to get a grasp of what these projects have to offer will have to get a hold of Go. As it often happens, the tools that we will consider a commodity in the future are being shaped by hyper-scalers today.

In summary, if your network automation activities have any of the following properties, you might consider Go as a tool for the job:

- Require being performant at scale.
- Have a strong use case for concurrent execution.
- Use generated data classes off of YANG models.
- Leverage Kubernetes control plane.
- Integrate with CNCF tools and projects.
- Make use of OpenConfig projects.

Echoing others, Go is not an ultimate answer or a replacement for Python/Java/and so on. It is, though, a programming language with a solid set of strong points, a large community, and a flourishing ecosystem. In my opinion, it has a bright future in the network automation domain, and this book should be an excellent aid for those who want to see the practical aspects of using Go for network automation today.

David Gee

David Gee is a Director of Product Management at Juniper Networks. He blogs at dave.dev, previously ipengineer.net. He is the creator of the JUNOS Terraform Automation Framework (JTAF), among other things. Twitter: @davedotdev

If you've built knowledge in the network space, chances are you've purchased and inhaled knowledge from *Cisco Press* books. These books, for the most part, are well structured and provide knowledge that opens up like a flower. For those looking to build automation knowledge, good sources of knowledge that are multi-vendor-friendly are hard to come by. The industry itself is fairly immature, and network engineers developing software skills vertically in the networking silo tend to make very questionable decisions. This isn't the fault of the network automation engineer but is due to a lack of discipline that's present in the industry. In plain-old networking, if you configure BGP badly, a session might not come up. If you accidentally leak prefixes, then someone will correct your knowledge pretty quickly. The next time you configure BGP, you probably won't make that mistake again!

Software discipline in the networking space is sorely needed, and many organizations are still in their nascent networking automation phase. Bad experiences in this phase normally are catastrophic for confidence levels and either confirm that it's too hard or light the runway for a great take-off. There are lots of people going to bootcamps still, and thanks to Udemy, Pluralsight, and a raft of other learning platforms, it's easier today than ever to get into software. This is a contentious topic and I want to be careful here, but software isn't all just throwing lines of code at something until it works on a knife edge. It's a discipline, a mindset, and requires rigor.

My journey toward a decade of Go

Go is a great language, and for many, it's a primary programming language as well as a tooling language. Go provides a "belts and braces approach" in which even the compiler nags you to do the right thing. Sure, you could write sloppy code, but the whole Go ecosystem is wired to help you not do that. Most of the IDEs on the market have great Go tooling and will further lint and format your code, kicking you into being a better developer. Mat Ryer of Grafana Labs and the "Go Time" podcast once said: "*Because of the Go tools, I can read other people's code and it feels familiar as if I'd written it.*" That's down to how the Go community has baked best practices into the toolchain. You get that for free.

For amusement, but also to make a point, I'm going to share a moment from my past career. I wrote C back in the day (C99) and wrote it on Microsoft Windows Notepad, linked it, and compiled it with individual tools into a binary, which then needed burning onto EPROMs for an embedded system. I managed thousands of lines of plain text, without so much as a hint of what was going to work at the time of writing. Test rigs helped, but the real world is always the truth. One day, I was called to an industrial unit where one of my systems had blown the lid off a water reservoir tank. In the moment and under pressure, I managed to find a bug because I'd written down the algorithm and left key comments in the code so I could follow under stress. Great tools and a solid engineering approach to writing code will save you from being fired or, even worse, being sued. If it was all spaghetti code (some of it was—I'm no hero), I'd have probably been imprisoned. Since then, we have great IDEs at our fingertips, and Go takes the best bits of C (in my opinion) and gives you a development journey that I've not found anywhere else. Ahead of even risking a production run, the compiler can tell me about race conditions, pointer problems, and a whole raft of things that I've been waiting decades for.

Beyond the IDE, compiler, and Go toolchain, Go lends itself to writing clear, readable, and maintainable code because of things such as error handling and desirable repetition. Avoiding magic is a key tenet, and you should be able to import a package and initiate it deterministically in your own code because of the discipline within the Go community.

Go offers so many out-of-the-box features, newcomers tend to get Go punch drunk. It's normal to see goroutines appearing everywhere and channels being used in situations where they're just not needed. Bill Kennedy of Ardan Labs has some great material on this, and if you think you need a goroutine, the chances are you probably do not. It's worth profiling your code with `pprof` before building things that you don't need and doing some benchmarks through Go's testing capabilities. Go in its simplest form will probably outperform your use case, and deciding to keep your design architecturally simple in the early days will prevent complex headaches in the future.

Go's type system

Go's type system can be strict to work with, but it provides the rigor and structure that you absolutely need. Network operating systems are normally based on structured data and things such as NETCONF engines have API schemas that are modeled from YANG. By consuming the **domain-specific language** (**DSL**) that defines the schema of the NOS data, you can generate one-to-one mappings against your Go code. The result is that by ingesting YANG and GPB, you gain predictable and reliable data structures, which are an important part of the API contract for interacting with a NOS. As network telemetry trends grow, a clear winner is working with GPB and gRPC. Good news! You can take the `.proto` files and get programmatic contract alignment for free when building client code. The same principle works for XML as it does for gRPC and GPB. There are many tools available for building data structures, and some IDEs have the capability to go from JSON to structs. Use the tools where they are available, but never dismiss the opportunity for entropy and drift. Version control is important for this very reason alone. As a final note on data encoding and schemas, XML is rich and programmatically powerful. JSON might be a cool kid thing, but XML is great to work with for generating configurations for platforms such as Junos. If you are comfortable with XML, working with NETCONF is one small stone's throw away. When building types with Go, encoding XML is just as easy as JSON. Here's an example of that:

```
package main
```

```
import (
	"encoding/json"
	"encoding/xml"
	"fmt"
)

type DataEncodingExample struct {
	/*
		Example payload
		{
			"_key": "blah",
			"_value": "42",
			"_type": "string",
		},
	*/
	Key   string `json:"_key",xml:"_key"`
	Value string `json:"_value",xml:"_value"`
	VType string `json:"_type",xml:"_type"`
}

func main() {
	dataInput := DataEncodingExample{
		Key:   "blah",
		Value: "42",
		VType: "string",
	}

	jsonEncoded, _ := json.Marshal(dataInput)
	xmlEncoded, _ := xml.Marshal(dataInput)
	// This is example code. What errors? :)

	fmt.Println("JSON Encoded: ", string(jsonEncoded))
	fmt.Println("XML Encoded: ", string(xmlEncoded))
}
```

The output is as follows:

```
JSON Encoded:   {"_key":"blah","_value":"42","_type":"string"}
XML Encoded:   <DataEncodingExample><Key>blah</Key><Value>42</
Value><VType>string</VType></DataEncodingExample>
```

A note on version control

On to version control, which is not only important for your own code but also important for Go's package management system. There have been more than 10 package management attempts from the core Go team, but as of version `1.13`, the Go module system feels like they finally got it right. If you're unfamiliar with `go mod` and its use, it's worth investing the time. Being able to deterministically rebuild a Go program with the correct package is of prime importance, and it's worth understanding how you can use semantic versioning and the `go mod` system to sturdy up your development habits. There are famous stories in the DevOps and SRE space about one patch version being off and code being entirely unpredictable. As great as those stories are when telling them at meet-ups, they aren't fun in the moment and can be avoided by locking your code to use specific versions and trusting that in CI/CD pipelines or build systems, your code will be re-composed the same way you composed it in development.

Growing your code

I'm thankful to have been an electronics engineer before I went into networking and learned assembly language and C before even so much as touching a CLI. I found it odd that I could make more money typing commands into a serial port than building a system with a serial port. Roll the calendar forward two decades (yikes), and many of my old habits are still in existence. If I begin to write a new tool or software service, I start by building out the kernel of the idea without implementation. This vehicle enables experimentation and learning about the problem space without lots of tedious code changes in the early phases of exploration. The algorithm kind of grows itself, and over time, I'll embed links to useful API code or comments I've found on forums and blogs, and so on:

```
package main

import (
	"context"
	"fmt"
	uuid2 "github.com/google/uuid"
	"github.com/sethvargo/go-envconfig"
	log "github.com/sirupsen/logrus"
)
```

```
const _VERSION = "0.0.1"

/*
This code logs into the auth service for X and then updates the
remote status with the local status measurement.

It is triggered when the remote state is changed.

Each invocation generates a UUID which can be used by the ops
team.
*/

type Config struct {
	APIUser string `env:"PROG1_API_USER_ID"`
	APIKey  string `env:"PROG1_API_USER_ID"`
}

// GetToken retrieves a JWT from the external auth service
func (c *Config) GetToken(URL, uuid string) (string, error) {
	// Initiate thing
	log.Info(fmt.Sprintf("system: updater, uuid: %v,
	 message: logging into device with key %v\n", uuid,
	 c.APIUser))
	// Imagine this is implemented!
	return "JWT 42.42.42", nil
}

func main() {
	// Set log level, normally this would be from config
	log.SetLevel(log.DebugLevel)

	// Get UUID for this instantiation
	uuid := uuid2.New().String()

	// Show the world what we are
	log.Info(fmt.Sprintf("system: updater, uuid: %v,
	 version: %v, maintainer: davedotdev\n", uuid,
```

```
        _VERSION))

       ctx := context.Background()

       // Get the config from env vars
       var c Config
       if err := envconfig.Process(ctx, &c); err != nil {
             log.Fatal(err)
       }

       // GetToken will get a JWT from the thing upstream
       token, err := c.GetToken(
              "https://example.com/api/v1/auth", uuid)
       if err != nil {
             log.Fatal(err)
       }

        log.Debug(fmt.Sprintf(
        "TODO: Got token from external provider: %v\n",
        token))

       log.Debug("TODO: Got the local state")

        log.Debug(
        "TODO: Logged in to remote service with token and updated
 the state")

       log.Debug(
        "TODO: Update success: ID from remote update is: 42")

       log.Debug("TODO: Our work here is done.")
}
```

The output is as follows:

```
go build
./main
```

```
INFO[0000] system: updater, uuid: 6cb60c9b-<snip>, version:
0.0.1, maintainer: davedotdev
INFO[0000] system: updater, uuid: 6cb60c9b-<snip>, message:
logging into device with key testuser
DEBU[0000] TODO: Got token from external provider: JWT 42.42.42
DEBU[0000] TODO: Got the local state
DEBU[0000] TODO: Logged in to remote service with token and
updated the state
DEBU[0000] TODO: Update success: ID from remote update is: 42
DEBU[0000] TODO: Our work here is done. Exit Go routines
cleanly if there are any.
```

A couple of items in the preceding code are worth mentioning. The first mention is on the use of external packages. I tend to standardize on a given project for a logging library and method of dealing with configuration. It makes the code easy to work with and predictable in its nature. Also, great libraries are gifts that keep on giving. Logrus is a great example of that. Want JSON? Not an issue. Want to change the log destination? Easy. Logging is not only important in development, but it's super important when you release a tool or put a software service into production. It might seem silly to have a UUID system in place for a low-use tool, but if it's a software service with many invocations per day, you can PayPal me a suitable gift when operations tell you how nice it is to follow what your creation does.

Comments

The value of comments is an age-old subject for shouty arguments. Be kind to the future version of yourself or any poor soul that has to maintain your code. Comments are worthless if they point out the obvious, and so I write a small variation of comment styles. They say *know your audience* when you write, and for reading code, the required expertise is a basic understanding of Go, and so you do not need to point out that a string is a string. Here are some pointers on what you could include:

- **Future hints**: This is when there is a known bottleneck or issue that's likely to arise at a certain user base or request rate but is not worth solving at the time.
- **To-do items**: When exploring problem spaces, there's nothing wrong with leaving mental hooks so that you can relocate your thoughts. They should reduce over time as the algorithm becomes more concrete, so remove them and improve the explanations in larger comment chunks as you work through your to-do list.
- When things get complex, write the algorithm out. It's like reading an exec summary in a corporate document. It's easier to understand what the code is trying to do from a tech memo comment than from reading the code, especially if it's complex and deals with things such as recursion. Always worth leaving a date too so that readers can reconcile versions against comments.

Being blindsided

Because writing in Go forces you into good habits, it can also blindside you. Go is massively powerful and packed with features that are quickly turned into invisible guard rails. Imagine interacting with an API that's been written in Python. Imagine also that the payload is encoded into a slice with each item being a small map—something simple, like this:

```
[
        {
                "key": "blah",
                "val": 42
        }
]
```

Immediately, we can see how to marshal and unmarshal, but a common gotcha, especially when interfacing between a strongly typed language and a dynamically typed language, is poor data type management discipline. The following example will trigger an error in Go when you attempt to marshal it because of the type system, but it's really common to see, unfortunately:

```
[
        {
                "key": "blah1",
                "key": 42
        },
        {
                "key": "blah2",
                "val": "42",
        },
]
```

Some software engineers handle these scenarios with TLV-style data encoding (see next), but if you're stuck with this problem, you can use Go's `reflection` capabilities to inspect the data and de-serialize it in a customized way for handling within your code. You could use reflection with the preceding code to then instantiate in types such as the following. This approach has saved my bacon more than once and is especially of use in dynamic data scenarios where languages such as Python make it dangerously easy. The user of the underscore is normally a hint that this is a TLV-style data instance and used for inter-process communication:

```
/*
        {
                "_key": "blah",
```

```
            "_value": "42",
            "_type": "string",
        },
*/

type BadDataManagement struct {
        Key   string `json:"_key"`
        Value string `json:"_value"`
        VType string `json:"_type"`
}
```

Go is a great language, and I implore you to work with standardized interfaces such as NETCONF, REST, and gRPC while making an effort to avoid silver-bullet *network API*-style packages and middleware. Simple rules such as avoiding magic will pay dividends in the future and, having a memory like a sieve, I try to remember that at all times if nothing else.

Writing this section has been an honor, and I believe this book paves the way for you to develop your own discipline, rigor, and skill for an industry that desperately needs it. Without lightning-rod efforts to provide learning paths, we'll find the network automation discipline heavily fragmented for years to come, and this book will help immensely with that journey. A huge thank you to the authors for letting me share these thoughts.

Daniel Hertzberg

Daniel is a Senior Technical Marketing Engineer at Arista Networks. He's been working within this field for double-digit years and has always had one foot in the door of networking and one foot in the door of automation/programmability. He writes Go on Visual Studio Code multiple times per week because of his success with network automation, cloud-native technologies, and OpenConfig.

I started off my automation not with network devices but with network overlays and network security with VMware NSX. NSX provides way too many options to click on to break the system. The same way that a network person could make a mistake and fat-finger a switch made it really easy for me to enter the same OSPF router ID within the same network... whoops! This was a REST API built with XML as an encoding and used Python requests to talk to it. At the time, most were using PowerShell to make this work, so even Python in this community was way outside the barriers of normalcy.

Fast forward a few years later—we started to see a lot of usage with vendor APIs. I found Python more or less at home given the amount of "getting started" examples that were out there simply importing the `requests` library and doing the typical RESTful thing—that is, sending a request and getting a response back. I found it pretty simplistic to generally work with all the normal Python objects such as dictionaries, lists, tuples, and so on.

Within every journey, you start to run into scaling problems, and there is no issue with Python if it works for what you are doing. I started getting more involved in cloud-native projects, Kubernetes, and OpenConfig. All things that ended up using Go. I felt the learning curve was a bit steeper than Python because the network community was not as into it as they were into Python. However, the benefits outweighed everything I knew about Python:

- Typed system
- Compiled system
- Concurrency
- Modules (`go mod` is so great to open it up and see what is being used across the entire project)
- No white spacing
- Garbage collection

I could probably add a bit more, but those are generally why I like Go so much. Having early access to this book and seeing the examples, I can see generations of network engineers picking this up rather easily and swapping out Python for Go.

Go overall has helped me tremendously in my career as customers are asking for more and more code written in Go for general networking projects including Kubernetes operators, network automation, and OpenConfig streaming. Best of luck, network gophers!

Marcus Hines

Marcus has spent his career focused on network device testing, test framework development, test automation and generally asking why things can't be done differently. He started his career as a Network Engineer and he now focuses on engineering productivity across his organization. He helps maintain most of the OpenConfig organization's repositories.

In a nutshell

I have become a very strong proponent of Go for general development for several key aspects:

- Ease of use of language-provided tooling
- Ramp-up speed for engineers joining projects
- Speed of compilation and multi-platform support
- Strongly typed language for static analysis with great build-time validations

Reasoning about automation

- **Testing and automation are basically the same thing.**

  Testing and automation can be distilled down to an ordered set of operations and validations to transform an input state and intent into an expected output state.

- **A stream of bytes is not an API.**

  SSH and shell scripts that contain vendor-specific details do not lend themselves to a heterogeneous environment.

- Flexibility on API definition, which focuses on iterative versioning with non-breaking changes.

  Go has strong first-class support for gRPC, which is a rich serialization and RPC framework with support for most popular programming languages.

- Automation should always only have one layer of templates and one layer of configuration. Everything else should be code.
- One automated test running continuously is worth 1,000 manual tests.
- Automation systems themselves need to be life - cycled.

  The first test developed for the system should be how to install, version, and tear down the system itself in a hermetic, repeatable way.

  Once you have that ecosystem, you can unlock the rest of your development team to quickly iterate on development with the trust they are not regressing the infrastructure.

Background

I have had a very long winding path to come to where I am today.

I started my network automation *scripting* back in TCL/Expect and Perl. Both of these ecosystems allowed for at least consistent repeated operations; however, everything else was a mess. Python added a robust ecosystem around libraries and version systems to allow for a more hermetic and repeatable world.

The Python code base, though, suffered from a couple of issues, which made it hard to maintain. The testing of the code itself was fairly straightforward. However, because of a lack of typing, we often had to write a lot of type validation into the code and could only find these errors during runtime. Also, the general focus on using mocking to drive up coverage numbers but not extensively testing the public contracts caused fairly brittle tests, which slowed development in the long term. I don't blame Python specifically for this, but it is very easy to fall into a pattern without the right tooling to enforce good practices.

I was introduced to Go around 2014 on a project and was quickly impressed with its strong typing, built-in tooling, and compilation speed. Before this, I had been working on a C++ test framework for a project. I was constantly frustrated with the complexity of building *flexible* C++ code; it had become a meta-programming nightmare of templates to generically support all of our use cases. Go fixed most of this by providing interface definitions for our use cases.

Since then, I have written three Go-based test frameworks for different organizations, all with different system needs. The first framework represented some unique challenges for solution testing. It required the ability to be open sourced. It needed to control components written by four different teams developing code in three different languages across two different build ecosystems. The tests themselves had to run on both Linux and Windows test runners. Go allowed us to develop this ecosystem using just standard Go tools for compilation.

The next framework was used for solution testing of a cloud-based Kubernetes ecosystem. We were able to make quick progress given the tooling and library support for k8s based projects. We could leverage infrastructure for cluster bring-up, k8s deployment, operator deployment, and application lifecycle.

The current framework I am involved with is Ondatra (see the *Further reading* section). This framework is focused on delivering an open source functional-, integration-, and solution-testing framework for network solutions. It is currently used by internal teams in my organization through feature profiles (see the *Further reading* section) for describing our network device requirements to vendors.

Ability to impact the industry

One last point I would like to make is the ability of individuals to change the industry.

This industry has long been dominated by vendors and the perception that the IETF will solve your problems. When it comes to automation, vendors are disincentivized to help. Every vendor-specific knob and API that can be created locks an operator further into a vendor solution that translates into **purchase orders** (**POs**) for them.

By starting to shape this industry around software automation and APIs, we are moving a network from an art to computer science. We are on the path to where network devices are nothing more than general-purpose compute with fancy network interface cards. With general APIs that can express intent, such as OpenConfig over gNMI, operators can build a single configuration and telemetry system that can support any number of vendors. With additional operational APIs around bootstrapping, security, software, and file management, operators can uniformly build their infrastructure. This becomes a very consistent testable layer that then can be used to test northbound services and downstream devices separately at the unit test layer. Building a strong layered test strategy gives you confidence and finds breakages much faster in your development cycle.

Don't wait for others to solve your needs; it won't happen. If you want something, demand it from the vendors. If they don't do it, demand it from a standards body. If they don't do it, take it upon yourself. Don't assume your idea is a bad one or that others have more understanding of the ecosystem than you do. Get into the open source world and pitch your ideas. The model of software development and collaboration has drastically changed over the last 20 years, let alone just in the last 5 years.

Network automation has many opportunities to develop ecosystems that can have a minimal number of transforms between operator intent and state on network devices.

Sneha Inguva

Sneha is a Software Engineer at Fastly on the network control and optimization team and a former Network Engineer at DigitalOcean.

My journey to writing networking code began on the internal Kubernetes and observability teams at DigitalOcean, a cloud hosting provider. Before I ever touched a line of network code or configuration logic, I learned that behind a planet-scale company is a multitude of distributed systems consisting of hundreds, if not thousands, of services, serviced by many teams of engineers. The process of building and deploying maintainable services required a proper CI/CD setup, monitoring, and actionable alerting. This was echoed in my experiences when I transitioned over to writing lower-level networking code in Go on various networking teams. When you are writing code that is meant to be deployed to thousands of hypervisors or servers in various locations around the world—and when that code controls fundamentals' ingress and egress networking—automation is key. This experience has continued at Fastly, a CDN provider with points of presence around the world.

Whether it is homegrown networking software or third-party OSS such as the BIRD routing daemon, I have learned that we absolutely need to be able to roll forward or roll back changes with ease. I am also a huge proponent of actionable alerts and runbooks; from experience, noisy alerts that are not directly tied to specific actions should never be pageable. I've also come to appreciate Go for what it offers when writing networking code; compared to languages such as C, it has been far easier to iterate code quickly and cross-compile applications for various platforms using Go. Go also has a useful network standard library and a growing ecosystem of packages that ease the process of writing code all the way from layer 2 and packet sockets to layer 7 using HTTP.

In summary, if I had to advise someone newly entering this field of networking and Go software engineering, I would say the following:

- My ethos when writing software at any large company is to keep it simple. Write such easily readable, modular, extensible, and well-documented code so that a new engineer well versed in Go but unfamiliar with the company's ecosystem would be able to easily join and contribute. I believe that excellent documentation and clear, simple code will always beat clever code.
- When it comes to CI/CD and Infrastructure as Code, there are numerous options available that often depend on the use case. Will the software be run as a binary on a host machine? Can it be containerized? Are we building Debian packages? Whatever it is you use, make sure it is easy to both deploy and roll back the version of a service with ease.
- Learn the idiosyncrasies of Go and have some agreed-upon best practices for company repositories.

- Though I absolutely appreciate third-party packages in the Go networking ecosystem (`netaddr`, `gobgp`, and so on), I also like to read through code and confirm my understanding of its functionality. This also often allows us to find bugs and upstream contributions.
- Make sure you have white-box monitoring and actionable alerts configured for your services.

And with these tips, I encourage everyone to embrace the Gopher life!

Antonio Ojea

Antonio Ojea is a Software Engineer at Red Hat, where he works on Kubernetes and other open source projects, mainly focused on cloud technologies, networking, and containers. He is currently a maintainer and contributor on the Kubernetes and KIND projects and has contributed in the past to other projects such as OpenStack and MidoNet.

During my early years as a professional, I started in the network department of a telecommunications company. We were responsible for the internal network and its services (DNS, email, WWW, and so on). At that time, our automation consisted basically of the following:

- **Configuration**: TCL/Expect scripts that connected to the network devices to apply different configurations
- **Monitoring**: Perl scripts that polled via SNMP the network devices and stored the data on **Round Robin Database** (**RRD**) files
- **Logging**: Using a central Syslog server dumping all logs to text files that were rotated periodically via `cron`
- **Alerting and reporting**: Processing text files with Perl, `cat`, `grep`, `cut`, `awk`, `sed`, `sort`, and so on, and sending the result via email

If we look back, in hindsight, it's incredible how much everything has improved and how interesting has been its evolution, especially in the open source area.

At the beginning of the 2000s, open source software was gathering momentum, the Apache license opened a new way for FOSS and corporations to interact, and there were already several stable Linux distributions providing the support, maintenance, security, and reliability required by enterprises.

During the 2000s, some projects started to flourish, improving the existing network automation. Some of them are still alive these days:

- **Really Awesome New Cisco confIg Differ** (**RANCID**): Monitors the device configurations and uses a versioning backend such as CVS, Subversion, or Git to maintain a history of changes.
- **Nagios**: It was kind of the industry standard for monitoring and alerting.

- **Cacti**: A complete network graphing solution designed to harness the power of RRDTool's data storage and graphing functionality.

However, it wasn't until the late 2000s that open source entered the spotlight, regulations were more clear about free software licenses, and the open source ecosystem was more solid and stable. Companies started to use and contribute to open source, attracted by the growth and change potential and the economic benefits in contrast to the existing licensing model of private software.

During this period, and driven by the necessity of businesses and companies to be more agile, the infrastructure becomes more flexible: virtual machines, containers, software-defined networks, and so on. All these changes cause an evolution in the industry. It's the dawn of the cloud, and network engineers start to have access to the networking data plane with technologies such as OpenFlow, or to the physical or virtual device configurations via APIs. The network becomes more open and programmable, creating unlimited opportunities for software developers.

My career was following this evolution. I started creating simple scripts and using other software projects to help me automate my work. However, once you realize you can build your own tools, collaborate with others to add the features that you need, and/or fix the limitations or bugs that are impacting you, you just can't stop. That's how I became a Kubernetes contributor and maintainer on SIG-Network. There is no secret: study, practice ... repeat.

Nowadays, and thanks to the explosion of open source projects and collaborative tools, it is easy to practice. Every project will be happy to have people willing to help, or you can just create your own project. There will always be someone that will be interested. The same is happening for studying; there is a lot of material accessible for everyone - videos, tutorials, and blogs - but I always recommend having some key books at hand, not just for reading, but also for consulting. Good books never age.

Remember, a programming language is just a tool. There is no ring to rule them all. There are tools you feel more comfortable with or are better suited for some kind of work or to solve some specific problem. Go is the core language for the container ecosystem; the main projects such as Kubernetes, Docker, and so on are built using Go. If you plan to work on network automation and containers, Go is definitively the appropriate language for you.

Carl Montanari

Carl defines himself as an ex(?) network person. He is a Python and Go developer, and creator of Scrapli(go), a Go package used in this book.

When I first started getting involved in the network automation community, the idea of anything but Python for network automation felt a bit insane. *Of course*, there were folks out there using things other than Python—maybe they had some Perl or Ruby, or maybe crazy folks had some C or something, but it really felt that Python was generally the *one ring to rule them all*. I leaned into Python, and, like many folks, I quickly fell in love. Python is a really neat language, and for somebody like me, without any kind of programming or computer science background, it served as an amazing and reasonably gentle introduction to the world of software.

For a good long while, I kind of felt like the network automation folks espousing Go were living in a fantasy land! Why would you need anything other than Python? Certainly, the speed/ease of development of Python outweighed the general speed of Go. Surely the much larger network automation ecosystem in Python was such a leg up that Go could never compete! Perhaps, I thought, the Go network automation advocates only had the newest fanciest gear that had 100% support for everything they could need to do with RESTCONF or gRPC. They probably also drank only the finest artisan coffees and beers and had enviable mustaches and/or colorful, fancy hair!

Naturally, these thoughts are all silly, and eventually, I started growing out a fancy mustache and learning Go. Just kidding—I can't grow a mustache, or at least not an enviable one, but I did dive into Go!

Of course, I never had any delusion that Python was truly the *one ring to rule them all*, but learning one language was hard enough, so perhaps I was just protecting my sanity from trying to learn another one! It's a bit unclear whether I've retained my sanity, but I do feel like I have learned quite a bit about Go over the past few years! For anyone that is on a journey like mine and looking to dig into Go, here are a few things I would recommend:

- Lean into the typing ecosystem in Python. `mypy` is awesome—you will catch bugs you had no idea you had. You will learn a ton about typing, and the best part: if your typing is all broken, your programs will still run! Being a pretty rabid-type hinting fan, I feel it helped me a ton when going into Go where it is required.
- Take the time to really understand interfaces and how to use them idiomatically. At first, for me, they were just kind of clunky abstract base classes, but of course, they really are more than that. While we're at it, make sure to understand the empty interface and how to use and abuse that!
- Stop trying to inherit all the things! This was (is?!) difficult for me—I quite fancied inheritance (perhaps too much, and perhaps that is a taboo nowadays anyway?), so it has been somewhat of a challenge at times to break away from that pattern. Sure, embed a struct here and there, but generally try to move away from that inheritance style mentality.
- Let the robots (linters) yell at you and tell you how bad your code is! I like `golangci-lint`, which is a linter aggregator that runs tons of linters against your code. Get a ton of errors, and search-engine-engineer your way to understanding why the error exists and how you can do better. While annoying, I've learned a ton from all the errors I've created this way!

I suspect Go will continue to become more and more commonplace in the network automation community. The benefits of language—speed, small footprint, compiled binary, and on and on—are hard to ignore. Moreover, as the network automation ecosystem continues to expand and grow, I believe that network automation roles will be increasingly software-centric, rather than network-centric or automation/software as an afterthought of a network role; as that happens, Go will be increasingly important for all the reasons espoused in this very book! Of course, just as Python is not the *one ring to rule them all*, neither will Go be, but both are tools you should absolutely have in your toolbelt... or some other worn-out platitude. Happy Gophering!

Brent Salisbury

Brent is a Principle Software Engineer with over 20 years of networking and compute experience. He started in network ops and architecture and gradually transitioned into network software development. He is as bullish as ever on the future of the prospects for young engineers entering the networking industry.

We have witnessed trends in networking come and go, and projects succeed and fail during a few innovation cycle booms and busts in the still-young life of the internet. Through these important iterations, one paradigm shift that will stick is the adoption of DevOps practices in networking. A core component of DevOps is automation. To scale network automation, it is important to have tools that are powerful yet not overly complex to use for the operator. The authors have done an excellent job laying out reasons Go has arguably become the de facto language for infrastructure programming over the past few years as libraries have matured, and some of the largest open source projects have been written in Go.

Whether you are a network engineer or a seasoned developer, it is often said a particular language is just a tool and we shouldn't grow too attached to one specific technology. While there is some truth in that premise, in the specific case of a language such as Go for networking, I would argue the right tool for the job is incredibly important. We are expecting a large swath of networking professionals to evolve into DevOps engineers for the network. If we are expecting a retooling of engineers' skill sets, we should make that path as easy as possible. The learning curve, packaging, and baseline performance of Go all benchmark exceptionally well as compared to peer languages, making it an excellent choice for both a newcomer and a seasoned developer for programming and automation.

Here are some recommendations for those getting started in the network programming and automation journey:

- Embrace open source.
- Learn Linux and Linux networking.
- Pick a language such as Go to start hacking.
- Get familiar with open source automation tools such as Ansible and Jinja.
- Learn how to use Git and its potential impact on configuration management.
- Start with a read-only project that won't do damage to the network as you are getting comfortable with automation and coding. Examples such as network monitoring/telemetry or configuration management/backups are relatively safe places to begin.
- Programmatically improve the understanding of the state of your network. Stop driving using the rear-view mirror!
- Learn about current developer tools and deployment mechanisms (Kubernetes, containers, popular libraries, and so on).
- Explore how to create CI/CD pipelines for your networks.

Start thinking of your network configurations as code. Automated outages are increasingly at the root of some of the more recent high-profile outages. Leverage your experience in operations, and create tests and safeguards to prevent common mistakes someone doing automation without a background in networking would not be aware of. Network engineers are not endangered species; it takes years to understand how networks work and how to build them at scale. By combining a new discipline such as programming, it makes you that much more valuable in being able to connect the increasingly complex environments in today's networks.

In closing, your goal should be to ensure the network is not a blocker of business velocity. Changes to the network taking weeks to implement must be a thing of the past. That is, of course, easier said than done, as network uptime is, and will always be, the number one metric a network team is going to be judged by. If I look at any projects, deployments, or products that I have done, the successful ones were where we took complexity and made it a little bit simpler. As networking professionals continue to evolve, powerful yet simple-to-use tools such as Go coupled with automation projects will be key enablers. Lastly, don't be afraid to fail. Find your strengths and work around your weaknesses. The network is a big boat and hard to steer, but I firmly believe we are tacking in the right direction with automation.

Maximilian Wilhelm

Maximilian—Max—Wilhelm is a Holistic (Network) Automation Evangelist, trying to bring software engineering methods to network automation, and helping to overcome vendor lock-in.

He developed a weakness for networking, IPv6, and routing early on and is an avid open source enthusiast, cofounder, maintainer, and contributor of Bio-Routing and ifupdown-ng, a regular speaker at open source and networking conferences, founder of the FrOSCon Network Track, and co-host of the virtualNOG.net meetings.

He's currently working as a Network Automation Engineer at Cloudflare and does a little moonlighting as a Senior Infrastructure Consultant. His second calling is being the lead architect behind the widely automated Freifunk Hochstift community network where he got his hands dirty with ifupdown2 as well as ifupdown-ng, VXLAN, Linux VRFs, BGP, and OSPF, plus infrastructure automation with Salt Stack, and has been afraid of commercial SDN solutions ever since.

A little bit of history

Coming from a Linux administrator/systems engineering background, I've been used to having home-grown automation solutions in place to manage a fleet of—for me at the time—a large number of servers and clients since my first job at the IT center of the Institute of Mathematics at Paderborn University in early 2004.

We had a locally developed software suite called SDeployment—written in Shell if I remember correctly—that was responsible for provisioning the correct software packages and desired configuration file state onto Linux-based servers and clients and enforcing the desired state to stay this way.

This even helped to detect an intruder who managed to exchange the `sshd` binary, which didn't have support for Kerberos, so he needed to change the `sshd_config`, which got overwritten after 1 hour and the service didn't start anymore.

At the time this was a huge benefit over solutions such as CFEngine, which could do incremental changes to configuration files but not maintain them holistically; Puppet had not been born yet (according to Wikipedia).

With the rise of Bcfg2, Puppet, Chef, Salt, and Ansible, we saw a shift from incremental configuration changes to intent-based configuration management in the wider industry, where the operator describes the desired state (intent) and writes templates to generate contents of entire configuration files, and the configuration management solution's task is to make this a reality and keep it this way.

Mental shift to holistic automation

The systems engineering/SRE world underwent this shift in thinking a long time ago, but it feels like the majority of network automation solutions are still following the idea of making incremental changes to the routers and switches out there, which, at the same time, might also be managed manually by operators typing (or copying) magic spells into a CLI.

This makes the device configuration the synchronization point, and we don't really have an idea of what this configuration will look like in full without checking back on the device.

I believe we, as network (automation) engineers, need to follow suit, make the mental shift to the holistic approach, let Perl, Shell, and Expect scripts be, and bring software engineering methods to network automation. This way, we are able to tackle the problems at hand at an abstract level and build solutions that can be reasoned with, tested on their own, and that scale to our needs (see *Chapter 5, Network Automation*).

For the most daunting problem of configuration management, this means plugging some of those systems together and building a solution that generates and owns the full device configuration.

The automation will likely rely on multiple inputs to gain full knowledge of the topology, operational overrides, subscribers, and services, as well as rules to derive the configuration from all of that.

This is following the overarching goal to do as few configuration changes as possible and leverage protocols such as BGP and BMP to extract/observe state or manipulate device state where more dynamic changes are required.

This is the way

Having all of this in the cards, the only API you need from a device is a function to upload a new complete configuration and let the device figure out the path from the current configuration to the new one.

Dealing with diverging configuration parts across the fleet, carefully cleaning up old approaches to configure X, doing incremental changes, and figuring out how to interact with a platform API, a dialect of NETCONF, YANG, and so on would all be from the past—wouldn't that be great?

I believe we have a bright future ahead of us!

That's where this great and inspiring book and Go come in!

With Go, you have a very solid foundation to build reliable, scalable, and fairly easily testable and observable software. Prometheus integration is at your fingertips.

This way, you can build tools to monitor your network (via BMP or streaming telemetry, for example), inject routes via BGP, or build your own holistic network config generator and deployment pipeline, as outlined previously.

Existing open source suites such as Bio-Routing can help you on the first part (using BMP/RIS) and act as the foundation to, for example, build a route-injector following your business logic.

The fact that you are reading this indicates you are looking into building your own automation solution to tackle your organization's needs—that's great!

If you can, please share it as open source and present it at your local NOG—or VirtualNOG—so that others can benefit and learn from it too. Good luck!

Matt Oswalt

Matt is a Systems Engineer at Cloudflare, where he works on proxies and control plane systems. He blogs at https://oswalt.dev and occasionally posts on Twitter as @Mierdin.

I'm grateful to have been exposed to software development as well as infrastructure technologies such as networking at roughly the same time in my life. While I had toyed around with the BASIC-esque language on my TI-82 calculator in high school (okay, *toyed* is a stretch—I created a rudimentary Galaga clone while failing Geometry) and taken a single semester of programming in Visual Basic, it wasn't until university that I first encountered Linux, networking, and a modern programming environment.

Over the next few years, I bounced back and forth between what seemed to be fairly isolated technical domains. Doing so often made me feel like a beginner in everything and an expert in nothing. I've had more than a few moments of anxiety, worrying that I'm not doing the right things in my career. In retrospect, however, this was the best experience I could have asked for. It kept me uncomfortable, and in this state, I honed the skill that I prize above all others, and that's my ability to learn. This skill has a snowball effect—having a formalized system of learning gives me the confidence to try new, more challenging things, which usually forces me to be even more rigorous and efficient in my learning process, and so on.

These days, there is a multitude of things to learn, and while it may be tempting to learn them all, we cannot. Something I'm still working on is my ability to seek out those skills that will really impact my career and the industry. In my experience, the kind of technologies and skills that have staying power are not always those that get the hype on social media or stars on GitHub—often, these are more fundamental technologies or ways of thinking that allow you to more quickly understand whatever the latest manifestation of those ideas might be.

If you're new in your career, or if you feel like you might be stagnating a bit but you're not sure where to go, hopefully the following advice is helpful to you:

- Stay curious. The work of learning is never finished. Don't get too focused on attaining certification *X* or being able to add technology *Y* to your resume—these are fleeting. Rather, take pride in building a continuously improving system of learning, and hone your own ability to acquire new skills efficiently.
- So much of what we tend to cling on to in our lives and careers is a crippling distraction. Separate the essential few from the trivial many and focus on what will allow you to make your highest level of contribution. It's far better to do a few things exceptionally well than to create a bounty of mediocre work.
- There are many more highly skilled engineers building efficient, scalable systems that you will never hear about; then, there are people posting about technology *X* on social media and getting *all the likes*. The vast majority of technology hot takes on social media aren't worth the bits used to transmit them.
- The technical skills that have the steepest learning curve can often (but do not always) have the biggest reward. Be very careful not to make career-limiting technical decisions based on how adoptable/approachable a technology may be; often, industry-changing innovations will not come with a perfect user experience at first, and the opportunities are much more plentiful for those who don't wait for the polished user manual. At the same time, do not fall into the trap of believing that the more complex or difficult to learn, the better it must be. As with most things in life, the truth is probably somewhere in the middle.
- No technology is a panacea; they were all designed with specific trade-offs in mind, including Go. If you haven't found the trade-offs, you haven't looked hard enough. Your job as an engineer is to understand these trade-offs and pick a technology that aligns best with the trade-offs you want to make in your current situation.

Happy learning!

Further reading

- *Decomposing Data Structures*: `https://gratuitous-arp.net/decomposing-complex-json-data-structures/`
- Ondatra: `https://github.com/openconfig/ondatra`
- Feature profiles: `https://github.com/openconfig/featureprofiles`
- FrOSCon Network Track: `https://myfirst.network`

12
Appendix : Building a Testing Environment

Every chapter of this book includes Go code examples to illustrate some points we make in the text. You can find all these Go programs in this book's GitHub repository (see the *Further reading* section of this chapter). While you don't have to execute them all, we believe that manually running the code and observing the result may help reinforce the learned material and explain the finer details.

The first part of this book, *Chapters 1* to *5*, includes relatively short code examples you can run in the Go Playground (*Further reading*) or on any computer with Go installed. For instructions on how to install Go, you can refer to *Chapter 1* or follow the official download and installation procedure (*Further reading*).

The rest of the book, starting from *Chapter 6*, assumes you can interact with a virtual topology, which we run in containers with the help of `containerlab` (*Further reading*). This *Appendix* documents the process of building a testing environment that includes the compatible version of `containerlab` and other related dependencies, to make sure you get a seamless experience running examples from any chapter of this book.

What is a testing environment?

The primary goal is to build an environment with the right set of hardware and software that meets the minimum requirements to execute the code examples. We base the requirements on the assumption that you're deploying a **virtual machine** (**VM**), as we realize you might not deploy this on a dedicated bare-metal server.

When it comes to deploying a VM for testing (testbed), you have two options, both of which we discuss later:

- You can deploy this VM in a self-hosted environment, such as VMware or **Kernel-based Virtual Machine** (**KVM**).
- You could use a cloud-hosted environment—for example, **Amazon Web Services** (**AWS**).

From the hardware perspective, we assume that the underlying CPU architecture is 64-bit x86, and our recommendation is to give the VM at least 2 vCPUs and 4 GB of RAM and ideally double that to make things a bit faster.

We describe all software provisioning and configuration in an Ansible playbook included in this book's GitHub repository (*Further reading*). We highly recommend you use the automated approach we have prepared for you to install all the dependencies to run the code examples in the book.

You can still install these packages on top of any Linux distribution—for example, **Windows Subsystem for Linux version 2** (**WSL 2**). In case you want to do the installation manually, we include a full list of dependencies here:

Package	Version
Go	1.18.1
`containerlab`	0.25.1
Docker	20.10.14
`ansible-core` (only required for *Chapter 7*)	2.12.5
Terraform (only required for *Chapter 7*)	1.1.9

Table 12.1 – Software dependencies

Step 1 – building a testing environment

In the following section, we describe the two automated ways of building a testing environment. If you are unsure which option is right for you, we recommend you pick the first one, as it has minimal external dependencies and is completely managed by a cloud service provider. This is also the only option that we (the authors of this book) can test and verify, and hence it should give you the most consistent experience.

Option 1 – cloud-hosted

We have picked AWS as the cloud service provider because of its popularity and general familiarity in our industry. Inside this book's GitHub repository (*Further reading*), we have included an Ansible playbook that completely automates all tasks required to create a VM in AWS. You are free to use any other cloud provider but you will have to do the provisioning manually.

The testing environment is a single Linux VM in AWS running `containerlab` to create container-based network topologies. The next diagram illustrates what the AWS environment looks like:

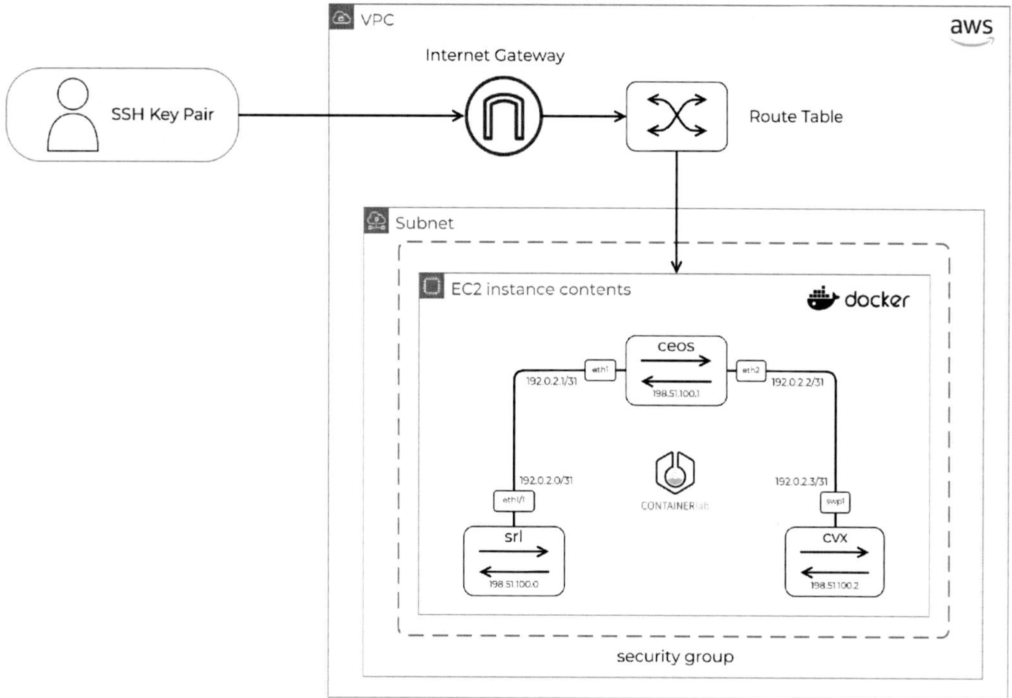

Figure 12.1 – Target environment

To conform with the hardware requirements stated earlier, we recommend you run at least a `t2.medium`-, ideally a `t2.large`-sized VM (**Elastic Compute Cloud** (**EC2**) instance). But the AWS Free Tier plan (*Further reading*) does not cover these instance types, so you should expect to incur some charges associated with the running of the VM. We assume you are familiar with the costs and billing structure of AWS and use financial common sense when working with a cloud-hosted environment.

Before you run the playbook, you need to make sure you meet the following requirements:

1. Create an AWS account (AWS Free Tier (*Further reading*)).
2. Create an AWS access key (AWS Programmatic access (*Further reading*)).
3. A Linux OS with the following packages:
   - Git
   - Docker
   - GNU Make

With all this in place, you can go ahead and clone the book's GitHub repository (*Further reading*) with the `git clone` command:

```
$ git clone https://github.com/PacktPublishing/Network-
Automation-with-Go
```

After you clone the repository, change directory to it.

Input variables

Before you can start the deployment, you need to supply your AWS account credentials (`AWS_ACCESS_KEY_ID` and `AWS_SECRET_ACCESS_KEY`). You do this by exporting a pair of environment variables containing the key ID and secret values, as follows. Check out AWS Programmatic access (*Further reading*) for instructions on how to create an access key:

```
$ export AWS_ACCESS_KEY_ID='…'
$ export AWS_SECRET_ACCESS_KEY='…'
```

Besides these required variables, there are other three optional input variables that you can adjust to fine-tune your deployment environment:

Name	Values
`AWS_DISTRO`	`fedora` or `ubuntu` (default: `fedora`)
`AWS_REGION`	One of the AWS Regions (default: `us-east-1`)
`VM_SIZE`	One of the AWS instance types (default: `t2.large`)

Table 12.2 – Testing VM options

If you choose to change any of these default values, you can do this the same way as the AWS access key. Here's an example:

```
$ export AWS_DISTRO=ubuntu
$ export AWS_REGION=eu-west-2
```

In that scenario, we selected Ubuntu as the Linux distribution of the VM and London (`eu-west-2`) as the AWS Region for deployment.

Deployment process

Once you have set all the required input variables, you can deploy the testing environment. From within the book repository directory, run the `make env-build` command, which deploys the VM and installs all the required software packages:

```
Network-Automation-with-Go$ make env-build
```

```
AWS_ACCESS_KEY_ID is AKIAVFPUEFZCFVFGXXXX
AWS_SECRET_ACCESS_KEY is **************************
Using /etc/ansible/ansible.cfg as config file

PLAY [Create EC2 instance] ************************************
***************************************************************
**********************************************************

TASK [Gathering Facts] ****************************************
***************************************************************
**********************************************************
ok: [localhost]

### ... <omitted for brevity > ... ###

TASK [Print out instance information for the user] ************
***************************************************************
**********************************************************
ok: [testbed] => {}

MSG:

['SSH: ssh -i lab-state/id_rsa fedora@ec2-54-86-51-96.
compute-1.amazonaws.com\n', 'To upload cEOS image: scp -i lab-
state/id_rsa ~/Downloads/cEOS64-lab-4.28.0F.tar fedora@ec2-54-
86-51-96.compute-1.amazonaws.com:./network-automation-with-
go\n']

PLAY RECAP ****************************************************
***************************************************************
**********************************************************
localhost                  :
ok=28   changed=9    unreachable=0    failed=0    skipped=3
rescued=0    ignored=0
testbed                    :
ok=36   changed=24   unreachable=0    failed=0    skipped=11
rescued=0    ignored=0
```

Assuming that the playbook has completed successfully, you can see the VM access details in the logs, as the preceding output shows. You can also view the connection details at any time after you've deployed the environment by running the `make env-show` command:

```
Network-Automation-with-Go$ make env-show
fedora@ec2-54-86-51-96.compute-1.amazonaws.com
```

Now, you can use this information to connect to the provisioned VM. The playbook generates an **Secure Shell** (**SSH**) private key (`lab-state/id_rsa`), so don't forget to always use it for SSH authentication:

```
Network-Automation-with-Go$ ssh -i lab-state/id_rsa fedora@ec2-
54-86-51-96.compute-1.amazonaws.com
fedora@testbed:~$  go version
go version go1.18.1 linux/amd64
fedora@testbed:~$  ls network-automation-with-go/
LICENSE  Makefile  README.
md  ch01  ch02  ch03  ch04  ch05  ch06
ch07  ch08  ch09
ch10  ch12  lab-state  topo-base  topo-full
```

You can connect to the VM and check the Go version installed and take a look at the files of the book's repository.

Option 2 – self-hosted

Another option is to create a VM in a private environment. This environment could be your personal computer running a hypervisor such as VirtualBox, an ESXi server, an OpenStack cluster, or something else as long as it can allocate the CPU and memory the VM requires to run the lab topology. The OS on the VM has to be either Ubuntu 22.04 or Fedora 35.

Once you have built the VM with SSH enabled, make sure you can SSH to the IP address of the VM and access it with its credentials. Then, change the Ansible inventory file (`inventory`) in the `ch12/testbed` folder (*Further reading*) of your personal computer's copy of this book's GitHub repository to point to your VM. It should look something like this:

```
# inventory
[local-vm]
192.168.122.18

[local-vm:vars]
ansible_user=fedora
```

```
ansible_password=fedora
ansible_sudo_pass=fedora
```

Include at least the IP address (`ansible_host`) to reach the VM, and the `ansible_user`, `ansible_password`, or `ansible_ssh_private_key_file` user credentials.

In the same `ch12/testbed` folder (*Further reading*), there is an Ansible playbook that calls the `configure_instance` role. Use this playbook to auto-configure your VM to run the book examples, like so:

```
# configure-local-vm.yml
- name: Configure Instance(s)
  hosts: local-vm
  gather_facts: true
  vars_files:
    - ./vars/go_inputs.yml
    - ./vars/clab_inputs.yml
    - ./vars/aws_common.yml

  roles:
    - {role: configure_instance, become: true}
```

The playbook filename is `configure-local-vm.yml` and the inventory filename is `inventory`, so from the `ch12/testbed` folder (*Further reading*), run `ansible-playbook configure-local-vm.yml -i inventory -v` to get the VM ready to go.

Step 2 – uploading container images

Not all networking vendors make it simple to access their container-based **network OSes** (**NOSes**). If you can't pull the image directly from a container registry such as Docker Hub, you might need to download the image from their website and upload it to the test VM. The only container image in the book that we can't pull from a public registry at the time of writing is Arista's **cEOS** image. Here, we describe the process of uploading this image into the testing environment.

The first thing you need to do is download the image from `arista.com` (*Further reading*). You should select the 64-bit cEOS image from the 4.28(F) train—for example, `cEOS64-lab-4.28.0F.tar`. You can copy the image to the test VM with the `scp` command using the generated SSH private key:

```
Network-Automation-with-Go$ scp -i lab-state/id_rsa ~/
Downloads/cEOS64-lab-4.28.0F.tar fedora@ec2-54-86-51-96.
compute-1.amazonaws.com:./network-automation-with-go
```

```
cEOS64-lab-4.28.0F.
tar                           100%  434MB  26.6MB/s   00:16
```

Then, SSH to the instance and import the image with the `docker` command:

```
Network-Automation-with-Go$ ssh -i lab-state/id_rsa fedora@ec2-54-86-51-96.compute-1.amazonaws.com
fedora@testbed:~$  cd network-automation-with-go
fedora@testbed:~$  docker import cEOS64-lab-4.28.0F.tar ceos:4.28
sha256:dcdc721054804ed4ea92f970b5923d8501c28526ef175242cfab0d158ac0085c
```

You can now use this image (`ceos:4.28`) in the `image` section of one or more routers in the topology file.

Step 3 – iInteracting with the testing environment

We recommend you start with a fresh build of a virtual network topology at the beginning of *Chapters 6* through *8*. To orchestrate the topologies, we use `containerlab`, which is available in the testing VM. `containerlab` offers a quick way to run arbitrary network topologies based on their definition provided in a human-readable YAML file.

> **Important Note**
>
> `containerlab` is written in Go and serves as a great example of an interactive CLI program that orchestrates local container resources.

You can find the following `base` topology definition file in the `topo-base` directory of this book's GitHub repository (*Further reading*):

```
name: netgo

topology:
  nodes:
    srl:
      kind: srl
      image: ghcr.io/nokia/srlinux:21.6.4
    ceos:
      kind: ceos
      image: ceos:4.28.0F
```

```
    startup-config: ceos-startup
  cvx:
    kind: cvx
    image: networkop/cx:5.0.0
    runtime: docker

links:
  - endpoints: ["srl:e1-1", "ceos:eth1"]
  - endpoints: ["cvx:swp1", "ceos:eth2"]
```

This YAML file defines a three-node topology, as the next diagram shows. One node runs Nokia SR Linux, another NVIDIA Cumulus Linux, and the last one runs Arista cEOS. In this scenario, all network devices come up with their default startup configurations, and throughout each chapter, we describe how to establish full end-to-end reachability between all three of them:

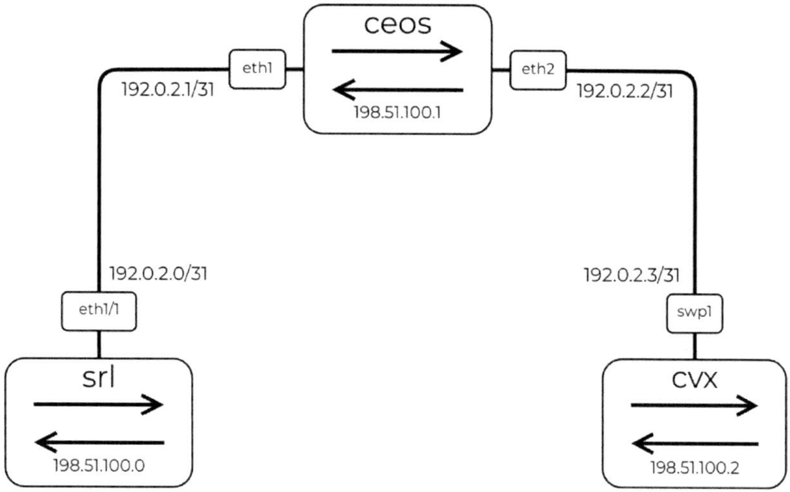

Figure 12.2 – "Base" network topology

The next two chapters (*Chapters 9* and *10*) rely on a slightly different version of the preceding topology. Unlike the `base` topology, the `full` topology comes up fully configured and includes an extra set of nodes to emulate physical servers attached to the network devices:

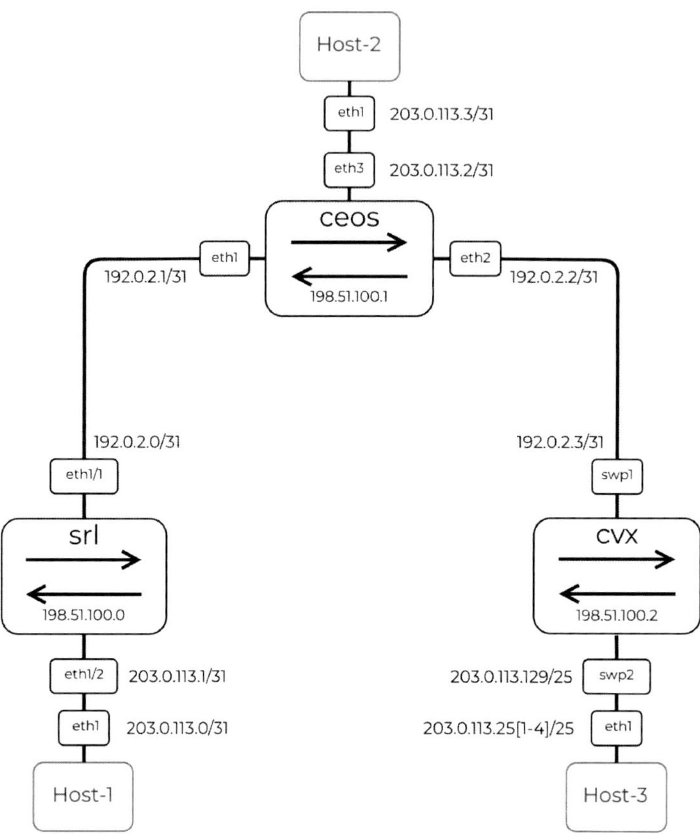

Figure 12.3 – "Full" network topology

These end hosts run different applications that interact with the existing network topology.

Launching a virtual network topology

You can use a `containerlab` binary to deploy the test topology. For convenience, we included a couple of `make` targets that you can use:

- `make lab-base` to create the `base` topology used in *Chapters 6* through *8*
- `make lab-full` to create the `full` topology used in *Chapters 9* and *10*

Here's an example of how you can create the `base` topology from inside the test VM:

```
fedora@testbed network-automation-with-go$ make lab-base
...
+---+-----------------+-------------+-------------
| # | Name            | Container ID | Image
+---+-----------------+-------------+-------------
| 1 | clab-netgo-ceos | fe422727f351 | ceos:4.28.0F
| 2 | clab-netgo-cvx  | 85e5b9135e1b | cx:5.0.0
| 3 | clab-netgo-srl  | 00106bef1d4e |srlinux:21.6.4
+---+-----------------+-------------+-------------
```

You now have `clab-netgo-ceos`, `clab-netgo-cvx` and `clab-netgo-srl` routers ready to go.

Connecting to the devices

`containerlab` uses Docker to run the containers. This means we can use standard Docker capabilities to connect to the devices—for example, you can use the `docker exec` command to start any process inside a container:

```
fedora@testbed:~$  docker exec -it clab-netgo-srl sr_cli
Welcome to the srlinux CLI.
A:srl# show version | grep Software
Software Version  : v21.6.4
```

`sr_cli` in the preceding example is the CLI process for an SR Linux device. The following table displays the "default shell" process for each virtual network device:

NOS	Command
Cumulus Linux	`bash` or `vtysh`
SR Linux	`sr_cli`
EOS	`Cli`

Table 12.3 – Device default shells

You can also use SSH to connect to the default shell. The next table provides the hostname and the corresponding credentials you can use to connect to each device:

Device	Username	Password
`clab-netgo-srl`	`admin`	`admin`
`clab-netgo-ceos`	`admin`	`admin`
`clab-netgo-cvx`	`cumulus`	`cumulus`

Table 12.4 – Device credentials

Here's how you can connect to Arista cEOS and Cumulus Linux, for example:

```
fedora@testbed:~$  ssh admin@clab-netgo-ceos
(admin@clab-netgo-ceos) Password: admin
ceos>en
ceos#exit
fedora@testbed:~$
fedora@testbed:~$  ssh cumulus@clab-netgo-cvx
cumulus@clab-netgo-cvx's password: cumulus

Welcome to NVIDIA Cumulus (R) Linux (R)

cumulus@cvx:mgmt:~$
```

Once you finish the chapter, you can destroy the topology.

Destroying the network topology

You can clean up both virtual network topologies using the `make cleanup` command:

```
fedora@testbed:~/network-automation-with-go$ make cleanup
```

The `make cleanup` command only cleans up the virtual network topology while all the cloud resources are still running.

Step 4 – cleaning up of the cloud-hosted environment

Once you're done working with the cloud-hosted testing environment, you can clean it up so that you don't pay for something you might no longer need. You can do this using another Ansible playbook that makes sure all the AWS resources you created before are now wiped out:

```
etwork-Automation-with-Go$ make env-delete
AWS_ACCESS_KEY_ID is AKIAVFPUEFZCFVFGXXXX
AWS_SECRET_ACCESS_KEY is *************************

PLAY [Delete EC2 instance] ************************************
***************************************************************
**********************************************************

TASK [Gathering Facts] ****************************************
***************************************************************
```

```
************************************************************
ok: [localhost]

### ... <omitted for brevity > ... ###

TASK [Cleanup state files] *************************************
*****************************************************************
************************************************************
changed: [localhost] => (item=.region)
changed: [localhost] => (item=.vm)

PLAY RECAP *****************************************************
*****************************************************************
************************************************************
localhost                  : ok=21   changed=8
 unreachable=0    failed=0    skipped=3
rescued=0    ignored=0
```

Further reading

- Book's GitHub repository: `https://github.com/PacktPublishing/Network-Automation-with-Go`
- Go Playground: `https://play.golang.org/`
- Official download and install procedure: `https://golang.org/doc/install#install`
- `containerlab`: `https://containerlab.dev/`
- AWS Free Tier: `https://aws.amazon.com/free/`
- AWS Programmatic access: `https://docs.aws.amazon.com/general/latest/gr/aws-sec-cred-types.html#access-keys-and-secret-access-keys`
- `ch12/testbed`: `https://github.com/PacktPublishing/Network-Automation-with-Go/blob/main/ch12/testbed`
- `ch12/testbed/inventory`: `https://github.com/PacktPublishing/Network-Automation-with-Go/blob/main/ch12/testbed/inventory`
- Arista: `https://www.arista.com/en/support/software-download`
- Beginner's Guide—Downloading Python: `https://wiki.python.org/moin/BeginnersGuide/Download`

- Installing Ansible with `pip`: `https://docs.ansible.com/ansible/latest/installation_guide/intro_installation.html#installing-ansible-with-pip`
- *Getting Started - Installing Git*: `https://git-scm.com/book/en/v2/Getting-Started-Installing-Git`
- Installing `pip`—*Supported Methods*: `https://pip.pypa.io/en/stable/installation/#supported-methods`
- Get Arista cEOS: `https://github.com/PacktPublishing/Network-Automation-with-Go/blob/main/ch12/testbed/get_arista_ceos.md`
- AWS access keys: `https://docs.aws.amazon.com/general/latest/gr/aws-sec-cred-types.html#access-keys-and-secret-access-keys`
- AWS Regions: `https://docs.aws.amazon.com/AWSEC2/latest/UserGuide/using-regions-availability-zones.html`
- AWS instance types: `https://aws.amazon.com/ec2/instance-types/`

Index

A

B

C

D

E

F

G

H

I

J

O

P

Q

R

S

T

U

V

W

X

Packt.com

Subscribe to our online digital library for full access to over 7,000 books and videos, as well as industry leading tools to help you plan your personal development and advance your career. For more information, please visit our website.

Why subscribe?

- Spend less time learning and more time coding with practical eBooks and Videos from over 4,000 industry professionals
- Improve your learning with Skill Plans built especially for you
- Get a free eBook or video every month
- Fully searchable for easy access to vital information
- Copy and paste, print, and bookmark content

Did you know that Packt offers eBook versions of every book published, with PDF and ePub files available? You can upgrade to the eBook version at packt.com and as a print book customer, you are entitled to a discount on the eBook copy. Get in touch with us at customercare@packtpub.com for more details.

At www.packt.com, you can also read a collection of free technical articles, sign up for a range of free newsletters, and receive exclusive discounts and offers on Packt books and eBooks.

Other Books You May Enjoy

If you enjoyed this book, you may be interested in these other books by Packt:

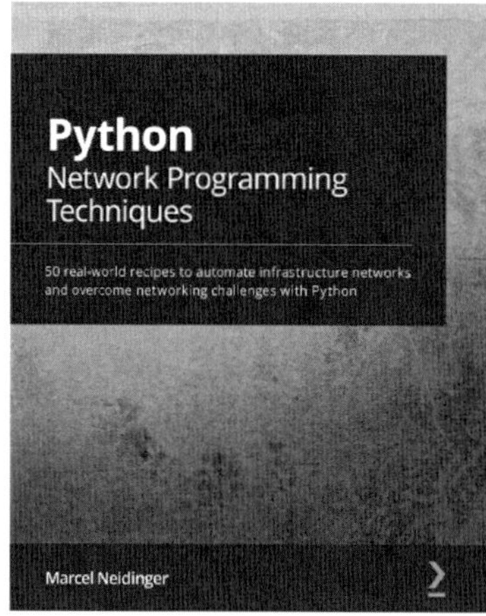

Python Network Programming Techniques

Marcel Neidinger

ISBN: 9781838646639

- Programmatically connect to network devices using SSH (secure shell) to execute commands
- Create complex configuration templates using Python
- Manage multi-vendor or multi-device environments using network controller APIs or unified interfaces
- Use model-driven programmability to retrieve and change device configurations
- Discover how to automate post modification network infrastructure tests
- Automate your network security using Python and Firepower APIs

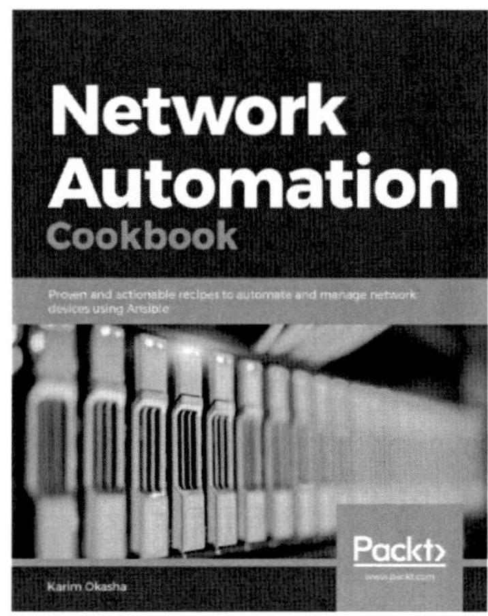

Network Automation Cookbook

Karim Okasha

ISBN: 9781789956481

- Understand the various components of Ansible
- Automate network resources in AWS, GCP, and Azure cloud solutions
- Use IaC concepts to design and build network solutions
- Automate network devices such as Cisco, Juniper, Arista, and F5
- Use NetBox to build network inventory and integrate it with Ansible
- Validate networks using Ansible and Batfish

Packt is searching for authors like you

If you're interested in becoming an author for Packt, please visit `authors.packtpub.com` and apply today. We have worked with thousands of developers and tech professionals, just like you, to help them share their insight with the global tech community. You can make a general application, apply for a specific hot topic that we are recruiting an author for, or submit your own idea.

Share Your Thoughts

Now you've finished *Network Automation with Go*, we'd love to hear your thoughts! Scan the QR code below to go straight to the Amazon review page for this book and share your feedback or leave a review on the site that you purchased it from.

`https://packt.link/r/1-800-56092-3`

Your review is important to us and the tech community and will help us make sure we're delivering excellent quality content.

Download a free PDF copy of this book

Thanks for purchasing this book!

Do you like to read on the go but are unable to carry your print books everywhere?

Is your eBook purchase not compatible with the device of your choice?

Don't worry, now with every Packt book you get a DRM-free PDF version of that book at no cost.

Read anywhere, any place, on any device. Search, copy, and paste code from your favorite technical books directly into your application.

The perks don't stop there, you can get exclusive access to discounts, newsletters, and great free content in your inbox daily

Follow these simple steps to get the benefits:

1. Scan the QR code or visit the link below

`https://packt.link/free-ebook/978-1-80056-092-5`

2. Submit your proof of purchase
3. That's it! We'll send your free PDF and other benefits to your email directly

Made in the USA
Coppell, TX
18 March 2023